The

CHRISTIAN
IMAGINATION

OTHER BOOKS BY LELAND RYKEN

A Dictionary of Biblical Imagery (coeditor)
Redeeming the Time: A Christian Approach to Work and Leisure
The Discerning Reader: Christian Perspectives on Literature and Theory
A Complete Literary Guide to the Bible (coeditor)
Contemporary Literary Theory: A Christian Appraisal (coeditor)
Realms of Gold: The Classics in Christian Perspective
The Liberated Imagination: Thinking Christianly About the Arts
Effective Bible Teaching (coauthor)
Work and Leisure in Christian Perspective
Words of Life: A Literary Introduction to the New Testament
Words of Delight: A Literary Introduction to the Bible
Worldly Saints: The Puritans as They Really Were
Culture in Christian Perspective
Windows to the World: Literature in Christian Perspective
The New Testament in Literary Criticism (editor)
How to Read the Bible as Literature
Milton and Scriptural Tradition (coeditor)
Triumphs of the Imagination
The Literature of the Bible
The Apocalyptic Vision in Paradise Lost

A WRITERS' PALETTE BOOK

The Practice *of* Faith in Literature and Writing

The

CHRISTIAN

IMAGINATION

Leland Ryken
EDITOR

REVISED & EXPANDED EDITION

WITH REFLECTIONS FROM J. R. R. TOLKIEN, FREDERICK BUECHNER,
ANNIE DILLARD, GEORGE MACDONALD, FRANCIS SCHAEFFER & OTHERS

SHAW BOOKS
AN IMPRINT OF WATERBROOK PRESS

The Christian Imagination
A SHAW BOOK
PUBLISHED BY WATERBROOK PRESS
2375 Telstar Drive, Suite 160
Colorado Springs, Colorado 80920
A division of Random House, Inc.

All Scripture quotations, unless otherwise indicated, are taken from the *Holy Bible,
New International Version®*. NIV®. Copyright © 1973, 1978, 1984 by International
Bible Society. Used by permission of Zondervan Publishing House. All rights reserved.
Scripture quotations marked (ESV) are taken from *The Holy Bible, English Standard
Version,* copyright © 2001 by Crossway Bibles, a division of Good News Publishers.
Used by permission. All rights reserved. Scripture quotations marked (KJV) are taken
from the *King James Version*. Scripture quotations marked (RSV) are taken from the
Revised Standard Version of the Bible, copyright © 1946, 1952, and 1971 by the Division
of Christian Education of the National Council of the Churches of Christ in the USA.
Used by permission.

For further acknowledgments please see page 463.

ISBN 0-87788-123-5 *2675 9158*
4-02
Copyright © 2002 by Leland Ryken

Portions of this book have been previously released by Baker Books under the same title.

Printed in the United States of America
2002—First Shaw Books Edition

10 9 8 7 6 5 4 3 2 1

For my grandchildren

Contents

Preface to the Revised Edition

The idea for this book came from the continuous requests that I received for copies of a book that I edited two decades ago titled *The Christian Imagination: Essays on Literature and the Arts*. While the present book contains relatively little overlap with its predecessor, it began with a similar impulse, which was to make available in a single volume the best that has been written about the announced subject.

The result is a book that covers all of the essential topics related to literature and writing as viewed from Christian perspectives. My guiding principle as a compiler of this anthology has been comprehensiveness: I have included both past and living authors, both writers of imaginative literature and literary critics, both poetry and narrative, and the interests of both writers and readers. I know of no other book that brings together this much information about Christianity and literature.

In terms of format, the main units of the book contain foundational essays and shorter excerpts labeled "viewpoints." In addition, five of the main units conclude with collections of choice excerpts on the respective topics.

Elizabeth Goudge, herself a compiler of anthologies, wrote in the preface to *A Book of Comfort*:

> And so of the making of books there is no end, and of the making of anthologies there seems particularly to be no end because we are all anthologists. The collection and hoarding of bits and pieces is basic to all animals, from the squirrel with his nuts…to the anthologist with his oddments stored up in his memory…. Anthology-making is therefore essentially selfish, like self-preservation…with the advantage of literature over nuts that it can be shared without personal loss to the hoarder.

In compiling this anthology I did, indeed, make sure that I included virtually all of my favorite passages, large and small, on the production and reading of literature—even to the extent of including short gems in boxed form throughout the essays of the book.

The book that follows is for lovers of literature, both readers and writers. It contains theory that will clarify thinking about the nature and value of literature. It is equally a practical book, filled with tips for reading and writing literature in the best ways possible. The keynote of the book is excellence— excellence in reading, in writing, in thinking about literature, in teaching and studying literature.

As the contributors to this volume declare, Christian writers and readers alike are free to revel in literature—in its ability to capture human experience, in its capacity to express truth, in its potential to provide the occasion for artistic enrichment and enjoyment. Here you will find a celebration, a discussion, an appreciation of the Christian imagination.

Part One

A Christian Philosophy
of Literature

An "aesthetic" is a philosophy of art. A "poetic" is a philosophy of literature, specifically. This unit of the book covers both. The perennial issues of art and literature that underlie the essays and excerpts that follow include these:

- What is the subject of art and literature?
- What is the relationship between art and life?
- What are the purpose, function, and effects of art and literature?
- How can art and literature be defended (the apologetic angle)?

When we attach the adjective *Christian* to the word *aesthetic,* a whole further set of considerations is set into motion. At heart, these considerations involve relating the issues of aesthetics to Christian doctrine and biblical example, thereby placing the issues into a context of Christian belief and experience. Since the ultimate source of Christian belief is the Bible, the Bible naturally assumes a central role in this enterprise.

The aim of this opening unit of the book is to introduce the leading themes of aesthetics and to provide a range of ways in which various Christian thinkers and writers have related these to Christian interests.

Christian Poetics,
Past and Present

Donald T. Williams

The story of Christian poetics—that is, of Christians thinking consciously as Christians about the nature and significance of literary art—is the tale of a movement struggling almost in spite of itself to come to grips with its own doctrine that human beings are created in the image of God. The faith was born into a pagan culture and has survived into a secular one which shows signs of returning to paganism. The church has perforce used the languages, the markets, and the forms of the surrounding culture. It has transformed them and been transformed by them. In the West, as the faith and the culture grew up together, this process has at times made them all but indistinguishable. "What has Athens to do with Jerusalem?" asked Tertullian; and the answers, while legion, have never been simple or easy.

Specifically, Christians have struggled to apply to literature the general New Testament principle about being in the world but not of it (John 17:11-16). They were rightly wary of a culture based on idolatry—hence of literature in general. But they could not escape the literary foundations of their own origin, or the fact that they, and all humankind, were created in the image of one who expressed his inmost nature from the beginning as the Word. This tension gives

DONALD T. WILLIAMS *teaches English and is the Director of the School of General Studies at Toccoa Falls College. One of his specialties is the literary theory of C. S. Lewis. His most recent books,* Inklings of Reality: Essays toward a Christian Philosophy of Letters *(Toccoa Falls College Press, 1996) and* The Disciple's Prayer *(Christian Publications, 1999), typify a career of straddling the border between the realms of theology and literature. The essay that appears here was first printed in* The Discerning Reader, *ed. David Barratt et al. (Baker, 1995).*

rise to the seeming contradictions of their collective response: condemning literature as dangerous at worst and a waste of time at best, while producing some of
the greatest poems the world has ever seen. And in the process, a few of them
have found in the *imago Dei* the only coherent explanation of why the human
race is, for better or worse, a tribe of incorrigible makers.

THE BEGINNINGS: AUGUSTINE

St. Augustine, the most profound and articulate of the early spokesmen, is in his
own writings a microcosm of their larger, continuing discussion. As such he
requires extended treatment. The negative side is more well known. In Book I of
the *Confessions* Augustine seems to look back on his study of Virgil with nothing
but regret for lost time. The exercise of imitating his poetic lies *(figmentorum
poeticorum)* was "mere smoke and wind"; Augustine's time would have been better spent on God's praises in Scripture than such "empty vanities"; his labor on
them was in effect nothing more than a "sacrifice offered up to the collapsed
angels" (51). He had wept for Dido who killed herself for love, while staying
dry-eyed over his own spiritual death, but now he thinks of his enjoyment of her
fictional sorrow as madness *(dementia)* (39-40). In Book III he confesses that
when he attended theatres in his youth he "sympathized together with the lovers
when they wickedly enjoyed one another" (103). To enjoy in tragedy that which
one would not willingly suffer in reality is "miserable madness" *(miserabilis insa-
nia)*. Literary experience does not lead to virtue because true mercy is practical.
The emotional catharsis of the theatre, though, is a sham, for by it one is not
"provoked to help the sufferer, but only invited to be sorry for him" (101).

The complaints are the familiar ones which would be repeated again and
again throughout history. The fictions of the poets are lies; they are a waste of
time, distracting us from more profitable pursuits; and they are an enticement to
evil. Yet even as we read these passages, we cannot believe that for Augustine
they tell the whole story. Where, we ask, would the felicitous style of the *Confessions* have come from if he had never studied the classics from the standpoint of
rhetorical analysis? And where would he have found such a perfect concrete
example for his point about the dolors of Dido? Indeed, if we just keep reading,
we find that there is more to Augustine's view of literature than at first meets
the eye.

Even in the *Confessions* we find hints of factors in Augustine's upbringing which help explain the vehemence of his negative statements and nuance our understanding of their significance. His education was rhetorical and sophistic; he was trained, in other words, to be a lawyer, a professional whose practice was to make the worse appear the better reason and to teach others to do the same. He was taught to scour the classics for examples of eloquence which could be used cynically to win court cases with no concern for the truth. And in this eloquence his "ambition was to be eminent, all out of a damnable and vainglorious end, puffed up with delight of human glory" (109). It is little wonder then that in his post-conversion reaction he felt compelled to toss out the baby of literature along with the bath-water of sophistry. Yet even the very terms of his rejection testify to the power of words well used.

It is evident on every page of his writings that Augustine was impacted for the good by his classical reading in spite of his cynical teachers and his own scruples, and sometimes he is not unaware of it. The pagan Cicero's *Hortensius* was a major influence leading to his conversion to Christ. It "quite altered my affection, turned my prayers to thyself, O Lord, and made me have clean other purposes and desires." It has this effect, he interestingly notes, because he made use of it not to "sharpen his tongue" but "for the matter of it" (109f). He had then, moments in which he recognized something in literature which the abuses that also exist ought not to deter us from seeking. Elsewhere he expounds the principle implicit here and defines explicitly what the something is:

> We [Christians] should not abandon music because of the superstitions of pagans if there is anything we can take from it that might help us understand the Holy Scriptures... Nor is there any reason we should refuse to study literature because it is said that Mercury discovered it. That the pagans have dedicated temples to Justice and Virtue and prefer to worship in the form of stone things which ought to be carried in the heart is no reason we should abandon justice and virtue. On the contrary, let everyone who is a good and true Christian understand that truth belongs to his Master, wherever it is found. (Howie 350-351)

Literature—even pagan literature—conveys truth and is therefore not to be despised. Unfortunately, the balance is provided by lesser-known treatises such as the *Christian Education*, leaving the negative impression of the *Confessions* unchallenged for most readers. Even in the *Confessions*, learning to read is a good thing, and even eloquence as such is admitted not to be inherently evil: "I blame not the words, which of themselves are like vessels choice and precious; but that wine of error that is in them" (Augustine 149). Clearly, the studies Augustine seems to reject have enhanced his ability to write the book in which he seems to reject them. The rationale for their use is worked out in the *Christian Education*.

Like the treasures of the ancient Egyptians, who possessed not only idols and heavy burdens, which the people of Israel hated and shunned, but also vessels and ornaments of silver and gold, and clothes, which on leaving Egypt the people of Israel, in order to make better use of them, surreptitiously claimed for themselves (they did this not on their own authority but at God's command...)—similarly all the branches of pagan learning contain not only false and superstitious fantasies...but also studies for liberated minds which are more appropriate to the service of the truth, and some very useful moral instruction.... These treasures...which were used wickedly and harmfully in the service of demons must be removed by Christians...and applied to their true function, that of preaching the gospel.

—AUGUSTINE, *De Doctrina Christiana*

How can Christians make use of the products of an idolatrous culture? In pagan learning, error and superstition are to be rejected. But pagan learning also included the liberal arts, which are servants of truth: "Now we may say that these elements are the pagans' gold and silver, which they did not create for themselves, but dug out of the mines of God's providence." Therefore, it is proper for Christians to "take all this away from them and turn it to its proper use in declaring the Gospel" (Howie 364). Even the infamous art of the rhetorician (we should remember that through the Renaissance, poetry was considered a species of rhetoric) is in itself morally neutral and capable of being used in the service of truth; therefore, "we should not blame the practice of eloquence but the perversity of those who put it to a bad use" (360). This being so, Christians have not only a right but also an obligation to learn and employ the art of rhetoric. Since it is "employed to support either truth or falsehood, who would venture to say that truth as represented by its defenders should take its stand unarmed?" The result of Christians abandoning the field would be that falsehood is expounded "briefly, clearly, and plausibly," but truth "in such a manner that it is boring…difficult to understand, and, in a word, hard to believe" (369).

In spite of eloquently expressed doubts, then, Augustine articulates a defense of Christian appropriation of and production of literature on the model of spoiling the Egyptians (see Ex. 11:2-3; 12:35-36). It is a limited and pragmatic approach: literature is valued for the truth (probably, for Augustine, propositional truth) it conveys and for the ways in which it can help us understand the Scriptures and proclaim the gospel. But it is a place to begin, and it adumbrates possibilities which would be developed later. When Augustine says that art makes truth plausible and its absence makes it "hard to believe," it is difficult not to hear the phrase resonating with Coleridge's "willing suspension of disbelief which constitutes poetic faith" and to see C. S. Lewis' magnificent attempts to make Christian truth believable by making it imaginable looming on the horizon. We should not, of course, press Augustine anachronistically in this direction, but perhaps in retrospect we can see the seeds of later developments already embedded there.

MEDIEVAL AND RENAISSANCE PERIODS

Augustine set the terms of the discussion and defined the tension which would characterize much of it down through the years. In the Middle Ages, criticism was mainly practical, focused on grammar, the classification of rhetorical tropes, and so on. Meanwhile, Christian writers wrestled with the issues in practical terms, embodying their Christian vision of the world in concrete images and moving stories. The *Beowulf* poet struggled with the relationship between his Christian faith and his Teutonic heritage and made a grand synthesis in which the heroic ideal was enlisted in a cosmic war of good and evil. Dante and Langland created concrete images which incarnated Christian doctrines allegorically so that they could bid their readers, as Sackville put it, to "come and behold, / To see with eye that erst in thought I roll'd" (Rollins and Baker 273). Anonymous lyricists captured the emotion of their faith in musical lines of beauty and simplicity. Chaucer gave us a humane and sympathetic portrait of "God's plenty" and then felt obligated to retract most of it before his death in a passage which still embarrasses his admirers and shows the Augustinian tension to be yet unresolved (Robinson 265). By the time of the Reformation, some serious polarization had set in.

Luther said that Reason was the devil's whore, but he also asked why the devil should have all the good music and noted that literary study equipped people as nothing else does to deal skillfully with Scripture. Calvin applied the new grammatico-historical exegesis to secular writing and Scripture alike and increased the number of quotations from Plato, Seneca and Cicero in the *Institutes* proportionally to the size of the work in each edition (Williams 78-103). Ironically, some of his followers would take Augustine's doubts about the value of secular literature, untempered by his more positive perspectives, and run with them to extreme and sometimes almost hysterical lengths.

I am persuaded that without knowledge of literature pure theology cannot at all endure, just as heretofore, when letters have declined and lain prostrate, theology, too, has wretchedly fallen and lain prostrate.... Certainly it is my desire that there shall be as many poets and rhetoricians as possible, because I see that by these studies as by no other means, people are wonderfully fitted for the grasping of sacred truth and for handling it skillfully and happily.

—MARTIN LUTHER, Letter to Eoban Hess

These objectors have been characterized, not entirely fairly, as Puritan. While Puritans took the lead in the drive to close the theatres, for example, not all who were sympathetic to the Puritan cause or the spiritual values they represented were in agreement with these objectives. Nor could all who raised them be classified, without anachronism, as Puritan. We find it as early as in that old humanist and gentle pedagogue Roger Ascham, who even as he praises the virtues of the (Greek and Latin) classics, inveighs against "books of chevalry," warning that "Mo papists be made by your merry books of Italy than by your earnest books of Louvain," and railing particularly against Malory's *Le Morte D'Arthur*, "the whole pleasure of which book standeth in two special points, in open manslaughter and bold bawdry." In Malory, "those be counted the noblest knights that do kill most men without any quarrel and commit foulest advoulteries by subtlest shifts" (Rollins and Baker 833).

When the Puritans do sound this note, even their later, more moderate spokesmen such as the usually sensible Richard Baxter (seventeenth century) sound extreme. Baxter advises Christian readers to read first the Bible, then books that apply it. If there is any time left, they may turn to history and science. But they must beware of the poison in "vain romances, play-books, and false stories, which may bewitch your fancies and corrupt your hearts." He buttresses such attacks with arguments: "Play-books, romances, and idle tales" keep more important things out of our minds; they divert us from serious thoughts of salvation; they are a waste of valuable time. Finally, he asks in a rhetorical flourish, "whether the greatest lovers of romances and plays, be the greatest lovers of the book of God, and of a holy life" (Baxter 56-57).

We have heard it all before, but now it is Augustine one-sided, without the balance of his more mature reflections. In Baxter's own youth, as he tells us in his autobiography, he had been "excessively addicted to plays" and "extremely bewitched with the love of romances, fables and old tales, which corrupted my affections and lost my time." So perhaps his suspicions are an understandable over-reaction to genuine excesses. But one might have expected the great Puritan casuist to remember the principle that *usus non tollit abusus;* the abuse does not overturn the right use.

Baxter's diatribe against literature cannot be called an advance, but such sentiments did perform one useful service: they provoked a reaction. It came from a Puritan who did not fit the caricatures. His name was Sir Philip Sidney, and what he wrote could be called an advance indeed. He called it *The Defence of Poesy.* It raised the discussion to heights which have seldom been reached again.

THE RENAISSANCE: SIR PHILIP SIDNEY

Responding in general to such scruples as we have noted and in particular to Stephen Gosson's *School of Abuse* (1579), Sidney wrote his *apologia* in the early 1580's, though it was not published until 1595. In it, he not only gives a thorough and brilliant refutation of the enemies of "poesy" (by which he means imaginative literature, whether in prose or verse) but also lays out a comprehensive vision of its place in the larger structure of learning and the Christian life. He leaves no stone unturned, appealing in luminous and eloquently cadenced prose to poesy's antiquity, its universality, and its effectiveness as a mnemonic device and as an enticement to and adornment of what his opponents consider more "serious" studies. In the process, he makes many of Augustine's positive points, distinguishing the right use from the abuse of literary art. He appeals to the example of Jesus and other biblical writers, who told stories (the parables) and wrote beautiful poetry (the Psalms, Song of Songs, *etc.*). But Sidney is not content merely to win a grudging admittance for literature to the curriculum; he will not stop until he has won it the highest place of all.

Sidney takes it for granted, along with his opponents, that the purpose of education is the acquisition not of knowledge only but of virtue as well. So then: the moral philosopher tells you the precept of virtue, what ought to be, but he does it so abstractly that he is "hard of utterance" and "misty to be conceived," so that one must "wade in him until he be old before he shall find sufficient cause to be honest." The historian, on the other hand, tells a concrete story we can relate to; but he is limited to what actually has been and cannot speak of what ought to be. The one gives an ideal but abstract precept, the other a concrete but flawed example. But "both, not having both, do both halt" (Rollins and Baker 610). How then do we get beyond this impasse?

> Now doth the peerless poet perform both: for whatsoever the philosopher saith should be done, he gives a perfect picture of it by someone by whom he presupposeth it was done; so as he coupleth the general notion with a particular example. A perfect picture, I say, for he yieldeth to the powers of the mind an image of that whereof the philosopher bestoweth but a wordish description, which doth neither strike, pierce, nor possess the sight of the soul as much as the other doth. *(Ibid)*

By combining the virtues of history and philosophy, the poet then becomes the "monarch" of the humane sciences, the most effective at achieving their end, virtuous action. He can give us better role models—and negative examples too—than can be supplied by real life in a fallen world. "Disdaining to be tied to any such subjection [to nature], lifted up by the vigor of his own invention," he makes in effect another nature (607). He has the freedom to do this because he is created in the image of the Creator. Greek and English rightly agree in calling the poet (from Greek *poiein,* to make) a maker, for people are most like God the Maker when they create a world and people it with significant characters out of their imagination. The very existence of literature, then, even when it is abused, is a powerful apology for the Christian doctrine of humanity and its creation in the image of God. Therefore, we should give right honor to the heavenly Maker of that maker, who, having made man to his own likeness, set him beyond and over all the works of that second nature: which in nothing he sheweth so much as in poetry, when with the force of a divine breath he bringeth things forth surpassing her doings. (608)

Here, then, is finally a profoundly Christian understanding of literature which does not merely salvage it for Christian use but finds the very ground of its being in explicitly Christian doctrine: creation, the *imago Dei,* the "cultural mandate" to subdue the earth. Christians alone understand why human beings, whether "literary" types or not, are impelled to make, tell, and hear stories. When Christians also do so, they are not so much spoiling the Egyptians as recovering their own patrimony. That is why we not only learn from literature but enjoy it: it delights as it teaches. And it conveys its kind of truth through the creation of concrete images which incarnate or embody ideas which would otherwise remain abstract and nebulous.

> But what, shall the abuse of a thing make the right use odious? Nay truly, though I yield that Poesy may not only be abused, but that being abused...it can do more hurt than any other army of words, yet shall it be so far from concluding that the abuse should give reproach to the abused, that contrariwise it is a good reason, that whatsoever, being abused, doth most harm, being rightly used...doth most good.
>
> —SIR PHILIP SIDNEY, *An Apology for Poetry*

Subsequent criticism, both Christian and secular, has confirmed Sidney's emphasis on the significance of the concrete image as an important way in which literature communicates. And the most profound moments in Christian reflection on literature since have simply followed up on hints Sidney gave us: that the principle of incarnation is why our images communicate so well; that the *imago Dei* is the key to our identity as poets as well as human beings. It is no exaggeration to call Sidney's *Defence* the fountainhead of modern Christian poetics. Those who do not begin with it are condemned to reinvent the wheel or to drag their load without one.

While Sidney gave us the foundation, there is yet a lot that can be built on it. Seventeenth-century devotional poets such as Donne explored the ability of unexpected metaphors to express the paradoxical mysteries of Christian truth and experience. George Herbert struggled to reconcile sparkling wit and simplicity in the service of edification, finally bringing his "lovely metaphors" to church "well dressed and clad" because "My God must have my best—even all I had" (Hutchinson 271-285). Poets such as Herbert increasingly looked to Scripture to provide both a justification for their writing and a model for how to pursue it. Milton, following Spenser's example, looked to both biblical and classical models as he created images of truth, virtue and vice (from Sabrina to the Son, from Comus to Satan) which function in precisely Sidneyan terms.

JOHN MILTON

Milton also buttressed Sidney's case with some powerful arguments of his own. The end of learning, he said, is to "repair the ruins of our first parents by regaining to know God aright, and out of that knowledge to love him, to imitate him, to be like him" by acquiring "true virtue" (Hughes 631). This reinforces and expands Sidney's point that the end of learning is virtuous action. While we are in the body, our understanding must "found itself on sensible things" and education must follow that method—which helps to explain the importance of concrete images for acquiring both understanding and virtue. The well-rounded Renaissance education Milton recommends then includes "a well-continued and judicial conversing among pure authors digested" *(Ibid)*. The salutary effects of literature then come only from a life-long habit of living with the minds of thoughtful and creative people in their books.

It is because of their connection with the mind of the author that books have such power, Milton explains, in a passage that essentially extends one of Sidney's points: if human beings are the image of a creative God, books are the image of such people:

> For books are not absolutely dead things, but do contain a potency of life in them to be as active as that should whose progeny they are; nay, they do preserve as in a vial the purest efficacy and extraction of that living intellect that bred them... [Hence] as good almost kill a man as kill a good book: who kills a man kills a reasonable creature, God's image; but he who destroys a good book kills reason itself, kills the image of God, as it were, in the eye. (720)

It is the "seasoned life of man" that is "preserved and stored up" in books *(Ibid)*. Part of what Milton valued in a good book then was contact with the mind of an author rendered otherwise inaccessible by distance or time. Such contact is precisely what much modern and postmodern criticism insists we cannot have. Perhaps a secular world view inevitably leads to a universe in which a text is merely a playing field for the reader's own intellectual athleticism. Perhaps only a Christian view (such as Milton's) of the *imago* descending from God to author to text can preserve the writing of literature as an act of communication. Perhaps some Christians have too easily accepted the dominance of reader-centered approaches when their own tradition could provide the basis for a more humane alternative. At any rate, Milton's language and its theological grounding may offer one reason many Christians still tend to be more sympathetic than other modern readers to author-centered approaches such as that of E. D. Hirsch.

[Literary] abilities, wheresoever they be found, are the inspired gift of God, rarely bestowed, but yet to some (though most abuse) in every nation; and are of power, beside the office of a pulpit, to inbreed and cherish in a great people the seeds of virtue and public civility, to allay the perturbations of the mind, and set the affections in right tune; to celebrate in glorious and lofty hymns the throne and equipage of God's almightiness..., [t]eaching over the whole book of sanctity and virtue through all the instances of example.

—JOHN MILTON, *The Reason of Church Government*

Milton also strengthens the rationale for refusing to ban literature on the grounds of its potential for abuse. His arguments against government censorship of some books tell equally against those who would eschew all books lest they be corrupted by them. Such attempts to bury our heads in the sand are smothered in terms of their own goals because virtue that is preserved only thus is "but a blank virtue, not a pure." In the real world after the fall, as in the literary worlds which represent it, good and evil are so intertwined that the responsibility of discernment cannot realistically be avoided. As a result,

What wisdom can there be to choose, what continence to forbear, without the knowledge of evil? He that can apprehend and consider vice with all her baits and seeming pleasures, and yet abstain, and yet distinguish, and yet prefer that which is truely better, he is the true warfaring Christian.

This is so because we "cannot praise a fugitive and cloistered virtue, unexercised and unbreathed, that never sallies out and sees her adversary, but slinks out of the race" (Hughes 728). Spenser's Guyon is a positive role model of uncloistered virtue who makes his authors a better teacher than Scotus or Aquinas. Thus Sidney's poet defeats the philosopher and the theologian. But even when a text promotes error, discernment is better than blindness, and "books promiscuously read" can help prepare us for life. If they do not, the fault lies not in the book but in the reader. Anyone who tried to avoid corruption by avoiding books only becomes a citizen of Mark Twain's Hadleyburg.

THE MODERN ERA

The eighteenth and nineteenth centuries saw advances in our understanding of literature, but few of them came from Christians speaking specifically as Christians. Dr. Johnson's observation that staying power—"length of duration and continuance of esteem"—is the ultimate criterion of literary greatness has itself stood the test of time (Tillotson 1066-1067). Wordsworth's attack on poetic diction, Coleridge's insights on the role of the imagination, and Keats' concept of negative capability have enriched our appreciation of the range of possibilities in literature. Arnold showed us how literature and its criticism could help us to see things as in themselves they really are and to discern the best that has been done and thought, but he succumbed to the post-Darwinian scepticism of his age so far as to make poetry more a substitute for faith than its servant.

In the twentieth century, the New Criticism focused constructively on the details of the text and sought to define the kind of knowledge literature offers in contradistinction to that which comes from the sciences, concluding that it was knowledge of human experience. On the other hand, its imbalanced emphasis on the autonomy of the text ironically opened the door to de[con]struction and other essentially anti-literary ways of reading. Christians participated in, benefited from, reacted against, and were influenced by many of these modern movements, but made few contributions to them that were motivated by their distinctively Christian world view as such.

In the meantime, a number of Christian thinkers from various traditions were profitably pursuing the idea that literature is a form of natural revelation parallel to the cosmos or conscience. Jesuit priest Gerard Manley Hopkins held that Nature is "news of God" and sought in his poetry to embody the "inscape"—the inner unity of being which a particular created thing has, for "I know the beauty of our Lord by it" (Gardner and MacKenzie xx-xxi). Conservative Protestant theologian A. H. Strong saw art giving testimony to "the fundamental conceptions of natural religion"; neo-Thomism emphasized art as a form of natural revelation; and liberal Protestant theologian Paul Tillich attempted to correlate "the questions posed by man's existential situation, expressed in his cultural creations," with the answers of the Christian message (Cary 35, 27). Michael Edwards is perhaps the best of the recent writers in this vein. "Literature occurs," he says, "because we inhabit a fallen world. Explicitly or obscurely, it is part of our dispute with that world" (Edwards 12). If the heavens declare the glory of God (Ps. 19:1) and the invisible things are understood by the things that are made (Rom. 1:20), then the things made by the creative member of the creation ought in a special way to bring the truths embodied in creation into focus. An eye that knows where to look should then be able to find in the recurring themes and structures of human literature (whether written by believers or not) an apology for and elucidation of biblical motifs. As Edwards puts it,

> If the biblical reading of life is in any way true, literature will be strongly drawn towards it. Eden, Fall, Transformation, in whatever guise, will emerge in literature as everywhere else. The dynamics of a literary work will be likely to derive from the Pascalian interplays of greatness and wretchedness, of wretchedness and renewal, of renewal and persisting wretchedness. *(Ibid)*

INKLINGS AND FRIENDS

To my mind, the most interesting contributions to Christian poetics in the twentieth century came from a group of friends centered in Oxford in mid-century, who, consciously or not, harked back to Sidney's themes and brought them to their fullest development. In 1938, J.R.R. Tolkien gave a lecture at St. Andrews University which was later published as "On Fairy Stories" (Tolkien 2-84). In it he provides a full critical vocabulary for Sidney's idea of the poet as maker made by the Maker: sub-creation for the process, primary creation for God's making, secondary creation for the poet's created world:

Although now long estranged
Man is not wholly lost, nor wholly changed.
Dis-graced he may be, yet not dethroned,
And keeps the rags of lordship once he owned:
Man, Sub-creator, the refracted Light
Through whom is splintered from a single white
To many hues, and endlessly combined
In living shapes that move from mind to mind. (54)

While the doctrine of sub-creation was created to explain certain features of fantasy literature, it is applicable to many other genres as well. Even in the most "realistic" fiction, the writer creates a world, peoples it with characters whose actions give its history significance, and determines the rules of its nature. And usually there will be a hero, a villain, a conflict, and some sort of resolution (which Tolkien called *eucatastrophe*), so that the secondary world echoes the primary creation in more ways than one. The hero, at great personal sacrifice, defeats the villain and rescues the damsel in distress, and they ride off into the sunset to live happily ever after: this basic plot we keep coming back to is salvation history writ small, as it were. As Edwards says, literature is "drawn" towards a biblical reading of life. Tolkien explains why: "We make still by the law in which we're made" (Tolkien 54).

In 1941, Dorothy L. Sayers provided a detailed analysis of that creative process in *The Mind of the Maker.* She developed the relevance of the *imago Dei* for understanding artistic creation in explicitly trinitarian terms. In every act of creation there is a controlling *idea* (the Father), the *energy* which incarnates that idea through craftsmanship in some medium (the Son), and the *power* to create a response in the reader (the Spirit). These three, while separate in identity, are yet one act of creation. So the ancient credal statements about the Trinity are factual claims about the mind of the maker created in his image. Sayers delves into the numerous literary examples, in what is one of the most fascinating accounts ever written both of the nature of literature and of the *imago Dei.* While some readers may feel she has a tendency to take a good idea too far, *The Mind of the Maker* remains an indispensable classic of Christian poetics.

The true work of art, then, is something new—*it is not primarily the copy or representation of anything. It may involve representation, but that is not what makes it a work of art.*

—DOROTHY SAYERS, "Towards a Christian Aesthetic"

C. S. Lewis never produced a major statement on literary theory from an explicitly Christian standpoint to rival Tolkien's or Sayers', but he gave us a constant stream of practical criticism from an implicitly Christian stance and a number of provocative essays that deal directly with the relationship between Christianity and literature. Probably best known is the essay "Christianity and Culture" (Lewis, *Christian Reflections* 12-36), superficial readings of which have given rise to the notion that Lewis had an "anti-culture bias" (Cary 16). Actually, he was making the point that idolization of culture (including literature) corrupts and destroys culture—a point he made more clearly in later essays (Lewis, *God in the Dock* 278-281, etc.). In "Christianity and Culture" he was engaged in the Augustinian task of defending the *innocence* of literary pursuits; in later writings he expanded his view of the positive *value* of reading.

Has [literature] any part to play in the life of the converted? I think so....
If all the cultural values, on the way up to Christianity, were dim antepasts and ectypes of the truth, we can recognize them as such still. And since we must rest and play, where can we do so better than here—in the suburbs of Jerusalem?

—C. S. LEWIS, "Christianity and Culture"

In the first place, literature enlarges our world of experience to include both more of the physical world and things not yet imagined, giving the "actual world" a "new dimension of depth" (Lewis, *Of Other Worlds* 29). This makes it possible for literature to strip Christian doctrines of their "stained glass" associations and make them appear in their "real potency" (37), a possibility Lewis himself realized in the Narnia series and the space trilogy. Then, too, literature can have something of the significance that Lewis denies it in "Christianity and Culture" through the creation of positive role models and the reinforcement of healthy "stock responses": life is sweet, death is bitter, and so on (Lewis, *C. S. Lewis: Poems* 1). "Since it is likely that [children] will meet cruel enemies, let them at least have heard of brave knights and heroic courage" (31). Finally, literature can cure our provincialism and fortify us in the "mere Christianity" which has remained constant through the ages, if we do not limit ourselves to the books of our own age (Lewis, *God in the Dock* 200-207). That literature will do these things is uncertain—much modern literature tries not to—but the literature of the ages *can* do so if we receive it sympathetically. In *An Experiment in Criticism* Lewis shows us how to do just that, in a book that demonstrates the possibility of a sane, reader-centered criticism which would not exclude the authority of the author.

OTHER VOICES

No one writer had more influence on modern thinking about literature than T. S. Eliot, whose conversion brought him back from the wasteland of modernity to dance at the still point of the turning world. Two major themes from his criticism compel our attention here. The first was a constant in both his modernist and Christian periods, though it makes best sense when grounded in the Christian worldview: the importance of rootedness in the literary *tradition* of the West for both intelligent reading and original writing. Many modernists and postmodernists tend to dismiss the "dead writers"—or at least their ideas—as irrelevant because "we know so much more than they did." "Precisely," Eliot replied, "and they are what we know" (Eliot, *Selected Essays* 6).

The second theme is the relation of *content* and literary value. Here, Eliot gradually moved from an early aestheticism in which he tended to rigorously separate the two toward an appreciation of the fact that ultimately literary greatness is inseparable from the value of the ideas expressed or implied. In 1927 he said that, from the standpoint of poetry, Dante's system of thought was "an irrelevant accident" (116). Just two years later he recognized that Dante's "His will is our peace" was "literally true," and that "it had more beauty for me now, when my own experience has deepened its meaning, than it did when I first read it," concluding that appreciation of poetry could not in practice be separated from personal belief after all (231). By 1935 Eliot was calling for literary criticism to be "completed by criticism from a definite ethical and theological standpoint" (354) and for Christians to produce both such criticism and also literary works themselves whose content was "unconsciously Christian."

A final important voice for twentieth-century Christian poetics belonged to an American local-color writer, the self-styled "hillbilly Thomist" Flannery O'Connor. Like Tillich and Edwards, she believed that great literature deals with ultimate concerns that are essentially theological; like Lewis, but in a totally different manner, she removed stained-glass associations so that the "action of grace" could be seen in new contexts with new power. In a small but powerful body of fiction she made the American South an image of the human condition seen in profoundly Christian terms. Her letters and critical writings are loaded with practical wisdom on how to embody the anagogical vision in concrete images which can speak to the modern reader.

CONCLUSION

Where, then, has this brief history of Christian thinking about literature brought us? Cary rightly notes that "the modern critic who wants to deal with literature from a Christian standpoint has not found direct precedents in the literary criticism of the past 150 years, which constitutes what is inevitably the critical milieu for him" (Cary 3-4). The Christian giants we have surveyed in the twentieth century definitely stood outside the mainstream. They all had roots sunk deep in a venerable and humane tradition which goes back to the ancients through Milton and Sidney and thus they preserve a way of reading and writing which has been able to resist the ideological fragmentation and de[con]struction which has followed the breakup of the hegemony of New Criticism.

In the pages of journals such as *Christianity and Literature*, explicitly Christian wrestling with literary questions continues. It represents a range from futile efforts to accommodate modernist and postmodernist perspectives to virile and living heirs of the right evangelical tradition descending, as I have argued, from Sir Philip Sidney. By grounding literary activity in a specifically Christian understanding of human nature, that evangelical tradition can give a coherent explanation of why people make worlds out of words and of the ways in which those worlds are valuable.

Perhaps our being reminded that there *is* a unique and distinctly Christian tradition of poetics could help us tap into its power once again. In America, evangelicals produce too many cheap imitations of Lewis and Tolkien on the one hand, and too many saccharine historical romances on the other. While such writers as Walter Wangerin Jr. and Calvin Miller have produced some interesting creative work, and such writers as Leland Ryken, Gene Edward Veith, and Michael Bauman have produced some incisive criticism, there is no one on the scene with the power of a Lewis, a Tolkien, a Sayers, or an O'Connor—much less a Milton. But the tradition that gave us those writers can give us more. As Francis Schaeffer reminded us, "The Christian is the one whose imagination should fly beyond the stars" (5).

Works Cited

Augustine, St. *Confessions.* Trans. William Watts. Cambridge: Harvard University Press, 1946.

Baxter, Richard. *The Practical Works of Richard Baxter.* vol. 1. *The Christian Directory.* London: George Virtue, 1838, 56-57

Cary, Norman Reed. *Christian Criticism in the Twentieth Century.* Port Washington: Kennicat, 1975.

Edwards, Michael. *Towards a Christian Poetics.* Grand Rapids: Eerdmans, 1984.

Eliot, T. S. "Dante." *Selected Essays.* New York: Harcourt, Brace & World, 1964. 199-237.

———. "Religion and Literature." *Selected Essays.* New York: Harcourt, Brace & World, 1964. 343-54.

———. "Shakespeare and the Stoicism of Seneca." *Selected Essays.* New York: Harcourt, Brace & World, 1964. 107-120.

———. "Tradition and the Individual Talent." *Selected Essays.* New York: Harcourt, Brace & World, 1964. 3-11.

Gardner, W. H. and N. H. MacKenzie eds. *The Poems of Gerard Manley Hopkins.* 4th ed. London: Oxford University Press, 1967.

Hirsch, E. D. *Validity in Interpretation.* New Haven: Yale University Press, 1967.

Howie, George, ed. *St. Augustine on Education.* Chicago: Regnery, 1996.

Hughes, Merritt Y., ed. *John Milton: Complete Poems and Major Prose.* Indianapolis: Bobbs-Merrill, 1957.

Hutchinson, F. E., ed. *The Works of George Herbert.* Oxford: Clarendon, 1941.

Lewis, C. S. "A Confession." *C. S. Lewis: Poems.* Ed. Walter Hooper. New York and London: Harcourt, Brace, Jovanovich, 1964.

———. *An Experiment in Criticism.* Cambridge: Cambridge University Press, 1969.

———. "Christianity and Culture." *Christian Reflections.* Ed. Walter Hooper. Grand Rapids: Eerdmans, 1967.

———. "First and Second Things." *God in the Dock.* Ed. Walter Hooper. Grand Rapids: Eerdmans, 1970. 278-81.

———. "On the Reading of Old Books." *God in the Dock.* Ed. Walter Hooper. Grand Rapids: Eerdmans, 1970. 200-207.

———. "On Three Ways of Writing for Children." *Of Other Worlds.* Ed. Walter H. Hooper. New York: Harcourt, Brace, Jovanovich, 1966. 22-34.

———. "Sometimes Fairy Stories Say Best What's to Be Said." *Of Other Worlds.* Ed. Walter Hooper. New York: Harcourt, Brace, Jovanovich, 1964. 35-38.

O'Connor, Flannery. *Mystery and Manners: Occasional Prose.* Ed. Sally and Robert Fitzgerald. New York: Farrar, Strauss and Giroux, 1961.

———. *The Complete Stories of Flannery O'Connor.* New York: Farrar, Strauss and Giroux, 1971.

———. *The Habit of Being: Letters of Flannery O'Connor.* Ed. Sally and Robert Fitzgerald. New York: Farrar, Straus and Giroux, 1961.

Robinson, F. N., ed. *The Works of Geoffrey Chaucer.* Boston: Houghton Mifflin, 1961.

Rollins, Hyder E. and Herschel Baker, eds. *The Renaissance in England.* Lexington: D. C. Heath, 1954.

Sayers, Dorothy L. *The Mind of the Maker.* London: Methuen, 1941.

Schaeffer, Francis. *Art and the Bible: Two Essays.* Downers Grove: InterVarsity Press, 1973.

Tillotson, Geoffrey, ed. *Eighteenth-Century English Literature.* New York: Harcourt, Brace and World, 1969.

Tolkien, J. R. R. "On Fairy Stories." *Essays Presented to Charles Williams.* Ed. C. S. Lewis. Oxford: Oxford University Press, 1947. Rpt. J. R. R. Tolkien, *The Tolkien Reader.* New York: Ballantine, 1966. 2-84.

Williams, Donald T. *Inklings of Reality: Essays Toward a Christian Philosophy of Letters.* Toccoa Falls, Georgia: Toccoa Falls College Press, 1996.

Thinking Christianly About Literature

Leland Ryken

"What has Ingeld to do with Christ?" That is what Alcuin wished to know in 797 when he saw the monks' fondness for fictional stories about heroes such as Beowulf and Ingeld. He put an end to such literary indulgence by laying down the rule, "Let the words of God be read aloud at table in your refectory. The reader should be heard there, not the flute-player; the Fathers of the Church, not the songs of the heathen" (Alcuin, qtd. in Duckett 209). Many Christians through the centuries have agreed with Alcuin's view of literature.

The apologists for literature surveyed in Donald Williams's essay in this volume disagreed with Alcuin's assessment, as do the contributors to this book. The purpose of the present essay is to provide a systematic overview of the leading issues that comprise a Christian poetic—a philosophy of literature.

Several broad generalizations are at once possible. A Christian poetic involves two things—a general *defense* of literature (a rationale for its importance in a Christian's life) and a *methodology* for relating one's actual reading or writing of literature to the Christian faith. It is also useful to keep in view that literature performs a threefold function: It presents human experience for contemplation, it offers an interpretation of that experience, and it presents form/technique/beauty for a reader's enjoyment. It is a time-honored axiom that literature is both useful and delightful.

A Christian philosophy of literature begins with the same agenda of issues that *any* philosophy of literature addresses. Its distinctive feature is that it relates these issues to the Christian faith. An understanding of at least four elements is essential to any philosophical discussion of literature: (1) There is a form of discourse that possesses properties that allow us to speak of it as literature. (2) One aspect of literature consists of form, beauty, technique, and creativity, and this aspect is self-rewarding as a form of enjoyment, entertainment, and aesthetic enrichment. (3) The content of literature has a lot to do with human experience, as distinct from abstract thought or ideas. (4) This should not, however, lead us to minimize the importance of perspective in literature, nor to deny that values and ideas are part of the literary enterprise.

THE NATURE OF LITERATURE

To speak of literature is to imply that it has identifiable traits that set it apart from other forms of discourse. This should be self-evident, but it is not. Through the centuries, Christians have tried to turn literature into something other than what it is. T. S. Eliot's dictum that literature should be allowed to be literature and "not defined in terms of something else" is always in need of reiteration (*Use of Poetry* 147).

Literature consists of words, first of all. Yet when Christians talk about literature, it would be easy to get the impression that literature consists of ideas. It does not. When a poet lamented his inability to write poetry even though he was "full of ideas," the French poet Mallarmé responded, "One does not make poetry with ideas, but with *words*" (quoted in Valéry 77). A proper respect for language is a prerequisite to producing and understanding literature. Christianity itself pushes us toward such a respect because it is a revealed religion whose authoritative truths are written in a book.

The bigger obstacle to letting literature be literature among Christians has been a naive belief that literature is somehow a direct rendition of reality. But literature is always life at the remove of art and the imagination. Literature is an imagined world having its own characteristics and its own integrity as a world created by human subcreators. The world of literature is a construct of the imagination that adheres to conventions that are always to some degree unlifelike and often openly fantastic. Literature takes reality and human experience as its starting point, transforms it by means of the imagination, and sends readers back to life with renewed understanding of it and zest for it because of their excursions into a purely imaginary realm.

Christians have traditionally found it difficult to grant integrity to this world of the imagination and have found ways to suppress or discredit the imaginary element in literature. One tendency has been to denigrate fiction and fantasy as being untruthful, frivolous, a waste of time, escapist, and something to be left behind with childhood. Others have tried to excise the imaginary aspect of literature by acting as though literature is a direct replica of everyday life, ignoring all that is unlifelike about it. The impulse to reduce literature to ideas has also been a perennially popular way for Christians to avoid the imaginary dimension of literature.

Literature will yield...what it has to give only if it is approached as literature.
—F. R. LEAVIS, *The Common Pursuit*

These responses misinterpret the nature of literature. Literature is built on a grand paradox: It is a make-believe world that nonetheless reminds us of real life and clarifies it for us. The eighteenth-century critic Samuel Johnson noted that the imitations of literature "are not mistaken for realities, but...bring realities to mind" (264). This is similar to artist Pablo Picasso's great aphorism that "art is a lie that makes us realize truth" (315).

Reading and writing literature depend on a respect for the ability of the imagination to embody truth. There is no valid reason for the perennial Christian preference of biography, history, and the newspaper to fiction and poetry. The former tell us what *happened,* while literature tells us what *happens.*

The example of the Bible, which is central to any attempt to formulate a Christian approach to literature, sanctions the imagination as a valid form of expressing truth. The Bible is in large part a work of imagination. Its most customary way of expressing truth is not the sermon or theological outline but the story, the poem, and the vision—all of them literary forms and products of the imagination (though not necessarily the fictional imagination). Literary conventions are present in the Bible from start to finish, even in the most historically factual parts.

LITERARY FORM AND CREATIVITY

Literature is a form of knowledge, but it is also an art form—the creation of technique and beauty for the sake of entertainment and aesthetic delight. A Christian approach to literature includes an endorsement of the artistic and pleasure-giving aspect of literature. A Christian view *should* stand as a corrective to the prevailing utilitarian spirit of a technological society, though in fact Christians have often perpetuated the utilitarian outlook to the disparagement of literature.

Faced with the charge of the nonusefulness of literature, Christian apologists for literature have tried to meet the argument on its own terms, showing that literature is useful after all. It teaches truth, apologists say, or it moves people to good moral behavior. While there is truth in these arguments, there is something inherently wrong with minimizing the aesthetic dimension of literature. A defense of beauty, form, and creativity can be rooted in biblical example and doctrine.

The doctrine of creation forms a good starting point. God himself is a creator, and the world he created is a world that is beautiful as well as utilitarian. This creative God made people in his image—that is, with a capacity for creativity and beauty. It is no wonder that Christian defenders of the arts have made much of creativity. Christian poet Chad Walsh writes that writers can see themselves "as a kind of earthly assistant to God…carrying on the delegated work of creation, making the fullness of creation fuller" (227).

> As image-bearer of God, man possesses the possibility both to create something beautiful, and to delight in it.
> —ABRAHAM KUYPER, Lectures on Calvinism

The example of the Bible confirms the importance of literary form and beauty. If the message of the Bible were all that mattered, there would have been no good reason for biblical poets to put their utterances into intricately patterned verse form, or for biblical storytellers to compose masterfully compact and carefully designed stories. In God's economy, the writers of the Bible did not have something better to do with their time and ability than to be artistic to the glory of God. The writer of Ecclesiastes speaks for other biblical authors as well as for himself when he tells us that he arranged his material "with great care," and that he "sought to find pleasing words" (Ecclesiastes 12:9-10, RSV) or "words of delight" (12:10, ESV).

This biblical endorsement of literary creativity is matched by its respect for beauty and enjoyment. When God formed paradise, the perfect human environment, he "made to grow every tree that is pleasant to the sight and good for food" (Genesis 2:9, RSV). God's design for human life, in other words, is aesthetic as well as utilitarian.

How can a person read literature to the glory of God? By enjoying the beauty that human creativity has produced and recognizing God as the ultimate source of this beauty and creativity. Christians do not need to defend literature, as most people have done, solely on the didactic grounds that it teaches us. Literature has a reason for being quite apart from that. In a Christian worldview, literature exists for more than our enjoyment, but not for less.

INCARNATION OF HUMAN EXPERIENCE

Along with the Christian doctrine of creation, the doctrine of the incarnation has most often been invoked in Christian philosophies of the arts, with the Christian sacraments close behind. It is not hard to see why the incarnation has loomed so large in Christian thinking about literature. In the words of C. S. Lewis, literature "too is a little incarnation, giving body to what had been before invisible and inaudible" (*Psalms* 5).

Although the terminology has differed from age to age, literary theory through the centuries has agreed that the subject of literature is human experience. The thing that sets literature off from philosophy and the "thought" disciplines is that it embodies human experience in concrete form rather than presenting abstract propositions. Literature gives the example rather than the precept. It embodies experience in event and character, in image and metaphor.

The writer's task, said Nathan Scott, is "to *stare,* to *look* at the created world, and to lure the rest of us into a similar act of contemplation" (52). Novelist Joseph Conrad said something similar: "My task...is, by the power of the written word to make you hear, to make you feel—it is, before all, to make you *see*" (19). Flannery O'Connor quipped, "The writer should never be ashamed of staring" (84).

The Christian doctrine of the incarnation and the Christian sacraments have provided a convenient analogy to literature, and perhaps even a sanction for it. Like the incarnation of Jesus and similar to the sacraments, literature embodies meaning in concrete form.

The incarnational nature of literature and the kind of knowledge that it gives us (an experiential knowledge of life as we live it) have important ramifications for thinking Christianly about literature. Western culture generally, as well as the Christian subculture specifically, has had an unwarranted tendency to think that abstract ideas and facts are the only valid type of knowledge that we possess. Literature challenges that bias, and so does the Bible. The Bible is not a theological outline with proof texts attached. It is an anthology of literature. When asked to define "neighbor," Jesus refused, telling a story instead (the parable of the Good Samaritan). Our fund of important knowledge is not limited to ideas but includes the characters and events of stories and the images and metaphors of poetry as well. In a startling challenge to our customary thinking in this regard, C. S. Lewis claimed that it is "a mistake to think that our experience in general can be communicated by precise and literal language and that there is a special class of experiences (say, emotions) which cannot. The truth seems to me the opposite" ("Language" 138).

> Poets are always telling us that grass is green, or thunder loud, or lips red.... This is the most remarkable of the powers of Poetic language: to convey to us the quality of experiences.
> —C. S. LEWIS, "The Language of Religion"

The incarnational nature of literature has important implications for settling the perennial question of whether literature tells the truth. One of the levels of truth in literature is truthfulness to human experience and external reality. Literature overwhelmingly tells the truth at this level. Writers are sensitive observers of reality. It is part of their craft to be such. Literature offers a kind of experiential knowledge and truth that everyone needs. Literature and the Bible alike tell us that we live by more than abstract ideas.

PERSPECTIVE IN LITERATURE

Literature does more than present human experience; it also interprets that experience. If one type of literary truth is representational truth based on the reality principle, another type is perspectival truth, consisting of ideas. At this level, literature embodies implied ideas and makes implicit truth claims.

The question of meaning in literature has always been somewhat problematic. Earlier centuries viewed literature as a branch of rhetoric or persuasion and made extravagant (and often unsupportable) claims for literature as a teacher of truth and moral influence. In the middle of the twentieth century, by contrast, literary theory was so preoccupied with literature as the embodiment of human experience that the ideational dimension of literature receded from view. More recently, deconstruction and related forms of skepticism have questioned the ability of literature to convey definite ideational meaning at all.

It is perhaps salutary to be reminded, then, that writers themselves intend to communicate meaning. A specimen statement is novelist Joyce Cary's claim that "a reader must never be left in doubt about the meaning of a story" (132). The assumption of meaning is simply one of the conventions of literature; in fact, a leading literary critic has labeled it "the rule of significance" and calls it "the primary convention of literature" (Culler 115). Writers are on the lookout not only for good story material but also for stories in which (to use the words of the nineteenth-century French poet Baudelaire) "the deep significance of life reveals itself" (quoted in Murry 30).

Writers intend meaning, and their works are a carefully contrived system of persuasion to get the reader to accept their view of the world. In other words, literature is *affective*. In the words of David Lodge, "The writer expresses what he knows by affecting the reader; the reader knows what is expressed by being receptive to affects" (65).

The Christian tradition has never been able to make up its mind about whether the affective persuasiveness of literature is good or bad. Augustine granted that literature is an affective influence, but he regarded this as bad because it moves people to embrace error rather than truth. Renaissance poet Sir Philip Sidney thought literature the most important of all disciplines because it moves people to virtue. Both viewpoints are right: Literature can persuade readers toward an acceptance of either truth or falsehood, and can be a prompter to either good or bad behavior.

What this means is that Christian readers must be discerning and self-conscious about their responses as they read. A Christian approach to literature involves a continuous testing of the spirits to see if they are from God, which brings us to the topic of assessing the intellectual and moral viewpoint of literary works.

All writers...must have, to compose any kind of story, some picture of the world, and of what is right and wrong in that world.

—Joyce Cary, *Art and Reality*

The keynote was sounded in a justly influential essay by T. S. Eliot (reprinted in this anthology), who wrote near the end of the essay, "What I believe to be incumbent upon all Christians is the duty of maintaining consciously certain standards and criteria of criticism over and above those applied by the rest of the world; and that by these criteria and standards everything that we read must be tested" (*Selected Essays* 353). At the outset of his essay Eliot spoke of how "literary criticism should be completed by criticism from a definite ethical and theological standpoint" (*Selected Essays* 343).

Several things are implied by Eliot's theory. One is that before we assess the truth or error of a work of literature we must let the work be itself as a work of literature. I would go so far as to call this a moral duty that we owe to a writer (a viewpoint shared by Peter Leithart's essay in this book). Furthermore, self-forgetfulness—getting beyond ourselves and our limited range of experience—is one of the chief rewards of reading literature. In fact, a degree of initial detachment from a work of literature is exactly what makes it useful for clarifying our own experience, for the simple reason that we cannot see something well if we are too close to it.

But self-forgetfulness must be followed by self-consciousness about who we are as readers. Once we have isolated the implied assertions of a literary work, we need to assess them by ordinary methods of philosophic and theological analysis. Works of literature can assert false ideas as well as true ones, and their artistic greatness does not guarantee their philosophic or moral truthfulness.

The intellectual usefulness of literature is not that it necessarily tells us the truth about an issue but rather that it serves as a catalyst to thinking about the great issues of life. If this is true, we can also see how misguided has been the frequent assumption that it is the task of Christian literary criticism to show *that* works of literature are Christian. The task is rather to assess *whether and to what degree* works are Christian in their viewpoint. Christian enthusiasts for literature too often seek to baptize every work of literature that they love.

Even when we judge a work of literature to be deficient in truth when measured by a Christian viewpoint, we should not dismiss the work wholesale. There are other aspects for which we can commend it. We can always be rapturous over the technique and beauty of a well-crafted story or poem. We can also value and affirm its truthfulness to life and human experience, even if the interpretive slant is wrong. As Christian readers we are free to approve part of a work without endorsing all of it, and conversely we can disagree with part of it without devaluing it entirely. On all of these matters, the record of Christians is not as good as one would wish.

If Christian readers are called to discern truth from error, surely the same responsibility rests on Christian writers. This responsibility might be discharged in two ways. On the one hand, since it is true that the content of writers' work "should be part of the habitual furniture of [their] minds" (Lewis, *Of Other Worlds* 34), it is crucial that the habitual furniture of a Christian writer be theologically and philosophically true rather than false. Secondly, writers need to be readers of their productions, and one of the high points of the essays and excerpts in this anthology is the full-fledged way in which the contributing fiction writers and poets have reflected on their own practices as writers.

CHRISTIAN READERS AND WRITERS

Modern literary theory has championed the idea of interpretive communities— readers and authors who share an agenda of interests, beliefs, and values. Christian readers and writers are one of these interpretive communities. Everyone sees the world and literature through the lens of his or her beliefs and experiences. Christians are no exception. As an interpretive community, Christians should not apologize for having a worldview through which they interpret the world and literature.

What, then, ought to characterize Christian writers and readers? What does the Christian faith offer to writers and readers? I begin with a caution: Christians are not necessarily better writers and readers than other people. The Christian faith does not privilege its adherents in that way. What Christianity provides instead is an agenda of concerns and working premises.

It is the whole person who responds to a poem or novel; and if that person is a believing Christian, then it is a believing Christian who judges.... Literary criticism is as much a personal matter, as much the product of a personal sense of life and value as literature itself.

—VINCENT BUCKLEY, *Poetry and Morality*

The most basic of all these presuppositions is the Christian view of authority and truth. Christians believe that the Bible and the system of doctrine derived from it are authoritative for thought and practice. Christian involvement in literature, therefore, begins with a belief that the Bible and its doctrine will determine how we should view literature itself and will provide a standard by which to measure the intellectual content and morality of literature that we read and write.

This is a way of saying that the Christian faith provides the right perspective from which to view the world and literature. One of the things that this perspective clarifies is the contradictions that we find in literature itself. The doctrines of common grace and general or natural revelation explain how unbelieving writers can produce works of truth and beauty. We do not have to inquire into a writer's orthodoxy to determine whether a novel or poem is worthy of praise. On the other side, the doctrines of the Fall and sin explain the abuses of literature that we see—the espousal of error, immorality of content and effect, degradation of subject matter, and deficiency of form.

The Christian faith also assures writers and readers of the importance of their enterprise. Christians believe that this is their Father's world. God's creation, including the creatures in it, have meaning and importance because God made them. The world is therefore worthy of the writer's portrayal and understanding and love. The same doctrine assures Christian readers that their interest in the portrayal of human experience in literature is not frivolous but essential.

Something similar is true of the enjoyment of literary creativity and beauty. God made people capable of creating. Art is God's gift to the artist (see especially two passages about the beautifying of the tabernacle in Exodus 31:1-11 and 35:30–36:2). This should deflect the ultimate praise from the subcreator to the Creator. The very form in which God inspired the writers of the Bible to write shows that the gift for literary composition bears God's imprint. The Christian reader is equally assured that enjoying the products of human creativity is one of the things that God intends for the human race.

Christians should neither undervalue nor overvalue literature. Literature is not exempt from artistic, moral, and intellectual criticism. Yet its gifts to the human race are immeasurable: artistic enrichment, pleasurable pastime, self-understanding, clarification of human experience, and, in its highest reaches, the expression of truth and beauty that can become worship of God.

When Alcuin asked what Ingeld has to do with Christ, he thought he was asking a rhetorical question that would disparage literature. After all, he was echoing, via similar questions voiced by Tertullian and Jerome, Paul's question, "What accord has Christ with Belial" (2 Corinthians 6:15, RSV)? If we rescue Alcuin's question from its intended scornful put-down of literature and turn his rhetorical question into a seriously intended invitation to discover the truth, we have nothing less than a doorway through which to enter fruitful discussion on a Christian philosophy of literature. What *does* Ingeld have to do with Christ? Looking at the question with thoughtfulness and appreciation, we find a rich array of answers.

Works Cited

Cary, Joyce. *Art and Reality.* Garden City, NY: Doubleday, 1961.

Conrad, Joseph. *The Nigger of the Narcissus.* New York: Collier, 1962.

Culler, Jonathan. *Structuralist Poetics: Structuralism, Linguistics, and the Study of Literature.* Ithaca: Cornell University Press, 1975.

Duckett, Eleanor S. *Alcuin, Friend of Charlemagne.* New York: Macmillan, 1951.

Eliot, T. S. *On Poetry and Poets.* New York: Farrar, Straus, and Cudahy, 1957.

———. *Selected Essays,* new edition. New York: Harcourt, Brace and Company. 1950.

———. *The Use of Poetry and the Use of Criticism.* Cambridge: Harvard University Press, 1933.

Johnson, Samuel. "Preface to Shakespeare." *Criticism: The Major Statements.* Ed. Charles Kaplan. New York: St. Martin's Press, 1975. 252-286.

Lewis, C. S. *Of Other Worlds and Other Essays.* Ed. Walter Hooper. New York: Harcourt Brace Jovanovich, 1966.

———. "The Language of Religion." *Christian Reflections.* Ed. Walter Hooper. Grand Rapids: 1967). 129-141.

———. *Reflections on the Psalms.* New York: Harcourt, 1958.

Lodge, David. *Language of Fiction.* London: Routledge and Kegan Paul, 1966.

Murry, J. Middleton. *The Problem of Style.* London: Oxford University Press, 1922.

O'Connor, Flannery. *Mystery and Manners.* Ed. Sally Fitzgerald and Robert Fitzgerald. New York: Farrar, Straus and Giroux, 1961.

Picasso, Pablo. "Picasso Speaks: A Statement by the Artist." *The Arts.* May 1923: 315-326.

Scott Jr., Nathan A., *Modern Literature and the Religious Frontier.* New York: Harper, 1958.

Valéry, Paul. "Poetry, Language and Thought." *The Modern Tradition: Backgrounds of Modern Literature.* Ed. Richard Ellmann and Charles Feidelson Jr. New York: Oxford University Press, 1965. 74-85.

Walsh, Chad. "A Hope for Literature." *The Climate of Faith in Modern Literature.* Ed. Nathan A. Scott Jr. New York: Seabury, 1964. 207-233.

Perspectives on Art

Francis A. Schaeffer

In what follows I wish to develop a Christian perspective on art in general. How should we as creators and enjoyers of beauty comprehend and evaluate it? There are, I believe, at least eleven distinct perspectives from which a Christian can consider and evaluate works of art. These perspectives do not exhaust the various aspects of art. The field of aesthetics is too rich for that. But they do cover a significant portion of what should be a Christian's understanding in this area.

1. The first is the most important: *A work of art has a value in itself.* For some this principle may seem too obvious to mention, but for many Christians it is unthinkable. And yet if we miss this point, we miss the very essence of art. Art is not something we merely analyze or value for its intellectual content. It is something to be enjoyed. The Bible says that the art work in the tabernacle and the temple was for beauty.

How should an artist begin to do his work as an artist? I would insist that he begin his work as an artist by setting out to make a work of art. What that would mean is different in sculpture and in poetry, for example, but in both cases the artist should be setting out to make a work of art.

Many modern artists, it seems to me, have forgotten the value that art has in itself. Much modern art is far too intellectual to be great art. I am thinking, for example, of artists such as Jasper Johns. Many modern artists seem not to see the

Francis A. Schaeffer *is best known as a towering evangelical apologist during the last three decades of the twentieth century. As director of L'Abri Fellowship in Switzerland, Schaeffer published an array of books that related the Christian faith to a wide range of intellectual disciplines and cultural forms. His most explicitly aesthetic statement is his monograph* Art and the Bible, *from which an excerpted version is presented here.*

distinction between man and non-man, and it is a part of lostness of modern man that they no longer see value in the work of art as a work of art.

I am afraid, however, that as evangelicals we have largely made the same mistake. Too often we think that a work of art has value only if we reduce it to a tract. This too is to view art solely as a message for the intellect.

Literature's world is a concrete human world of immediate experience. The poet uses images and objects and sensations much more than he uses abstract ideas; the novelist is concerned with telling stories, not with working out arguments.

—NORTHROP FRYE, *The Education Imagination*

There are, I believe, three basic possibilities concerning the nature of a work of art. The first view is the relatively recent theory of art for art's sake. This is the notion that art is just *there,* and that is all there is to it. You can't talk about it, you can't analyze it, it doesn't say anything. This view is, I think, quite misguided. No great artist functions on the level of art for art's sake alone.

The second possibility is that art is only an embodiment of a message, a vehicle for the propagation of a particular message about the world, or the artist, or man, or whatever. This view has been held by Christians as well as non-Christians, the difference between the two versions being the nature of the message which the art embodies. But, as I have said, this view reduces art to an intellectual statement and the work of art as a work of art disappears.

The third basic notion of the nature of art—the one I think is right, the one that really produces great art and the possibility of great art—is that the artist makes a body of work and this body of work shows his world view. No one, for example, who understands Michelangelo or Leonardo can look at their work without understanding something of their respective world views. Nonetheless, these artists began by making works of art, and then their world views showed through the body of their work. I emphasize the body of an artist's work because it is impossible for any single painting, for example, to reflect the totality of an artist's view of reality. But when we see a collection of an artist's paintings or a series of a poet's poems or a number of a novelist's novels, both the outline and some of the details of the artist's conception of life shine through.

How then should an artist begin to do his work? I would insist that he begin by setting out *to make a work of art.* He should say to himself, "I am going to make a work of art." Perspective number one is that a work of art is first of all a work of art.

2. *Art forms add strength to the world which shows through, no matter what the world view is or whether the world view is true or false.* Think, for example, of a side of beef hanging in a butcher shop. It just hangs there. But if you go to the Louvre and look at Rembrandt's painting, "Side of Beef Hanging in a Butcher Shop," it's very different. It's startling to come upon this particular work because it says a lot more than its title. Rembrandt's art causes us to see the side of beef in a concentrated way, and, speaking for myself, after looking and looking at his picture, I have never been able to look at a side of beef in a butcher shop with the superficiality I did before. How much stronger is Rembrandt's painting than merely the label, A Side of Beef.

Aesthetic perfection in a work of fiction carries with it a certain felt tension of tone which not only awes the reader, so that he judges the work to be absolutely excellent, but also inspires him to consider it more deeply.

—ANNIE DILLARD, *Living by Fiction*

In literature, there is a parallel. Good prose as an art form has something bad prose does not. Further, poetry has something good prose does not. We may have long discussions on what is added, but the fact that there are distinct differences is clear. Even in the Bible the poetry adds a dimension lacking in the prose. In fact, the effect of any proposition, whether true or false, can be heightened if it is expressed in poetry or in artistic prose rather than in bald, formulaic statement.

3. *In all forms of writing, both poetry and prose, it makes a tremendous difference whether there is a continuity or a discontinuity with the normal definitions of words in normal syntax.* Many modern writers make a concerted effort to disassociate the language of their works from the normal use of language in which there is a normal definition of words and a normal use of syntax. If there is no continuity with the way in which language is normally used, then there is no way for a reader or an audience to know what the author is saying.

What is true in literature is also true in painting and sculpture. The common symbolic vocabulary that belongs to all men (the artists and the viewers) is the world around us, namely God's world. That symbolic vocabulary in the representational arts stands parallel to normal grammar and normal syntax in the literary arts. When, therefore, there is no attempt on the part of an artist to use this symbolic vocabulary at all, then communication is impossible here, too. There is then no way for anyone to know what the artist is saying. My point is not that making this sort of art is immoral or anti-Christian but rather that a dimension is lost.

Totally abstract art stands in an undefined relationship with the viewer, for the viewer is completely alienated from the painter. There is a huge wall between them. The painter and the viewer stand separated from each other in a greater alienation than Giacometti could ever show in his alienated figures. There is a distinct limitation to totally abstract art.

4. *The fact that something is a work of art does not make it sacred.* Heidegger in *What Is Philosophy?* came finally to the view that there are small beings, namely people, who verbalize, and therefore we can hope that Being has some meaning. His great cry at the end of this book is to listen to the poet. Heidegger is not saying that we should listen to the content of what the poets say, because one can find two different poets who give absolutely opposite content; this doesn't matter. The poet became Heidegger's upper-story optimistic hope.

As Christians, we must see that just because an artist—even a great artist—portrays a world view in writing or on canvas, it does not mean that we should automatically accept that world view. Art may heighten the impact of the world view (in fact, we can count on this), but it does not make something true. The truth of a world view presented by an artist must be judged on grounds other than artistic greatness.

5. What kind of judgment does one apply, then, to a work of art? *I believe that there are four basic standards: (a) technical excellence, (b) validity, (c) intellectual content, the world view which comes through, and (d) the integration of content and vehicle.*

I will discuss *technical excellence* in relationship to painting because it is easy to point out through this medium what I mean. Here one considers the use of color, form, balance, and texture of the paint, the handling of lines, the unity of the canvas, and so forth. In each of these there can be varying degrees of technical excellence. By recognizing technical excellence as an aspect of an art work, we are often able to say that while we do not agree with such and such an artist's world view, he is nonetheless a great artist.

We are not being true to the artist as a man if we consider his art work junk simply because we differ with his outlook on life. Christian schools, Christian parents, and Christian pastors often have turned off young people at just this point. Because the schools, the pastors, and the parents did not make a distinction between technical excellence and content, the whole of much great art has been rejected with scorn and ridicule. Instead, if the artist's technical excellence is high, he is to be praised for this, even if we differ with his world view. Man must be treated fairly as man. Technical excellence is, therefore, an important criterion.

Validity is the second criterion. By validity I mean whether an artist is true to himself and to his world view or whether he makes his art only for money or for the sake of being accepted. If an artist makes an art work solely for a patron—whether that patron is the ancient noble, the modern art gallery to which the artist wants access, or the modern art critics of the moment—his work does not have validity. The modern forms of "the patron" are more destructive than even that of the old noble.

The third criterion for the judgment of a work of art is its *content,* that which reflects the world view of the artist. As far as a Christian is concerned, the world view that is shown through a body of art must be seen ultimately in terms of the Scripture. The artist's world view is not to be free from the judgment of the Word of God. In this the artist is like a scientist. The scientist may wear a white coat and be considered an "authority" by society, but where his statements impinge upon what God has given us in Scripture, they come under the ultimate authority of his Word. An artist may wear a painter's smock and be considered almost a holy man, yet where his work shows his world view, it must be judged by its relationship to the Christian world view.

I think we can now see how it is possible to make such judgments concerning the work of art. If we stand as Christians before a man's canvas and recognize that he is a great artist in technical excellence and validity—if in fact he is—and if we have been fair with him as a man and as an artist, then we can say that his world view is wrong. We can judge this view on the same basis as we judge the views of anybody else—philosopher, common man, laborer, business man, or whatever.

Some artists may not know that they are revealing a world view. Nonetheless, a world view usually does show through. Even those works which were constructed under the principle of art for art's sake often imply a world view. Even the world view that there is no meaning is a message. In any case, whether the artist is conscious of the world view or not, to the extent that it is there it must come under the judgment of the Word of God.

True painting...is full of the spirit that moves the brush.
—GEORGE SAND, letter to Gustave Flaubert

To tell a story...is to create a world, adopt an attitude, suggest a behavior.
—JOHN SHEA, *Stories of God*

There is a corollary to this third criterion. We should realize that if something untrue or immoral is stated in great art it can be far more destructive and devastating than if it is expressed in poor art or prosaic statement. Much of the crude art commonly produced by the underground press is laden with destructive messages, but the art is so poor that it does not have much force. But the greater the artistic expression, the more important it is to consciously bring it and its world view under the judgment of Christ and the Bible.

The common reaction among many, however, is just the opposite. Ordinarily, many seem to feel that the greater the art, the less we ought to be critical of its world view. This we must reverse.

There is a second corollary related to judging the content of an art work: It is possible for a non-Christian writer or painter to write and paint according to a Christian world view even though he himself is not a Christian. To understand this, we must distinguish between two meanings of the word *Christian*. The first and essential meaning is that a person who has accepted Christ as his Savior and has thus passed form death to life, from the kingdom of darkness to the kingdom of God by being born again. But if a number of people really are Christians, then they bring forth a kind of consensus that exists apart from themselves, and sometimes non-Christians paint and write within the framework of that consensus even though they as individuals are not Christians.

The fourth criterion for judging a work of art involves how well the artist has *suited the vehicle to the message.* For those art works which are truly great, there is a correlation between the style and the content. The greatest art fits together the vehicle that is being used and the message that is being said.

A recent example is found in T. S. Eliot's "The Waste Land." When Eliot published this in 1922, he became a hero to the modern poets, because for the first time he dared to make the form of his poetry fit the nature of the world as he saw it, namely, broken, unrelated, ruptured. What was that form? A collection of shattered fragments of language and images and allusions drawn seemingly haphazardly from all manner of literature, philosophy, and religious writings from the ancients to the present. But modern poets were pleased, for they now had a poetic form to fit the modern world view of unrelatedness.

6. *Art forms can be used for any type of message from pure fantasy to detailed history.* Because a work of art is in the form of fantasy or epic or painting does not mean that there is no propositional content. Just as one can have propositional statements in prose, there can be propositional statements in poetry; in painting, in virtually any art form.

7. Many Christians, especially those unused to viewing the arts and thinking about them, reject contemporary painting and contemporary poetry not because of their world view but simply because they feel threatened by a new art form. It is perfectly legitimate for a Christian to reject a particular work of art intellectually, that is, because he knows what is being said by it. But it is another thing to reject the work of art simply because the style is different from that which we are used to. In short: *Styles of art form change and there is nothing wrong with this.*

As a matter of fact, change is one difference between life and death. There is no living language which does not undergo constant change. The languages which do not change, Latin, for example, are dead. As long as one has a living art, its forms will change. The past art forms, therefore, are not necessarily the right ones for today or tomorrow. To demand the art forms of yesterday in either word systems or art is a bourgeois error. It cannot be assumed that if a Christian painter becomes "more Christian" he will necessarily become more and more like Rembrandt. This would be like saying that if the preacher really makes it next Sunday morning, he will preach to us in Chaucerian English. Then we'll really listen!

Not only will there be a change in art forms and language as time processes, but there will be a difference in art forms coming from various geographical locations and from different cultures. Take, for example, Hebrew poetry. It has alliteration and parallelism and other such rhetorical forms, but it hardly ever rhymes. Does this mean it is not poetry? Or does it mean that English poetry is wrong when it rhymes? Surely not. Rather, each art form in each culture must find its own proper relationship between world view and style.

Then what about the Christian's art? Here three things should be stressed. First, Christian art today should be twentieth-century art. Art changes. Language changes. The preacher's preaching today must be twentieth-century language communication, or there will be an obstacle to being understood. And if a Christian's art is not twentieth-century art, it is an obstacle to his being heard. It makes him different where there is no necessity for difference. A Christian should not, therefore, strive to copy Rembrandt or Browning.

Second, Christian art should differ from country to country. Why did we ever force the Africans to use Gothic architecture? It's a meaningless exercise. All we succeeded in doing was making Christianity foreign to the African. If a Christian artist is Japanese, his paintings should be Japanese; if Nidian, Indian.

Third, the body of a Christian artist's work should reflect the Christian world view. In short, if you are a young Christian artist, you should be working in the art forms of the twentieth century, showing the marks of the culture out of which you have come, reflecting your own country and your own contemporariness and embodying something of the nature of the world as seen from a Christian standpoint.

8. While a Christian artist should be modern in his art, he does face certain difficulties. First, we must distinguish carefully between style and message. Let me say firmly that *there is no such thing as a godly style or an ungodly style.* The more one tries to make such a distinction, the more confusing it becomes.

Yet while there is no such thing as a godly or ungodly style, we must not be misled or naive in thinking that various styles have no relation whatsoever to the content or the message of the work of art. Styles themselves are developed as symbol systems or vehicles for certain world views or messages. In the Renaissance, for example, one finds distinctively different styles from those which characterize art in the Middle Ages. It does not take much education in the history of art to recognize that what Filippo Lippi was saying about the nature of the Virgin Mary is different from what was being said in paintings done before the Renaissance. Art in the Renaissance became more natural and less iconographic. In our own day, men like Picasso and T. S. Eliot developed new styles in order to speak a new message.

Think, for example, of T. S. Eliot's form of poetry in "The Waste Land." The fragmented form matches the vision of fragmented man. But it is intriguing that after T. S. Eliot became a Christian, for example in "The Journey of the Magi," he did not use quite this same form. Rather, he adapted it for the message he was now giving—a message with a Christian character. But he didn't entirely give up the form; he didn't go back to Tennyson; rather, he adapted the form that he used in "The Waste Land," changing it to fit the message that he was now giving. In other words, T. S. Eliot the Christian wrote somewhat differently than T. S. Eliot the "modern man."

The form in which a world view is given can either weaken or strengthen the content, even if the viewer or reader does not in every case analyze this completely. In other words, depending upon the vehicle you use, though an audience may not notice, you will be moving either toward your world view or away from your world view.

In conclusion, therefore, often we will use twentieth-century art forms, but we must be careful to keep them from distorting the world view which is distinctively ours as Christians. In one way styles are completely neutral. But in another way they must not be used in an unthinking, naive way.

9. *The Christian world view can be divided into what I call a major and a minor theme.* (The terms *major* and *minor,* as I am using them, have no relationship to their use in music.) First, the *minor theme* is the abnormality of the revolting world. This falls into two parts: (a) Men who have revolted from God and not come back to Christ are eternally lost; they see their meaninglessness in the present and they are right from their own standpoint. (b) There is a defeated and sinful side to the Christian's life. If we are at all honest, we must admit that in this life there is no such thing as totally victorious living. In every one of us there are those things which are sinful and deceiving and, while we may see substantial healing, in this life we do not come to perfection.

The *major theme* is the opposite of the minor; it is the meaningfulness and purposefulness of life. From the Christian viewpoint, this falls into two headings, (a) metaphysics and (b) morals. In the area of metaphysics (of being, of existence, including the existence of every person) God is there, God exists. Therefore, all is not absurd. Furthermore, man is made in God's image and so man has significance. The major theme is an optimism in the area of being: everything is not absurd, there is meaning.

There is also a major theme in relation to morals. Christianity gives a moral solution on the basis of the fact that God exists and has a character which is the law of the universe. There is therefore an absolute in regard to morals. It is not that there is a moral law beyond God that binds both God and man, but that God himself has a character and this character is reflected in the moral law of the universe. Thus when a person realizes his inadequacy before God and feels guilty, he has a basis not simply for the feeling but for the reality of guilt. Man's dilemma is not just that he is finite and God is infinite, but that he is a sinner guilty before a holy God. But then he recognizes that God has given him a solution to this in the life, death, and resurrection of Christ. Man is fallen and flawed, but he is redeemable on the basis of Christ's work. This is beautiful. This is optimism. And this optimism has a sufficient base.

Notice that the Christian and his art have a place for the minor theme because man is lost and abnormal and the Christian has his own defeats. There is not only victory and song in my life. But the Christian and his art don't end there. Life goes on to the major theme because there is an optimistic answer. This is important for the kind of art Christians are to produce. First of all, Christian art needs to recognize the minor theme, the defeated aspect to even the Christian life. If our Christian art only emphasizes the major theme, then it is not fully Christian but simply romantic art. And let us say with sorrow that for years our Sunday school literature has been romantic in its art and has had very little to do with genuine Christian art. Older Christians may wonder what is wrong with this art and wonder why their kids are turned off by it, but the answer is simple. It's romantic. It's based on the notion that Christianity has only an optimistic note.

On the other hand, it is possible for a Christian to so major on the minor theme, emphasizing the lostness of man and the abnormality of the universe, that he is equally unbiblical. There may be exceptions where a Christian artist feels it his calling to picture only the negative, but in general for the Christian, the major theme is to be dominant—though it must exist in relationship to the minor.

10. *Christian art is by no means always religious art, that is, art which deals with religious themes.* Consider God the Creator. Is God's creation totally involved with religious subjects? What about the universe? the birds? the trees? the mountains? What about the birds song? and the sound of the wind in the trees? When God created out of nothing by his spoken word, he did not just create "religious" objects. And in the Bible, as we have seen, God commanded the artist, working within God's own creation, to fashion statues of oxen and lions and carvings of almond blossoms for the tabernacle and the temple.

We should remember that the Bible contains the Song of Solomon, the love song between a man and a woman, and it contains David's song to Israel's national heroes. Neither subject is religious. But God's creation—the mountains, the trees, the birds, and the birds' songs—are also non-religious art. Think about that. If God made the flowers, they are worth painting and writing about. If God made the birds, they are worth painting. If God made the sky, the sky is worth painting. If God made the ocean, indeed, it's worth writing poetry about. It is worth man's while to create works upon the basis of the great works God has already created.

There are no prescriptions for subject matter. There is no need for a Christian to illustrate biblical stories or biblical truth, though he may of course choose to do so. An artist has the right to choose a subject that he thinks worthwhile.

—H. R. Rookmaaker, "Letter to a Christian Artist"

This whole notion is rooted in the realization that Christianity is not just involved with "salvation" but with the total man in the total world. The Christian message begins with the existence of God forever and then with creation. It does not begin with salvation. We must be thankful for salvation, but the Christian message is more than that. Man has a value because he is made in the image of God and thus man as man is an important subject for Christian art. Man as man—with his emotions, his feelings, his body, his life—this is important subject matter for poetry and novels. I'm not talking here about man's lostness but about his humanness. In God's world the individual counts. Therefore, Christian art should deal with the individual.

Christian art is the expression of the whole life of the whole person who is a Christian. What a Christian portrays in his art is the totality of life. Art is not to be solely a vehicle for some sort of self-conscious evangelism.

If, therefore, Christianity has so much to say about the arts and to the artist, why is it that recently we have produced so little Christian art? I should think the answer would now be clear. We have not produced Christian art because we have forgotten most of what Christianity says about the arts.

Christians, for example, ought not to be threatened by fantasy and imagination. Great painting is not "photographic"; think of the Old Testament art commanded by God. There were blue pomegranates on the robes of the priest who went into the Holy of Holies. In nature there are no blue pomegranates. Christian artists do not need to be threatened by fantasy and imagination, for they have a basis for knowing the difference between them and the real world "out there." The Christian is the really free person—he is free to have imagination. This too is our heritage. The Christian is the one whose imagination should fly beyond the stars.

A Christian artist does not need to concentrate on religious subjects. After all, religious themes may be completely non-Christian. Religious subjects are no guarantee that a work of art is Christian. On the other hand, the art of an artist who never paints the head of Christ, never once paints an open tomb, may be magnificent Christian art. For some artists there is a place for religious themes, but an artist does not need to be conscience-stricken if he does not paint in this area. Some Christian artists will never use religious themes. This is a freedom the artist has in Christ under the leadership of the Holy Spirit.

11. *Every artist has the problem of making an individual work of art and, as well, building up a total body of work.* No artist can say everything he might want to say or build everything he might want to build into a single work. It is true that some art forms, such as the epic and the novel, lend themselves to larger conceptions and more complex treatments, but even there not everything that an artist wants to do can be done in one piece. Therefore, we cannot judge an artist's work from one piece. No art critic or art historian can do that. We must

judge an artist's performance and an artist's world view on the basis of as much of that artist's work as we can.

If you are a Christian artist, therefore, you must not freeze up just because you can't do everything at once. Don't be afraid to write a love poem simply because you cannot put into it everything of the Christian message. Yet, if a man is to be an artist, his goal should be in a lifetime to produce a wide and deep body of work.

Viewpoint: Annie Dillard

Literature As an Art Object

The art object does not do to us; rather, it presents to us. What does it present? It presents an object for study and contemplation. Why should we study and contemplate this object more than any other, more than a pebble or a pelican? After all, the art object wholly lacks certain qualities which we prize. Its components may lack simple material presence—mass and extension—such as we find in the components of pebbles. As a total object, the art object lacks life, the capacity to grow and change and reproduce, spontaneity, mobility, warmth, senses and sensations, appetite, and other such fine things which any pelican possesses. Nevertheless, the art object may represent these things. And in the manner of its representing—in its surface and in its structure—the art object may present, embody, and enact certain additional qualities as much as, or even more than, we prize the qualities of pebbles and pelicans, or we would never read or sketch on the beach. We find in art objects qualities in which the great world and its parts seem often wanting: human significance, human order, reason, mind, causality, boundary, harmony, perfection, coherence, purity, purpose, and permanence.

In *Fiction and the Figures of Life*, William Gass says, and I concur, "The aim of the artist ought to be to bring into the world objects which do not already exist there, and objects which are especially worthy of love." Always crucial to these thoughts is the caveat that art is lovable and has beauty neither according to its novelty as a newborn object on earth nor according to the lovableness and beauty of the worldly objects it represents, but only according to its internal merits as art. Thus painting has turned from pretty ladies; thus a photographer makes little progress in his art until he ceases making prints of beautiful or lovable objects (like leaves or slaves), the aesthetic or moral virtues of which he attempts to borrow or heist. Similarly, fiction's function is not to people the earth with lovable folk and their dramatic doings in order to widen our acquaintance and cheer our stay on the planet. In *A Dance to the Music of Time,* Anthony Powell manufactures the representation of a person named Kenneth Widmerpool, who is neither beautiful nor lovable. As an artifice, he is both. Graham Greene's *Brighton Rock* is about as crafted a novel as you will find. Its subject, which it presents with unflagging intensity, is human evil. It is very, very good. So also is *Ship of Fools,* so is *The Good Soldier.* As objects, these works possess integrity, intelligence, harmony, and so forth, although their characters and events may not. These points are widely understood; I beg indulgence for mentioning them again.

Art remakes the world according to sense. The art object is a controlled context whose parts cohere within an order according to which they may be understood. Context is meaning.

—Living by Fiction

Viewpoint: C. S. Lewis

We Demand Windows

What then is the good of—what is even the defence for—occupying our hearts with stories of what never happened and entering vicariously into feelings which we should try to avoid having in our own person? Or of fixing our inner eye earnestly on things that can never exist...? The nearest I have yet got to an answer is that we seek an enlargement of our being. We want to be more than ourselves. Each of us by nature sees the whole world from one point of view with a perspective and a selectiveness peculiar to himself.... We want to see with other eyes, to imagine with other imaginations, to feel with other hearts, as well as with our own.... We demand windows. Literature as Logos is a series of windows, even of doors....

> *I believe that the purpose of reading literature is to exercise or incite one's imagination; specifically, one's ability to imagine being different.... The pleasure of reading literature arises from the exercise of one's imagination, a going out from one's self toward other lives, other forms of life, past, present, and perhaps future. This denotes its relation to sympathy, fellowship, the spirituality and morality of being human.*
>
> —DENIS DONAGHUE, *The Practice of Reading*

In love we escape from our self into one other. In the moral sphere, every act of justice or charity involves putting ourselves in the other person's place and thus transcending our own competitive particularity.... The primary impulse of each is to maintain and aggrandise himself. The secondary impulse is to go out of the self, to correct its provincialism and heal its loneliness. In love, in virtue, in the pursuit of knowledge, and in the reception of the arts, we are doing this. Obviously this process can be described either as an enlargement or as a temporary annihilation of the self. But that is an old paradox; 'he that loseth his life shall save it'....

This, so far as I can see, is the specific value or good of literature considered as Logos; it admits us to experiences other than our own.... Those of us who have been true readers all our life seldom fully realise the enormous extension of our being which we owe to authors. We realise it best when we talk with an unliterary friend.... My own eyes are not enough for me, I will see through those of others. Reality, even seen through the eyes of many, is not enough. I will see what others have invented....

Literary experience heals the wound, without undermining the privilege, of individuality.... In reading great literature I become a thousand men and yet remain myself. Like the night sky in the Greek poem, I see with a myriad eyes, but it is still I who see. Here, as in worship, in love, in moral action, and in knowing, I transcend myself; and am never more myself than when I do.

—An Experiment in Criticism
Cambridge: Cambridge University Press, 1961

Christian Art

By the words "Christian Art" I do not mean *Church art....* I mean Christian art in the sense of art which bears within it the character of Christianity.... Christian art is defined by the one in whom it exists and by the spirit from which it issues: one says "Christian art" or the "art of a Christian," as one says...the "art of man." It is the art of redeemed humanity. It is planted in the Christian soul, by the side of the running waters, under the sky of the theological virtues, amidst the breezes of the seven gifts of the Spirit. It is natural that it should bear Christian fruit.

Everything belongs to it, the sacred as well as the profane. It is at home wherever the ingenuity and the joy of man extend. Symphony or ballet, film or novel, landscape or still-life, puppet-show libretto or opera, it can just as well appear in any of these as in the stained-glass windows and statues of churches.

But it may be objected.... Is not art pagan by birth and tied to sin—just as man is a sinner by birth? But grace heals wounded nature. Do not say that a Christian art is impossible. Say rather that it is difficult, doubly difficult—fourfold difficult, because it is difficult to be an artist and very difficult to be a Christian, and because the total difficulty is not simply the sum but the product of these two difficulties multiplied by one another: for it is a question of harmonizing two absolutes. Say that the difficulty becomes tremendous when the entire age lives far from Christ, for the artist is greatly dependent upon the spirit of his time. But has courage ever been lacking on earth?...

If you want to make a Christian work, then *be* Christian, and simply try to make a beautiful work, into which your heart will pass; do not try to "make Christian."

Do not make the absurd attempt to dissociate in yourself the artist and the Christian. They are one, if you *are* truly Christian, and if your art is not isolated from your soul by some system of aesthetics. But apply only the artist to the work; precisely because the artist and the Christian are one, the work will derive wholly from each of them.

Do not *separate* your art from your faith. But leave *distinct* what is distinct. Do not try to blend by force what life unites so well. If you were to make of your aesthetic an article of faith, you would spoil your faith. If you were to make of your devotion a rule of artistic activity, or if you were to turn desire to edify into a method of your art, you would spoil your art.

The entire soul of the artist reaches and rules his work, but it must reach it and rule it only *through the artistic habitus.* Art tolerates no division here.... Christian work would have the artist, as artist, free.

Nevertheless art will be Christian, and will reveal in its beauty the interior reflection of the radiance of grace, only if it overflows from a heart suffused by grace. For the virtue of art which reaches it and rules it directly, presupposes that the appetite is rightly disposed with regard to the beauty of the work. And if the beauty of the work is Christian, it is because the appetite of the artist is rightly disposed with regard to such a beauty, and because in the soul of the artist Christ is present through love. The quality of the work is here the reflection of the love from which it issues, and which moves the virtue of art instrumentally.... It would therefore be futile to try to find a technique, a style, a system of rules or a way of working which would be those of Christian art. The art which germinates and grows in Christian man can admit of an infinity of them. But these forms of art will all have a family likeness, and all of them will differ substantially from non-Christian forms of art.

—Art and Scholasticism
Notre Dame: University of Notre Dame Press, 1974

REFLECTIONS ON
AN UNDERSTANDING
OF LITERATURE

When we are at a play, or looking at a painting or a statue, or reading a story, the imaginary work must have such an effect on us that it enlarges our own sense of reality.

—Madeleine L'Engle, *Walking on Water*

Students value literature as a means of enlarging their knowledge of the world, because through literature they acquire not so much additional information as additional experience.... Literature provides a living-through, not simply knowledge about: not the fact that lovers have died young and fair, but a living-through of *Romeo and Juliet;* not theories about Rome, but a living-through of the conflicts in *Julius Caesar.*

—Marie Rosenblatt, *Literature as Exploration*

Nothing human is alien to me.

—Terence

Literature was born not the day when a boy crying wolf, wolf came running out of the Neanderthal valley with a big gray wolf at his heels; literature was born on the day when a boy came crying wolf, wolf and there was no wolf behind him.

—Vladimir Nabokov, *Lectures on Literature*

The poet's job is not to tell you what happened, but what happens: not what did take place, but the kind of thing that always does take place.

—Northrop Frye, *The Educated Imagination*

The primary job that any writer faces is to tell you a story of human experience—I mean by that, universal mutual experience, the anguishes and troubles and gifts of the human heart, which is universal, without regard to race or time or condition.

—William Faulkner, *Faulkner at West Point*

Literature is news that stays news.

—Ezra Pound, *ABC of Reading*

My assumption is that the story of any one of us is in some measure the story of us all.

—Frederick Buechner, *Listening to Your Life*

The poet is not a man who asks me to look at *him;* he is a man who says "look at that" and points.

—C. S. Lewis, *The Personal Heresy*

Abelard raised a very foolish question when he asked: "What has Horace to do with the Psalter, Virgil with the Gospel, Cicero with the Apostle?" The answer is simply that Horace, Virgil, and Cicero clarify the human situation to which the salvation of God is addressed through Psalter, Gospel, and Apostle.

—Roland M. Frye, *Perspective on Man:
Literature and the Christian Tradition*

The writer…is the world's interpreter…. The critic is interested in the novel; the novelist is interested in his neighbors. Perhaps even more than in his own techniques, then, the writer is interested in knowing the world in order to make real and honest sense of it. He worries the world and probes it; he collects the world and collates.

—Annie Dillard, *Living by Fiction*

I'm always highly irritated by people who imply that writing fiction is an escape from reality. It is a plunge into reality.

—Flannery O'Connor, "The Nature and Aim of Fiction"

Literature, then, serves to deepen and to extend human greatness through the nurture of beauty, understanding, and compassion. In none of these ways, of course, can literature, unless it be the literature of the Christian faith, lead us to the City of God, but it may make our life in the city of man far more a thing of joy and meaning and humanity, and that in itself is no small achievement. Great literature may not be a Jacob's ladder by which we can climb to heaven, but it provides an invaluable staff with which to walk the earth.

—Roland M. Frye, *Perspective on Man:*
Literature and the Christian Tradition

The deeds of Achilles or Roland were told of because they were exceptionally and improbably heroic;…the saint's life, because he was exceptionally and improbably heroic…. Attention is fixed on…the more than ordinary terror, splendour, wonder, pit, or absurdity of a particular case.

—C. S. Lewis, *An Experiment in Criticism*

Life and literature, then, are both conventionalized, and of the conventions of literature about all we can say is that they don't much resemble the conditions of life.

—Northrop Frye, *The Educated Imagination*

For this is quite the final goal of art: to recover this world by giving it to be seen as it is.

—Jean-Paul Sartre, *What Is Literature?*

Literature gives us forms for our feelings.... [One of the functions of literary form is] to facilitate perception—to silhouette the material with the desired degree of clarity.

—Simon Lesser, *Fiction and the Unconscious*

It is the function of all art to give us some perception of an order in life, by imposing an order upon it.

—T. S. Eliot, *On Poetry and Poets*

A well-known writer got collared by a university student who asked, "Do you think I could be a writer?" "Well," the writer said, "I don't know.... Do you like sentences?"

—Annie Dillard, *The Writing Life*

Art is one of the means by which man grapples with and assimilates reality.

—Ralph Fox, *The Novel and the People*

It is easy to forget that the man who writes a good love sonnet needs not only to be enamoured of a woman, but also to be enamoured of the Sonnet.

—C. S. Lewis, *A Preface to Paradise Lost*

You use a glass mirror to see your face; you use works of art to see your soul.

—George Bernard Shaw, *Back to Methuselah*

A poem is the very image of life expressed in its eternal truth.
                    —Percy B. Shelley, *A Defence of Poetry*

The primary job that any writer faces is to tell you a story of human experience—I mean by that, universal mutual experience, the anguishes and troubles and gifts of the human heart, which is universal, without regard to race or time or condition.
                    —William Faulkner, *Faulkner at West Point*

The fairy tale reveals a truly nonsexist world, because we are all, male and female, both the younger son and the true princess.... And the fairy tale assures us, regardless of our gender, "You are the younger son. You are the true princess. You are the enchanted beast."
                    —Madeleine L'Engle, *The Rock That Is Higher*

A poem...begins in delight and ends in wisdom [and]...a clarification of life.... For me the initial delight is in the surprise of remembering something I didn't know I knew.... There is a glad recognition of the long lost.
                    —Robert Frost, "The Figure a Poem Makes"

Part Two

Imagination, Beauty, and Creativity

The oldest theory of art belongs to the Greeks, who regarded art as an imitation (mimesis) of reality. The strength of that theory is that it explains the way in which art takes its materials from real life. After dominating aesthetic theory for at least twenty centuries, the theory of art as imitation showed its limitations, especially in its inability to account for the creative element in artistic composition and the ways in which works of art and literature are unlifelike and imaginary.

Beginning with the Romantic movement of the nineteenth century, therefore, the imagination replaced imitation as the preferred way of conceptualizing the relationship between art and life, and of explaining human creativity as an ingredient in literary composition. In this tradition, the imagination means several things—our image-making and image-perceiving capacity, the creative faculty, the contemplative act, the ability to synthesize disparate details into a single whole, and the human capacity for artistic form and beauty.

All of these themes will be prominent in the essays and excerpts that follow in this unit. Additionally, these issues are related to Christian concerns, thereby yielding a composite picture of the Christian imagination.

The Christian Imagination

Janine Langan

The eye is the lamp of the body. So, if your eye is healthy, your whole body will be full of light; but if your eye is unhealthy, your whole body will be full of darkness. If then the light in you is darkness, how great is the darkness! (Matthew 6:23, NRSV).

Never have so many been educated so long as in today's North America. Yet, despite Northrop Frye's warnings about the dangers of ideological manipulation in his brilliant *The Educated Imagination,* our schools generally put little stress on educating imaginations. We tend to think of the imagination as "ice cream on the cake"—as flight, fancy, distraction, decoration. And education, of course, should focus on the fundamentals. My contention is that there is nothing more fundamental than the imagination, and that our loss of respect for it is directly linked to religious apathy.

This neglect is well pictured by Diderot's *Encyclopedia* (first published in 1751), one of the intellectual wedges that opened the revolutionary floodgates in eighteenth-century France. Its frontispiece represents the unveiling of truth by reason and philosophy. Imagination flits in on Truth's left, bringing a wreath of flowers to "embellish and crown her;" satirical poetry reclines at her feet, bare-breasted and waving a fool's wand. Theology kneels in front of Truth, a big book

JANINE LANGAN *is Professor Emerita of Christianity and Culture at the University of Toronto, where she teaches courses on the Christian imagination in a program that she founded twenty-four years ago. She also teaches at St. Augustine's Seminary and lecures widely on Christianity, the arts, and the media. She has published on Mallarmé, Dante, Dostoevsky, de Beauvoir, Teilhard de Chardin, Christian art, and Catholic education.*

in hand. Shading her eyes from the radiance of Truth, she looks away from her to the heavens, seriously impeding by her weighty presence the unveiling activity of philosophy. At their feet, the sciences, technologies and arts happily interact.

I fear that we still share this view of imagination's role in society: distracting, charming, and filling practical life with all the superficial and superfluous delights made possible by technology, the daughter of right reason. The imagination, most of us really think, prettily crowns our conquest of the world; but reason, in the background, does all the serious work. Critics and artists have challenged this view again and again. From George Steiner *(Real Presences)* to Anne Carson in a recent interview with the *Globe and Mail,* these advocates keep pointing out that the imagination is our fundamental mode of insertion in the world, and that therefore it has deep religious implications.

THE IMAGINATION: OUR PRIMARY INTERFACE WITH THE WORLD

The imagination makes images out of the chaotic influx of our sense perceptions. We tend to stress the artificial and free-floating dimension of the process, as evidenced by the way in which the dictionary defines imagination as "forming a mental concept of what is not actually present to the senses." We forget that none of our conscious intercourse with the world around us is free from the imagination's input. As Rudolph Arnheim points out in *Visual Thinking,* seeing itself banks on the imaging, simplifying, and interpretative power of the imagination. Its project is to propose a picture of the world in which we can fit, with which we can interact. It is purposive and selective; it proposes patterns. Any imaging of the world already orients our response to what it offers, and our perceptions already seduce, repel, and fascinate before the will and the intellect kick in. Hence the importance of a healthy imagination: We access all reality, past, present and future, through its screen. It colors our view of ourselves in the world from the ground up.

The constructs of the imagination tell us things about human life that we don't get in any other way.

—NORTHROP FRYE, *The Educated Imagination*

Our ancestors were highly conscious of this fact. They thought of imagination as a faculty which prepares the food of thought from raw sense given, as the inescapable interpreter of reality, and they took its power very seriously. The word *imagination* originally denoted "the operation of the mind generally, thought, opinion." Regrettably, this dimension of the word's meaning is now "obsolete," as the dictionary puts it.

Yet what is more fundamental to our being the astonishing species that we are than this amazing gift? What is more central to our freedom than this ability to distance ourselves from oppressive givens in order to re-interpret them, to give them meaning and digest them so as to live them out with dignity? Without this ability to empathize with situations different from our own, could we love the otherness of the other with the necessary respect? To say nothing of the most striking aspect of our imagination: creativity, a gift that makes us, for all our weakness, just lower than the angels. Do we not imagine God primarily as the creative artist whose work our imagination admires and echoes, however weakly? Has not humanity always experienced creative imagination as participation in divine life?

This word—this idea of Art as creation *is, I believe, the one important contribution that Christianity has made to aesthetics. Unfortunately, we are apt to use the words "creation" and "creativeness" very vaguely and loosely, because we do not relate them properly to our theology. But it is significant that the Greeks had not this word in their aesthetic at all. They looked on a work of art as a kind of* techné, *a manufacture. Neither, for that matter, was the word in their theology—they did not look on history as the continual act of God fulfilling itself in creation.*

—DOROTHY SAYERS, "Towards a Christian Aesthetic"

Imagining is an act of hope, a challenge to fate, an effort to take matters in hand and to accept our unique role as human beings, "in the world but not of it." It is the weaver of culture. Artists create the language we use to intuit each other's thoughts, the very forms through which we transmit our insights, worship together, galvanize each other to common action. As the destruction of images in the Reformation demonstrated, loss of community follows upon the loss of common images.

To all this, there is a frightful corollary. Free to play with the givens, to reject or distort input, at the interface between our senses and ourselves, our imagination has a terrible power over our inner life, over the decisions we make. Hence Pascal's fearful respect for that faculty: We must seduce imagination in others if we wish to transmit our message to them; we must tame and guard our own imagination if we wish to attend properly to reality. For the imagination always totters between that Wisdom, which played at the feet of the Creator before the stars sang together, and madness.

EDUCATING CHRISTIAN IMAGINATIONS

Educating the imagination—or controlling it—is thus of primordial importance. The secular world knows this. Advertisers, politicians, and totalitarian regimes have developed a science of this faculty, and a whole technology through which to manipulate it.

Logically, Christians should be well armed against such manipulation. They are heirs to the greatest imaginative tradition alive on this planet. In Christian theology, imaging has pride of place. Adam is defined as created in the image of God. The Incarnation, the very heart of Salvation, is imaging: Paul preaches Christ as "the image of the invisible God" (Colossians 1:15). Being a Christian is being called to further imaging. That Divine Image must be transmitted in ever new contexts, in words, in stone, in paint, above all in flesh, our own flesh, in His body, the church. "And we all, with unveiled face, beholding the glory of the Lord, are being changed into his likeness from one degree of glory to another; for this comes from the Lord who is the Spirit" (2 Corinthians 3:18, RSV).

The Christian imagination, if true to this theology, is paradoxical and strikingly original. I would like here to propose a few catchwords to point out aspects of this originality: The Christian imagination is anti-Gnostic, typological, iconic, sacramental, and eschatological.

Imagination demands an image.
                    —G. K. CHESTERTON, "The Soul in Every Legend"

First, the Christian imagination is *anti-Gnostic*. The Judeo-Christian imagination is not a flight from physical reality; it is not an aristocratic exercise in personal insight; and it detests myth, which despises history. It refuses to separate salvation from creation, the life of the spirit from its inception in the flesh. As Irenaeus put it, Christ did not produce wine at Cana out of a hat; he simply transmuted already-created water into wine, for the joy of all present. In the world to come, nothing good from this one will be lost, only transformed.

A Christian imagination does not see the world as a prison from which the soul must escape, but as the stage of humanity's interaction with its God. This world makes sense. God made it with a plan of His own; it is the imagination's role to delight in this plan and explore each person's role in it. Neither is the Christian imagination suicidal; it does not seek to climb its way back to "dark with brightness" glory lost at birth by the fallen individual. It certainly does not thrive in Rimbaud's famous *dérèglement de tous les sens* ("throwing all the senses out of kilter"). Rather, it gratefully anchors itself in the gift of reality, seeking to decipher its message, not to get drunk on it. From its encounter with a man-God, it has been taught to experience life, not as imprisonment in the flesh, but as the generation of a body for resurrection. It sees reality, not as a horror to abolish, but as an ongoing revelation to orchestrate in praise, as an unfolding mystery in which we have a role. To the Christian imagination, history is not meaningless clashes, but the saga of God's kingdom, the very arena of personal and communal "divinisation," to use the term of the Greek Fathers.

As a result, the Christian imagination has manifested itself from the very first as *typological.* It sees every moment in this kingdom-saga as linked mysteriously to every other, and it envisions itself as actor in this drama. It reads life as a meaningful history, the structure of which (that "plan hidden since the beginning of the world") was revealed in Christ. Counter to the *Sesame Street* culture of three minute bites, the Christian imagination is a storytelling imagination. In every era, in every life, it recognizes the creation-death-resurrection pattern epitomized in Christ's life. And it interprets every event as an essential moment in the movement of time toward eternity.

The first Christian art is joyful expression of that vision. Jonah, Noah, the three children in the furnace, Cana, the healing of the paralytic, and eucharistic banquets echo each other on catacomb walls. All of these real events point to the same reality, so tangible here among the resurrected dead, the ongoing salvation of humanity by its God, the Good Shepherd of Israel.

William Kilpatrick, in an analysis of the role of popular music in contemporary education *(Why Johnny Can't Tell Right from Wrong),* proposes as a criterion for good music the question, Does it tell a story? However silly this may sound at first, it points out that the Christian imagination does not thrive in the disconnected instant, that it does not seek intense shock nor orchestrate instant gratification. Rather it seeks to recognize the stamp of eternity in every present, and to reinsert the lived moment in the whole sweep of human history.

The Middle Ages developed a technique to practice typological interpretation of the Bible: First read carefully the text you wish to grasp, then ask three questions: How does this jive with Christ's experience? What does this imply about what I should do next? What does this reveal about God's promise to me, in other words, what dare I hope for? One of the great American writers of the last century, Flannery O'Connor, practiced this technique in order to write:

> The writer whose point of view is catholic in the widest sense of the term reads nature the same way medieval commentators read Scripture. They found three levels of meaning in the literal level of the sacred text—the allegorical, in which one thing stands for another; the moral, which has to do with what should be done; and the anagogical, which has to do with the Divine life and our participation in it, the level of Grace. (468-9)

When teaching film, I have found that students are intensely excited when introduced to this method as a mode of interpretation.

Furthermore, the Christian imagination is *iconic*. It seeks to reflect faithfully the face of the Beloved. For six centuries at least, until the thirteenth century in the West, to this day in the East, Christian art saw itself as an attempt to let that face impress itself in matter, *acheiropoietos*, unsullied by human manipulation. Icon painting called for ascetic preparation of the imagination. Wide open to inspiration, the painter had to silence his own quirks, the better to be that lyre on which the spirit plays. He trained himself to minimize his own storms, the better to reflect, in a smooth mirror, the presence offering itself to him. The iconic imagination wishes its individuality erased, the better to allow Christ's person to take over. It seeks transparency so as to orient the viewer to the self-revealing Invisible One and establish contact with the *prototype* of its work. It offers itself to the fire of love like glowing iron, sure of the divine power to transfigure matter, to glorify the body. It has one aim, Marian in nature: to give flesh here and now to the Holy One.

The most seminal of modern artists—Cezanne, Mondrian, Rouault, to name but a few—took, in fact, a similar road. They, too, refused to revel in their own desires, or to court personal fame, seeking instead to give shape, not to an idol, but to Being revealing itself to us.

Let us take note of a new word that has crept into the argument by way of Christian theology—the word Image. *Suppose, having rejected the words "copy," "imitation" and "representation" as inadequate, we substitute the word "image" and say that what the artist is doing is* to image forth *something or the other, and connect that with St. Paul's phrase: "God...hath spoken to us by His Son, the brightness of this glory and* express image of His person. *"—Something which, by, being an image, expresses* that which *it images.*

—DOROTHY SAYERS, "Towards a Christian Aesthetic"

And the public, too, still thirsts for the Beloved's face. How else explain the lasting popularity of Dostoevsky's tale of the Grand Inquisitor, or the overwhelming response of people everywhere to Mother Teresa's and to the present Pope's call to "Come and see." It is the Christian imagination's role to keep this thirst intense, by recalling that face, re-presenting it over and over again.

Again, the Christian imagination is *sacramental.* From the fifteenth to the eighteenth centuries, many of the greatest Christian art works were altarpieces, orchestrating the miracle of God's "Real Presence," rejoicing in the call to participate in His supper, bringing pictures to the altar, like the bread to be consecrated, fruit of the earth and work of human hands. Artists saw art as having a priestly role whose purpose was to gather glimpses of God throughout His universe and to give this beauty back to its author.

We encounter the sacramental imagination in Gerard Manley Hopkins, whose poem "Hurrahing in Harvest" is one of the most beautiful Eucharistic poems. Roaming through the fields under the late summer sky, Hopkins discovers the splendor of his vocation as poet: The Savior had been there to be "gleaned" all along, with only

> the beholder
> Wanting; which two when they once meet,
> The heart rears wings bold and bolder
> And hurls for him, O half hurls earth for him off under his feet.

For the sacramental imagination, nothing in the world is silent. As Hopkins writes in "As Kingfishers Catch Fire," "Each mortal thing...deals out that being indoors each one dwells," while "Christ plays in ten thousand places, lovely in limbs and lovely in eyes not his." Annie Dillard, too, writes sacramentally. The imaginative bent of Hopkins and Dillard was Duns Scotus" kind of imagination, which Augustine described already in the fourth century:

> These things we see, and we see that each of them is good, and that all of them together are very good. Your works praise you, to the end that we may love you, and we love you to the end that your works may praise you. (367)

Praise, *Eucharist:* Such is the priestly role of the imagination.

Finally, the Christian imagination is *eschatological,* attuned to Christ's parables, those shocking and amazing tales. It perceives the paradox at the heart of creation, which must find fulfillment in another, new and incommensurable world. Such an imagination is at home everywhere and nowhere, and never loses its sense of humor. Like Don Quixote's, its logic is both seductive and explosive. Leaving common sense behind, it yearns for grace's necessary earthquakes. It is haunted by Christ's sentence, "I have come to bring fire on the earth, and how I wish it were already kindled!" (Luke 12:49). For the Christian imagination is born of conversion, and as Flannery O'Connor put it, "I don't know if anybody can be converted without seeing themselves in a kind of blasting annihilating light, a blast that will last a lifetime" (427). Like Walker Percy's work, O'Connor's demonstrates what a contemporary eschatological imagination sounds like: terrible, passionate, and comic at once.

CONTEMPORARY CHALLENGES TO THE CHRISTIAN IMAGINATION

The imagination is too original, too personal, and too creative to be "trained." But, like all things human, it is fragile; we must foster and protect it. We are today under extreme de-Christianizing pressure. Never has imaging been so central to a culture as it is to ours. And never has it been so blatantly disconnected from any transcendence. The images offered by contemporary culture have these traits:

- They are anti-eschatological. They no longer hint at the hidden joy, beyond imagining, which this world prefaces. They provide only the pleasure they promise.

- They are anti-eucharistic. No longer do they seek to reveal the Being, the "inscape" hidden in all we encounter, so that we may rejoice in it and give praise. Today, rather, the word *image* suggests mask, superficiality, deception, artificiality.

- They are anti-iconic. No longer is the image sought as a means by which to contact an "other," its divine prototype. Instead it is used as a tool of self-idolatry.

- They are anti-typological. No longer is the imagination asked to weave the lived moment in a shared, real history. It is usually called to provide escape into virtual reality.

It is no use pretending that with the Fall behind us the imagination is not, like all man's other powers, liable to corruption and disease and death.... The imagination is at present in a very bad way indeed. It receives no proper food, no love....

—ELIZABETH SEWELL, "The Death of the Imagination"

Whether it wishes to or not, modern information technology tempts us to disconnect the products of our imagination—words, sounds, image—from any objective truth, from any personal responsibility, from any shared project. The more obviously imaginary, the more attractive. Artists are valued for their ability to cut all ties with real life, to play wildly with hacked up segments of experience. And the internet fascinates as a potential way finally to "dis-embody" ourselves without dying.

How far this all is from Dostoevsky's passionate dedication to art as a search for *Pravda,* a truth that is also justice, and which must be shared and built in community. We must learn again that vision is not for private consumption. My vision is my vocation; the world is waiting for it to find concrete form. So few people, alas, still perceive the art in which they participate—music, films—as an arena for exchange of visions, for discovery of our common human vocation. Few would understand what Robert Young, a contemporary Vancouver artist, means when he says, "I paint what must be painted now."

Many of our contemporaries think of art—painting, music, drama, film— simply as relaxation or personal therapy. They use their imaginations to flee into their mental cocoons, to weave a personal lifestyle not open to discussion. We are developing solipsistic imaginations, perhaps as our last escape hatch from political correctness: If beauty is a matter of taste, and imagination a way to let out steam, everything goes. Whatever! And no one else needs criticize my private lifestyle.

AN EXAMINATION OF CONSCIENCE: WHAT OF OUR OWN IMAGININGS?

We need to challenge this marginalization of what is perhaps the most vital of our faculties. It must be reattached to the realm of ethics, of truth, of love. All Christians should include the imagination in their examinations of conscience. Its health is vital to the soul's health.

Are we using responsibly our own imaginative faculty, or have we let ourselves be hijacked by the clichés and propaganda with which we are continually bombarded? When planning our future, are we writing our own biography, or xeroxing a script? If we are externally but parroting political correctness, what is our imagination concocting down below? Is there a connection between the success of a culture of pornography and violence and this failure to do our own responsible imaging of reality and self?

As a Christian, I am responsible for the furniture of my mind and imagination.
　　　　　　　　—FRANK GAEBELEIN, "Christian Responsibility in the Arts"

Is our image of "the state of the world" and of our role in it in any way shaped by the fact we are Christians? What fundamental grid do we work from as we project meaning on bare "facts" to navigate our lives? Does our world fundamentally taste sour? Do we look at it through rose tinted glasses? Or is it the bare stage of our unexpected encounters with the mystery of God? Nothing reveals more forcefully one's true view of God than the quality of one's imaginings.

Is our self-image affected by our Christianity? What vision of our own story silently shapes our reactions and decisions? Are we patiently fleshing out the face Christ is showing to the world through us? Do we recognize that preparing the public imagination for Christ's return is our personal responsibility, not the Church's problem, for we *are* the Church?

Such are the questions we should be asking each other if we wish to reeducate ourselves and help new generations to become imaginative Christians. For all of us are indeed responsible for the shape of tomorrow's Christianity. It is being forged at home, in our schools, at university, through the media. As responsible artists, citizens, parents, friends, or educators, we must oversee the resulting formation of the next generation's imaginations, as well as monitor our own.

SOME GUIDELINES FROM DANTE ON REEDUCATING THE IMAGINATION

Much has been written recently on the importance of developing the ability to criticize the mass of material with which we are constantly bombarded. And it is certainly important to learn to reject cliché responses. Precooked imaginative projections must be challenged, starting with Disney's invasion of children's very playtime and self-image. We must all learn early to smell out the hidden agenda of imagination manipulators of every stripe.

Critical training, however, is but chipping at the top of the iceberg. It does not deal with the core of the problem facing Christian imaginations, namely, a failure to recognize and shoulder one's own unique vocation, to activate one's own creativity, for the sake of all.

Instead of coming to the imagination's rescue, the Church has panicked at its antics. As a result, we have let the imagination de-Christianize, losing in the process the conquests of centuries of education. Yet the Judeo-Christian tradition is an expert in such matters.... It has waged a millennial struggle for the imagination of humanity, with astonishing success.... Our problem is thus not bolstering the imagination, but educating it, reconnecting it to its origin and end; Christians would say, baptizing a power in us all which nothing can destroy.

—JANINE LANGAN, "Truth, Justice, and the Modern Imagination"

The Divine Comedy records the imaginative reeducation of a very great Christian poet, Dante, by a very great pagan poet, Virgil. Virgil's first lesson is a blunt one (*Inferno* ii, 43-49):

"If I have understood what you have said"
Replied the shade of that great-hearted one,

"Your soul has been assailed by cowardice,
Which often weighs so heavily on a man—
Distracting him from honorable trial—
As phantoms frighten beasts when shadows fall."

It takes great courage to do one's own imagining, a courage based on aware-ness of the greatness of one's call. Young and old, we all need to be so encour-aged, by a real respect for our unique personal vocation. We all should be prodded to discover, on our own, patterns in reality that have not already been mapped out. The young especially must be helped to take responsibility for what they glimpse—hints of beauty, visions of the future germinating in the present. And they must be pushed to project these insights in their own words and images for others to share. This does not mean applauding any and all of their dadaist flings. It means rather helping them to focus what they see. It means inciting them to clarify their own response to the world. It means helping them deal with their fears and destructive instincts, in order to discover their own capacity to insert themselves joyfully into the world—to give thanks for it—to participate in its transformation. It also means helping them acquire the vocabulary, visual and verbal, the basic disciplines and techniques, which make imaging possible.

Secondly, imaginations thrive only when led out of all-too-tempting solip-sism. Dante needed Virgil, because personal tragedies had repelled him into soli-tude. Life looked to him like a desert of self-pity, anguish, and silence. He was trapped alone in an imagination incapable even of remembering his encounter with Beatrice, an imagination in the grip of despair. He needed a human being to launch his return to the land of the living by reorienting his imagination to the possibility of joy, which is creative love. Why could Virgil help? Because he was Dante's all-too-human brother and understood his plight. Virgil's own imaginative conquest of meaning out of harsh experience inspired Dante to emulate him and to stop moping. Not all of us are as gifted as Virgil, but we all can introduce others to potential Virgils: In a two-thousand-year-old tradition, there are many from which to choose.

And one need not even search that far. Virgil's greatest impact on Dante was helping him to un-forget his own original encounter with love, the "Beatrice experience" that introduced him to *caritas*. There is no more powerful "educating" than calling the attention of others to their own experience of grace, of *communio*. Everyone needs to fertilize such gifts and bring them to fruition.

In the imagination the body must have its rights, the senses and the heart as well perhaps—see how in the Bible, the phrase runs "the imagination of the thoughts of man's heart."... Body and mind have somehow to find freedom here in the imagination, and because of that, the conditions of free activity will be different from those of the reason alone.

—ELIZABETH SEWELL, "The Death of the Imagination"

Finally, reeducation of the Christian imagination begins with a reality check. We need to explode Santa Claus. I mentioned the eschatological nature of a Christian imagination. To many North Americans, however, Christianity seems soppy. That is because they have not seen the real goods. True Christian imaging meets violence head-on, mine and the world's, but also God's. Dragged through hell, Dante is forced to admit the harshness of our human world, where senses, imagination, heart, and intellect are sick with sin, its own punishment. He must acknowledge the deadly games the imagination tends to play, from encouraging the illusion that sex fulfills our deepest desire, to luring others into the icy pit of its own despair. The Christian imagination must pass through this baptism. It must face the reality of Job's cry, the cry of God's crucifixion, and of our participation in it. Once this is recognized, faith becomes not only possible, but necessary; it can never again be rose-water belief in Santa Claus. No one needs padding from reality; we must learn early to see both its reflected glory and its ultimate inability to fit our wishes. We must learn early to seek God within the wounds that reality inflicts. There is indeed no better educator of the imagination than Job, since he ended up "seeing" God! The healthy imagination, rooted in contrition, is fully open to painful change; it is always ready to accept the new, however dazzling to human eyes.

THE CHURCH, KEY PARTNER IN IMAGINATIVE EDUCATION

It is fascinating to watch Dante's view of Being in the world transforming as he climbs. He first meets God's self-revelation as an obstacle—incomprehensible, terrifying words carved in stone, in murky darkness. He then experiences that revelation as a firm and steep mountain under his feet, a mountain which orients his ascent during the day and cradles him at night. He is finally sucked into its ever more intense light, immersed in fireworks too wonderful to describe. Eventually, nothing is left to image or say. Even *The Divine Comedy* must end in silence. But that silence is the silence of the stars, as the poet is drawn into the reality of love's eternal dance.

The imagination is not its own end, just as art is not for art's sake. It is an instrument of encounter, at the service of life—one's own and that of others. Virtuous Virgil, the ultimate secular artist, is not, it turns out, the main facilitator of Dante's ascent, but Life itself is the facilitator—divine life, infused in humanity. In Purgatory already, Virgil is often superseded by the church militant and its rituals. In Paradise, he disappears altogether, replaced by Beatrice, Bernard, and all the saints in between. They help Dante internalize virtues which make the difference between a secular and a Christian imagination: faith, hope, and charity. Throughout Purgatory, Dante is steeped in the church's art: its prayer, music, ritual. In Paradise, he is asked to participate in it personally—to ask questions, thank, give glory, meditate, desire, and finally to witness creatively, in his own words, to the divine gifts he himself received: in other words, to write *The Divine Comedy*.

Surely there is here valid advice for all Christians. The individual imagination thrives on active participation in the church's sacramental imagination. It feeds on admiration of its art, its architecture, its poetry, its ritual, and the myriad community structures it has developed through the centuries. The liturgy, said Jaroslav Pelikan, is the digestive system of the church. It is the process by which we prepare the raw givens of creation and history so they may become, in Christ, our Eucharist. What better wellspring than the Eucharist for the faith which grounds all creativity, for the hope which lets us glimpse eternity dawning in today's world, and for the charity which fuels our imagination's tackling of history?

MEETING BEAUTY

"Procreating in Beauty" is the role of the imagination, wedded to creation, says Jacques Maritain. "Beauty will save the world," proposed Dostoevsky. We are far from such a dream in a world where beauty contests are demeaning, and ugliness is perceived as liberation from aesthetic totalitarianism. Much of twentieth-century art seeks no "procreation in beauty," but rather strives to conquer and to create, torturing nature in the process.

Of course, beauty, we painfully found out last century, is much too ambiguous to save the world. But as Mitya Karamazov saw, it is a major arena on which the fight for salvation is waged in the human heart: "Beauty is mysterious as well as Terrible. God and the devil are fighting there, and the battlefield is the heart of man" (97). The imagination is thus a fundamental way to share in God's life.

The dismissal of beauty is quite a dangerous thing—if not for art, which cannot *in reality divorce beauty, at least for humanity.... The dehumanizing process...can be overcome. Art in this connection has an outstanding mission. It is the most natural power of healing and agent of spiritualization needed by the human community.... Art, as long as it remains art, cannot help being intent on beauty.*

—JACQUES MARITAIN, *Creative Intuition in Art and Poetry*

In his *Letter to Artists* of 1999 (henceforth *L.A.*), John Paul II meditates on this analogy between the life of the imagination and God's own life. Artistic contemplation echoes the sympathy or *pathos* with which God looked on to this creation and saw that it was good. We all need such moments of "divinelike" passionate rest; we should help each other to notice beauty and to respond to it with "pathos." Our wonder before the beauty of the world is a Sabbath prayer which, in John Paul II's words, "reconciles the world to God" (*L.A.* 14). At the same time, it is potentially one of the deepest experiences of community. Instinctively we all know there is a difference between private pleasure and rejoicing in beauty, even if we apply this distinction poorly. We know the contrast between matters of taste and moments which "unite humanity, one in admiration," as the Pope puts it (*L.A.* 11). Who has not called even an anonymous passerby to join in a moment of epiphany, or mourned the inability of a beloved to share it? Delight in beauty is not self-indulgence; it is the most disinterested response we can make to the world. Educating the imagination is progressively weaning from personal taste, from projection of one's desires, to prepare for such contemplative breakthroughs.

The experience of beauty does not glut; it leaves us tantalized. Beauty is cruel, says the secular artist. It "stirs our hidden nostalgia for God," says John Paul II. We must be sure to expose our students to real beauty which does not glut, not to the cute or the pretty. Much is at stake: Every encounter with true beauty is "a kind of appeal to the mystery," "the mystery of the incarnate God and the mystery of man" (*L.A.* 10). All artists know this. As Alex Coleville, an openly atheistic Canadian artist, put it in an interview with the *National Post,* "Art is fueled by the desire to give meaning to one's life, joined by the fleeting vision of beauty and the mysterious unity of things." This mystery is elusive. All artists experience "the gap between the work of their hands and the dazzling perfection of the beauty glimpsed in the ardor of the creative moment…the splendor which flared for a moment before the eyes of their spirit" (*L.A.* 6). All deep experience of beauty is indeed poignantly prescient of eternity.

The pace of modern life and its comfortable cocooning leave little occasion for encounters with real beauty. It is every adult's responsibility to provide such occasions for young minds around them, through contact with nature, with history in the making, with great art, with wonderful people. Little by little, these youths will learn to find similar moments on their own. We may hope that, like Francis of Assisi, they will become able "in things of beauty [to contemplate] the one who is supremely beautiful." Then, "led by the footprints they find in creatures, they [will follow] the Beloved everywhere" (Bonaventure, *Legenda Maior,* IX, 1). If we succeed in sending others in search for beauty, it may indeed lead them "to that infinite Ocean of beauty where wonder becomes awe, exhilaration, unspeakable joy" (*L.A.* 16).

> *For as God is infinitely the greatest Being, so he is allowed to be infinitely the most beautiful and excellent: and all the beauty to be found throughout the whole creation is but the reflection of the diffused beams of that Being who hath an infinite fulness of brightness and glory; God…is the foundation and fountain all being and all beauty.*
> —JONATHAN EDWARDS, *The Nature of True Virtue*

Which is why the church needs artists, and artists need the church. The Pope, quoting Chenu, emphasizes that art works are not mere illustrations of dogma, but "genuine sources of theology" (*L.A.* 11). And there is more. Life itself is a work of art, the most vital product of our imaginings:

Not all are called to be artists in the specific sense of the term. Yet…all men and women are entrusted with the task of crafting their own life: in a certain sense, they are to make of it a work of art, a masterpiece. It is important to recognize the distinction, but also the connection, between these two aspects of human activity. (*L.A.* 2)

Indeed, the discipline but also the audacity of art are wonderful pointers to what our Christian vocation is all about. What is true of art is true of life. We are never self-made. We cannot create or re-create by ourselves. Like the imagination, we live off inspiration. Judeo-Christianity is rooted in this revelation. Since the dawn of the first day when "the earth was without form and void, and darkness was upon the face of the deep; and the Spirit of God was moving over the face of the waters" (Genesis 1:2, RSV), "the Spirit has been the mysterious Artist of the universe" (*L.A.* 15). This includes us minor artists. Grasping this message crowns any Christian education of the imagination. "O man," says St. Irenaeus of Lyons,

it is not you who make God, but rather God who makes you. Wait patiently for the hand of your Artist, who makes all things at the proper time. Present him with a heart that is supple and docile, preserve the imprint that this artist has given you, protect in yourself the Water that comes from Him, without which you will harden and lose the trace of his fingers. In preserving the modeling, you will mount up toward perfection, for the art of God will cover what in you is only clay. His hands have fashioned in you your very substance; he will adorn you with gold and silver, inside and out, and the King himself will be captured by your beauty. (*Against Heresies*, IV, 39, 2)

The highest role of human imagination is humble cooperation with this modeling of our own face by God Himself. Thank heavens, education of the Christian imagination is, first and foremost, in His hands.

Works Cited

Arnheim, Rudolf. *Visual Thinking*. Berkeley: University of California Press, 1969.

Augustine, Saint. *Confessions*. Trans. John K. Ryan. Garden City: Image Books, 1960.

Dante Alighieri. *The Divine Comedy*. Trans. Allen Mandelbaum. Toronto: Bantam Books, 1986.

Dostoevsky, Fyodor. *The Brothers Karamazov.* Trans. Constance Garnett. Ed. Ralph E. Matlaw. New York: W. W. Norton, 1976.

John Paul II. *Letter to Artists.* Vatican City, 1999.

Kilpatrick, William. *Why Johnny Can't Tell Right from Wrong.* New York: Simon and Schuster, 1992.

Maritain, Jacques. *Creative Intuition in Art and Poetry.* Meridian, New York: Scarborough, 1973.

O'Connor, Flannery. *The Habit of Being.* Ed. Sally Fitzgerald. New York: Noonday Press, 1995.

Steiner, George. *Real Presences.* Chicago: University of Chicago Press, 1989.

Beauty and the Creative Impulse

Luci Shaw

What Secret Purple Wisdom

What word informs the world,
and moves the worm along in his blind tunnel?

What secret purple wisdom tells the iris edges
to unfold in frills? What juiced and emerald thrill

urges the sap until the bud resolves
its tight riddle? What irresistible command

unfurls this cloud above this greening hill,
or one more wave—its spreading foam and foil—

across the flats of sand? What minor thrust
of energy issues up from humus in a froth

of ferns? Delicate as a laser, it filigrees
the snow, the stars. Listen close—What silver sound

thaws winter into spring? Speaks clamor into singing?
Gives love for loneliness? It is this

unterrestrial pulse, deep as heaven, that folds us
in its tingling embrace, gongs in our echo hearts.

(From *The Angles of Light,* Shaw Books, 2000, 27)

Does this poem suggest to you that color, shape, sound, growth, and pattern are important? That they have something to do with what we call beauty? That beauty is given from a Source beyond us?

I have come to believe that beauty is something inherent in creation (and by creation I mean the environment, the created universe in which we live). A sense of the beautiful is so integral, so deeply a part of who we are and what we enjoy as human beings, that we may easily take it for granted. Often flawed, or marred, or distorted as a result of human depravity and failure, beauty is still visible in the fingerprints of the Creator on the natural world, in the wilderness, and in human beings who reflect the Creator's beauty.

Only the individual twisted by wrong choices and destructive relationships into perversity and emptiness will create and worship ugliness. Beauty is perhaps one of the few things that constantly calls us back to God, that reminds us of a standard of goodness, vitality, and reality that embodies the beautiful. The Benedictines hold that beauty is "truth shining into being," a principle adopted by John Keats in his famous line "beauty is truth, truth beauty." In this sense beauty is redemptive and powerful. It can motivate us to turn a corner, to pursue a new objective. It awakens a new awareness in us because it is often surprising enough to startle, showing up in unexpected forms and places. Beauty was one of the three Platonic ideals—companion of Truth and Goodness. For Plato, being human meant having to deal with these ideals, because beauty is no abstraction. It is always tied to the real, the observable. It is there to be seen, felt, experienced.

The church has given considerable attention to Truth and Goodness, to theology and ethics. But too often beauty has escaped us, or we have tried to escape from it. This is partly because of its innovative, experimental aspect, its way of reaching for originality or a new way of expressing an old standard. In many Christian circles this is felt to be dangerous; the pursuit of beauty is seen merely as an option, and a seductive one at that, because beauty can neither be controlled nor programmed. As Eugene Peterson has said, "It works out of the unconscious, is not practical, cannot be quantified, is not efficient, and cannot

LUCI SHAW *is a poet, essayist, and teacher. She has authored a number of prose books, seven volumes of poetry (including* Polishing the Petoskey Stone, Writing the River, *and* The Angles of Light*), and an anthology of incarnation poetry entitled* A Widening Light. *Writer in residence at Regent College, Vancouver, Canada, she lives with her husband in Bellingham, Washington.*

be 'used' for very long without corrupting either the art or the artist" (from a personal letter, 1999).

But beauty gives pleasure. It awakens in us sensations which may have lain dormant. It arrives through the windows of our souls, our five senses—hearing (music, the small sounds of the rain forest, thunder, birdsong), sight (landscapes, colors, textures, contrasts, the micro- and the macrocosm), touch (the nerves of our fingers are tuned to smooth, rough, silky, oily, warm, chilled, frosty), taste (cinnamon rolls, good coffee, vintage wine, toffee, mint jelly, roast beef with horseradish), or smell (roses, bread baking, Chanel #5, newly cut grass). The messages of beauty through the senses, when combined with the responses of our reasoning intelligence, achieve meaning or significance for us. These messages lodge in our minds and memories. They print themselves like pictures on our imaginations and do their transforming work in us, reminding us, if we are aware, of the One behind the messages.

[The imagination] lifts the veil from the hidden beauty of the world.…
[It] turns all things to loveliness; it exalts the beauty of that which is most
beautiful, and it adds beauty to that which is most deformed.
—PERCY BYSSHE SHELLEY, *A Defence of Poetry*

I have vowed never to cut myself off from beauty. Dallas Willard counsels us to "cultivate the beautiful." For me it is part of the *via affirmativa,* the "way of celebration." It is God's grace in action, the invisible made visible, the Word made flesh and dwelling with me, grace in astonishing three-dimensional color with better-than-Dolby sound, and fragrance, taste, and texture thrown in to make it even more memorable.

But though beauty is intensely personal, experienced moment by moment in individuals with vastly differing tastes and standards, I love to think of beauty's universality. Around the globe we all gasp at the sight of wild breakers sending up violent white curtains of foam as they crash on the coastal rocks. We breathe in the silent greenness of a meadow after rain, with its moist fragrances. We marvel at the icy glory of the Antarctic, the subtle earth tones of the painted deserts of Arizona and New Mexico and the Kalahari. We call our neighbor on the phone to witness with us a double rainbow over the lake, or the golden glory of the sun setting behind spectacular purple clouds (as I did just the other day).

Similarly with music: I love its infinite variety of possibilities, the diversity of notes and tempos, of assonance and dissonance, of intensity and dynamic range. Mozart's extraordinary orchestration of melody is beautiful, as is the music-making of Palestrina, and Respighi, and John Rutter. (Add your own favorites to this list, either classical or contemporary.) Bach is beautiful. For me, much of Bach's beauty is linked to his celebration of the Creator's work and worth. He marked his scores "soli gloria deo"—Glory to God alone.

BEAUTY'S IMPROVISATION

Composers of the Baroque period were known for their ability to improvise and produce masterpieces of polyphonic complexity. Domenico Scarlatti's fugue in G minor, "The Cat's Fugue," is an example. The story is that Scarlatti's cat leaped up onto the piano keyboard in his studio and in walking along the keys struck a random and unlikely series of notes, out of which the composer fashioned his fugue. By a creative act, Scarlatti brought order, beauty, grace, and meaning out of accident. And that is an act of redemption. Bringing order and beauty out of disorder and chaos, and meaning out of the meanest of circumstances, is God-work, in which we may be co-creators. Sometimes we are called to turn things around, to view reality from a fresh angle, as in the following poem:

Diamonds That Leap

When the leaf fell and brushed my hand
I began to reverse the world. I asked:
What if this warped willow leaf, yellow,

scaled with age, could smooth
to a green blade, then flicker into
the knot of a spring twig, like

a grass snake's tail disappearing, slick
and chill, into his home? That one question—
it was a whirlpool, pulling in

others: What about a river?
Might its waters rush up these indigo
hills of Shenandoah and split to a scatter

of diamonds that leap to their rain
clouds, homing? Can a love
shrink back and back to like,

then to the crack of a small, investigative
smile? Could God ever suck away creation
into his mouth, like a word regretted,

and start us over?

(From *Writing the River,* Pinon Press, 1994, 32)

As a writer, as a keeper of a daily reflective journal, I find that as soon as I
put words and ideas onto paper in my notebook, or type them into my computer, they begin to gather to themselves more images, more words and ideas. As
I write, I have the sensation of being at the center of a small vortex of enlarging
connections, as in the poem above, and my pen or my fingers on the keyboard
move faster and faster to keep pace with them.

---

*The artist must be obedient to the work.... I believe that each work of art,
whether it is a work of great genius, or something very small, comes to the
artist and says, "Here I am. Enflesh me. Give birth to me." And the artist
either says, "My soul doth magnify the Lord," and willingly becomes the
bearer of the work, or refuses.*

—MADELEINE L'ENGLE, *Walking on Water*

This growing cluster of words and images reflects not an externally imposed
outline, or system, or a preconceived plan, but a more organic development, a
kind of evolution from a very small beginning—a leaf, a seed idea, a phrase, a
vivid image. Words, ideas, images, all of which have enormous imaginative and
emotive power, seem to gain a life of their own, fleshing themselves out and making a way for themselves as they stretch and expand, with our minds and writing
instruments following, becoming merely a kind of substrate to record them and
shape them as they develop.

Cogitation (which means "together shaking"—the dance of thought with
imagination, a cerebral pas de deux) accompanies any art, such as musical

composition or dance or painting, rather than preceding it. What does this mean, in practical terms, for any artist involved in creative work? For me, it means that I follow ideas and images. If an image shows up, often uninvited, unexpected, I am called to stop everything and pay attention. And the word *pay* is significant. There's a cost to it, in time, in energy. But the rewards are great. When a poem is finished after many drafts, when it has settled into what it was meant to be, I sometimes echo Dorothy Sayers who exclaimed, on finishing a novel, "I feel like God on the Seventh Day!"

A few years back I signed a book contract with a well-known publisher. I was assigned to provide a piece on "cultivating the interior life." I also had a problem—the difficulty of writing a book based on someone else's formula or image. It took a considerable time before the idea kindled into life and became my own. The book eventually caught fire in my mind and ended up as a truly creative project, but my assigned metaphor—the soul as a garden to be cultivated—had to germinate internally, like a fetus in the womb, so that it became *my* metaphor, not my editor's! Knowing that I write poetry, friends often will call me with an idea for a poem, or an image which they think has poetic possibilities. I appreciate their generosity in sharing their ideas, but if that is the image that has sprung into life for them, it should be *their* poem!

I tend to write poetry from enthusiasm rather than discipline, or rather, the discipline does not take the form of sitting down at a set time every day and saying, "Today I will write a sonnet." Rather, a compelling iambic phrase will come to me, calling out, "Write me!" And I can't help but obey. Or a comparison or contrast occurs to me in my reading of another poet, or in the Sunday sermon, or a phrase floats into my mind unbidden as I write my journal, which is where most of my seed poems are recorded. Sometimes I am overcome, as I walk out of my front door early in the morning, with the beauty of mist drifting between the mountains and over the lake before me, shifting and reshaping itself, for true beauty is not static. I am compelled either to photograph it or write about it before it evaporates.

When I am actively being moved into creativity, I find myself drawing the writing out of myself much as a spider draws silk from her own abdomen to fashion her delicate, intricate web. The writing is integral to my own thinking and living. I often say that should I lose my current journal, filled with intensely personal responses, events, emotions, images, and ideas, I would feel that I had lost a part of myself. My *self.*

Beauty isn't always carefully planned and programmed. Sometimes it's just a matter of slowing down and giving the mind and soul time to be reflective and responsive, and then looking, or listening, and going with what is seen or heard. The writing, the music, the painting, the art will begin to open doors as it advances, without my always knowing where it is going or what the end result will be.

Henri Nouwen commented (in an essay on *Theological Ideas in Education*), "Most students...feel that they must first have something to say before they can put it down on paper. For them writing is little more than recording a preexistent thought. But...*writing is a process in which we discover what lives in us. The writing itself reveals what is alive.*" In William Saroyan's words, "The task of the writer is to create a rich, immediate, usable past."

The deepest satisfaction of writing is precisely that it opens up new spaces within us of which we were not aware before we started to write. To write is to embark on a journey whose final destination we do not know. Thus, creative writing requires a real act of trust. We have to say to ourselves, "I do not yet know what I carry in my heart, but I trust that it will emerge as I write." Writing is like giving away the few loaves and fishes one has, in trust that they will multiply in the giving. Once we dare to "give away" on paper the few thoughts that come to us, we start discovering how much is hidden underneath...and gradually come in touch with our own riches.

—HENRI NOUWEN, *Theological Ideas in Education*

OVERCOMING CHAOS

On my refrigerator I used to have the collection of words on magnetic strips known as Magnetic Poetry. From the hundreds of randomly chosen available words, one or two interesting ones might come into focus for me from the metal surface, calling to be singled out—*sausage,* say, or *manipulate,* or *repulsive.* Or *incubate.* Here's a combination of some words that appealed to me:

Ice Box Poem

Dreaming,
I shake the enormous moment,
whisper static language into life,
manipulate blue shadows in the sun,
crush peaches for juice warm as blood,
swim essential jungles,
always incubate the image.

You line them up—strange juxtapositions of words and phrases that attract other words or prefixes or suffixes into their magnetic field. These surprising combinations of nouns and verbs with a few articles and conjunctions and a couple of adjectives paint a new picture, or suggest some unplanned kind of relationship which shifts or jells as other words are added or subtracted. Order is overcoming randomness much as when Scarlatti's cat's strange, staggered, haphazard theme melted in the composer's mind and fingers, as he felt a pattern emerging and followed its flow, forming a fugue in which beauty, order, and meaning suggested itself.

As I. A. Richards put it, "Poetry is a perfectly possible means of overcoming chaos." Poetry, drama, sculpture, painting, architecture, gardening, any creative art, or act, like music, gives chaos the chance of *disintegrating back* into a kind of primal order or meaning that we call beauty.

We go far astray if we regard beauty as mere ornament or decoration, as a filigree attached to the surface of life.... Beauty is not excrescent to the general well-being of man, but essential to it.... Beauty, at base, is the result of the creative activity of God, and artistic beauty is...a humanly created revelation.

—ROLAND M. FRYE, *Perspective on Man: Literature and the Christian Tradition*

In an article about life on the prairies, I read about a prairie woman in 1870 who wrote in her diary a note about her quilt-making: "I make them warm to keep my family from freezing; I make them beautiful to keep my heart from breaking." My heart went out to her. To construct a quilt is to make beauty and meaning out of life's scrappy leftovers. The image in that wry entry was power-ful. I felt caught in its force as I wrote the following poem:

Quilt-Maker

To keep a husband and five children warm,
she quilts them covers thick as drifts against
the door. Through every fleshy square white threads
needle their almost invisible tracks; her hours
count each small suture that holds together
the raw-cut, uncolored edges of her life.

She pieces each one beautiful and summer bright
to thaw her frozen soul. Under her fingers
the scraps grow to green birds and purple
improbable leaves; deeper than calico, her mid-winter
mind bursts into flowers. She watches them unfold
between the double stars, the wedding rings.

(From *Polishing the Petoskey Stone*, Shaw Books, 1990, 33)

Sometimes beauty becomes almost a matter of survival. Without it, a part of us shrivels and dies. Frederick Buechner says of beauty, "It is to the spirit what food is to the flesh. It fills an emptiness in you that nothing else under the sun can."

Human beings cannot be human without some field of fancy or imagina-tion; some vague idea of the romance of life and even some holiday of the mind in a romance that is a refuge from life.

—G. K. CHESTERON, "Fiction as Food"

When the world was created, it might have seemed to be enough to have it *work*. To include beauty seems unnecessary for a mechanistic universe. We have been given a sense of the beautiful which can be regarded as gratuitous. Which it is—a gift of pure grace. And our own creation of beautiful things links us with our Creator. God was the first Quilter of prairies, the primal Painter (night skies, ferns, thunderheads, snow on cedars), the archetypal metal Sculptor (mountain ranges, icebergs), the Composer who heard the whales' strange, sonorous clickings and songs in his head long before there were whales to sound them, the Playwright who plotted the sweeping drama of Creation, Incarnation, Redemption, the Poet whose Word said it all.

God made us human beings in his image; we participate in creative intelligence, giftedness, originality. We each have the faculty of imagination deep within us, waiting, like a seed, to be watered and fertilized. Imagination gives us pictures by which to see things the way they *can* be, or the way they *are*, underneath. The prairie woman, hemmed into her sod house with her small children by months of sub-zero cold and snow, used her imagination redemptively. Around the traditional quilt patterns—double stars, wedding rings—her imagination pieced in the exuberant flowers and leaves that redeemed the long winter, that brought her soul back to life. She created beauty and richness from the ordinary stuff, even the castoffs, of her life.

BEAUTY AS SACRAMENT

At that point, in that redemptive action, beauty becomes sacramental, that is, it is pointing beyond itself to something even larger, truer, more potent. As Eugene Peterson says in *Leap Over a Wall*, "There's more to beauty than we can account for empirically. In that *more* and *beyond*, we discern God." And it is then that we can worship God "in the beauty of holiness."

Eugene Peterson theorizes that the vocation of the artist is to awaken our sensitivity of beauty, "most exquisitely beauty in the human body, with its fulfillment in the human face." This reminds me of Annie Dillard's comment for *Life* magazine on, of all things, the meaning of life: "We are here to witness and abet creation. To notice each thing so each thing gets noticed. Together we notice not only each mountain shadow and each stone on the beach but we notice each other's beautiful face and complex nature so that creation need not play to an empty house." Beauty is there to be noticed. Too often it is taken for granted because we are moving too fast to take it in and allow it to deliver its message in us. We need to pay attention. To show indifference to beauty is an insult to its Creator. And it is to be seen in every person who fulfills George Herbert's ideal (expressed in his poem "The Windows") that man

is a brittle crazy glass:
Yet in thy temple thou dost him afford
This glorious and transcendent place,
To be a window through thy grace.

That is, beauty is not merely a matter of face and figure, or personality, but a totality of human graces which may enflesh aspects of the divine shining through individuals as through a series of windows.

There's a long tradition in the Christian life, most developed in Eastern Orthodoxy, of honoring beauty as a witness to God and a call to prayer. Beauty is never only what our senses report to us but always also a sign of what's just beyond our senses—an innerness and depth. There's more to beauty than we can account for empirically. In that more and beyond, we discern God. Artists who wake up our jaded senses and help us attend to these matters are gospel evangelists.… In the presence of the beautiful we intuitively respond in delight, wanting to be involved, getting near, entering in—tapping our feet, humming along, touching, kissing, meditating, contemplating, imitating, believing, praying. It's the very nature of our five senses to pull us into whatever is there—scent, rhythm, texture, vision. And it's the vocation of the artist to activate our senses so that they do just that. Beauty in bird and flower, in rock and cloud. Beauty in ocean and mountain, in star and sand. Beauty in storm and meadow, in laughter and play. But most exquisitely beauty in the human body, with its fulfillment in the human face. Instinctively…we recognize that there's more to beauty than what we discern with our senses. That beauty is never "skin deep," but always revelatory of goodness and truth. Beauty releases light into our awareness so that we're conscious of the beauty of the Lord.

—EUGENE PETERSON, *Leap over a Wall*

Emerson said, "We ascribe beauty to that which is simple, which has no superfluous parts; which exactly answers its end." At which point beauty and function are joined, which is, I suspect, what God intended all along. But I also suspect that the simplicity that Emerson commends is not quite as simple as he makes out. Beauty is also rich and complex, constantly shifting, appearing in different guises to different people. Our human standards of beauty continually renew themselves, as new stylistic combinations are invented and discarded, which is what keeps the fashion industry going.

CREATED TO CREATE

Beauty is the business of the artist, the one who creates in the image of the Creator. But it is also the delight of every ordinary human being, because we are all created, in God's image, to create. Children who have not yet been trapped and trammeled by inhibition or self-consciousness often seem free to express their feelings in art that is more intuitive and spontaneous than that of adults. But have you ever heard of anyone who has not, at some point in his or her life, yielded to the creative impulse? Doodled? Decorated an Easter egg or a Christmas tree? Landscaped a garden plot? Written a poem or song to the object of their affections? And didn't you, as you got dressed this very morning—*you, getting dressed, this morning*—pay some attention not only to being warm and comfortable and decently covered, but also, to some degree, attractive? We care how we look. And that concern is not just part of the human mating ritual. It's because appearances often reflect something deeper, about who we are.

When we move into a new home or apartment, most of us make some effort to harmonize the color scheme, the wallpaper, to effect a pleasing arrangement of the furniture. Even in our offices, we'll bring in a potted plant and a pictorial calendar to add some life and color to an otherwise drab cubicle. And haven't we ever danced and jumped up and down when we were too excited to simply walk? Or whistled and sung when speaking was inadequate for the happiness we were feeling?

This practical modern world is prone to conceive beauty as an extraneous luxury.... We do not think of it as an integral and inseparable element of our living, as did the Greeks; or as did the Christians for many centuries. Yet something deep and instinctive within us hungers for the beauty of holiness, as well as for its truth and its righteousness.... Beauty is an indispensable and logical part of practice and worship in the religious life.

—CHARLES G. OSGOOD, *Poetry as a Means of Grace*

Years ago, I was talking with my Uncle Max, a hard-working, shrewd, practical New Zealand apple farmer. Hearing that a new book of my poems had just been published he asked me, with genuine bewilderment, "But—what *good* is a poem? What earthly use is it? Why can't you say what you want to say in a straightforward way that people can understand?"

I was nonplussed. How *do* you explain poetry, or any form of art or creative work, to someone for whom it has little appeal and no meaning? Uncle Max's idea of beauty was probably summed up in the form of a well-pruned apple tree, or a perfectly formed, ripe Cox's Orange Pippin, the hybridized apple for which his orchards were famed.

The same question may be asked about any art form—"What good is it?" What does it accomplish? Why does beauty, and the art we make of it, exist in the first place?

Years later, I think I know how I could have answered him—that poetry, and any art, says something in a way that nothing else can, and that something that art communicates is so qualitatively different that it demands a radically different expression. Where linear, logical thinking may produce prose with a specific function—information or historical record or critical analysis or entertainment or instruction or narrative—poetry and art select and reflect on a small slice of human experience and lay it out there, a gift to anyone who is willing to look at it, savor it, and enter into the artist's experience. The poet communicates experience in images and forms so precisely tailored, so personal, so multileveled that the insights go far beyond bare facts or mere usefulness.

David Jones put it this way: "Man is a creature whose end is extra-mundane and whose nature is to make things and that the things made are not only things of mundane requirement but are of necessity the signs of something other. Further, that an element of the gratuitous adheres to this making" (*Epoch and Artist*). It is true that much art has no practical use. Where prose may teach us how to solve a problem or outline the stages of a romantic relationship, poetry lets us in, cognitively, to how it feels to be overwhelmed with amazement or what it feels like to be in love. Poetry, as well as any of the arts, is my soul crying out to your soul, "There's something here that has leapt into life for me. This is what I'm seeing, hearing, feeling. It's so uniquely marvelous that I want to share it with you. Can you see it? Can you feel it too?"

Alexander Solzhenitzyn, in his lecture on being awarded the Nobel prize for literature, said, "Archeologists have not yet discovered any stage of human existence without art. Even in the half-light before the dawn of humanity we received this gift from Hands we did not manage to discern. Nor have most of us managed to ask: Why was this gift given to us, and what are we to do with it?"

And out of the ground the LORD God made to grow every tree that is pleasant to the sight and good for food.

—GENESIS 2:9, RSV

And in every culture, in every period of human history, all the decoration of human dwellings and artifacts and bodies, and the elaboration of song and story into music and literature, are graphic demonstrations of the human impulse which moves beyond purely practical necessities—usefulness—toward something that we call beauty, which is expressed and communicated to others in art.

Art is what we say, what we sing, what we show about the beauty that is bubbling up within us like a pot on the boil. It cries out for recognition and response. Because it is so significant, so full of wonder to us—this upwelling from our creative imaginations—we want to show and share it with kindred spirits. And so we have poetry readings and art galleries and concerts and square dances and films and fashion shows and coffee-table books.

But why? Where do such impulses toward the beautiful spring from? Why are they so universal? For the Christian believer, it is significant that though we each know that we have been uniquely "made" by God, we sense that we are not merely mechanisms whose sole purpose is to function efficiently, sustaining physical life, performing mental and physical work as part of our social infrastructure, and reproducing ourselves in an endless cycle.

We who believe we bear God's image must realize that that image includes the capacity to imagine and create, because God is himself an imaginative Creator. Though we cannot produce something out of nothing, as God did, we can combine the elements and forms available to us in striking and original ways that arise out of the unique human ability (designed and built into us by God) to imagine, to see pictures in our heads. And beyond that, to remember things from our past that no longer exist, and mentally to invent (imagine) things that have as yet no reality, to hear sounds and rhythms and recognize patterns, and to translate them into forms which will strike a chord in the hearts of other human beings. In art and creativity we make visible to others the beauty and meaning God has first pictured, or introduced, into our own imaginations. In that sense we are each a small extension of the mind of God.

The characteristic common to God and man is apparently that: the desire and the ability to make things up.

—DOROTHY SAYERS, *The Mind of the Maker*

Yes, beauty matters. It is important to God. He loves it! Why else would he shape and color fish, birds, insects, rocks, plants, and people with such rich diversity? As my friend Elizabeth Rooney said, "Imagine making something as useful as a tree, as efficient at converting sunlight into food and fuel, as huge and tough as a white oak that can live 300 years, and then decorating it in spring with tiny pink leaves and pale green tassels of blossoms."

And beyond his primary creation of our vividly beautiful universe, with all its sounds and colors and smells and textures, God also seems to be interested in helping his people both create and appreciate beauty. One example, in which human beings reflect or imitate God's own love for the beautiful, and in which they co-create with the Creator, is seen in Exodus 31:1-11. Here Bezalel's intelligent craftsmanship and his ability in design are said to be the direct results of his infilling by the Spirit of God. Spirit-filled Bezalel, and his helper, Oholiab, also gifted with "ability to do every sort of work done by a craftsman or...skilled designer" are models for artist Christians today. I find this to be true on a very practical level. Often, in the process of writing an article or a poem or an essay, I find myself "stuck," confused, or unable to know in which direction the writing wants to go. That's when I cry "Help!" and ask the Holy Spirit to guide my listening, my thinking, my creating, into channels that will bring me to the heart of truth for the work. I become a servant of the word, rather than its controller. And listening obedience, rather than preplanning, becomes my *modus operandi*.

We tend to think of our Creator in terms of the infinitely large, a deity of cosmic and supercosmic proportions. But not only do we have a God who creates mountains, oceans, planets, galaxies, universes. For our God, even the smallest details are significant, details like a mustard seed, a single pearl, a sparrow, a hair on a human head, an olive leaf in a dove's mouth, drops of blood on a doorframe, a coin in the mouth of a fish. In the Exodus story, Yahweh's attention to detail is evident in the design and implementation of the tabernacle. In Exodus 28 and following we find an abundance of careful description and planning for the tabernacle and its furnishings that goes on for pages and pages!

Think, for a moment, on the priestly garments. In Exodus 28:40: "And for Aaron's sons you shall make coats and girdles and caps; you shall make them for glory and for beauty." In other words, glory to reflect Yahweh's splendor, and beauty, or adornment, because God delighted in it and wanted his people to enjoy it too. As Gene Edward Veith has said in *The Gift of Art*, "Beauty is an appropriate end in itself—the garments were to be made *for* beauty. The inventor of color, of form, of texture, the author of all natural beauties, values the aesthetic dimension *for its own sake*. According to the clear statements of Scripture, art has its place in the will of God."

The primal artistic act was God's creation of the universe out of chaos, shaping the formless into form; and every artist since, on a lesser scale, has sought to imitate him.

—LAURENCE PERRINE, *Sound and Sense*

In Exodus 28:31-35, a passage describing the priest's garments, we find pattern, color and sound all working together. As Francis Schaeffer once observed, "The making of the Tabernacle involved almost every form of representational art known to humanity. But because God is also the God of creative imagination, of metaphor and symbol, of parable and analogy, the design of the Tabernacle, and later of the Temple, was packed with symbolism. The design and placement of furnishings and vessels, the use of different materials such as linen, goatskins, silver, brass, gold, acacia wood, and the ceremonies prescribed for the worship of God in these sacred precincts, the system of sacrifices and oblations, all had meaning *beyond themselves*."

This is the essence of the sacramental—that material things remind us of and point us to the things we cannot see but which have ultimate and eternal reality.

Of course, it is sadly true that, as with any gift of God, imagination and its enfleshment in art may be wrenched into something degraded and degrading. Because art speaks so powerfully to our inner beings and emotions, it carries with it a freight of inherent risk, a potential for evil as well as for good. I was fascinated to read the chapter in Exodus that follows the description of Bezalel's spiritually motivated artistic work. In that close yet paradoxical juxtaposition, we learn of Aaron's deliberate molding of a gold calf-figure designed to replace God in the worship of the people—the very thing prohibited by the second commandment which specifically forbade the making of "a graven image, or any likeness of any thing in heaven or earth."

Some have taken such a mandate as a prohibition against all art. But it would seem that the idolatry enters not in the fashioning of the images or likenesses, but in the worship of them. As Veith says: "To assume that the second commandment forbids any representational art would contradict the orders give for the construction of the Tabernacle and the Temple which called for cast or engraved figures of such objects as leaves, flowers, branches, chains, cherubim and oxen…. But we must not worship art, or create art to be worshiped."

Stripped of religious and moral values, many contemporary artists who are self-conscious and creative, knowing that they *are*, but not knowing the *why*, see themselves as results of a cosmic accident. Much postmodern art, fiction, poetry, music, drama, and film represents the result of this unknowing and the fragmentation, cynicism, and personal chaos that result from it.

The tragedy is that so many Christians, in their revulsion at the perverse aspects of such art, shun all art, even that which may spring from a God-honoring imagination or a Christocentric consciousness. The other "Christian" alternative is a conservatism that responds only to *kitsch,* a sentimental art of the Hallmark greeting card variety that cheapens true sentiment, turning it into sweetness and light or mere moralistic propaganda—no teeth, no guts, no muscle, no reality. No real Christianity either, if we consider the Creator's work as our powerful, radical model.

But *kitsch* is easy. It is as accessible as a Thomas Kinkade painting, and as stereotypical. It is manipulative and narcotic, and by contrast it makes true art seem difficult or complicated. For true art is not all sweet reasonableness. It may project outrage, or make a creative statement as hyperbolic as Jesus' "if your eye causes you to sin, pluck it out; if your right hand causes you to sin, hack it off and throw it away." Such an image is *meant* to jolt, to shock, to sting, to push truth into our awareness in ways that show the freshness, originality, and surprise of the Creator. Consider the following:

The Foolishness of God

Perform impossibilities
or perish. Thrust out now
the unseasonal ripe figs
among your leaves. Expect
the mountain to be moved.
Hate parents, friends, and all
materiality. Love every enemy.
Forgive more times than seventy-
seven. Camel-like, squeeze by
into the kingdom through
the needle's eye. All fear quell.
Hack off your hand, or else,
unbloodied, go to hell.

Thus the divine unreason.
Despairing you may cry,
with earthy logic—How?
And I, your God, reply:
Leap from your weedy shallows.
Dive into the moving water.
Eye-less, learn to see
truly. Find in my folly your
true sanity. Then, Spirit-driven,
run on my narrow way, sure
as a child. Probe, hold
my unhealed hand, and
bloody, enter heaven.

(From *Polishing the Petoskey Stone*, Shaw Books, 1990, 198)

We were each, in the image of our Creator, created to create, to call others back to beauty, and the truth about God's nature, to stop and cry to someone preoccupied or distracted with the superficial, "Look!" or "Listen!" when, in something beautiful and meaningful we hear a message from beyond us, and worship in holiness our Creator who in his unlimited grace, calls us to become co-creators of beauty.

Viewpoint: George MacDonald

The Imagination:
Its Function and Its Culture

The word *imagination*...means an *imaging* or a making of likenesses. The imagination is that faculty which gives form to thought.... It is, therefore, that faculty in man which is likest to the prime operation of the power of God, and has, therefore, been called the *creative* faculty, and its exercise *creation*. *Poet* means *maker.* We must not forget, however, that between creator and poet lies the one unpassable gulf which distinguishes—far be it from us to say *divides*—all that is God's from all that is man's...; between that which makes in its own image and that which is made in that image. It is better to keep the word *creation* for that calling out of nothing which is the imagination of God; except it be as an occasional symbolic expression...of the likeness of man's work to the work of his maker.... The imagination of man is made in the image of the imagination of God. Everything of man must have been of God first....

The imagination...can present us with new thought-forms—new, that is, as revelations of thought. It has created none of the material that goes to make these forms. Nor does it work upon raw material. But it takes forms already existing, and gathers them about a thought so much higher than they, that it can group and subordinate and harmonize them into a whole which shall represent, unveil that thought. The nature of this process we will illustrate by an examination of the well-known *Bugle Song* in Tennyson's "Princess."...

Is not this a new form to the thought—a form which makes us feel the truth of it afresh? And every new embodiment of a known truth must be a new and wider revelation.... This operation of the imagination in choosing, gathering, and vitally combining the material of a new revelation, may be well illustrated from a certain employment of the poetic faculty in which our greatest poets have delighted. Perceiving truth half hidden and half revealed in the slow speech and stammering tongue of men who have gone before them, they have taken up the unfinished form and completed it; they have, as it were, rescued the soul of meaning from its prison of uninformed crudity.... Shakespeare's keen eye suggested many such a rescue from the tomb—of a tale drearily told— a tale which no one now would read save for the glorified form in which he has re-embodied its true contents....

"But although good results may appear in a few from the indulgence of the imagination, how will it be with the many?"

We answer that the antidote to indulgence is development, not restraint, and that such is the duty of the wise servant of Him who made the imagination.

"But will most...rise to those useful uses of the imagination? Are they to more likely to exercise it in building castles in the air to the neglect of houses on the earth? And as the world affords such poor scope for the ideal, will not this habit breed vain desires and vain regrets? Is it not better, therefore, to keep to that which is known, and leave the rest?..."

"Is the world so poor?" we ask in return. The less reason, then, to be satisfied with it; the more reason to rise above it, into the region of the true, of the eternal, of things as God thinks them.... And as to keeping to that which is known and leaving the rest—how many affairs of this world are so well-defined, so capable of being clearly understood, as not to have large spaces of uncertainty, whose very correlate faculty is the imagination? Indeed it must, in most things, work after some fashion, filling the gaps after some possible plan, before action can even begin. In very truth, a wise imagination, which is the presence of the spirit of God, is the best guide that man or woman can have; for it is not the things we see the most clearly that influence us the most powerfully; undefined, yet vivid visions of something beyond, something which eye has not seen nor ear heard, have far more influence than any logical sequences whereby the same things may be demonstrated to the intellect....

Is there, therefore, no faculty for those infinite lands of uncertainty lying all about the sphere hollowed out of the dark by the glimmering lamp of knowledge? Are they not the natural property of the imagination? there, *for* it, that it may have room to grow? there, that the man may learn to imagine greatly like god who made him, himself discovering their mysteries...?

The end of imagination is *harmony.* A right imagination, being the reflex of the creation, will fall in with the divine order of things as the highest form of its own operation.... The reveries even of the wise man will make him stronger for his work; his dreaming as well as his thinking will render him sorry for past failure, and hopeful of future success....

If we speak of direct means for the culture of the imagination, the whole is comprised in two words—food and exercise.... And first as for the food.

Goethe has told us that the way to develop the aesthetic faculty is to have constantly before our eyes, that is, in the room we most frequent, some work of the best attainable art. This will teach us to refuse the evil and choose the good. It will plant itself in our minds and become our counsellor.... In the culture of the imagination, books, although not the only, are the readiest means of supplying the food convenient for it.... In books, we not only have store of all results of the imagination, but in them, as in her workshop, we may behold her embodying before our very eyes, in music of speech, in wonder of words, till her work, like a golden dish set with shining jewels, and adorned by the hands of the cunning workmen, stands finished before us. In this kind, then, the best must be set before the learner, that he may eat and not be satisfied; for the finest products of the imagination are of the best nourishment for the beginnings of that imagination.

—"The Imagination: Its Functions and Its Culture"
A Dish of Orts
London: Edwin Dalton, 1908

Viewpoint: Clyde S. Kilby

The Bible as a Work of Imagination

I want to base what I have to say on three facts which I think indisputable.

The first is the Bible belongs to literature; that is, it is a piece of art. Does it make any difference that the Book we look upon as holy comes to us in literary form rather than in the form of abstract doctrine or systematic theology? Is the poetry of the Bible a fact plus an artistic decoration? If we summarize the Twenty-third Psalm to declare that God cares for his children as a good shepherd cares for his sheep, do the poetry and the prose summary amount to the same thing? If so, why the poetry in the first place? What change takes place when a piece of poetry is turned into a piece of doctrine or of practical exhortation?

How is the divine inspiration of the Bible related to the great oddity that the longest of the Psalms was written in the form of an acrostic? Was the acrostic form from God or only from the poet?... Did God inspire the form or only the content of the Bible? Is its form only a man-made incidental? Should Christian teachers ever encourage students to read the Bible as literature?

Why the "indirection" of saying that a godly man is like a tree planted by the rivers of water, and the extreme exaggeration of saying that the floods and the trees of the fields clap their hands and sing? Are such expressions to be dismissed as mere adornments, embroidery, as feathers—perhaps very pretty ones—that are to be removed from the turkey before its caloric and real meaning can come into existence?

Why isn't the Bible plain, expository, concrete? Why those numerous and difficult paradoxes flung at the readers...? Why the...frequent wordplay even in our Lord's own language? All of which suggests the literary quality of the Bible.

The second indisputable fact is that, because one—and possibly the greatest—ingredient of literature is imagination, we must say that the Bible is an imaginative book. There is no literature without imagination—strong, honest, often daring imagination.

The third indisputable fact is that the greatest artist of all, the greatest imaginer of all, is the one who appears at the opening of Genesis. Esthetics has to do with form, design, harmony, beauty. Perhaps the key word is "form." Now the earth, says Genesis, was without form. God shaped the creation into form—light and darkness, the heavens, the teeming waters, the multitudinous fauna and flora.... And we are told that he looked upon each thing he had shaped and saw that it was good. The whole he saw to be "*very* good." Even after the fall of man the Bible treats nature as beautiful, with God as its maker and wielder.... God did not, as so many of us, think that the esthetic was an incidental for leisure time.

—"Christian Imagination"
Christian Herald, 1969

Creating Narnia

Some people seem to think that I began by asking myself how I could say something about Christianity to children; then fixed on the fairy tale as an instrument; then collected information about child-psychology and decided what age group I'd write for; then drew up a list of basic Christian truths and hammered out "allegories" to embody them. This is all pure moonshine. I couldn't write in that way at all. Everything began with images; a faun carrying an umbrella, a queen on a sledge, a magnificent lion. At first there wasn't even anything Christian about them; that element pushed itself in of its own accord. It was part of the bubbling.

Then came the Form. As these images sorted themselves into events (i.e., became a story) they seemed to demand no love interest and no close psychology. But the Form which excludes these things is the fairy tale. And the moment I thought of that I fell in love with the Form itself: its brevity, its severe restraints on description, its flexible traditionalism, its inflexible hostility to all analysis, digression, reflections and "gas." I was now enamoured of it. Its very limitations of vocabulary became an attraction; as the hardness of the stone pleases the sculptor or the difficulty of the sonnet delights the sonneteer.

On that side (as Author) I wrote fairy tales because the Fairy Tale seemed the ideal Form for the stuff I had to say....

All my seven Narnian books, and my three science fiction books, began with seeing pictures in my head. At first they were not a story, just pictures. The *Lion* all began with a picture of a Faun carrying an umbrella and parcels in a snowy wood. This picture had been in my mind since I was about sixteen. Then one day, when I was about forty, I said to myself: "Let's try to make a story about it."

At first I had very little idea how the story would go. But then suddenly Aslan came bounding into it. I think I had been having a good many dreams of lions about that time. Apart from that, I don't know where the Lion came from or why He came. But once He was there He pulled the whole story together, and soon He pulled the six other Narnian stories in after Him.

So you see that, in a sense, I know very little about how this story was born. That is, I don't know where the pictures came from. And I don't believe anyone knows exactly how he "makes things up." Making up is a very mysterious thing. When you "have an idea" could you tell anyone exactly *how* you thought of it?"

—*Of Other Worlds*
New York: Harcourt Brace Jovanovich, 1966

Viewpoint: Denise Levertov

Work and Inspiration: Inviting the Muse

Poems come into being in two ways. There are those which are—or used to be—spoken of as *inspired;* poems which seem to appear out of nowhere, complete or very nearly so; which are quickly written without conscious premeditation, taking the writer by surprise. These are often the best poems; at least, a large proportion of those that *I* have been "given" in this way are the poems I myself prefer and which readers, without knowledge of their history, have singled out for praise. Such poems often seem to have that aura of authority, of the incontrovertible, that air of being mysteriously lit from within their substance, which is exactly what a poet strives to attain in the poems that are hard to write. But though the inspired poem is something any poet naturally feels awed by and grateful for, nevertheless if one wrote only such poems one would have, as it were, no occupation; and so most writers, surely, are glad that some of their work requires the labor for which they are constitutionally fitted. For the artist—every kind of artist, and, I feel sure, not only the artist but everyone engaged in any kind of creative activity—is as enamored of the process of making as of the thing made.

There is nothing one can say directly concerning the coming into being of "given" or "inspired" poems, because there is no conscious process to be described. However, in considering what happens in writing poems which have a known history, I have come to feel convinced that they are not of a radically different order; it is simply that in the "given" poem *the same kind of work* has gone on below, or I would prefer to say beyond, the threshold of consciousness. The labor we call conscious is, if the poem is a good one, or rather if the poet knows how to work, not a matter of use of the intellect divorced from other factors but of the intuitive interplay of various mental and physical factors, just as in unconscious procreative activity; it is *conscious* in that we are aware of it, but not in the sense of being deliberate and controlled by the rational will (though of course reason and will can and should play their modest part too).

The two manifestations of this underlyingly identical process can both occur in the composition of a single poem. Either sections of a poem emerge "right" the first time, while other sections require much revision; or…many drafts and revisions can prepare the way for a poem which at the last leaps from the pen and requires little or no revision, but which is emphatically not simply a final draft and indeed bears practically no resemblance to the earlier "versions" which make it possible. In such a case conscious work has led to the unpredictable inspiration.

—The Poet in the World
New York: New Directions, 1973

REFLECTIONS ON
LITERARY COMPOSITION

The best novels, and the best part of a novel, is a creation ex nihilo. Unlike God, the novelist does not start with nothing and make something of it. He starts with himself.

—Walker Percy, interview

A book begins with falling in love. You lose your heart to a place, a house, an avenue of trees, or with a character who walks in and takes sudden and complete possession of you. Imagination glows, and there is the seed of your book.

—Elizabeth Goudge, *The Joy of Snow*

Memory exercised in a particular way is the natural gift of poetic genius. The poet, above all else, is a person who never forgets certain sense-impressions which he has experienced and which he can re-live again and again as though with all their original freshness. All poets have this highly developed sensitive apparatus of memory, and they are usually aware of experiences which happened to them at the earliest age and which retain their pristine significance through-out life.... There is evidence for the importance of this kind of memory in all the creative arts.... The imagination itself is an exercise of memory. There is nothing we imagine which we do not already know. And our ability to imagine is our ability to remember what we have already once experienced and to apply it to some different situation.

—Stephen Spender, "The Making of a Poem"

The Muses are the daughters of Mnemosyne, Memory. It is my antique conviction that the Greeks knew what they were talking about—that to make the

Muses the daughters of Memory is to express a fundamental perception of the way in which Creativity operates.... When Homer talks of the Muses, he has nothing to say about Inspiration.... Creative thinking of any kind requires more than just knowing where to look things up; you have to know they're there before you know you need them. The mind is the greatest of computers, and it works its marvels best when well stored—with facts: names, dates, events, sequences—and also with language: words, phrases, sentences, the tongues of men and of angels.... Memory is not the enemy of Inspiration, or of thought either. Today, as always, it is the essential prerequisite of both.

—Clara Claiborne Park, "The Mother of the Muses:
In Praise of Memory"

Any discipline can help your writing: logic, mathematics, theology, and of course and particularly drawing. Anything that helps you to see, anything that makes you look. The writer should never be ashamed of staring. There is nothing that doesn't require his attention.

—Flannery O'Connor, *Mystery and Manners*

A writer needs three things, experience, observation, and imagination, any two of which, at times any one of which, can supply the lack of the others. With me a story usually begins with a single idea or memory or mental picture. The writing of the story is simply a matter of working up to that moment, to explain why it happened or what it caused to follow.

—William Faulkner, interview

Once a spectator said, after Jack Nicklaus had chipped a shot in from a sand trap, "That's pretty lucky." Nicklaus is supposed to have replied, "Right. But I notice the more I practice, the luckier I get." If you write often, perhaps every day, you will stay in shape and will be better able to receive those good poems...and get them down. Lucky accidents seldom happen to writers who don't work.... The hard work you do on one poem is put in on all poems. The hard work on the first poem is responsible for the sudden ease of the second. If you just sit around waiting for the easy ones, nothing will come.

—Richard Hugo, *The Triggering Town*

The writer...has no predisposed outlook; he seldom observes deliberately. He sees what he did not intend to see; he remembers what does not seem wholly possible. Inattentive learner in the schoolroom of life, he keeps some faculty free to veer and wander. His is the roving eye. By that roving eye is his subject found.... Writers do not find subjects; subjects find them. There is not so much a search as a state of open susceptibility.... Temperamentally, the writer exists on happenings, on contacts, conflicts, action and reaction, speed, pressure, tension. Were he a contemplative purely, he would not write. His moments of intake are inadvertent.

—Elizabeth Bowen, *The Search for a Story*

There had [originally] been no Joshua in my plot at all. I had a choice at that moment. I could ignore Joshua, refuse to allow him into my story. Or I could have faith in the creative process and listen to Joshua. This meant a great deal of rewriting—probably 150 or more pages. I cannot now imagine the book without Joshua, and I know that it is a much better book because of him. But where he came from I cannot say. He was a sheer gift of grace. It has been pointed out to me that Joshua is a Christian figure, and of course the name Joshua is a form of Jesus. But if I had consciously thought, "I will put a Christian figure into my book," I could not possibly have done it.

—Madeleine L'Engle, *Walking on Water*

A poem can be said to have two subjects, the initiating or triggering subject, which starts the poem or "causes" the poem to be written, and the real or generated subject, which the poem comes to say or mean, and which is generated or discovered in the poem during the writing.... Young poets find it difficult to free themselves from the initiating subject. The poet puts down the title:

"Autumn Rain." He finds two or three good lines about Autumn Rain. Then things start to break down. He cannot find anything more to say about Autumn Rain so he starts making up things, he strains, he goes abstract, he starts telling us the meaning of what he has already said. The mistake he is making, of course, is that he feels obligated to go on talking about Autumn Rain, because that, he feels, is the subject. Well, it isn't the subject. You don't know what the subject is, and the moment you run out of things to say about Autumn Rain start talking about something else. In fact, it's a good idea to talk about something else before you run out of things to say about Autumn Rain.

—Richard Hugo, *The Triggering Town*

The focus comes at random moments which no one can understand, least of all the author. For me, they usually follow great effort. To me, these illuminations are the grace of labor.... After months of confusion and labor, when the idea has flowered, the collusion is Divine. It always comes from the subconscious and cannot be controlled. For a whole year I worked on *The Heart Is a Lonely Hunter* without understanding it at all.

—Carson McCullers, "The Flowering Dream: Notes on Writing," in *The Mortgaged Heart*

There are four principles [of writing] which I see as important. The first is to read widely, not in order to copy someone else's style, but to learn to appreciate and recognize good writing, and to see how the best writers have achieved their result.... Practise writing in whatever form; the craft is learned by practising it.... Increase your vocabulary; the raw material of the writer is words and the more we have available and can use effectively and with confidence the better. Welcome experience. This means going through life with all senses open: observing, feeling, relating to other people. Nothing that happens to a writer need ever be lost.

—P. D. James, *Time to Be in Earnest*

Part Three

To Teach and Delight

The Roman writer Horace bequeathed one of the most foundational of all principles of literary theory when he defined a twofold function for literature. Horace's Latin formula was *utile et dulci*. The first of these denotes the usefulness of literature. Through the centuries this has been variously formulated as teaching, moving the reader toward right moral behavior, embodying truth, and expressing wisdom. This cluster of meanings obviously points to the didactic ("teaching") function of literature and is based on a utilitarian defense of literature.

Horace's word *dulci* literally means sweet, pleasant, or delightful. Through the centuries it has been formulated with such descriptors as enjoyment, pleasure, delight, and entertainment. To defend literature on such grounds is to conduct a hedonistic defense of literature.

This section of the book is shaped by Horace's famous dictum. Gene Veith's essay addresses the instructive side of literature under the umbrella of worldview, and his essay is buttressed by an excerpt that provides a practical methodology for discerning and analyzing worldviews in works of literature. The second essay analyzes the importance and nature of the pleasure that both readers and writers derive from the literary enterprise.

Reading and Writing Worldviews

Gene Edward Veith Jr.

T he mark of strictly literary reading, as opposed to scientific or otherwise informative reading," observed C. S. Lewis, "is that we need not believe or approve" what is said (136). The assumptions and values different books project in their writings may be mutually exclusive, and yet it is possible for readers, who themselves have their own assumptions and values, to enjoy and profit from reading them all. Why is this, Lewis asks?

"The nearest I have yet got to an answer is that we seek an enlargement of our being. We want to be more than ourselves. Each of us by nature sees the whole world from one point of view with a perspective and a selectiveness peculiar to himself." This is necessary, but it is also limiting. "We want to see with other eyes, to imagine with other imaginations, to feel with other hearts, as well as with our own" (137). Lewis argues that this is the key value of literature, whether it is fantasy or realism, sophisticated or popular. Literature is a point of entry into "other worlds," to use the title of one of his literary and critical collections.

A fantasy world may be wholly imaginary, yet it can move us strangely (as the fantasies of George MacDonald and others moved Lewis in the direction of Christianity). Reading old books, Lewis showed, is a way of transcending our chronological captivity to our one little time and place, freeing us from

GENE EDWARD VEITH JR. *is Professor of English at Concordia University in Wisconsin. He is the general editor of Crossway's "Focal Point" series, a line of books dealing with worldview issues from a Christian perspective. He is the author of ten books, including* Postmodern Times: A Christian Guide to Contemporary Thought and Culture; State of the Arts: From Bezalel to Mapplethorpe; *and* Reading Between the Lines: A Christian Guide to Literature.

the intellectual and imaginative constraints of the one that we happen to inhabit.

What Lewis is describing is the way literature projects a "worldview." The very act of writing involves the articulation of meanings—drawn from the author's beliefs, assumptions, and imaginative constructions—that constitute a little world, which readers, by letting the language play in their own minds as they read, can access in their own terms.

Lewis's formulation might seem to be an invitation to relativism. A reader might be someone who jumps from one world to another, like an intergalactic tourist, visiting for a while and "enlarging his being" with what the world has to offer, then blasting off to somewhere else, but having no world of his own. Many readers are, in fact, like that. But Lewis, being a Christian, knew of a real world, a habitation that was "not made with hands" as human worlds are (2 Corinthians 5:1, RSV).

For Christians, attending to worldviews is not only a way of understanding other worlds: it is a means of critique. The Bible teaches a worldview of its own, which Christians learn to explore and to apply. This worldview is necessarily in tension with merely human ideologies, tainted as they are by sin, the Fall, and the primal attempts to evade God.

To judge between one ethos *and another, it is necessary to have got inside both, and if literary history does not help us to do so it is a great waste of labour.*

—C. S. LEWIS, *English Literature in the Sixteenth Century Excluding Drama*

Reading with worldviews in mind—both one's own and that projected by the text—allows Christians to engage works in their own terms, while also interacting with them theologically. On its simplest level, worldview criticism—not just with literature but with every kind of cultural expression, from psychological theories to political programs—involves the ancient spiritual discipline of discernment. Christians oblivious to the diverse worldviews that are everywhere around them end up absorbing stances and attitudes that are incompatible with their faith, consuming whatever their culture has to offer them (self-help books, TV talk shows, political ads, postmodern novels) uncritically. Worldview criticism helps them to sort through the cultural barrage, accepting what is compatible with their faith while setting aside the ideas, morality, and assumptions that violate their deepest convictions.

This does not mean, though, that worldview criticism should consist merely of reducing a work to its constituent ideas, then accepting or rejecting the work accordingly. This is, in fact, how some Christians use worldview analysis. A work with a Christian worldview is to be read and appreciated. A work that embodies some non-Christian worldview is, if not rejected entirely, consigned to the status of visual aid, an illustrative example to show how bad a particular philosophy can be. Worldview criticism becomes a heuristic device for detecting errors, whether in a poem, a TV show, or some other cultural phenomenon.

To be sure, worldview criticism is a helpful heuristic device for detecting theological errors in cultural artifacts, a concern that Christians neglect to their peril. But attention to the worldviews that underlie a work of literature is by no means incompatible with an aesthetic and sympathetic engagement with a work of art. The way a work projects its worldview and the effectiveness of its imaginative communication of that worldview bring us back into the realm of aesthetics. Worldview criticism does not mean simply "criticizing worldviews"; rather, for Christians, it is a way to engage constructively the whole range of human expression from a Christian perspective.

WELTANSCHAUUNG

The term *worldview* is essentially an English translation of the German *Weltanschauung* (literally, "world perception"). The concept has its origins in nineteenth-century German philosophy, in Hegel's work on historical and intellectual change, and in the work of Kant, who argued that human perception is shaped by preexisting mental categories. Friedrich Schiller and, especially, Wilhelm Dilthey showed how knowledge and consciousness are shaped by the particular *Weltanschauung* of a people or of an era.

It was in this philosophical climate that continental Calvinist thinkers began applying the concept in a theological way. The succession of human ideologies that marks human history is, indeed, a succession of humanly devised worldviews. These ways of looking at existence—the varying assumptions about the nature of reality, the basis of morality, what human nature is like—are not so much consciously held philosophies. Rather, they are presuppositions, habits of thinking that are taken for granted and that serve as the basis for other perceptions. Because the human intellect is fallen, secular knowledge is always partial and in a state of change, and we are in constant need of God's revelation—the Word of God—which alone is the ground of truth.

If one is making a table it is possible that one's relationship to the Battle of Hastings or to the Nicene Creed might have little bearing on the form of the table to be made; but if one is making a sonnet such kinds of relationships becomes factors of more evident importance.

—DAVID JONES, Preface to *The Anathemata*

Furthermore, the Word of God itself sets forth a worldview. The Bible speaks not just of ethereal "spiritual" truths; rather, it reveals truths about the nature of existence that speak to every dimension of life. The Dutch theologian Abraham Kuyper worked out the parameters and implications of the Christian worldview (see, for example, his book *Christianity: A Total World and Life System*) and then attempted to apply it to the social problems of the Netherlands, which, at one point, made him head of state.

This Reformed tradition of worldview thinking also bore fruit in a particular approach to apologetics. Reason alone can never bring anyone to faith, as Calvinists have always insisted, no matter how strong the evidence for the truth of Christianity. Faith is a gift of God, a creation of the Holy Spirit in the heart of a totally depraved sinner. Cornelius Van Til, of Westminster Theological Seminary in Philadelphia, maintained that human beings are bound in their thinking to what is allowed in their worldviews. Naturalists who believe that the physical universe is all there is rule out miracles at the very outset. Their worldview will not permit them to accept a miracle even if they see it with their own eyes. Everything they believe is accounted for in terms of the closed system of their worldview, which, by definition, can have no room for God.

The evangelist, though, can help naturalists discover the inadequacy of their worldview, showing how it contradicts the deepest truths of life. They can be shown how naturalism, logically pursued, has a way of excluding the love they feel for family, or how it cannot help them face death, or how such a meaningless universe violates their own sense of justice and moral ideals. To use Francis

Schaeffer's term, the evangelist "takes the roof off," exposing unbelievers to the consequences of their worldview. Broken, desperate, and bereft of the most treasured assumptions, they can then be confronted with the claims of Christ, and, by God's grace, come to faith and be transformed by the renewing of their mind in accord with the Word of God.

In the 1960s, Francis Schaeffer helped popularize Van Til's apologetics and Dutch worldview thinking for American evangelicals. Young people who studied with him at L'Abri in Switzerland began to self-consciously consider what the biblical worldview consisted of, and what its implications might be for the arts and for culture as a whole. Schaeffer's friend Hans Rookmaaker applied worldview thinking to the arts, and his protegé James Sire used literary examples as a way to explain worldview thinking in *The Universe Next Door*. More and more books—written for the church at large rather than academics—began to apply worldview analysis to field after field. Unlike most academic endeavors, worldview criticism came out of the ivory towers and was taken up by the masses of ordinary Christians, carried out in Bible studies, youth groups, and activist committees, to the point that it inspired something of a backlash at many Christian colleges, with many Christian scholars lumping it together with the "narrow-minded fundamentalism" they were seeking to enlighten.

Though worldview criticism was mainly being pursued by conservative Christians who were using it as a weapon to refute the spirit of the age, irony of ironies—something very like it emerged in mainline secular academy. The *Weltanschauung* of the philosophers was taken over by the cultural anthropologists, who became more and more interested in describing and analyzing cultural worldviews. Historians of science, such as Thomas Kuhn, pointed out how scientific progress consists of the construction of explanatory paradigms, and how those paradigms keep shifting. Postmodernists began insisting that perception, knowledge, and truth itself is culturally conditioned, that we are captive to our cultural and linguistic and ideological "prison house"; that is to say, expressed more mildly, our worldview. As New Historicists and feminists unmasked the hidden social contexts and power ideologies implicit in literary texts, deconstructionists employed the "hermeneutics of suspicion" to uncover their hidden worldview contradictions. The deconstructionists were, in effect, "taking the roof off" of a literary text, what Francis Schaeffer did to unbelievers.

Worldview criticism became intellectually respectable again. That is, for all of its Christian affinities, it began to fit with the prevailing worldviews.

WHAT IS A WORLDVIEW?

A worldview has to do with both beliefs and the assumptions that underlie those beliefs. It is often articulated self-consciously by philosophers, but it is often more a matter of culture. People may acquire a worldview from their reading, education, or religious commitments, but more often they simply absorb certain ways of looking at reality from their surroundings and the social groups to which they belong. (One of the insights of worldview critics is that the ideas of the philosophers themselves are often correlated to the cultural climate of their time, that ideas do have cultural consequences and, conversely, that they can have cultural causes.) On the most basic level, worldviews involve the different assumptions about what is true and false, right and wrong, important and unimportant.

Worldviews can best be determined, according to James Sire, by answering questions like these:

1. *What is prime reality—the really real?* To this we might answer: God, or the gods, or the material cosmos.

2. *What is the nature of external reality, that is, the world around us?...* Whether we see the world as created or autonomous, as chaotic or orderly, as matter or spirit, or whether we emphasize our subjective, personal relationship to the world or its objectivity apart from us.

3. *What is a human being?...* A highly complex machine, a sleeping god, a person made in the image of God, a "naked ape."

4. *What happens to a person at death?...* Personal extinction or transformation to a higher state or departure to a shadowy existence on "the other side."

5. *Why is it* possible *to know anything at all?...* That we are made in the image of an all-knowing God or that consciousness and rationality developed under the contingencies of survival in a long process of evolution.

6. *How do we* know *what is right and wrong?...* We are made in the image of a God whose character is good, or right and wrong are

determined by human choice alone, or the notions simply developed under an impetus toward cultural or physical survival.

7. *What is the* meaning *of human history?.* . . To realize the purposes of God or the gods, to make a paradise on earth, to prepare a people for a life in community with a loving and holy God. (18)

Sire takes an openly philosophical approach, dealing with issues of epistemology, metaphysics, ethics, and teleology, which he proceeds to apply to non-philosophical expressions, such as literature. And though they might seem to be focusing on western intellectual history, his seven questions can take us deeply into the *Weltanschauung* of other cultures as well. For example, while most Westerners of whatever persuasion can usually agree that there is an external, objective universe, Eastern monism teaches that what we perceive is an illusion, not a creation by God, but a deceptive web spun by a demon. The Western assumptions of an orderly nature, comprehensible by rational laws, is revealed to be a cultural understanding—that is, a worldview, and one influenced by the biblical notion that God created the universe and saw that it was good.

The novelist. . .can only reply in the context of his own world view. . . . I speak in a Christian context. That is to say, I do not conceive it my vocation to preach the Christian faith in a novel, but as it happens, my world view is informed by a certain belief about man's nature and destiny which cannot fail to be central to any novel I write.

—WALKER PERCY, *The Message in the Bottle*

Nancy Pearcey and Chuck Colson, in their analysis of contemporary culture, approach worldviews by applying a distinctly Christian paradigm: Creation ("Where did we come from and who are we?"); the Fall ("What has gone wrong with the world?"); Redemption ("What can we do to fix it?"); Restoration ("How now shall we live?"). Christianity has answers to these questions, but so do non-Christian, even nonreligious ways of thinking. Today's secular, naturalistic scientific establishment does have a distinct position on creation, and its insistence that nature is essentially random and undirected has a bearing on their view of social problems (the Fall), ways to address them (Redemption), and how we must live in a random universe (Restoration). Marxism does have a thoroughly worked-out position on what has gone wrong with the world (a Fall), how it is to be fixed (Redemption), and how we should live in light of economic oppression (Restoration). In their book *How Now Shall We Live?* Colson and Pearcey offer a wide-ranging critique of contemporary culture, finding at the root of many of our problems worldview issues that only the Bible can successfully address.

It needs to be stressed that worldview is not the same as theology. Though a particular theology—say, the Calvinist understanding of divine providence, or the premillenialist notion that the world is constantly in decay until Christ comes—may indeed promote particular views of the world among its followers, to speak of the "Christian worldview" or the "biblical worldview" is generally much broader. Protestants and Catholics hold contrary and mutually incompatible doctrinal positions on issue after issue, but they generally hold a very similar worldview. They would agree on the basic assumptions that the universe is the creation of a transcendent yet personal God, that human beings are valuable yet fallen, that morality is a matter of transcendent absolutes grounded in God Himself, and the like. Jewish writers also will tend to project a worldview that grows out of the biblical way of looking at reality.

Thomas Jefferson was no Christian, but the worldview implicit in the Declaration of Independence is consonant with biblical assumptions: "We hold these truths to be self-evident, that all men are created equal, that they are endowed by their Creator with certain inalienable Rights, that among these are Life, Liberty, and the pursuit of Happiness." For Jefferson, these truths are "self-evident," and worldview has to do with beliefs that need not be proven, that are taken for granted. He grounds his political document in a view of Creation, which includes the reality of a personal Creator who is the source of transcendent moral truth. This Creator has made human beings, all of whom are equal before Him, and are endowed with rights that are "inalienable," grounded in His transcendent character, so that no one, or no society, can take them away.

Certainly, Christians of the time might disagree with Jefferson, but his ideas, however revolutionary, rest on a worldview that includes God, the creation, and the transcendence of the moral law. Today, of course, the worldview has shifted, and it is a fair question to ask whether a society for whom these ideas are no longer "self-evident" can maintain the kind of government he envisioned.

If human beings had no Creator, but are the product of random mutations, selected according to the survival of the fittest, can rights be "inalienable"? If the rights to life, liberty, and the pursuit of happiness are not endowed by the Creator, they must be a social construction, bestowed by the state or the culture. And what the state grants, the state can take away.

Although Jefferson was working with the raw materials of a biblical worldview, he was busy in his spare time scissoring the miracles out of the New Testament and criticizing the very notion of a revealed religion. The Declaration of Independence is not a "Christian" document—it says nothing about salvation in Christ, the Gospel which alone can make a Christian. And Christianity is not unitary; people of the same worldview have assumed many different political systems. Different ideologies, different cultural situations, and the specific historical conditions are still in play. And yet, the Declaration of Independence could never have been written in a culture untouched by the Bible.

WORLDVIEW IN LITERATURE

Literature presents a worldview from the inside. Reading a poem or a novel puts the reader inside the author's consciousness. The author's assumptions, emotional reactions, priorities, and sense of what is important are part of the texture of the work. The reader has access to the author's imagination, and thus to the author's worldview. It is not that authors are deliberately writing about their philosophy of life, ticking off answers to Sire's seven questions. Rather, they are writing about exciting stories or love or tragedy or something funny. Nevertheless, in doing so, they are presenting their subjects through the lens of their particular view of the world, that is, through their worldview.

To get this coherence of meaning as a set of ordered values in a work of art, the writer selects his facts. He arranges their order to suit his own conception of values.... All writers have, and must have to compose any kind of story, some picture of the world, and of what is right and wrong in that world.

—JOYCE CARY, *Art and Reality*

Some scholars have devoted themselves to the reconstruction of the intellectual and cultural contexts—the worldviews—of particular literary periods, as a way to explain an author's references and sensibility. For example, E. M. W. Tillyard's *The Elizabethan World Picture* (1944), D. W. Robertson's *Preface to Chaucer: Studies in Medieval Perspective* (1963) and, of course, C. S. Lewis's *The Discarded Image: An Introduction to Medieval and Renaissance Literature* (1964) are all "introductions" that serve as helpful guides in reading literature from times utterly unlike our own.

It is fashionable to criticize such books today for positing a "unitary" view of these periods, whereas in point of fact the Middle Ages and the Renaissance and every other era were times of conflicting voices, with marginalized people speaking out against the established power structures, and so on. Maybe so, but the conflicting voices constitute conflicting worldviews, so that the postmodernist scholars end up doing worldview criticism of their own, though focusing on social constructions more than intellectual philosophies. Needless to say, the contemporary critical interest in issues of gender, sexual orientation, economic classes, and power relationships as they relate to literature is also reflective of *our* century's worldviews. Thus worldview criticism remains a necessary prolegomena to literary studies.

The gold contained in the great books is a collection of world views. An effective method for mining these world views requires that the reader make only two assumptions and answer two questions. First, he must assume that any world view has a central concept or value.… Second, the reader must assume that all the other elements in the world view will derive their significance and worth from their relation to the central concept or value.

—RICHARD STEVENS and THOMAS J. MUSIAL,
Reading, Discussing, and Writing about the Great Books

But the real value of the approach comes not so much from the global analyses of thought forms, but from the way worldview criticism can serve as an entry into specific works of literature. Worldview criticism is a way to turn just about any work of literature into what is, in effect, a religious text, making it speak about ultimate issues, whether in harmony or in contrast to Christian beliefs. This is wholly legitimate, in my opinion, though without care this approach can lend itself to "using" literature, which C. S. Lewis warns about, rather than "receiving" it. At any rate, worldview criticism is at its most illuminating when it deals with sheerly secular texts, those that are not about ultimate philosophies at all, but which nevertheless betray a view of the universe. Consider, for example, some love poems.

The sonnets of Shakespeare have roots deep in the medieval tradition of courtly love, which might be described in worldview terms as a melange of neo-platonism, displaced pagan goddess worship, and a twisted cultural view of marriage in which the upper class married for property and loved on the side. The connection between romantic love and adultery, explicated even by Lewis in *The Allegory of Love* and his writings on Spenser, might be seen as a counter-view, a subversive subtext, to the "medieval world picture" hailed by many as a model of a unified Christian civilization. (On the other hand, one could argue that romantic love was reintegrated into the Christian worldview, pointing to Chaucer's "Franklin's Tale" and Dante's *Comedy*, the latter read with the help of Charles Williams's *The Figure of Beatrice*.)

Shakespeare's sonnets, though, manage also to mock that tradition of romantic verse—"My Mistress' eyes are nothing like the sun." That sonnet (130), with others, contrasts the idealizations of romantic love—its self-conscious conventions and its glorification of love apart from even knowing the person—with what it means to love an actual human being in the real world ("My mistress when she walks treads on the ground"). The whole sonnet sequence deals with the conflicts between Platonic love and Aristotelian lust, along with the guilt the latter brings ("Th' expense of spirit in a waste of shame / Is lust in action" [129]). The poems are filled with jealousy, self-loathing, abject adoration, hurt feelings, and inextricable soap opera complications and psychosexual confusions, what with the Fair Man and the Dark Lady (20, 134, 144). But take a particular poem and it resonates with a sense of eternity, transcendent values, and the immortal worth of the soul—worldview convictions that make the poems possible.

"Let me not to the marriage of true minds admit impediments" (116) relates love to marriage in a very nonmedieval way. More strikingly, in exploring the difference between true love, which is permanent, lasting even when "rosy lips and cheeks" are mowed down by the scythe of Time, and false love, which keeps changing and which seeks to change the other person, it addresses today's divorce culture more than it did his own times. The advice is almost strange, being given in a time when young noblemen, such as the Fair Friend being addressed, married for dynastically more important reasons than for love, but also when there was almost no question of "falling out of love" and getting a divorce. And yet here, in the late sixteenth century, Shakespeare is writing about how marriage involves unconditional love and how love—as opposed to love that is not love—never lets go. The love that "looks on tempests and is never shaken," that is not "Time's fool," that "alters not" is what married love is all about. Shakespeare is, in fact, admitting "impediments" to the marriage—an allusion to the wedding service in the Book of Common Prayer, where it asks if anyone knows any "impediments" why this marriage should not take place. The poem is warning his friend not to be drawn into marriage by the mere transient beauty of a young woman, but to understand the transcendent quality of love, as a real mutually accepting relationship, which is the lasting ground of marriage.

According to the worldview projected by this poem, love is no mere feeling, nor a choice, nor a consuming passion, as it is in other poems with other world-views. Rather, it is a kind of transcendent absolute. It is described as being *above* the "tempests" of life; it is an "ever-fixéd mark," "a star" that guides the lost ship, which knows it is there, even when it cannot be perceived (which is what the navigational jargon is referring to). Indeed all of Shakespeare's sonnets, including the more sinful and possibly homoerotic ones, have this assumption about what love is, a love that transcends time, history, and death itself (for example, 18, 55, 123). It would be impossible for this poem to have been written by an author who was an existentialist, for whom there are no transcendent absolutes, or a Darwinist, or a postmodernist. Shakespeare's universe, which makes possible his view of love, is that of Christianity. This is evident in the poem "Let Me Not to the Marriage of True Minds Admit Impediments," with its opening allusion to the wedding liturgy, and in the double biblical allusion in line 12 that is the poem's climax: Love "alters not," he says, "But bears it out even to the edge of doom." The first half of the line recalls 1 Corinthians 13:7, how love "bears all things." The effect is to bring into the poem the whole chapter on the Christian love that goes far beyond marriage to embrace all of the ways Christians are to relate to each other and the love of God for human beings that consists of sheer grace. The end of the line is apocalyptic, a reference to Doomsday, the very end of time, when Christ will return, as the Bridegroom to His bride, the church.

No less romantic, though, than Shakespeare's sonnets is Matthew Arnold's "Dover Beach." This is also a marriage poem, having been written in 1851 on the occasion of the author's honeymoon. He calls his bride—"Come to the window, sweet is the night air!"—to enjoy the "moon-blanched" landscape of the ocean, the beach, and the white cliffs. But the mood turns melancholy, as the constant crashing of the waves, which has gone on forever, heard too by the long-dead Sophocles, makes him think of "the ebb and flow / Of human misery." Like Shakespeare, he relates love and time, but now time makes human life seem small and insignificant. Then the receding of the tide makes him reflect about how "The Sea of Faith," though once at full tide, is now in this Victorian age receding, so that "now I only hear / Its melancholy, long, withdrawing roar." Looking ahead to their new life together and whatever the future might hold in this nascent modern, faith-free age, the poet rejects the typical Victorian trust in progress and sees before them only bleakness, emptiness, and darkness. But these throw into higher relief the necessity of their love:

> Ah, love, let us be true
> To one another! For the world, which seems
> To lie before us like a land of dreams,
> So various, so beautiful, so new,
> Hath really neither joy, nor love, nor light,
> Nor certitude, nor peace, nor help for pain;
> And we are here as on a darkling plain
> Swept with confused alarms of struggle and flight,
> Where ignorant armies clash by night.

The artist wants to give shape to…the primary data of experience…. But, of course, he cannot discover such a pattern unless he has a vantage point from which to view experience and by means of which his insights may be given order and proportion. Which is to say that he can transmute the viscous stuff of existential reality into the order of significant form only in accordance with what are his most fundamental beliefs about what is radically significant in life.

—Nathan A. Scott Jr., *Modern Literature and the Religious Frontier*

The world, bereft of faith, is not, in fact, a land of limitless dreams; the age ahead seems various, beautiful, and new, but it "really" is bereft of joy, love, light, certitude, peace, and help for pain. But it is *because* there is no external meaning in the world, that the lovers must "be true to one another!" Their love is all they have. Arnold foresees a world of confusions in conflict, of struggle and running away, ignorant clashes in a world growing darker and darker. But this means that their love is intensified, a personal assertion of meaning in a world which, among other things, "hath not...love." The contrast with Shakespeare's notion of love, which does exist outside and beyond the lovers as a star above the tempests, could hardly be greater.

Arnold's poem, in asserting how an individual creates his own personal meaning through his own commitments in a meaningless world, anticipates existentialism by a century. Not only that, in a time when Victorians tended to view the future with blithe optimism, in a worldview shaped by a facile notion of inevitable progress, Arnold anticipated the failures of the twentieth century in the middle of the nineteenth. More than that, Arnold's poem offers a foretaste of the lack of "certitude," the struggles, the ignorant armies clashing in the dark that feels like postmodernism.

Notice that writers do not always simply embody the worldview of their times, at least the best writers do not. They may well be reacting against the dominant worldviews that are around them, or positing an alternate worldview, or extending a worldview into new spaces.

Notice too that the greatness of the poet is not determined by the worldview that the poet holds. A skillful poet, such as Arnold, makes his worldview vivid, conveying a perspective that is honestly and imaginatively realized, which we readers can enter into and at least sympathize with, whether we agree with his worldview or not. And surely Arnold the agnostic is a greater writer than most Christian writers today, who cannot convey their own worldview in a way that helps anyone, even a nonbeliever, enter into it and taste its breadth, mystery, and depth.

WORKING FROM A WORLDVIEW

The question remains, How does worldview manifest itself from the writer's point of view? The question may be especially urgent for Christian writers: Does my worldview emerge naturally, in the course of my writing—whether I am writing a story, a poem, or a piece of scholarship—or should I consciously work in the elements of a biblical worldview?

Certainly, the most telling ways worldview shapes a work are in the unself-conscious assumptions about life that emerge—not just consciously held, strenuously contended for ideas, but those that are prereflective, taken for granted. Certainly, the themes of literature often deal with the "big ideas," and these are legitimate subjects for every writer, non-Christian and Christian alike. But the author's worldview exists also beneath the surface. The worldview is a precondition for an ideology; it constitutes the mind-set that allows a person to embrace a particular ideology. Only a materialist can be a true Marxist. By the same token, a Christian sensibility may be evident in a writer like Chaucer, even when he is writing utterly secular or even ribald tales: Even in his dirty jokes, the biblical assumptions about the worth of the human soul and the reality of the fall can be discerned. (That writing his scatological fabliaux also made Chaucer feel guilty, as evident in his end-of-life "Retraction," shows that the author believed in Christian morality, even though he felt that his writings sometimes violated it.)

We are told that novelists must not preach. This is nonsense. All serious artists preach—they are perfectly convinced of the truth as they see it, and they write to communicate that truth.... For a reader must never be left in doubt about the meaning of a story.

—Joyce Cary, *Art and Reality*

Though expressing a worldview is not necessarily something an author must work at, but happens naturally in the normal course of expression, a Christian writer has another issue. A Christian is called to live out his or her faith in daily life. Christians are called to grow in their faith, which involves putting to death their natural inclinations and surrendering more and more to the Holy Spirit. This process of sanctification is a constant conflict, an unsteady series of victories and failures that is never complete or perfected in this life. Though sanctification is a natural outgrowth of justification—not a new "salvation by works" after a one-time forgiveness at conversion—it certainly involves an active obedience to God's Word. The doctrine of vocation, in turn, teaches that Christians are to see their work—determined by their God-given talents, opportunities, and stations in life—as arenas for Christian service. For a Christian, being a writer is a vocation, a calling from God. So Christian writers will indeed have the impulse to consciously embody their understanding of the Word of God and to work out the implications of their faith in their writings.

Does this limit the Christian writer? Does this predetermine what he or she will see, and thus preclude creativity, originality, and the articulation of new ideas or new expressions? When it does, the Christian writer is underestimating what the biblical worldview actually is. It must dawn on anyone who seriously studies worldview, whether as a reader or a writer, that the Christian worldview is, in fact, bigger, broader, and more comprehensive than any of the humanly devised *weltanschauungs*.

The non-Christian worldviews, to give them credit, are more than erroneous philosophies. They usually contain at least a grain of truth. The problem is that human philosophies tend to be partial. The full truth, as God reveals it, is complex and comprehensive. It has been said that human reason works with "either/or." Christianity works with "both/and." Human reason would say that Jesus Christ must be either God or a man. Christian revelation says that He is *both* God *and* man. Human beings are *both* images of God *and* miserable sinners. The same paradoxes are evident when we talk about the Trinity, Law and gospel, grace and freedom, and the nature of the sacraments. The great doctrines of Christianity constitute a framework for knowledge that allows us to take the best of human insights, while balancing them with a larger vision.

Everything in the story should arise from the whole cast of the author's mind.... The matter of our story should be a part of the habitual furniture of our minds.

—C. S. LEWIS, *Of Other Worlds*

Christians can agree with the Eastern thinkers on the comparative insignificance of the physical realm compared to the spiritual. We can even agree that God is immanent, that, in the Holy Spirit, He indwells those who believe in Him. We can even agree on the importance of self-denial and rejection of the world. We cannot go as far as the Easterners do, however. *Both* the spiritual *and* the physical are important. God is *both* immanent *and* transcendent. We affirm *both* the strict demands of the Law *and* the free forgiveness of the gospel.

With the Enlightenment, we agree that the universe is marvelously and intricately ordered. We agree that reason is important. We agree that as individuals, we are part of a larger system. We also agree with the romantics, that nature is beautiful and mysterious. Emotions are also important. Individuals have value in themselves. If you put the Enlightenment together with romanticism, you will have something close to a Christian perspective on these issues.

With the materialists, we can affirm that nature is limited. There is violence and conflict in the natural order. Nature is not the source of moral values. We can agree that human beings are often beastlike in their craven sinfulness. The Bible teaches that both human beings and nature were ravaged by the Fall. We cannot agree, though, that the physical universe is all there is. Matter is real, but God is real too, and human beings, for all of their animality, bear His image.

With the existentialists, we can agree that, apart from God, there is no meaning in a person's life. This is the fruit of the Fall, what it means to be lost. We sympathize with the honesty and responsibility of the great existentialist thinkers. And yet, we affirm that there is objective meaning in God. We do not create Him; He creates us. The issue is not our will, but God's will. Truth is not relative, but revealed.

The sequence of human worldviews cannot all be true. An Enlightenment rationalist could not agree with a romantic; an existentialist would disagree with both of them. And yet, the biblical worldview gives us a framework for learning from each perspective. A Christian can learn from a rationalist, a romantic, and an existentialist without falling into their errors and without falling into relativism. A Christian knows that human answers are always partial, and thus not be committed exclusively to human half-truths. Knowing that human philosophies keep changing, a Christian can keep learning.

Christianity can give inspiration and direction to the intellectual life. The doctrines of Creation and Incarnation charge both the sciences and the humanities with divine significance. The biblical worldview also gives balance. If Christian doctrine works by "both/and," Christian scholarship works by "yes/but."

When we read a book that assumes that human beings have unlimited potential, we can say *yes*. Human beings by virtue of the divine image can do great things. *But* we will not buy the theory completely. Human beings are also sinners. There are limits. When we next read a book that says human beings are merely animals, determined by their heredity and environment, we can say *yes*. Human beings as sinners are a wretched lot; our wills, in bondage to sin, are not free. *But* we are more than animals; we have immortal souls; we have been redeemed. The same pattern is evident as Christians confront other scholarly issues. (*Yes,* human beings are insignificant creatures in a vast universe; *but* we have transcendent value. *Yes,* history is a record of human atrocities; *but* God redeems history. *Yes,* the scientific method is valid; *but* there are truths that elude science.) The two secular writers will not be able to agree with each other, but a Christian can learn from them both without taking either one too seriously.

Christianity offers a worldview and a framework for learning about other worldviews. Far from being narrow-minded, Christianity is mind-expanding, as it breaks us out of the confines of our limited perspectives. "I have heard it said that belief in Christian dogma is a hindrance to the writer," observed the great Christian novelist Flannery O'Connor, "but I myself have found nothing further from the truth. Actually it forces the storyteller to observe. It is not a set of rules which fixes what he sees in the world. It affects his writing primarily by guaranteeing his respect for mystery" (804).

Works Cited

Colson, Charles and Nancy Pearcey. *How Now Shall We Live?* Wheaton, Ill.: Tyndale House, 1999.

Lewis, C. S. *The Discarded Image: An Introduction to Medieval and Renaissance Literature.* London: Cambridge UP, 1964.

———. *An Experiment in Criticism.* London: Cambridge UP, 1961.

O'Connor, Flannery. "The Fiction Writer and His Country." In *Collected Works.* New York: The Library of America, 1988.

Robertson, D. W. *Preface to Chaucer: Studies in Medieval Perspective.* Princeton, N.J.: Princeton UP, 1963.

Sire, James. *The Universe Next Door.* Downers Grove, Ill.: InterVarsity Press, 1988.

Tillyard, E. M. W. *The Elizabethan World Picture.* New York: MacMillan, 1944.

"Words of Delight": A Hedonistic Defense of Literature

Leland Ryken

The Roman author Horace bequeathed the famous formula *utili et dulci* ("useful and delightful") to describe the two-fold function of literature, but he was actually popularizing a view that can be traced all the way back to the Bible. When the writer of Ecclesiastes states his philosophy of composition, he does so in terms of content and technique, teaching and delighting. Here is the passage (Ecclesiastes 12:9-10, ESV):

> Besides being wise, the Preacher also taught the people knowledge, weighing and studying and arranging many proverbs with great care. The Preacher sought to find words of delight, and uprightly he wrote words of truth.

Through the centuries, the words *wisdom* and *delight* have commended themselves to writers as the most evocative way in which to express the duality of literature. Percy Shelley spoke of poetry as "a fountain for ever overflowing with the waters of wisdom and delight" *(A Defence of Poetry)*. Robert Frost claimed that a poem "begins in delight and ends in wisdom" (22).

Despite the conventional pairing of words that name the usefulness and delight of literature, the hedonistic defense of literature has been largely asserted and taken for granted rather than explained and defended. Though they pay lip service to the delightfulness of literature, most theorists through the years have said little about the pleasure-giving aspect of literature, and it has not infrequently been an object of attack. Sir Philip Sidney, author of perhaps the greatest Christian apology for literature *(Apology for Poesy* [1595]), shows which way the wind is blowing when he speaks of "delightful teaching" as the chief glory of literature. In Sidney's formula, the emphasis falls on the noun, with the adjective bearing a subordinate role. This accords with the emphasis in Sidney's treatise as a whole, as Sidney finally rests his case for the importance of literature with a utilitarian exaltation of the power of literature to move its readers to good moral behavior. The writer is hailed as "the right popular philosopher." Later theorists have generally echoed Sidney's implied hierarchy of values: for Samuel Johnson "the end of poetry is to instruct by pleasing" *(Preface to Shakespeare)*, for Shelley poets are "the unacknowledged legislators of the world," and for Matthew Arnold the essence of literature is its status as "a criticism of life" *(Wordsworth)*.

Through the centuries, the hedonistic defense of literature has had to contend with a utilitarian or functional outlook that belittles anything that is not directly useful in mastering the physical demands of life. The utilitarian disparagement of the arts has been a frequent ingredient in Christian attitudes toward literature. But it has been equally true of non-Christian theories of literature and the arts, never more so than in our own technological culture. When applied to the arts, this mind-set either disparages the arts altogether or values them only for their ideas and usable content.

A Christian worldview stands opposed to such a reduction of life to the directly utilitarian. God did not create a purely functional world. Instead he planted a garden in which the trees were "pleasant to the sight" as well as "good for food" (Genesis 2:9, RSV). The writer of Psalm 19 valued nature, not because it was useful to him, but because it gave him the opportunity to contemplate the beauty and handiwork of God.

THE PLEASURES OF READING

The best starting point for getting an angle on the pleasure-giving aspect of literature is not to theorize about it but to proceed empirically, simply observing what happens when we read, hear, or view literature, and correspondingly why we seek out literary occasions. One of the oldest accounts of how people actually experience literature can be found in the passages in Homer's *Odyssey* that describe the performances of epic. Here is one of the descriptions:

> "What a pleasure it is, my lord," Odysseus said, "to hear a singer like this, with a divine voice! I declare it is just the perfection of gracious life: good cheer and good temper everywhere, rows of guests enjoying themselves heartily and lis-

tening to the music, plenty to eat on the table, wine ready in the great bowl, and the butler ready to fill your cup whenever you want it. I think that is the best thing men can have."

Obviously the performance of an epic was a form of after-dinner entertainment. Its function was communal enjoyment in a courtly setting. In fact, the regularity with which epics were performed when visiting dignitaries arrived suggests that it was a preeminent form of entertainment in ancient societies. To say that the most apparent function of an epic recital was entertainment is not to preclude the possibility that epic might have also served a didactic function. Obviously, though, people did not attend the performance of an epic in the spirit and with the expectations that people bring to hearing a sermon or attending a lecture. They first of all expected to be entertained.

Every good book should be entertaining. A good book will be more; it must not be less. Entertainment...is like a qualifying examination. If a fiction can't provide even that, we may be excused from inquiry into its higher qualities.

—C. S. Lewis, *An Experiment in Criticism*

It is an easy step from the after-dinner epic performance in Homer's *Odyssey* to our own experiences as readers of literature. While readers gravitate to literature for many reasons, enjoyment or pleasure is nearly always the leading motivation. Literature is something we pursue in our leisure time. While we also do utilitarian things in our free time, there are reasons for assigning reading a story or attending a play or reading a poem to the category of entertainment. Reading a novel is felt by most readers to have more in common with a stroll in the park than studying a textbook, and more in common with going on vacation than working in the kitchen or office. Watching a play is closer to attending a ball game than listening to a lecture.

We can learn a lot about the nature of literature by paying attention to what prompts people to seek literature in the first place. The overwhelming majority of people (not counting those who are enrolled in a literature course or wish to impress a friend) go to literature for enjoyment, entertainment, and what we might call the refreshment value of literature. People read literature because they want to, not because they are required to do so. Someone who wrote a book-length study of the psychological forces that lead people to read fiction concluded that "man is an indefatigable seeker of pleasure" (Lesser 21).

We can also profitably notice *when* people read literature or go to see a play. They do so during their leisure time—in the evening, on the weekend, during a break from work, while on vacation. Even our posture and surroundings are typically relaxed when we read literature. We might normally read a textbook or an owner's manual at a desk or table, but we probably read a novel or short story in an easy chair.

If we turn from these considerations of why, when, and how we typically read imaginative literature to its effects, the pleasure principle again emerges as important. The works that we finish reading and later reread obviously strike us as pleasurable. The delight and appeal of stories, for example, is well known. One of the most universal human impulses can be summed up in the four words, "Tell me a story." It is no wonder that Sir Philip Sidney described the story-teller as someone with the enchanting power to hold "children from play, and old men from the chimney corner" *(Apology for Poesy)*. In a similar vein, Owen Barfield, in speaking of the pleasures of poetry, describes "the old, authentic thrill, which is so strong that it binds some men to their libraries for a lifetime" (171). I remember how liberating I found a comment by Charles Williams that "*Paradise Lost* is much more fun written in blank verse than it would be in prose.... Let us have all the delights of which we are capable" (5).

THE NATURE OF LITERATURE

It is easy to see why readers find literature a source of enjoyment and refreshment: These effects are rooted in the nature of literature itself. Literature is an art form—a craft or skill. Robert Frost called poetry "a performance in words" (quoted in Drew 84). Great literature pleases and awes us with its display of literary form, technique, and inventiveness. Someone has rightly said that "our primal aesthetical experience is...a response of enchantment to 'beauty' (in a very wide sense of the term)" (Kolnai 340). A literary scholar who surveyed the three areas in which modern criticism has found the value of literature identified one of the areas as "a group of closely related ideas about form...treated as a...function of the imagination: beauty, form, art, style, craftsmanship, structure, the perfect and isolated object" (Kernan 35).

Artistic joy or delight is one of the purposes of literature. The purpose of expository writing such as we find in a newspaper, textbook, or informational book is primarily practical. Such writing does its job best if it is transparent as a medium, not calling attention to itself but pointing beyond itself to a body of information. Whatever pleasure we might find in such a book or article is likely to be the pleasure of having learned something, and even if we admire the writer's style, we are unlikely to claim that we have read the book (and even less likely to reread it) because we relish the writer's technique. Literature, by contrast, always adds an aesthetic purpose to the practical one. Its very form aims to give pleasure. Literary style and technique call attention to themselves and are experienced as something gratuitous, going beyond the functional needs of communication, possessing a refreshment or entertaining value that is self-rewarding. C. S. Lewis once wrote of literature that "every episode, explanation, description, dialogue—ideally every sentence—must be pleasurable for its own sake" (*Experiment* 84).

Much bad criticism, indeed, results from the efforts of critics to get a work-time result out of something that never aimed at producing more than pleasure.

—C. S. Lewis, *Christian Reflections*

THE TESTIMONY OF WRITERS

Readers and viewers want literature to be an enjoyable use of leisure time. The nature of literature explains why literature lends itself to enjoyment and entertainment. To these two considerations we can add the testimony of writers. T. S. Eliot, for example, called literature "superior amusement" (viii). W. H. Auden said that when young writers would tell him that they wanted to write poetry, he would ask, "Why do you want to write poetry?" According to Auden, "If the young man answers: 'I have important things I want to say,' then he is not a poet. If he answers: 'I like hanging around words listening to what they say,' then maybe he is going to be a poet" (171). Jean-Paul Sartre theorized that "the writer, like all other artists, aims at giving his reader...aesthetic joy" (58). Horace wrote, "That is how it is with poetry: created and developed to give joy to human hearts" *(The Art of Poetry)*. Matthew Arnold said regarding poetry that "it is demanded, not only that it shall interest, but also that it shall inspirit and rejoice the reader: that it shall…infuse delight" (Preface to *Poems*).

Last fall I received a letter from a student who said she would be "graciously appreciative" if I would tell her "just what enlightenment" I expected her to get from each of my stories.… I wrote her back to forget about the enlightenment and just try to enjoy them.

—FLANNERY O'CONNOR, *Mystery and Manners*

As we will see, the refreshment value of literature is not limited to its form and beauty as distinct from its content, but the entertainment value of literature depends chiefly on technique. When writers make statements about the craft of their writing, they are giving implicit testimony to their desire that their work be a delight to their audience. Dylan Thomas, for example, claimed,

> I like to treat words as a craftsman does his wood or stone…to hew, carve, mold, coil, polish, and plane them into patterns, sequences, sculptures, fugues of sound.… I, myself, do not read poetry for anything but pleasure. (185-186, 190)

Gerard Manley Hopkins claimed that the form of a poem exists "for its own sake and interest even over and above its interest of meaning" (38).

Writers do not, of course, claim that literature is *only* entertaining. Robert Frost expressed the majority viewpoint when he wrote that a poem "begins in delight and ends in wisdom.… It begins in delight…and ends in a clarification of life" (22). The useful and entertaining functions of literature are complementary, not incompatible.

Writers' theoretic endorsement of the pleasure of literature is corroborated by their practices. Great writers—indeed, great artists—drive themselves to perfect their form. Leonardo da Vinci drew over a thousand hands in his attempt to capture the ideal beauty of the human form. Ernest Hemingway rewrote the conclusion to *A Farewell to Arms* seventeen times in an effort to "get it right" (Baker 97). Dylan Thomas made over two hundred manuscript versions of his poem "Fern Hill" (Ackerman 123-124). It was not the ideas that Hemingway and Thomas were trying to perfect; it was the beauty and perfection of the form.

If we ask what difference the pleasure-giving element of literature makes to a writer in the act of composition, the answer may be a little less obvious than when we ask the same question about readers in the act of reading. After all, composition is hard work. It is also a very intuitive process. If asked what difference it makes to the creative process to know that literature is intended to give pleasure, most (not all) writers would be hard pressed to answer the question. Upon reflection, most would probably claim to be preoccupied with truth and content during the process of composition. As Annie Dillard puts it, "The writer is certainly interested in the art of fiction, but perhaps less so than the critic is. The critic is interested in the novel; the novelist is interested in his neighbors. Perhaps even more than in his own techniques, then, the writer is interested in knowing the world in order to make real and honest sense of it" (*Living by Fiction* 151).

But writers do have a stake in the pleasures of literature in at least two ways— as the bringers of pleasure to readers and as participants in the pleasures of composition. To be a source of pleasure, a story, play, or poem needs first of all to be entertaining, and this pushes a writer to the refinement of technique and the creation of beauty. It is the same Annie Dillard who said that the novelist is more interested in making sense of the world than in the art and technique of writing who also theorized that "the more literary the book—the more purely verbal, crafted sentence by sentence, the more imaginative, reasoned, and deep—the more likely people are to read it" (*Writing Life* 19). Might we say that successful writers have an intuitive Nielsen rating system inside them that leads them to give readers what they want? And if it is true that readers go to literature in the first place for the entertainment and pleasures that it affords, writers show by their attention to the artistry and beauty of their work that they accept the giving of pleasure as a leading part of their vocation. Even so didactic a poet as William Wordsworth surprises us by saying that "the Poet writes under one restriction only, namely, the necessity of giving immediate pleasure" (*Preface to Lyrical Ballads*).

Secondly, writers not only bring pleasure to their audience; they also experience joy in their vocation and craft. The enjoyment of readers and viewers has a counterpart in the joys of creation experienced by the writer in the act of composition. Of course composition is hard work—"elaborate and painful toil," Dante called it (quoted Scott-James 126). In his poem "Adam's Curse," William Butler Yeats ranks the poet's work as one of the three great labors that prove that "there is no fine thing / Since Adam's fall but needs much laboring." And yet authors keep giving us glimpses of the joy that they find in the act of creation. We catch the hint in Madeleine L'Engle's comment that

> when we are writing, or painting or composing, we are, during the time of creativity, freed from normal restrictions, and are opened to a wider world, where colours are brighter, sounds clearer, and people more wondrously complex than we normally realize. (101)

If there is enjoyment in the reading of literature, we can rest assured that there was joy in the creating of it beforehand.

We sense the writer's pleasure in Denise Levertov's attack on the notion of the suffering writer:

> A secret artists share—but it's so secret they don't talk about it even to each other—is the strange ease and pleasure there is in their work.... I feel ashamed, often, hearing that stuff about suffering.... All the time we have, we lucky ones, this amazing secret, the way vision slides on, like a well-talcumed kid glove, to enclose on in its words.... For those who have the luck to be so engaged—by nature, by their natures, their destinies—is there any *pleasure* deeper...? (214-216)

One of the recurrent themes of Mihaly Csikszentmihalyi's massive study of human creativity is the enjoyment that creative people derive from their work. A playwright once responded to the question why he wrote plays with the quip, "For the glory of God and fun."

I got into this row, big, at the novel conference at Harvard, when...we had a novelist get up and speak about the responsibilities of the novelist. I was with Anthony West on the stage and I was gradually getting into hysterics.... "All right," I said at the end of it, "if there are any of my students here I'd like them to remember that writing is fun." That's the reason you do it, because you enjoy it, and you read it because you enjoy it.... You do it for exactly the same reason that you paint pictures or play with the kids. It's a creative activity.

—FRANK O'CONNOR, interview

From writers' comments and practices we can infer that it is one of their intentions to entertain and please their readers and viewers. C. S. Lewis picks up on this principle of intention when he writes, "A great deal (not all) of our literature was made to be read lightly, for entertainment. If we do not read it, in a sense, for fun…we are not using it as it was meant to be used" (*Reflections* 34).

WHAT KINDS OF PLEASURE?

If we begin to reflect on the kinds of pleasure and refreshment that literature offers its recipients, the list keeps expanding. Some of the pleasures of imaginative literature are ones that apply equally to other kinds of reading, though usually not in the same way or to the same degree. But the composite picture of the delights of literature explains the unique hold of literature upon those who have developed a taste for it. As I turn to an anatomy of the kinds of pleasure that literature affords, I should note in passing that many of the time-honored theories of literature—theories like art as mimesis (imitation), catharsis (emotional equilibrium), imagination—can be construed in part as attempts to explain the pleasures that the human race has found in literature and art.

We can begin with the intellectual pleasures of literature, which stem from the ideas embodied in it. The ideational richness and profundity of literature varies widely from work to work and genre to genre, and the degree to which the ideas of literature are an important source of pleasure varies from reader to reader. Two types of intellectual pleasure may be identified. One is the intellectual stimulation that comes when a work of literature raises issues in such a way as to activate us to think about them. At this level, whether we agree or disagree with the author's ideas is less important than the way in which the work serves as a catalyst to our thinking about important issues of life. For thinking people, this is a source of pleasure. Ralph Waldo Emerson said that the poet has the power of "rejoicing the intellect" *(The Poet)*, while R. A. Scott-James claimed the writer's "joy is the joy that arises from discerning the truth" (343).

"No ideas but in things" does not mean no ideas.
—DENISE LEVERTOV, *The Poet in the World.*

The other kind of intellectual pleasure comes when a work espouses ideas with which we agree. In such instances our encounters with the ideas in a work are a celebration of truth as we understand it. Malcolm Muggeridge recorded the pleasure of encountering the Christian vision in literature this way: "Books like *Resurrection* and *The Brothers Karamazov* give me an almost overpowering sense of how uniquely marvelous a Christian way of looking at life is, and a passionate desire to share it" (79).

While ideas are the forte of expository writing more than literary writing, lifelong readers of literature can attest that many of the most powerful ideas in their lives are ones that they encountered first or most memorably in literature. Matthew Arnold championed this view of literature when he wrote, "It is important…to hold fast to this:…that the greatness of a poet lies in his powerful and beautiful application of ideas to life" *(Wordsworth)*. We should note that in Arnold's formula it is not the disembodied ideas that constitute their power in literature. It is their *application* to real life that makes them live in literature, and furthermore they cannot be divorced from the aesthetic criterion of their being presented in a form that is *beautiful.*

A second pleasure to be derived from literature is the pleasure of seeing human experience accurately embodied so it can be contemplated and vicariously lived. More than anything else, literature is an embodiment of human experience. Truthfulness to reality is the kind of truth that literature offers in the greatest abundance. People are affirming creatures in this regard, and they enjoy seeing human experience captured in a form that they can recognize as being truthful to the way things are. Aristotle long ago observed this, speaking of the "universal…pleasure felt in things imitated" in a work of art *(The Poetics)*. Ralph Waldo Emerson correctly observed that all people "stand in need of expression," and yet "adequate expression is rare"; writers supply the gift of expression to the human race, being "natural sayers, sent into the world to the end of expression" *(The Poet)*. Taking human experience as its subject, literature is both a mirror in which we see ourselves and our experiences and a window through which we observe the world of things and people. When C. S. Lewis wrote about literature that "we demand windows" *(Experiment* 138), he linked it to the notion that "we delight to enter into" other people's beliefs, passions, and imaginations. Many writers and critics through the centuries have defined the nature of literature in terms of leading a reader to *see* human experience accurately, thereby pointing to one of the greatest pleasures of reading literature—the pleasure of "right seeing."

In addition to intellectual and representational pleasure, literature offers aesthetic pleasure—the pleasure that we derive from beauty and artistry. It is a large part of what the arts offer to the human race. Even definitions of beauty usually link beauty to pleasure, as in the famous medieval definition of beauty as *id quod visum placet*—"that which, being seen, pleases." This might well remind us of John Keats's famous aphorism that "a thing of beauty is a joy forever" (*Endymion*, Book 1), and of Coleridge's formula that the "immediate purpose" of poetry is "pleasure through the medium of beauty" *(On the Principles of Genial Criticism Concerning the Fine Arts)*. Russian novelist Boris Pasternak once claimed that "a literary creation can appeal to us in all sorts of ways—by its theme, subject, situations, characters. But above all it appeals to us by the presence in it of art" *(Doctor Zhivago)*. Beauty is in itself nonutilitarian and therefore appreciated and valued as self-rewarding. Emerson said that "beauty is its own excuse for being' ("The Rhodora"). H. R. Rookmaaker gave this a Christian twist when he claimed that "art needs no justification.... Art has a meaning as art because God thought it good to give art and beauty to humanity" (229-230).

Apart of course from those who invest their money in things of beauty, nobody wants works of art for their own sake; what is wanted in them is the pleasure of seeing them, of reading them, of hearing them.

—Etienne Gilson, *The Arts of the Beautiful*

The pleasures of literature, moreover, include the pleasures of contemplation. This contemplation exists on several levels. Any literary experience involves a reader, listener, or viewer whose attention is riveted on the work itself. Part of this attention flows to the aesthetic properties of the work. In addition, because the subject of literature is human experience, experiencing a work of literature always lures the audience into an act of contemplating human experience. The writer's vocation, claims Nathan A. Scott, "is to *stare*, to *look* at the created world, and to lure the rest of us into a similar act of contemplation" (52). When we assimilate literature, we contemplate ourselves and our own experiences, external reality, the social world of people, and in some instances the spiritual world.

Yet another category of literary pleasure is emotional or affective pleasure. A prime function of literature is to awaken feelings, especially in the form of longing for the good and aversion to what is evil or terrifying. Shelley held as an ideal that in our encounters with literature "the good affections are strengthened," resulting in "an exalted calm" *(A Defence of Poetry)*, a sentiment similar to Wordsworth's view that readers of literature can find their "affections strengthened and purified" *(Preface to Lyrical Ballads)*. In addition to the pleasure of having good affections strengthened, the affective pleasures of literature belong to a process that throughout literary history has most often been known as catharsis—the calming of the emotions into a state of repose and equilibrium (Adnan Abdulla's book *Catharsis in Literature* shows how pervasive the concept has been, in a wide range of formulations, throughout the history of literary theory). Milton claimed that at its best literature has the ability to "allay the perturbations of the mind, and set the affections [emotions] in right tune" *(The Reason of Church Government)*. Matthew Arnold claimed that poetry possesses "the power of so dealing with things as to awaken in us a wonderfully full, new, and intimate sense of them. When this sense is awakened in us…we feel ourselves to be in contact with the essential nature of those objects…and to be in harmony with them; and this feeling calms and satisfies us as no other can" *(Maurice de Guérin)*. More recently, Sven Birkerts has praised literature for the state that it induces—a state in which "all is clear and right" and in which one feels "a sense of being for once in accord with time" (83).

Writers construct a space where readers come to meditate alone.
—JOHN E. BECKER, "Science and the Sacred: From Walden to Tinker Creek"

The pleasures of literature also include the pleasures of imagination. For people whose philosophy of literature is based primarily on the imagination, to speak of the pleasures of the imagination is to cover virtually all that one might say about the pleasures of literature. Apart from that, surely all philosophies of literature can agree that much of the pleasure that we derive from literature, whether as writers or readers, is the power of transport that literature affords— the knack that literature has of whisking us away from our own time and place to another time and place. Our ability to imagine something beyond the actual is what makes this pleasure of transport possible.

We can rightly speak of the holiday spirit that inheres in the literary experience. Writers themselves have sometimes used the image of the journey to express the pleasures of transport that literature offers. John Keats spoke of traveling in the realms of gold ("On First Reading Chapman's Homer"). Emily Dickinson wrote in a similar vein, "There is no frigate like a book / To take us lands away." Everyone needs beneficial escapes from actual reality; it is one of the rights to which the human race is entitled. As Marie Rosenblatt says in defending literary escape from its derogatory sense, "Anything that offers refreshment and lessening of tension may have its value in helping us to resume our practical lives with renewed vigor" (39; compare the view of C. S. Lewis that escaping into an imagined world "paradoxically enough, strengthens our relish for real life. This excursion into the preposterous sends us back with renewed pleasure to the actual" ["On Stories"]).

Now there is a clear sense in which all reading whatever is an escape. It involves a temporary transference of the mind from our actual surroundings to things merely imagined or conceived. This happens when we read history or science no less than when we read fictions. All such escape is from the same thing; immediate, concrete actuality. The important question is what we escape to....

Escape, then, is common to many good and bad kinds of reading. By adding –ism to it, we suggest, I suppose, a confirmed habit of escaping too often, or for too long, or into the wrong things, or using escape as a substitute for action where action is appropriate, and thus neglecting real opportunities and evading real obligations. If so, we must judge each case on its merits. Escape is not necessarily joined to escapism.

—C. S. Lewis, *An Experiment in Criticism*

Yet another category of pleasure that we derive from literature is verbal pleasure—the pleasure that comes from our reading and hearing beautiful language skillfully employed. What, after all, captures us most in the following description of sunrise as captured by Mark Twain *(Life on the Mississippi)*? "The dawn creeps in stealthily; the solid walls of black forest soften to gray, and vast stretches of the river open up and reveal themselves; the water is glass-smooth, gives off spectral wreaths of white mist." From what do we derive the pleasure in the following description by Charles Dickens *(Great Expectations)*?

The June weather was delicious. The sky was blue, the larks were soaring high over the green corn. I thought all that countryside more beautiful and peaceful by far than I had ever known it to be yet…. They awakened a tender emotion in me; for my heart was softened by my return, and such a change had come to pass, that I felt like one who was toiling home barefoot from distant travel, and whose wanderings had lasted many years.

What pleases us beyond even the experiences evoked is the writer's skill with words—the linguistic feat of saying something in a way that dazzles and delights us. When Robert Frost speaks of poetry as "a performance *in words*" (italics mine), he implicitly confirms language as the medium with which the poet performs and in which we take delight. The formula that best expresses the verbal pleasure of literature comes from the writer of Ecclesiastes when he speaks of how he "sought to find words of delight" (Ecclesiastes 12:10, ESV; New English Bible: "he chose his words to give pleasure").

We demand of a great poem…what I should call Deliciousness— what the older critics often called simply 'Beauty'. The poem must please the senses, directly by its rhythms and phonetic texture, indirectly by its images.
                                          —C. S. LEWIS, "Williams and the Arthuriad"

Not all of our travels in the realms of gold (John Keats's metaphor for the experience of reading literature) offer spiritual pleasure, but for Christian readers a great deal of their reading includes this pleasure. What I have chiefly in mind is the way in which literature provides the materials and occasion for encountering God and spiritual experience as we read literature. Literature that espouses a Christian view of life is the chief repository of such an encounter. Within that body of literature, the devotional lyric of course looms large, but narrative and drama are just as capable of becoming the occasion for such spiritual pleasure. Spiritual perception and communion with God are ultimately located within the reader or viewer who assimilates a work of literature, and it is therefore possible for a Christian to encounter God in literature that does not embody a Christian viewpoint and that in fact may have been written by a non-Christian with an anti-Christian agenda and perspective.

CHRISTIAN HEDONISM

I have thus far implicitly defended the pleasures of literature on broadly human-istic grounds. Does the Christian faith have anything distinctive to say on the matter? It does. A person with a Christian worldview has a reason to value enjoyment and the enlightened use of leisure time in ways that the human race at large does not. Christians are the last people in the world who should feel guilty about the enjoyment of literature. As C. S. Lewis correctly stated, the Christian "has no objection to comedies that merely amuse and tales that merely refresh…. We can play, as we can eat, to the glory of God" (*Reflections* 33-34).

If we are looking for a biblical endorsement of enjoyment and pleasure, the doctrine of Creation is a good starting place. Christians affirm in their creed that God is "Maker of heaven and earth." The Bible tells us, moreover, that people are created in the image or likeness of God. Abraham Kuyper concluded from this that "as image-bearer of God, man possesses the possibility both to create something beautiful and to delight in it" (142).

We might also note the precise kind of world that God created. He made a world that is beautiful as well as functional (Genesis 2:9). From a utilitarian point of view, God did not need to create a world filled with colors and beautiful shapes that delight the human senses. He could have created everything in a drab gray color. It is obvious that God made provision for the quality of human life, not simply its survival. At the heart of God's creation lies the pleasure principle, as John Piper has documented in two books with the intriguing titles *Desiring God: Meditations of a Christian Hedonist* and *The Pleasures of God: Meditations on God's Delight in Being God* (Portland: Multnomah, 1986, 1991).

While the pleasures of literature are not solely the domain of beauty, it is this aspect of literature (however we name it) that is the particular locus of the pleasure that literature offers to us. In a host of ways, not least of which is the example of the Bible itself, the Bible shows us that God values beauty. The classic texts are the passages in Exodus 35–39 that describe the building of the tabernacle. We read here that it was God himself who called the chief artist and "filled him with the Spirit of God, with ability, with intelligence, with knowl-edge, and with all craftsmanship, to devise artistic designs, to work in gold and silver and bronze, in cutting stones for setting, and in carving wood, for work in every skilled craft" (Exodus 35:31-33, RSV).

As with beauty, so with pleasure itself. Pleasure and its synonyms are one of the recurrent motifs in the Psalms, but the endorsement of pleasure is evident in less obvious ways in virtually every part of the Bible. As the article on pleasure in *A Dictionary of Biblical Imagery* traces the pleasure motif in the Bible, it turns out that the Bible's positive pleasures extend to virtually every area of life—nature, worship, romantic love, family life, community and sociability, God himself (651-654). In fact, the Bible is enveloped with the pleasure principle, beginning as it does with a perfect garden and ending with an eternal life of bliss in a celestial city. The *locus classicus* for the biblical endorsement of pleasure is the God-centered passages in the book of Ecclesiastes. One of these passages states,

> Behold, what I have seen to be good and to be fitting is to eat and drink and find enjoyment in all the toil with which one toils under the sun the few days of his life which God has given him, for this is his lot. Every man also to whom God has given wealth and possessions and power to enjoy them, and to accept his lot and find enjoyment in his toil—this is the gift of God. (Ecclesiastes 5:18-19, RSV)

These same sentiments are reiterated in a classic New Testament passage in which Paul comments on wealthy people. Paul's advice to Timothy is as follows: "Charge them that are rich in this world, that they be not highminded, nor trust in uncertain riches, but in the living God, who giveth us richly all things to enjoy" (1 Timothy 6:17, KJV). This key verse establishes three important principles regarding enjoyment: (1) God is the giver of all good things; (2) he gives people these things to enjoy; and (3) the misuse of them consists not in enjoyment of them but in trusting them or making idols of them.

The biblical doctrine of heaven also exalts pleasure. If heaven is the place where there is no more pain (Revelation 21:4), C. S. Lewis can correctly assert that "all pleasure is in itself a good and pain in itself an evil; if not, then the whole Christian tradition about heaven and hell and the passion of our Lord seems to have no meaning" (*Reflections* 21).

A person's attitude toward pleasure is actually a comment on his or her estimate of God. To assume that God dislikes pleasure and enjoyment is to charge him with being sadistic toward his creatures. The Bible, of course, does not allow such a conclusion. Someone has aptly written that "God is not a celestial

Scrooge who hates to see his children enjoy themselves. Rather, he is the kind of Father who is ready to say, 'Let us eat and make merry; for this my son was dead and is alive again; he was lost and is found' (Luke 15:24)" (Geisler 11).

What does the biblical affirmation of beauty and enjoyment have to do with the reading and production of literature? Primarily it validates the enjoyment of literature as a Christian activity. When we enjoy the beauty of a sonnet or the artistry of an epic or the fictional inventiveness of a novel, we are enjoying a quality of which God is the ultimate source and performing an act similar to God's enjoyment of his own creation. The way to show gratitude for a gift is to enjoy it. Literature and art are God's gifts to the human race. One of the liberating effects of letting ourselves "go" as we enjoy literature is to realize that we can partly affirm the value of literature whose content or worldview we dislike. If God is the ultimate source of all beauty and artistry, then the artistic dimension of literature is the point at which Christians can be unreserved in their enthusiasm for the works of non-Christian writers. John Milton gradually came to deplore the ethical viewpoint of pagan authors, but he noted that "their art I still applauded" *(Apology for Smectymnuus)*. Werner Jaeger, in his book on the classical tradition, claimed that "it was the Christians who finally taught men to appraise poetry by a purely aesthetic standard—a standard which enabled them to reject most of the moral and religious teaching of the classical poets as false and ungodly, while accepting the formal elements in their work as instructive and aesthetically delightful" (34).

Reading is not only a pleasure in itself, with its concomitants of stillness, quietness and forgetfulness of self, but in what we read many of our other comforts are present with us.

—ELIZABETH GOUDGE, *A Book of Comfort*

The modern age has generally regarded the arts as dispensable because they are nonutilitarian. But if we look honestly and deeply within the human spirit as created by God, we will find a hunger for human creativity, for artistry, for beauty. And if we look beyond the human spirit to the God of all beauty and creativity, we will conclude that literature and the arts are not the unnecessary pursuit of an idle moment.

Literature is one of the things that can satisfy the human urge for enjoyment—enjoyment of beauty, of truth, of life itself. Writers aim to please as well
as to edify, and they construct their works accordingly. The result is that for both
writers and readers, literature is "created and developed to give joy to human
hearts" (Horace), possessing the power to "inspirit and rejoice the reader…and
infuse delight" (Matthew Arnold).

Works Cited

Abdulla, Adnan K. *Catharsis in Literature.* Bloomington: Indiana University Press,
    1985.

Ackerman, John. *Dylan Thomas: His Life and Work.* London: Oxford University Press,
    1964.

Auden, W. H. "Squares and Oblongs." *Poets at Work.* Ed. Charles D. Abbott. New
    York: Harcourt, Brace, 1948. 163-181.

Baker, William Carlos. *Hemingway: The Writer as Artist.* Princeton: Princeton Univer-
    sity Press, 1952.

Barfield, Owen. *Poetic Diction: A Study in Meaning.* New York: McGraw-Hill, 1964.

Birkerts, Sven. *The Gutenberg Elegies.* New York: Fawcett Columbine, 1994.

Csikszentmihalyi, Mihaly. *Creativity: Flow and the Psychology of Discovery and
    Invention.* New York: HarperCollins, 1996.

A Dictionary of Biblical Imagery. Ed. Leland Ryken *et al.* Downers Grove: InterVarsity,
    1998.

Dillard, Annie. *Living by Fiction.* New York: Harper and Row, 1982.

———. *The Writing Life.* New York: Harper and Row, 1989.

Drew, Elizabeth. *Poetry: A Modern Guide to Its Understanding.* New York: Dell, 1959.

Eliot, T. S. *The Sacred Wood.* London: Methuen, 1920, 1960.

Frost, Robert. "The Figure a Poem Makes." *Writers on Writing.* Ed. Walter Allen.
    Boston: The Writer, 1948). 22-23.

Geisler, Norman. "The Christian as Pleasure-Seeker." *Christianity Today.* 25 September
    1975: 8-12.

Hopkins, Gerard Manley. "Poetry and Verse." *Gerard Manley Hopkins: The Major
    Poems.* Ed. Walford Davies. London: J. M. Dent and Sons, 1979.

Jaeger, Werner. *Paideia: The Ideals of Greek Culture.* Trans Gilbert Highet. New York: Oxford University Press, 1939. Volume 1.

Kernan, Alvin. "The Idea of Literature." *New Literary History* 5 (1973): 31-40.

Kolnai, Aurel. "Contrasting the Ethical with the Aesthetical." *British Journal of Aesthetics* 12 (1972): 331-344.

Kuyper, Abraham. *Lectures on Calvinism.* Grand Rapids: William B. Eerdmans, 1953.

L'Engle, Madeleine. *Walking on Water: Reflections on Faith and Art.* Wheaton: Harold Shaw, 1980.

Lesser, Simon. *Fiction and the Unconscious.* 1957. Chicago: University of Chicago Press, 1975.

Levertov, Denise. *The Poet in the World.* New York: New Directions, 1973.

Lewis, C. S. *An Experiment in Criticism.* Cambridge: Cambridge University Press, 1961.

———. *Christian Reflections.* Ed. Walter Hooper. Grand Rapids: William B. Eerdmans, 1967.

Muggeridge, Malcolm. *Jesus Rediscovered.* Garden City: Doubleday, 1969.

Rookmaaker, H. R. *Modern Art and the Death of a Culture.* Downers Grove: InterVarsity, 1970.

Rosenblatt, Marie. *Literature as Exploration.* 3rd ed. New York: Modern Language Association, 1976.

Sartre, Jean-Paul. *What Is Literature?* Trans. Bernard Frechtman. New York: Philosophical Library, 1949.

Scott Jr., Nathan A., *Modern Literature and the Religious Frontier.* New York: Harper and Brothers, 1958.

Scott-James, R. A. *The Making of Literature.* London: Martin Secker, 1928.

Thomas, Dylan. "Poetic Manifesto." *The Poet's Work.* Ed. Reginald Gibbons. Boston: Houghton Mifflin, 1979). 184-190.

Williams, Charles. *Reason and Beauty in the Poetic Mind.* Oxford: Oxford University Press, 1933.

Viewpoint: Richard Stevens and Thomas J. Musial

Reading Fiction for Meaning

We seek a method of reading that does not disregard fiction as an enjoyable and artistic product, but still allows, even encourages, an intellectual awareness of the several meanings of the work....

In particular, how can we most efficiently [determine the intellectual meanings of] a story? First the reader determines the characteristics of the hero, that is, he identifies what kind of man he is. This involves noting what the hero says, does, and thinks, and how other characters react to him.... The reader must understand the moral quality of the hero as quickly as possible.... Secondly, the reader identifies what kind of moral trial or experiment the hero attempted or suffered. A more common way of putting this is to say he must determine the line of action or plot....We can say, for example, that the *Odyssey,* an epic of many incidents, is the story of a proud and strong man who is trying to get home....

Third, the reader discovers what results from such a person trying to accomplish what he tried. What can be learned from the *Odyssey* about Odysseus' trying what he tried in the way he tried it? Man does not accomplish what he wishes until he has fulfilled his destiny by the greatest care to the powers that he is subject to....

The last matter to discover is the kind of world contained in the fiction. The world may be one which contains such beings as angels, gods, sprites, nymphs (the worlds of Homer, Virgil, Goethe), or it may exclude such creatures from existence (the worlds of Sherwood Anderson, Ernest Hemingway, John Steinbeck). The world may allow men certain powers, for example, freedom to change, grow, or control themselves (as in Shakespeare's plays), or it may deny them (as in those of Jonson). The world may be a meaningful place governed by strict metaphysical necessities (Dante), or it may be metaphysically meaningless and have none but capricious relationships (Euripides, Camus).

—Reading, Discussing, and Writing about the Great Books
Boston: Houghton Mifflin, 1970

Part Four

The Christian Writer

This unit and the next will fall into place if we are aware that four ingredients converge in any literary situation. These can be pictured as follows:

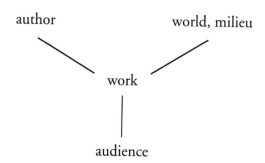

As this diagram shows, works of literature are not self-contained. A complete understanding of them requires that we relate them to other things. The focus of this section is on one of these relationships—that between a work and the author who produced it.

There are several good reasons to inquire into the author's role in the literary enterprise. Writers themselves benefit from all helpful information about their task and methods. Readers, in turn, can have both their understanding and appreciation of literature enhanced by information about the writer's work. Furthermore, statements about the writer's task often yield very helpful insights into literature itself and are, in fact, one of the best repositories of literary theory. Finally, despite attempts to excise the author's intention from literary interpretation, writers are always a presiding presence in their works.

When we speak of the *Christian* writer, specifically, we imply that Christian writers do some things (not all things) differently from or in addition to what writers more generally do. As the following essays and excerpts will show, the statements of Christian writers themselves prove particularly helpful.

Novelist and Believer

Flannery O'Connor

B eing a novelist and not a philosopher or theologian, I shall have to enter this discussion at a much lower level and proceed along a much narrower course than that held up to us here as desirable. It has been suggested that for the purposes of this symposium, we conceive religion broadly as an expression of man's ultimate concern rather than identify it with institutional Judaism or Christianity or with "going to church."

I see the utility of this. It's an attempt to enlarge your ideas of what religion is and of how the religious need may be expressed in the art of our time; but there is always the danger that in trying to enlarge the ideas of students, we will evaporate them instead, and I think nothing in this world lends itself to quick vaporization so much as the religious concern.

As a novelist, the major part of my task is to make everything, even an ultimate concern, as solid, as concrete, as specific as possible. The novelist begins his work where human knowledge begins—with the senses; he works through the limitations of matter, and unless he is writing fantasy, he has to stay within the concrete possibilities of his culture. He is bound by his particular past and by those institutions and traditions that this past has left to his society. The Judeo-Christian tradition has formed us in the West; we are bound to it by ties which may often be invisible, but which are there nevertheless. It has formed the shape of our secularism; it has formed even the shape of modern atheism. For my part,

FLANNERY O'CONNOR *(1925–1964) is most widely known as a writer of two novels and thirty-two short stories. A Catholic by theological persuasion, her greatest literary subject was the rural, Protestant South. She was also an astute literary critic and theorist, and no book is more important in the ongoing discussion of how literature relates to the Christian faith than* Mystery and Manners *(Farrar, Straus, and Giroux, 1961), from which the following essay is taken.*

I shall have to remain well within the Judeo-Christian tradition. I shall have to speak, without apology, of the Church, even when the Church is absent; of Christ, even when Christ is not recognized.

If one spoke as a scientist, I believe it would be possible to disregard large parts of the personality and speak simply as a scientist, but when one speaks as a novelist, he must speak as he writes—with the whole personality. Many contend that the job of the novelist is to show us how man feels, and they say that this is an operation in which his own commitments intrude not at all. The novelist, we are told, is looking for a symbol to express feeling, and whether he be a Jew or Christian or Buddhist or whatever makes no difference to the aptness of the symbol. Pain is pain, joy is joy, love is love, and these human emotions are stronger than any mere religious belief; they are what they are and the novelist shows them as they are. This is all well and good so far as it goes, but it just does not go as far as the novel goes. Great fiction involves the whole range of human judgment; it is not simply an imitation of feeling. The good novelist not only finds a symbol for feeling, he finds a symbol and a way of lodging it which tells the intelligent reader whether this feeling is adequate or inadequate, whether it is moral or immoral, whether it is good or evil. And his theology, even in its most remote reaches, will have a direct bearing on this.

A whole moral universe is implicit in the plot of Peter Rabbit.... *Writers' deep and often unconsidered beliefs about the nature of the world...underlie the fictions they create, and these beliefs can often be teased out from the story and held up to ridicule or respect.*

—JILL PATON WALSH, "The Lords of Time"

It makes a great difference to the look of a novel whether its author believes that the world came late into being and continues to come by a creative act of God, or whether he believes that the world and ourselves are the product of a cosmic accident. It makes a great difference to his novel whether he believes that we are created in God's image, or whether he believes we create God in our own. It makes a great difference whether he believes that our wills are free, or bound like those of the other animals.

St. Augustine wrote that the things of the world pour forth from God in a double way: intellectually into the minds of the angels and physically into the world of things. To the person who believes this—as the Western world did up until a few centuries ago—this physical, sensible world is good because it proceeds from a divine source. The artist usually knows this by instinct; his senses, which are used to penetrating the concrete, tell him so. When Conrad said that his aim as an artist was to render the highest possible justice to the visible universe, he was speaking with the novelist's surest instinct. The artist penetrates the concrete world in order to find at its depths the image of its source, the image of ultimate reality. This in no way hinders his perception of evil but rather sharpens it, for only when the natural world is seen as good does evil become intelligible as a destructive force and a necessary result of our freedom.

For the last few centuries we have lived in a world which has been increasingly convinced that the reaches of reality end very close to the surface, that there is no ultimate divine source, that the things of the world do not pour forth from God in a double way, or at all. For nearly two centuries the popular spirit of each succeeding generation has tended more and more to the view that the mysteries of life will eventually fall before the mind of man. Many modern novelists have been more concerned with the processes of consciousness than with the objective world outside the mind. In twentieth-century fiction it increasingly happens that a meaningless, absurd world impinges upon the sacred consciousness of author or character; author and character seldom now go out to explore and penetrate a world in which the sacred is reflected.

What I do wish to affirm is that the whole of modern literature is corrupted by what I call Secularism, that it is simply unaware of, simply cannot understand the meaning of, the primacy of the supernatural over the natural life: of something which I assume to be our primary concern.... The greater part of our reading matter is coming to be written by people who not only have no such belief, but are even ignorant of the fact that there are still people in the world so "backward" or so "eccentric" as to continue to believe.

—T. S. Eliot, "Religion and Literature"

Nevertheless, the novelist always has to create a world and a believable one. The virtues of art, like the virtues of faith, are such that they reach beyond the limitations of the intellect, beyond any mere theory that a writer may entertain.

If the novelist is doing what as an artist he is bound to do, he will inevitably suggest that image of ultimate reality as it can be glimpsed in some aspect of the human situation. In this sense, art reveals, and the theologian has learned that he can't ignore it. In many universities, you will find departments of theology vigorously courting departments of English. The theologian is interested specifically in the modern novel because there he sees reflected the man of our time, the unbeliever, who is nevertheless grappling in a desperate and usually honest way with intense problems of the spirit.

We live in an unbelieving age but one which is markedly and lopsidedly spiritual. There is one type of modern man who recognizes spirit in himself but who fails to recognize a being outside himself whom he can adore as Creator and Lord; consequently he has become his own ultimate concern. He says with Swinburne, "Glory to man in the highest, for he is the master of things," or with Steinbeck, "In the end was the word and the word was with men." For him, man has his own natural spirit of courage and dignity and pride and must consider it a point of honor to be satisfied with this.

There is another type of modern man who recognizes a divine being not himself, but who does not believe that this being can be known anagogically or defined dogmatically or received sacramentally. Spirit and matter are separated for him. Man wanders about, caught in a maze of guilt he can't identify, trying to reach a God he can't approach, a God powerless to approach him.

And there is another type of modern man who can neither believe nor contain himself in unbelief and who searches desperately, feeling about in all experience for the lost God.

At its best our age is an age of searchers and discoverers, and at its worst, an age that has domesticated despair and learned to live with it happily. The fiction which celebrates this last state will be the least likely to transcend its limitations, for when the religious need is banished successfully, it usually atrophies, even in the novelist. The sense of mystery vanishes. A kind of reverse evolution takes place, and the whole range of feeling is dulled.

The searchers are another matter. Pascal wrote in his notebook, "If I had not known you, I would not have found you." These unbelieving searchers have their effect even upon those of us who do believe. We begin to examine our own religious notions, to sound them for genuineness, to purify them in the heat of our unbelieving neighbor's anguish. What Christian novelist could compare his concern to Camus'? We have to look in much of the fiction of our time for a kind of sub-religion which expresses its ultimate concern in images that have not yet broken through to show any recognition of a God who has revealed himself. As great as much of this fiction is, as much as it reveals a wholehearted effort to find the only true ultimate concern, as much as in many cases it represents religious values of a high order, I do not believe that it can adequately represent in fiction the central religious experience. That, after all, concerns a relationship with a supreme being recognized through faith. It is the experience of an encounter, of a kind of knowledge which affects the believer's every action. It is Pascal's experience after his conversion and not before.

What I say here would be much more in line with the spirit of our times if I could speak to you about the experience of such novelists as Hemingway and Kafka and Gide and Camus, but all my own experience has been that of the writer who believes, again in Pascal's words, in the "God of Abraham, Isaac, and Jacob and not of the philosophers and scholars." This is an unlimited God and one who has revealed himself specifically. It is one who became man and rose from the dead. It is one who confounds the senses and the sensibilities, one known early on as a stumbling block. There is no way to gloss over this specification or to make it more acceptable to modern thought. This God is the object of ultimate concern and he has a name.

The problem of the novelist who wishes to write about a man's encounter with this God is how he shall make the experience—which is both natural and supernatural—understandable, and credible, to his reader. In any age this would be a problem, but in our own, it is a well-nigh insurmountable one. Today's audience is one in which religious feeling has become, if not atrophied, at least vaporous and sentimental. When Emerson decided, in 1832, that he could no longer celebrate the Lord's Supper unless the bread and wine were removed, an important step in the vaporization of religion in America was taken, and the spirit of that step has continued apace. When the physical fact is separated from the spiritual reality, the dissolution of belief is eventually inevitable.

The novelist doesn't write to express himself, he doesn't write simply to render a vision he believes true, rather he renders his vision so that it can be transferred, as nearly whole as possible, to his reader. You can safely ignore the reader's taste, but you can't ignore his nature, you can't ignore his limited patience. Your problem is going to be difficult in direct proportion as your beliefs depart from his.

When I write a novel in which the central action is a baptism, I am very well aware that for a majority of my readers, baptism is a meaningless rite, and so in my novel I have to see that this baptism carries enough awe and mystery to jar the reader into some kind of emotional recognition of its significance. To this end I have to bend the whole novel—its language, its structure, its action. I have to make the reader feel, in his bones if nowhere else, that something is going on here that counts. Distortion in this case is an instrument; exaggeration has a purpose, and the whole structure of the story or novel has been made what it is because of belief. This is not the kind of distortion that destroys; it is the kind that reveals, or should reveal.

Some good stories...turn upon the fortunes of men.... Other good stories turn on the perennially interesting topic of character in men.... Or a good story may have its chief appeal in the sheer surface delineation, the absorbing detail and concreteness of the portrayal. In none of such fictions, however, do we necessarily have man and the enigma of man adequately presented. What especially may be missing is some sense of that secret of his being where he is...sensitive not only to external approval and disapproval but to internal peace or shame.

—AMOS N. WILDER, *Early Christian Rhetoric*

Students often have the idea that the process at work here is one which hinders honesty. They think that inevitably the writer, instead of seeing what is, will see only what he believes. It is perfectly possible, of course, that this will happen. Ever since there have been such things as novels, the world has been flooded with bad fiction for which the religious impulse has been responsible. The sorry religious novel comes about when the writer supposes that because of his belief, he is somehow dispensed from the obligation to penetrate concrete reality. He will think that the eyes of the Church or of the Bible or of his particular theology have already done the seeing for him, and that his business is to rearrange this essential vision into satisfying patterns, getting himself as little dirty in the process as possible. His feeling about this may have been made more definite by one of those Manichean-type theologies which sees the natural world as unworthy of penetration. But the real novelist, the one with an instinct for what he is about, knows that he cannot approach the infinite directly, that he must penetrate the natural human world as it is. The more sacramental his theology, the more encouragement he will get from it to do just that.

The supernatural is an embarrassment today even to many of the churches. The naturalistic bias has so well saturated our society that the reader doesn't realize that he has to shift his sights to read fiction which treats of an encounter with God. Let me leave the novelist and talk for a moment about his reader.

This reader has first to get rid of a purely sociological point of view. In the thirties we passed through a period in American letters when social criticism and social realism were considered by many to be the most important aspects of fiction. We still suffer with a hangover from that period. I launched a character, Hazel Motes, whose presiding passion was to rid himself of a conviction that Jesus had redeemed him. Southern degeneracy never entered my head, but Hazel said "I seen" and "I taken" and he was from East Tennessee, and so the general reader's explanation for him was that he must represent some social problem peculiar to that part of the benighted South.

Ten years, however, have made some difference in our attitude toward fiction. The sociological tendency has abated in that particular form and survived in another just as bad. This is the notion that the fiction writer is after the typical. I don't know how many letters I have received telling me that the South is not at all the way I depict it; some tell me that Protestantism in the South is not at all the way I portray it, that a Southern Protestant would never be concerned, as Hazel Motes is, with penitential practices. Of course, as a novelist I've never wanted to characterize the typical South or typical Protestantism. The South and the religion found there are extremely fluid and offer enough variety to give the novelist the widest range of possibilities imaginable, for the novelist is bound by the reasonable possibilities, not the probabilities, of his culture.

There is an even worse bias than these two, and that is the clinical bias, the prejudice that sees everything strange as a case study in the abnormal. Freud brought to light many truths, but his psychology is not an adequate instrument for understanding the religious encounter or the fiction that describes it. Any psychological or cultural or economic determination may be useful up to a point; indeed, such facts can't be ignored, but the novelist will be interested in them only as he is able to go through them to give us a sense of something beyond them. The more we learn about ourselves, the deeper into the unknown we push the frontiers of fiction.

I have observed that most of the best religious fiction of our time is most shocking precisely to those readers who claim to have an intense interest in finding more "spiritual purpose"—as they like to put it—in modern novels than they can at present detect in them. Today's reader, if he believes in grace at all, sees it as something which can be separated from nature and served to him raw as Instant Uplift. This reader's favorite word is compassion. I don't wish to defame the word. There is a better sense in which it can be used but seldom is— the sense of being in travail with and for creation in its subjection to vanity. This is a sense which implies a recognition of sin; this is a suffering-with, but one which blunts no edges and makes no excuses. When infused into novels, it is often forbidding. Our age doesn't go for it.

I have said a great deal about the religious sense that the modern audience lacks, and by way of objection to this, you may point out to me that there is a real return of intellectuals in our time to an interest in and a respect for religion. I believe that this is true. What this interest in religion will result in for the future remains to be seen. It may, together with the new spirit of ecumenism that we see everywhere around us, herald a new religious age, or it may simply be that religion will suffer the ultimate degradation and become, for a little time, fashionable. Whatever it means for the future, I don't believe that our present society is one whose basic beliefs are religious, except in the South. In any case, you can't have effective allegory in times when people are swept this way and that by momentary convictions, because everyone will read it differently. You can't indicate moral values when morality changes with what is being done, because there is no accepted basis for judgment. And you cannot show the operation of grace when grace is cut off from nature or when the very possibility of grace is denied, because no one will have the least idea of what you are about.

The novel has concerned itself with the strokes of fate, with good and bad fortune, with social interchanges, with the conflict of passions, with characters, but not at all with the essence of the human being. To carry the drama over to the moral place—this...was the task of Christianity.

—ANDRÉ GIDE, *Les Faux-Monnayeurs*

The serious writer has always taken the flaw in human nature for his starting point, usually the flaw in an otherwise admirable character. Drama usually bases itself on the bedrock of original sin, whether the writer thinks in theological terms or not. Then, too, any character in a serious novel is supposed to carry a burden of meaning larger than himself. The novelist doesn't write about people in a vacuum; he writes about people in a world where something is obviously lacking, where there is the general mystery of incompleteness and the particular tragedy of our own times to be demonstrated, and the novelist tries to give you, within the form of the book, a total experience of human nature at any time. For this reason the greatest dramas naturally involve the salvation or loss of the soul. Where there is no belief in the soul, there is very little drama. The Christian novelist is distinguished from his pagan colleagues by recognizing sin as sin. According to his heritage he sees it not as sickness or an accident of environment, but as a responsible choice of offense against God which involves his eternal future. Either one is serious about salvation or one is not. And it is well to realize that the maximum amount of seriousness admits the maximum amount of comedy. Only if we are secure in our beliefs can we see the comical side of the universe. One reason a great deal of our contemporary fiction is humorless is because so many of these writers are relativists and have to be continually justifying the actions of their characters on a sliding scale of values.

Our salvation is a drama played out with the devil, a devil who is not simply generalized evil, but an evil intelligence determined on its own supremacy. I think that if writers with a religious view of the world excel these days in the depiction of evil, it is because they have to make its nature unmistakable to their particular audience.

The novelist and the believer, when they are not the same man, yet have many traits in common—a distrust of the abstract, a respect for boundaries, a desire to penetrate the surface of reality and to find in each thing the spirit which makes it itself and holds the world together. But I don't believe that we shall have great religious fiction until we have again that happy combination of believing artist and believing society. Until that time, the novelist will have to do the best he can in travail with the world he has. He may find in the end that instead of reflecting the image at the heart of things, he has only reflected our broken condition and, through it, the face of the devil we are possessed by. This is a modest achievement, but perhaps a necessary one.

The Advantages of the Christian Faith for a Writer

Chad Walsh

THE GIFTS CONFERRED BY THE CHRISTIAN FAITH

Some writers have discovered, and I think more will discover, that Christianity offers them the best pair of eyes. This is not the main reason for being a Christian—one should not worship Christ merely in order to write a *Hamlet*—but the discovery remains valid. To change the metaphor, the Christian lives in the roomiest house that seems to be available. Writers who become Christians discover that they have only their negations to lose. The affirmations that other faiths make, Christians can mostly second—with appropriate footnotes, of course. Their negations must be denied.

What advantages are there for writers in being a Christian? I am speaking now of advantages to them *as writers,* not *as people.* In the first place, Christianity gives writers whereon to stand, an ordering of their own personal lives that makes intellectual and emotional sense. It also gives them a perspective on their work as a writer. They can honestly see themselves as a kind of earthly assistant to God (so can the carpenter), carrying on the delegated work of creation, making the fullness of creation fuller. At the same time, they are saved from the romantic tendency toward idolatry. Art is not religion. A writer is not a god or

CHAD WALSH *(1914–1991) spent his career as Professor of English at Beloit College, where he cofounded the Beloit Poetry Journal. He published books on C. S. Lewis, Christian apologetics, the Bible, and utopian literature. He wrote numerous essays of literary criticism and is best known for his volumes of poetry.*

godling. There is wisdom and illumination but not salvation in a sonnet. Thus the work of any writer is set in proper proportion. Just as a husband and wife have a deeper marriage if they see their love as a human reflection of God's love, but do not make gods of each other, and do not equate the ceremonies of the marriage-bed with the love upon the Cross, so authors write better (for the inner setting of their work is founded on true relationships) if they give themselves to their work in a spirit of deadly serious playfulness and do not pretend to themselves and others that they are a temple builder and the high priest and divinity of the temple.

I have heard it said that belief in Christian dogma is a hindrance to the writer, but I myself have found nothing further from the truth. Actually, it frees the story-teller to observe.

—FLANNERY O'CONNOR, *Mystery and Manners*

Christianity offers also to the writer, as it does to every person, a community. The old organic communities are visibly dissolving. I do not think this process can be reversed. Perhaps it should not be. In the organic communities, the individual was born into a world of inescapable relationships and duties. As the organic community crumbles into the vague society of the social contract and voluntary relationships, there is a gain in freedom. One must select, one must take the initiative to establish relationships, rather than merely inherit them. New dimensions of liberty—frightening, it is true—are opened up. In terror at their new freedom, people hastily erect clumsy substitutes for the old organic bonds: they invent ideologies and stage mass rallies; they organize interlocking committees and hire sociologists to create an ersatz togetherness. But a Communist rally or a community square dance planned by a committee with sociological goals in mind is not the same thing as the old organic community, which was like an extended family. One can be as lonely in a planned demonstration or a community-sponsored fun night as in a solitary cell.

Angels or demons with flaming swords bar the way back. The Church offers a way forward, beyond mere individualism, beyond mere organization. It is a voluntary community of those who have caught some glimmering of what God means in Christ and how Christ unites all who accept the Accepter. Thus in the Church, at its best, there is both the flowering of individuality and also the sense of belonging, of being accepted, of forgiving, of being forgiven, of loving and being loved.

Admittedly, the average parish church does not bear much visible resemblance to the community of voluntary love and acceptance and mutual responsibility that I have briefly sketched. It is too much like the world about it. It bears traces of the old organic society, now in decay; it is sometimes an anarchy of solitary individuals who come together and worship as though each were in a lonely, separate room; or at times it feverishly generates a synthetic sense of community by activities, activities, and activities. Those who have the peculiarly Christian sense of community are likely to be a minority, a kind of third order or *ecclesia in ecclesia*. Thus it may be that writers will find their "community" not so much in the parish church as in that "scattered brotherhood" of persons whom he meets here and there, comes to know, and in whom they find a hint of what it means to be centered in Christ and therefore members one of another.

Any genuine community, whether localized or diffused, is a home. Living in it, drawing strength from it, writers can move back and forth into the surrounding and interpenetrating world, and yet always have solid ground under their feet. Paradoxically, the firmer their sense of community, the less fearfully they will throw themselves into society as a whole. They will be enabled to love it more, to study it with more compassion and interest, for they will not be afraid of absorption and destruction by it. And, yet another paradox, they will find strong evidence that in the apparently non-Christian or very vaguely Christian society, the secret Christ is at work. The scattered brotherhood will come to include, for Christians, men and women who do not recognize the Master they nevertheless serve.

WHAT CHRISTIANITY OFFERS TO A WRITER

Most of the gifts I have so far mentioned are those equally precious to the housewife, the business executive, and the writer. But there are some gifts that are especially valuable to the writer. The poet, for instance, is reassured that his preoccupation with sensory observations is not a frivolous study. Things are real; they are real because God made them; and, because he made them, they are important and worthy of study and even a proper portion of love. Not only did God make things. He built us so that we perceive them as much through our animal senses as our minds; the mind must turn to the senses to have something to feed upon. The color and smell of a rose are not irrelevant or illusory. We were constructed so that we come into communion with the rose through its color, fragrance, and the thorns that scratch. Compared to the rose that the senses perceive, the rose of the botanist—still more the rose of the physicist—is a construct or abstraction, true in its own way, but not the rose that we are built to admire and love.

The beginning of human knowledge is through the senses, and the fiction writer begins where human perception begins. He appeals through the senses, and you cannot appeal to the senses with abstractions.

—FLANNERY O'CONNOR, "The Nature and Aim of Fiction"

The novelist and playwright receive the assurance that people's social and psychological life and his entire historical existence are meaningful. History becomes part of a cosmic drama, reaching backward to the moment outside of time when the command, "Let there be," was spoken into the void, leading forward toward a culmination that is destined but not compelled; a culmination that by some mysterious paradox lies both inside and outside history and calls forth man's deepest freedom in working with what will surely come to *pass.*

There is another gift that Christianity bestows. In some systems of thought, diversity dissolves into a totality of one kind or another. Sciences move steadily toward mathematics as the All. Hindu thought, so far as I understand it, has no meaningful place for diversity. The teeming variety of this earth is a strange and passing thing, eventually to be merged once more with the All. To Christian eyes, diversity is a good thing in itself, for God made diversity. He did not create "trees"; he created pines, oaks, and ginkoes. The animals are as fantastically varied as the impish drawings of a surrealist. The temperaments of people are as varied as the forms of animals. Christianity aims not at the bypassing of individuality and absorption back into the All, but at fulfillment and redemption of the individual. Salvation is not absorption but relationship. If Hamlet and Lear are both in heaven, it is not because they have become indistinguishable nor because they have lost individual consciousness and are now merged as raindrops in the ocean of God. No, each is more himself than ever, but each self is a redeemed self, oriented to turn with love to God and his creatures. In sum, Christianity is concerned with the fulfillment of personality, not its negation.

We are called to be children of God, and a child is not a father. Novelists are not being frivolous when they take their characters seriously.

Another way in which Christian eyes aid writers is simply that they can make greater sense of the towering heights and dizzy abysses of the human drama. They do not have to explain them away. They need not elucidate Hitler as a throwback to the anthropoids or St. Francis as a complex manifestation of the herd instinct. They see in people both the angels and the demons at work, as well as the simpler imperatives of the animal nature. And they observe, and experience, a drama with eternal stakes. The stakes are not merely the welfare or destruction of society, but the drama of individual damnation and salvation. It is a drama with no foregone conclusions. In real life, as in a good novel, the spectator is kept guessing up to the end.

I have found, in short, from reading my own writing, that my subject in fiction is the action of grace in territory held largely by the devil.... If you believe in the Redemption, your ultimate vision is one of hope.

—FLANNERY O'CONNOR, *Mystery and Manners*

So much for some of the special gifts and graces that a writer can receive when his or her eyes are baptized. Christian faith is no substitute for talent, for genius. But if a writer has that, the new eyes can aid him or her in seeing more, understanding more, saying more.

THE CHRISTIAN WRITER'S AUDIENCE

But to whom shall Christian writers say it? Are Christian writers of the near future doomed to be esoteric, coterie figures, speaking only to those who share their pair of eyes? It is possible that this is the case, but I am hopeful that Christian writers can reach many others. If it is true that the soul is *naturaliter christiana,* Christian insight should not be without response among non-Christians. Many an agnostic is deeply moved by Dante; there is Graham Greene, whose novels are meaningful to thousands who reject his theology. If the Christian faith provides the roomiest dwelling; if Christian eyes can see more and see it more exactly, it should follow that the truth a Christian writer can portray will somehow get through, because it will ring true even in men who consciously reject the faith that offers the new eyes.

I could be mistaken in this. It may be that for the next few generations the Christian writer is condemned to write for a coterie. This is more likely to happen with the playwright than anyone else. The playwright requires a certain community of reaction. The people sitting in the theater need to have enough in common so that they will respond with some unanimity to the play. If their assumptions and ingrained attitudes are too different, it may be impossible to arouse the spontaneous symphony of individual responses that great plays call forth when there is common ground between playwright and audience. Conceivably, Christian playwrights may have to develop their own audience in Church circles. I do not believe this is the case, but it could be so.

The case of the novelist and the poet is more hopeful. Except for public readings of poetry (almost a form of drama) these two types of literature are read by individuals in their solitude. There is not the necessity to arouse a group response. A person reading a novel or a poem can mull it over, let it sink in, and respond to it at his or her own speed. If the soul is Christian by nature, it can take its time and slowly gasp whatever insight is offered.

Christian dogma will aid the artist, not by giving him a privileged and special subject-matter but rather by defining for him a perspective from which "full light" can be had on all subject matters.
—Roy Battenhouse, "The Relation of Theology to Literary Criticism"

At this point I have the uneasy feeling that some readers may assume I expect Christian writers to produce "Christian literature." If by that they mean books in which such words as God, Christ, soul, etc., frequently occur; or books dealing with Church life, ministers, devout souls, etc.—they are mistaken. Christian writers do not necessarily deal directly with anything that would be labeled "Christian." Their plots and characters may be precisely those one would find in a naturalistic or existential novel. It is again the angle of vision, the nuances that a different pair of eyes can yield, a way of understanding, not subject matter.

A HOPE FOR LITERATURE

I have tried to state the "Hope for literature" in modest and tentative terms. One must not claim too much nor hope too much. If there is to be a great literature, it will come about first of all because great talents arise. In the future, as in the past, many of these may be non-Christians. Their insights will often be more probing than those of devout but less gifted Christian authors. In a sense, a real sense, they may write books more radically "Christian" than many Christians have the skill to write.

But, for Christian and non-Christian alike, this is a world moving into a period when all foundations are increasingly shaken and new foundations are perhaps being built without our quite knowing the building material we are using. Science, for good or evil—that is our choice—is doubling and re-doubling the wager. The old dream of world brotherhood is becoming a possibility, a mirage, an absolute necessity all simultaneously. Humankind is called upon to achieve the impossible or perish. The nineteenth-century world order, as hierarchical with its distinction of "civilized" and "primitive" nations as the social hierarchy of the Middle Ages, is dissolving in fire, blood, and strident shouts for equality and dignity in tongues only recently reduced to alphabetical form. Meanwhile, the space vehicles are probing the heavens, and who knows what adventures of the spirit lie barely beyond tomorrow's newspaper, when the first contact is made with intelligences independent of our parochial earth? Closer to home, all the advances of science make a human being more a marvel, more an impenetrable mystery, than ever before. The final frontier is ourselves.

It could be another Elizabethan age, a century of outer and inner explorations, while everywhere the relations among men and between men and whatever they call God are being reordered. Like the Elizabethan age, it is already a time dominated by voices of pessimism, at the very moment when men are acting with frantic energy and, for good or evil, are doing mighty deeds.

Writers will continue to write. They will have much to write about. It may be that the Christian faith will help some of them to see more, see it more truly. This is a hope, not a certainty; but when was hope ever the name for a sure thing?

On Writing One's Place: Writing Bluesville

Reggie Young

If you ever write of
Bluesville,
never
let me know, un-
less you alter
your conceptions

Is a rose
always
a rose?
—"June Bug" Bailey, "The Bluesville Boogie"

ON HAVING *SOMETHING* TO READ FROM YOUR OWN WORLD
A woman who worked as a secretary for one of the administrators at my university offered to help type my dissertation. This woman, Mrs. Wilson, volunteered
to type during her lunch break and after hours not only because she and I were
both black, but because we were part of the same *community*. Back then, in the
1980s, which was, obviously, not very long ago, there were few African Americans in most mainstream colleges and universities, but there was a sense of community that existed among most of us who were at this particular institution in

---

REGGIE YOUNG *is a former faculty member at Wheaton College and has taught literature and cre-*
ative writing at Hamilton College, Louisiana State University, and Villanova University. The
recipient of a Pew Fellowship in 2000, he is author of a forthcoming critical book entitled Liberating Literacies: Righteous Resistance and Secular Redemption in African American Expressive
Works *(St. Martin's Press). His creative and scholarly works have appeared in numerous journals.*

various capacities and at different levels, even though few of us knew each other away from campus.

Our sense of community was based, in part, on the fact that if you were African American, with the exception of some of the students who were more interested in partying than anything else and the few remaining militants left over from the 1960s, you belonged to a church, or a church claimed you, even if you were out of church at that time. Although issues of faith were not always central to our discussions, our faith in the God who had seen the previous generations of our culture through everything from slavery to Jim Crow and the turbulent 1960s was our unspoken common bond. Mrs. Wilson's investment of time and effort in my degree was something that would not benefit her financially, but as a mother with children in the same school system in Chicago that I attended, she knew that my success and the success of others like me might have a positive influence on the young adults of the neighborhood since in our community there was little tradition of individuals graduating from college, especially with advanced degrees, or writing novels. Unlike the basketball player Charles Barkley, we knew we were role models, whether we wanted to be or not.

Not long after Mrs. Wilson started typing my manuscript, she became interested in the material she read as she worked from her keyboard. My dissertation was a novel that is now titled *Salvation Song* (as a dissertation it was titled *Crimes in Bluesville*), and it contained a selection of my own poems that were placed in the novel to represent the perspective of J. P. Bailey, better known as June Bug, a young inner-city youth who serves as the novel's central character. Mrs. Wilson did not have much of a background in literature, and had read few novels and poems except those she had to read back in high school, and she admitted she was not sure she understood some of the material she was typing due to the narrative's experimental, nonlinear form. She found it hard to understand why a novel's plot should be organized any differently from the plot of a good detective movie, but one day she smiled as she handed me a pile of pages she had just typed onto a disk and said, "After reading your book, at least people will know we exist."

My novel is set in the community where I once lived and where Mrs. Wilson still lives. It is full of characters who represent the kinds of people I remember from growing up on Chicago's West Side, such as Miss Lucinda the Hoodoo-Lady, Monkey Jr., Mae Ellen, Sleepy Martin, the militants Snake and

Shabaka, Miss Beets, June Bug's Big Momma, the detectives Executioner St. Jacques and Cryptsealer Cambridge, the Black Avengers (June Bug's gang), the Cobras, Vice-Lords, Mau-Maus, and the Uppity Bunch. Knowing that the finished dissertation would be available to the public through university libraries and that I hoped to publish it one day after I finished graduate school, to Mrs. Wilson, the members of my own family, and many of the residents of our neighborhood, the completion of the work and its approval by my dissertation committee was as significant as if the book were about to be published by a major publishing house. Few people were willing to actually commit themselves to reading it, but people from all around the area inquired about obtaining copies to sit on display in their front rooms.

It is by the nature of itself that fiction is all bound up in the local. The internal reason for that is surely that feelings *are bound up in place....
Fiction depends for its life on place.*

—EUDORA WELTY, *Place in Fiction*

Although Mrs. Wilson and I were both from the West Side—I was from North Lawndale and she was from the neighboring Garfield—it was one of the few times she had read *anything* about the West Side, except for the depressing stories about the area's crime and poverty which often ran in the local newspapers, and it was definitely the first time she had ever heard of stories and poems about that part of town. Her enthusiasm stemmed from her belief that my novel might one day help to put the West Side on the map and would give those who live there a sense of place in the world. After all, Chicago's South Side African American community has a longstanding reputation in the nation's consciousness that is surpassed only by New York's Harlem, and for decades it has maintained its own cultural and civic institutions and businesses. The South Side even saw one of its own, Harold Washington, elected to serve as the mayor of the entire city. Mrs. Wilson stressed how my novel might help to give the young people on the West Side a sense of pride if they knew it is a book about where they are from, and it might also encourage them to have a greater appreciation of books since "they'll have something to read from their own world for once, seeing how difficult it is to understand everyone else's when you don't have a basis for understanding your own."

A CALLING TO WRITE BLUESVILLE

A few years earlier, I had read a book titled *An Autobiography of Black Chicago* by Dempsey Travis, a popular South Side businessman. After I saw how Travis's book for the most part excluded my particular part of *black* Chicago (as most works on the African American experience in Chicago had done), I felt a calling to write about Chicago's West Side in my own work. Those who know anything about black Chicago can testify about the rivalry that once existed between the West Side and South Side, and that West Siders used to feel as if they were looked down upon by their South Side brethren. In fact, while I was growing up, if you ventured into one of the neighborhoods on the other side of the city, you feared for your safety because you felt as if you were in enemy territory. The tribal differences between the two were mostly a result of perceived class and caste differences. I have written several poems on this matter, including one titled "Tribal Differences," and these differences in the larger African American community are also of thematic importance to my novel.

My reason for reflecting back on this earlier period and my motivation for making Chicago's West Side African American community a place of importance in my work is because of a request I received one day from Leland Ryken, my colleague at the time at Wheaton College and the editor of this volume. Professor Ryken was teaching a senior seminar on "Literature and Place," and he asked me to discuss the importance of place in my writing. Around that time, I received an announcement from a college in Minnesota that advertised a summer conference for writers titled "Earth Songs: Writing About Place and Community." The pamphlet offered the following statement in its description: "The conference will explore visions of place and voices of landscape. Workshops will focus on oral and written traditions as they affect writing about place, landscapes, and family histories." While appearing before Professor Ryken's students several days later, I showed them the conference announcement and explained that it is also my goal as a writer to explore the voices and visions of a place I write about as Bluesville, the metaphorical name I use for the community where I grew up, one not based solely on a type of music but on the culture itself.

I knew that some students in the class might find themselves puzzled by my use of the name Bluesville, since the word *blues* is such a loaded term. Like many others from families who yearned for upward mobility in American society, especially from among the more socially conservative Christian families in our immediate neighborhood, I found myself influenced to view the blues as backward and demeaning. At a time when African Americans were trying to prove their dignity and self-worth to the larger culture, we felt the blues made us all look pagan. As a youth, I was embarrassed by the blues and did not want to associate with those whose behavior reflected the fact that they were from what might best be described as blues families—families who, as far as we knew, did not go to church each Sunday and were headed by men and sometimes women who drank in public and used bad language without showing an ounce of shame.

> *Always locate the reader in time and space—again and again. Beginning writers rush in to feelings, to interior lives. Instead, stick to surface appearances; hit the five senses; give the history of the person and place, and the look of the person and the place. Use first and last names. As you write, stick everything in a place and a time.*
>
> —ANNIE DILLARD, "Notes for Young Writers"

As I grew older, the prejudice I had against the blues and those we thought of as blues people began to wane, and I started feeling uncomfortable with the reputation I had developed among my peers who thought I was a "square" because I had always kept my distance from them. In order to "fit in" with those in the neighborhood whom I had once shunned, I found myself acting less and less like the upright young man I was expected to be by my family, because it was an almost impossible task to avoid violating family rules while trying to gain the respect of those who did not have similar restrictions on their behavior. My first published story, "Concrete Rituals," which also serves as the opening chapter of *Salvation Song,* is about such a youth, one who was named Jim Finn in the opening drafts but who was later renamed June Bug. The story is autobiographical, as are many other aspects of the novel, but not in a literal sense, since many of June Bug's exploits are very different from those I experienced as a boy. He does not represent the specific experiences of my youth, but his characterization does figuratively convey the reality of my life as a young boy from a Christian background growing up in the blues culture of Chicago's West Side.

For example, June Bug is a poor athlete, but he tries, nevertheless, to play in the games of basketball on the area's schoolyard courts because it is one way he can earn the respect he desires in the eyes of the other neighborhood youths.

During a game in which his "respectable" gang, the Colored Avengers (later to become the "Black Avengers" after it becomes "hip" for African Americans to call themselves black during the mid-1960s), takes on the notorious Moonwalkers, he realizes Me-Me, a girl he dislikes because she wears glasses and looks like a bookworm, has "all four of her eyes" on him. Since he desperately wants to shed his own reputation as a bookworm, he remarks, "After all I done did to make people in the 'hood see that I ain't no straitlaced square, I ain't about to be seen messing around with nobody like her. In Bluesville, you get respected more for being an average hucklebutt than you do for being a Mr. Peabody." His language in this part of the novel is contrived, because his Big Momma raised him to speak what people in the community call "good English," as opposed to speaking as though he had never read a book or attended school. On the other hand, it is important to note that June Bug actually speaks in the kind of vernacular that he uses to narrate the tale because he *does* read books, and because he has read one book in particular: Mark Twain's *The Adventures of Huckleberry Finn*.

The location of his story in time and space is the first problem that confronts a novelist, and the way in which he solves the problem has a great deal to do with the success or failure of his novel.

—CAROLINE GORDON, *How to Read a Novel*

NARRATIVE ROOTS AND THE HARMONY OF VOICE AND PLACE

In originally conceiving June Bug's character as a Jim Finn, I was influenced by Twain's depiction of Huck in his novel, because his characterization influenced me to explore my own youthful rebellions against what I perceived to be convention and social norms. Like Huck, I was also an observer and participant during a long journey, only mine was not a literal journey down a river as was Huck's, but an episodic journey down the metaphorical River Bluesville, the name I used to characterize the metaphorical pathway that I traveled during a particular stage of my life. Huck, in his heart, was a good guy, but he rebelled against the attempts of his guardian the Widow Douglas and her sister, Miss Watson (who influenced the characterization of June Bug's Big Momma), to socialize him in a way that might make him appear to be square or like a chump in the eyes of Tom Sawyer and the other boys he looked up to.

When I studied *Huckleberry Finn* in college, I realized I had experienced several similar trials of conscience during my youth as Huck did in the course of Twain's novel. Calling my character Jim Finn was not only an attempt to call attention to the influence of Twain's character, but also to point out that my Huck was a black version, since Jim was the escaped slave whom Huck tried to help reach freedom, ironically, by sailing down the Mississippi River deeper and deeper into the slave-holding South. (A scholar later published a book titled *Was Huck Black?* which argues that Huck Finn's voice and certain aspects of his character were influenced by the slaves Mark Twain lived around during his own youth.)

Twain also wrote about what might be described as a blues culture in such works as *Huckleberry Finn* and *Pudd'nhead Wilson*. If a blues culture actually exists, it must be understood as a cultural style and social perspective that grew out of the antebellum South and the peculiar interactions that took place between enslaved blacks and their white masters. Blues is America's first folk music, and its influence can be seen in country-and-western and other musical expressions that are largely associated with nonblacks. My work might be set in a northern urban blues landscape, but Twain depicted areas where various forms of the blues were born.

Nothing can happen nowhere. The locale of the happening always colours the happening, and often, to a degree, shapes it…. Scene is only justified in the novel where it can be shown, or at least felt, to act upon action or character.
—ELIZABETH BOWEN, "Pictures and Conversations"

Just as the Mississippi River is used as a literal geographical location in so much of Twain's writings, it also represents a metaphorical dimension, something T. S. Eliot discusses in his famous introduction to the 1950 edition of *The Adventures of Huckleberry Finn*. Many of Twain's best-loved works are grounded in the river culture, and it is from this particular grounding that these works evolved. When I started writing fiction, I looked for something from my reality of living in what I thought of as a bluesville community to ground my work and to help establish it as an ongoing reality for my future writings, but there are no rivers in Lawndale, nothing nearly as impressive or powerful, since "broad shouldered" Chicago, as Carl Sandberg portrayed it, is a place of human construction as opposed to one of natural beauty and growth. Twain's description of the river's landscape is still one of the most remarkable in the history of literature, especially the details he presents about the plant life that Huck observed along the river and in the surrounding countryside.

But I came from a place that used to be referred to sarcastically as a "concrete jungle" by its residents, because very little grew there except for deterioration. I knew hardly anything about azaleas, lilies, junipers, and daffodils, because other than grass in a few toupee-size yards and the city trees that lined the streets of some blocks, very little grew in our neighborhood. In fact, according to one of the poems in *Salvation Song* titled "Recollections,"

> In Bluesville there grows dandelions
> to the world, Bluesville's flower is a weed
> but being from Bluesville a person knows
> a dandelion is a ghetto rose.

"Recollections" is the concluding poem in the novel and represents June Bug's reflections of his life in Bluesville when he returns to the community after attending college. But even earlier in the narrative, he has dandelions on his mind. In an exchange with his friend Monkey Jr., June Bug says,

> You mean to tell me you've never stopped to think about all of the dandelions you see growing in this park? They're everywhere, the same way the old folks used to talk about cane stalks and cotton in the south. I guess dandelions are the cane stalks and cotton plants of the north all in one, only we ain't got to pick them, and they ain't just in the park—they grow all over the 'hood, spreading like wild fire, consuming everything in their way.

Although Monkey Jr. tells him, "Aw, come on, man. You know I ain't thinking about no dandelions right now...at least, not as long as I ain't got to eat 'em," June Bug replies:

> But Monk, look around you.... You don't see flowers around here anymore. You don't even see much grass. The only things that grow in this whole neighborhood nowadays are weeds and vacant lots. You ever notice how every time

something gets burnt down, torn down, or abandoned around here, you never see anything new going up to take its place?

In a sense, the physical landscape where *Salvation Song* is set is opposite to the one used by Twain, but the exploration of those kinds of environmental differences and their effect on a youthful male protagonist is a key aspect of the novel.

In reading, one should notice and fondle details.... The reader must [try] to get clear the specific world the author places at his disposal. We must see things and hear things, we must visualize the rooms, the clothes, the manners of an author's people.
—VLADIMIR NABOKOV, "Good Readers and Good Writers"

I did not have a river that I could use for my character to send him off into various episodic adventures as Twain did with Huck, but I did have a street that seemed as wide as a river to me. I lived just one block down from Ogden Avenue, a street that cuts diagonally across Chicago, in contrast to most other streets, which run in straight lines from North to South and East to West. There were no river boats on Ogden Avenue, of course, but there were plenty of buses and big trucks—river boats and barges in the imagination of a city boy. Ogden Avenue became my river. It remains today a very large thruway that has six lanes, with long narrow islands dividing the express lanes of traffic from the local lanes on both sides of the avenue. Ogden runs from the heart of Chicago far out into what were then the undeveloped rural areas of the outlying counties where few city kids had ever ventured. Today those lands are mostly filled with suburban sprawl. Although the novel eventually took a different shape and form, it was intended to depict the adventures of a boy who runs away from his domineering guardian by hitching rides on trucks and buses up and down the gigantic thoroughfare he thought of as the dried up River Bluesville, venturing into one neighborhood after another and often barely escaping trouble before making it back to Ogden Avenue to look for another ride. In the completed novel, my character does not take a ride down the River Bluesville as I originally intended, but the metaphor was important because from it the novel developed its own organic shape and form.

Starting as a modern day Huck Finn in black face, figuratively speaking, and as one who faced a number of Huck-like crises of consciousness, my June Bug grew to become more of a cross between George Bailey of *It's a Wonderful Life* and the youthful protagonist in Ralph Ellison's *Invisible Man.* Like Ellison's character, June Bug is almost totally naive, but like George Bailey he has a good heart, though needing a bit of direction from a guardian angel, a character named Azusa Beets in my novel. But the River Bluesville, which flowed out of my reading of *Huckleberry Finn,* is the fertile ground from which *Salvation Song's* narrative took root and grew.

WRITING MY WORLD INTO BEING

It took me years and years to realize it, along with a considerable amount of softening of my own heart, but eventually I realized that the blues epitomized the very voice of the community landscape from where I came. People are the most important element of any cultural landscape, and I would write to give the people of my Bluesville visibility in a society where they have been too often overlooked. It was never my goal to politicize their plight, but simply to reveal their existence as a viable aspect of the larger human experience. Long before I attempted to compose a novel, I wrote of these people in poetry—not poems for the sake of a timeless aesthetic beauty, but functional poems regarding a particular community of people in a specific place and time. Because of the influence of my work as reporter for student newspapers in both high school and college, many of the poems I wrote included stories about such Bluesville occurrences as an alley baseball game being invaded by a drunken gang whose members look like snakes in black leather jackets and processed hair, a mother's reaction after seeing her son lying prone in the street after a hit-and-run by a "happy hour" driver from the suburbs, and winos going to cast votes after receiving "gift certificates" from their ward committeeman for bottles of Wild Irish Rose at the Bucket-of-Blood.

Besides furnishing a plausible abode for the novel's world of feeling, place has a good deal to do with making the characters real.

—EUDORA WELTY, *Place in Fiction*

The blues were once considered the music of the down-and-out, although now it is the domain of ritzy blues clubs owned by yuppie entrepreneurs who promote the blues as the party music of the sexually affluent. But the blues in their natural element are also tragic, which is why two of the earliest poems I published in magazines and journals are about fire. In fact, the title of my dissertation came from "Crimes in Bluesville," a poem about families who are forced to deal with the ordeal of having their heat cut off by an unmerciful gas company. In the early 1980s when unemployment in Bluesville seemed to touch far too many households, a lot of people were trying to find creative ways to stay warm. The voice in the poem lists some of the ways people respond to a lack of heat in their homes:

Sometimes,
we light the oven
those of us with gas
or turn on an old 'lectric heater
after running an extension cord
next door
we even burn old wooden chairs
in the tub, or
bring a garbage can in and
let it be our fireplace

Houses burning down in Bluesville are not a once-in-a-while occurrence, which is why the last stanza ironically states "Too often / we are the burning story in / the morning news."

Although my family was fortunate to avoid such catastrophes, there were several times when neighborhood fires did touch our lives. One time in particular was when an apartment building caught fire while six children from my family's church were home alone as their single mother beat the pavement looking for work. The pain of seeing so many young lives aborted so senselessly left the entire community numb for weeks. Some wanted to blame God, arguing that if He was the one who made rich people rich, that He was also the one who inflicted the poor with poverty. A week after the tragedy, I was asked to speak at a memorial service that the organizers thought might help bring a sense of relief to the community. I knew that God hadn't forsaken those children, and I wanted to find a way to put what had happened in a different perspective. The Bible is clear in expressing the special love that Jesus has for children, and also our need to develop a childlike faith, and I wanted to find a way to communicate those truths in a way that the preacher could not for the benefit of those who had shut themselves off from his voice. As a result, I wrote "Saviors," which begins,

Little kids are
a lot like Jesus, they
often die of sins
not their own; like
the ones who die in
Bluesville praying:

"Father God, please
save us cause
Momma's gone"

The poem asks us to consider whether the deaths of the young ones might have helped save the mother from temptation, since in her desperation for work she had not only left the church but was being wooed by some of the darker elements of the streets. She allowed neighbors to take her children off to church each week, but she refused to have anything to do with religion before their deaths. My intention was not to suggest that it was God's design to take six innocent lives for the purpose of bringing one wayward soul back into the church, but to show that God can use even the most tragic situation to serve His purpose and glory. The poem ends,

Mercy be to
little children who
often die of sins
not their own

Sometimes they suffer
sacrifice of life, to be
resurrected in holy
smoke

This may not be sociologically sound or theologically correct, but, like the blues, it was composed to meet the needs of people at a certain point in time. It attempted to make those who were affected by the tragedy to consider mercy, and to realize that only by being merciful in our thoughts about the ones who died could we find mercy for ourselves in our efforts to achieve a sense of reconciliation and release.

Writers are not always the best critics of their own work, and I must confess that other than describing the situation that gave birth to "Saviors" I am not the best person to address the poem's actual meaning. I do know, however, that there is no other thing that I have done in my life as a writer or in any other role that has been so powerfully received by a group of people. When I read the poem from the pulpit of Douglas Park Missionary Baptist Church, the audience was not silent as you might expect in such a solemn public gathering, but there was also no applause after I finished reading the poem because applause would have been inappropriate; after all, the people were not there to be entertained. But even as I introduced the piece and read its title, there were the scattered utterings that one expects to hear in a black religious gathering, and I found myself involved with the audience in that old building where I had been baptized as a boy in a call and response performance in which those who were assembled there encouraged me and urged me to give them more and more, until at the very end a chorus of "amen" and "teach, brother" rang out in the small but packed sanctuary.

What is…a writer going to take his "country" to be? The word usually used by literary folk in this connection would be "world," but the word "country" will do; in fact, being homely, it will do better, for it suggests more. It suggests everything from the actual countryside that the novelist describes, on to and through the peculiar characteristics of his region and his nation, and on, through, and under all of these to his true country, which the writer with Christian convictions will consider to be what is eternal and absolute.
—FLANNERY O'CONNOR, "The Fiction Writer and His Country"

It would be silly to try to argue that "Saviors" is a significant poem to anyone but those who were in that room or who lived in that neighborhood at that time, but it was written to serve a specific function at a specific time and place and for a particular group of people. In that context it served its purpose—it helped those who were demoralized by the situation to leave the burden of the tragic fire behind them. After the service, people thanked me and all through the night they asked for a copy of the poem. I went to a print shop and had the poem copied next to a photograph of the children, and everyone wanted a copy, including people who were not in attendance during the service, and some who did not even know the children or their mother. Weeks after the event, I still ran into individuals on the streets of Bluesville who would greet me by saying "I still remember that poem," or "Mercy be to little children."

A long blues poem near the end of *Salvation Song* depicts the salvation experience that June Bug undergoes during a meeting in a vacant lot near his house. In "Praise in Bluesville," June Bug and his small gang invade a Saturday morning worship service headed by the Reverend Red Clay Jones, a down-home, Mississippi Delta backwoods preacher who ministers to the needs of those in the community. Because of a large boulder that sits at the far end of the lot and serves as a makeshift altar, the people in the area call the church without walls Tabernacle Rock. Much of the narrative shows June Bug in rebellion against his grandmother's faith, and his reason for showing up at Reverend Jones's meeting with his friends is to ridicule the ritual ceremony and the people who left their houses in response to the itinerant preacher's call to

Come on down peoples
bring all yo' worries 'n pain cause
greater is He that is workin in me
'n I feels the spirit coming on.

But the boys initially find the open-air ritual to be backward and demeaning, especially the down-home style of music sung by Reverend Jones to a guitar, tambourine, and harp. To them, the music sounds more like the blues—"the devil's music"—than the formal gospel music of which they are more familiar and which they believe sounds more reverent. In response to Reverend Jones and the seemingly crude nature of the service, June Bug states

We laughed,
we circled that old dude, his fraud
in our eyes; we spat in
his offering cup, slapped hands

like we were somebody's saviors, then we waved
our arms, waved our arms to disperse
the crowd

All we got in response was some of them

ya'll must be some fools

eyeballs in return

That dude, he didn't do nothing
but smile

Reverend Jones responds by teaching the "boyz" that "God made the music." He informs them that "the devil ain't never made a doggone thing / and we taking back the music / Glory to God!" He then performs a literal salvation song—a blues-style rendition of Psalm 100—that is instrumental in the youths' overcoming their attitudes of indignation, especially when they hear Reverend Jones sing "it is He that hath / made us," which makes them realize "we didn't / make ourselves."

"Praise in Bluesville" is a performance piece that works most effectively when readers allow themselves to hear the blues cadence of Reverend Jones's voice, along with the guitar, tambourine, and harp that accompany his rendition of Psalm 100. The service illustrates how vestiges of the bush arbor worship practices of earlier generations of African Americans still influence their religious rites today. Many of the people in attendance are humbled as they listen to the words and the sounds, and at the song's conclusion the boys in the gang all realize their own insufficiencies and get "saved."

The poem, as well as the novel as a whole, is a work of spiritual realism. Spiritual realism might best be considered in light of Flannery O'Connor's statement that "the deeper kinds of realism are less and less understandable." It is the primary element in the spirituals that were composed by antebellum slaves, despite the arguments of those who claim that the songs were little more than a series of social codes. In the spiritual realism handed down by African slaves, a harmony between the sacred and the secular still exists, at least in the artistic imagination, and can be thought of as a place where the sacred and the secular—the spirituals and the blues—intersect in people's lives. Not everyone's needs can be fully met in the traditional services of mainline denominational churches, so gatherings in less likely places are important in helping the gospel reach the lives of those who have been otherwise neglected. Those were the kinds of people to which Reverend Jones ministered in his work as an evangelist of the streets. June Bug received salvation, therefore, through a ministry led by the kind of person that he (and I) had once been taught to disdain.

PARTICULAR "POSTAGE-STAMPS" OF PLACE

One of the most significant aspects of my education as a student and my work as a scholar and writer has been my discovery of the blues as one of the truest and most meaningful voices of the black cultural landscape in the United States, and the most genuine forms of expression that I could use to capture the essence of the place where I once lived. It was only after I coined the term Bluesville that I felt for the first time that I had truly become a writer, because I discovered a place with stories that needed to be revealed to the world in poetry, fiction, and essays like the one I am presently writing, stories that few others could tell.

I was trying to talk about people, using the only tool I knew, which was the country that I knew…. I discovered that my own little postage stamp of native soil was worth writing about and that I would never live long enough to exhaust it.

—WILLIAM FAULKNER, interview

Although I felt called to write the stories of Bluesville, I had to first learn that such stories are sometimes most effectively told by limiting the scope of the tale. Although young writers often attempt to make their work appear universal by offering generic time and place settings, it takes a writer who is an experienced student of literature to discover, as James Joyce did in his works set in Ireland, that the universal is best expressed when grounded in the particular. So Bluesville became my unique and peculiar place, one on which I could concentrate, to borrow from Faulkner, as my own little "postage-stamp" of concrete and asphalt. Since then, Bluesville has developed into my own Yoknapatawpha, an area of about twenty square blocks that I have tried to write into the consciousness of those who might not ever consider the realities of the people who live in such a place.

Viewpoint: Walker Percy

On Being a Catholic Novelist

Of course the deeper themes of my novels are religious. When you speak of religion, it's almost impossible for a novelist because you have to use the standard words like "God" and "salvation" and "baptism," "faith," and the words are pretty well used up. They're old words. They're still good words, but the trick of the novelist, as the Psalmist said, is to sing a new song, use new words.... The so-called Catholic or Christian novelist nowadays...has to do what Joyce did: he has to practice his art in cunning and in secrecy and achieve his objective by indirect methods....

What is a Catholic novelist? Is he a novelist who happens to be a Catholic, or is he a novelist who is first a Catholic before he's a novelist? All I can say is, as a writer, you have a certain view of man, a certain view of the way it is, and even if you don't recognize it or even if you disavow such a view, you can't escape that view or lack of view. I think your writing is going to reflect this. I think my writings reflect a certain basic orientation toward, although they're not really controlled by, Catholic dogma.

What we call the Catholic novel is not necessarily about a Christianized or catholicized world, but simply...one in which the truth as Christians know it has been used as a light to see the world by.... The Catholic novel can't be categorized by subject matter, but only by what it assumes about human and divine reality.

—FLANNERY O'CONNOR, *Mystery and Manners*

As I say, it's a view of man, that man is neither an organism controlled by his environment, not a creature controlled by the forces of history as the Marxists would say, nor is he a detached, wholly objective, angelic being who views the world in a God-like way and makes pronouncements only to himself or to an elite group of people. No, he's somewhere between the angels and the beasts. He's a strange creature whom both Thomas Aquinas and Marcel called *homo viator*, man the wayfarer, man the wanderer. So, to me, the Catholic view of man as pilgrim, in transit, in journey, is very compatible with the vocation of a novelist because a novelist is writing about man in transit, man as pilgrim...

And by the same token, nothing is worse than a bad Catholic novel. Nothing is worse than a novel which seeks to edify the reader....

I didn't really begin to write until after I became a Catholic. I would agree with Flannery O'Connor that my Catholicism is not only not a hindrance but a *help* in my work. It's a way of seeing the world. I don't think my writings are meant to preach Catholicism, but the novel can't help but be informed by a certain point of view—and this happens to be a Catholic point of view....

I've always been a polemicist and a moralist. I mean moralist in a large sense, of saying this is the way the world *ought* to be and not the way it is. As I got interested in philosophy and language and linguistics I began writing articles and was able to get them published. But, number one, I didn't make any money, and, number two, nobody read them. So I thought...wouldn't it be nice to write a *novel* saying the same thing, maybe even saying it better.... I saw how it was possible to translate my ideas into concrete situations. But nothing would be worse than a so-called philosophical or religious novel which simply used a story and a plot and characters in order to get over a certain idea. On the other hand, a novel in which the characters are real, the situation is real, the action is real, and which also expressed a certain point of view is what I was getting at....

Life is a mystery, love is a delight. Therefore I take it as axiomatic that one should settle for nothing less than the infinite mystery and the infinite delight, i.e., God.

—*Conversations with Walker Percy*
Ed. Lewis A. Lawson and Victor A. Kramer
Jackson: University Press of Mississippi, 1985

Part Five

The Christian Reader

The elevation of the reader was a major literary trend of the later twentieth century. Its legacy continues today. This unit is concerned partly with issues and methods that are distinctive to Christian interests. Specific questions that are addressed include the following:

- What activities do Christian readers share with all good readers?
- What is distinctive to the interests of Christian readers?
- How do various theories of reading fare when viewed in a Christian light?
- How might Christian readers improve their reading, in keeping with their Christian commitments?
- What are the rewards of reading?

From the discussion that follows, there emerges a composite portrait of the ideal Christian reader.

Because this book was compiled partly with book lovers in view, this section includes a compilation of excerpts on the joys of reading books.

Religion and Literature

T. S. Eliot

What I have to say is largely in support of the following propositions: Literary criticism should be completed by criticism from a definite ethical and theological standpoint. In so far as in any age there is common agreement on ethical and theological matters, so far can literary criticism be substantive. In ages like our own, in which there is no such common agreement, it is the more necessary for Christian readers to scrutinize their reading, especially of works of imagination, with explicit ethical and theological standards. The "greatness" of literature cannot be determined solely by literary standards; though we must remember that whether it is literature or not can be determined only by literary standards.

We have tacitly assumed, for some centuries past, that there is no relation between literature and theology. This is not to deny that literature—I mean, again, primarily works of imagination—has been, is, and probably always will be judged by some moral standards. But moral judgments of literary works are made only according to the moral code accepted by each generation, whether it lives according to that code or not. In an age which accepts some precise Christian theology, the common code may be fairly orthodox: though even in such periods the common code may exalt such concepts as "honour," "glory" or "revenge" to a position quite intolerable to Christianity. The dramatic ethics of

THOMAS STEARNS ELIOT *was one the foremost literary influences in English and American literature during much of the twentieth century. His numerous works cover a broad spectrum—literary criticism and theory, poetry, drama, and occasional theological and philosophical essays. In all of these fields, his mature viewpoint was Christian, sometimes overtly (as in the essay reprinted here), sometimes implicitly. Eliot's landmark essay "Religion and Literature" was originally published in 1932.*

the Elizabethan Age offers an interesting study. But when the common code is detached from its theological background, and is consequently more and more merely a matter of habit, it is exposed both to prejudice and to change. At such times morals are open to being altered *by* literature; so that we find in practice that what is "objectionable" in literature is merely what the present age is not used to. It is a commonplace that what shocks one generation is accepted quite calmly by the next. This adaptability to change of moral standards is sometimes greeted with satisfaction as an evidence of human perfectibility: whereas it is only evidence of what unsubstantial foundations people's moral judgments have.

I am not concerned here with religious literature but with the application of our religion to the criticism of any literature. It may be as well, however, to distinguish first what I consider to be the three senses in which we can speak of "religious literature." The first is that of which we say that it is "religious literature" in the same way that we speak of "historical literature" or of "scientific literature." I mean that we can treat the Authorized translation of the Bible, or the works of Jeremy Taylor, as literature, in the same way that we treat the historical writing of Clarendon or of Gibbon—our two great English historians—as literature; or Bradley's *Logic,* or Buffon's *Natural History.* All of these writers were men who, incidentally to their religious, or historical, or philosophic purpose, had a gift of language which makes them delightful to read to all those who can enjoy language well written, even if they are unconcerned with the objects which the writers had in view. And I would add that though a scientific, or historical, or theological, or philosophic work which is also "literature," may become superannuated as anything but literature, yet it is not likely to be "literature" unless it had its scientific or other value for its own time. While I acknowledge the legitimacy of this enjoyment, I am more acutely aware of its abuse. The persons who enjoy these writings solely because of their literary merit are essentially parasites; and we know that parasites, when they become too numerous, are pests. I could fulminate against the men of letters who have gone into ecstasies over "the Bible as literature," the Bible as "the noblest monument of English prose." Those who talk of the Bible as a "monument of English prose" are merely admiring it as a monument over the grave of Christianity. I must try to avoid the by-paths of my discourse: it is enough to suggest that just as the work of Clarendon, or Gibbon, or Buffon, or Bradley would be of inferior literary value if it were insignificant as history, science and philosophy respectively, so the Bible has had a *literary* influence upon English literature not because it has been considered as literature, but because it has been considered as the report of the Word of God. And the fact that men of letters now discuss it as "literature" probably indicates the end of its "literary" influence.

The second kind of relation of religion to literature is that which is found in what is called "religious" or "devotional" poetry. Now what is the usual attitude of the lover of poetry—and I mean the person who is a genuine and first-hand enjoyer and appreciator of poetry, not the person who follows the admirations of others—towards this department of poetry. I believe, all that may be implied in his calling it a *department*. He believes, not always explicitly, that when you qualify poetry as "religious" you are indicating very clear limitations. For the great majority of people who love poetry, "*religious* poetry" is a variety of minor poetry: the religious poet is not a poet who is treating the whole subject matter of poetry in a religious spirit, but a poet who is dealing with a confined part of this subject matter: who is leaving out what men consider their major passions, and thereby confessing his ignorance of them. I think that this is the real attitude of most poetry lovers towards such poets as Vaughan, or Southwell, or Crashaw, or George Herbert, or Gerard Hopkins.

But what is more, I am ready to admit that up to a point these critics are right. For there is a kind of poetry, such as most of the work of the authors I have mentioned, which is the product of a special religious awareness, which may exist without the general awareness which we expect of the major poet. In some poets, or in some of their works, this general awareness may have existed; but the preliminary steps which represent it may have been suppressed, and only the end-product presented. Between these, and those in which the religious or devotional genius represents the *special* and limited awareness, it may be very difficult to discriminate. I do not pretend to offer Vaughan, or Southwell, or George Herbert, or Hopkins as major poets: I feel sure that the first three, at least, are poets of this limited awareness. They are not great religious poets in the sense in which Dante, or Corneille, or Racine, even in those of their plays which do not touch upon Christian themes, are great Christian religious poets. Or even in the sense in which Villon and Baudelaire, with all their imperfections and delinquencies, are Christian poets. Since the time of Chaucer, Christian poetry (in the sense in which I shall mean it) has been limited in England almost exclusively to minor poetry.

I repeat that when I am considering Religion and Literature, I speak of these things only to make clear that I am not concerned primarily with Religious Literature. I am concerned with what should be the relation between Religion and all Literature. Therefore the third type of "religious literature" may be more quickly passed over. I mean the literary works of men who are sincerely desirous of forwarding the cause of religion: that which may come under the heading of Propaganda. I am thinking, of course, of such delightful fiction as Mr. Chesterton's *Man Who Was Thursday*, or his *Father Brown*. No one admires and enjoys these things more than I do; I would only remark that when the same effect is aimed at by zealous persons of less talent than Mr. Chesterton the effect is negative. But my point is that such writings do not enter into any serious consideration of the relation of Religion and Literature: because they are conscious operations in a world in which it is assumed that Religion and Literature are not related. It is a conscious and limited relating. What I want is a literature which should be unconsciously, rather than deliberately and defiantly, Christian: because the work of Mr. Chesterton has its point from appearing in a world which is definitely not Christian.

I am convinced that we fail to realize how completely, and yet how irrationally, we separate our literary from our religious judgments. If there could be a complete separation, perhaps it might not matter: but the separation is not, and never can be, complete. If we exemplify literature by the novel—for the novel is the form in which literature affects the greatest number—we may remark this gradual secularization of literature during at least the last three hundred years. Bunyan, and to some extent Defoe, had moral purposes: the former is beyond suspicion, the latter may be suspect. But since Defoe the secularization of the novel has been continuous. There have been three chief phases. In the first, the novel took the Faith, in its contemporary version, for granted, and omitted it from its picture of life. Fielding, Dickens and Thackeray belong to this phase. In the second, it doubted, worried about, or contested the Faith. To this phase belong George Eliot, George Meredith and Thomas Hardy. To the third phase, in which we are living, belong nearly all contemporary novelists except Mr. James Joyce. It is the phase of those who have never heard the Christian Faith spoken of as anything but an anachronism.

Now, do people in general hold a definite opinion, that is to say religious or anti-religious; and do they read novels, or poetry for that matter, with a separate compartment of their minds? The common ground between religion and fiction is behaviour. Our religion imposes our ethics, our judgment and criticism of ourselves, and our behaviour toward our fellow men. The fiction that we read affects our behaviour towards our fellow men, affects our patterns of ourselves. When we read of human beings behaving in certain ways, with the approval of the author, who gives his benediction to this behaviour by his attitude toward the result of the behaviour arranged by himself, we can be influenced towards behaving in the same way. When the contemporary novelist is an individual thinking for himself in isolation, he may have something important to offer to those who are able to receive it. He who is alone may speak to the individual. But the majority of novelists are persons drifting in the stream, only a little faster. They have some sensitiveness, but little intellect.

We are expected to be broadminded about literature, to put aside prejudice or conviction, and to look at fiction as fiction and at drama as drama. With what is inaccurately called "censorship" in this country—with what is much more difficult to cope with than an official censorship, because it represents the opinions of individuals in an irresponsible democracy, I have very little sympathy; partly because it so often suppresses the wrong books, and partly because it is little more effective than Prohibition of Liquor; partly because it is one manifestation of the desire that state control should take the place of decent domestic influence; and wholly because it acts only from custom and habit, not from decided theological and moral principles. Incidentally, it gives people a false sense of security in leading them to believe that books which are not suppressed are harmless. Whether there *is* such a thing as a harmless book I am not sure: but there very likely are books so utterly unreadable as to be incapable of injuring anybody. But it is certain that a book is not harmless merely because no one is consciously offended by it. And if we, as readers, keep our religious and moral convictions in one compartment, and take our reading merely for entertainment, or on a higher plane, for aesthetic pleasure, I would point out that the author, whatever his conscious intentions in writing, in practice recognizes no such distinctions. The author of a work of imagination is trying to affect us wholly, as human beings, whether he knows it or not; and we are affected by it, as human beings, whether we intend to be or not. I suppose that everything we

eat has some other effect upon us than merely the pleasure of taste and mastica-
tion; it affects us during the process of assimilation and digestion; and I believe
that exactly the same is true of anything we read.

---

*Of course, it is the whole person who responds to a poem or novel; and if
that person is a believing Christian, then it is a believing Christian who
judges; one can't...pretend to be something one is not.... Literary criticism
is as much a personal matter, as much the product of a personal sense of life
and value as literature itself.*

—VINCENT BUCKLEY, *Poetry and Morality*

The fact that what we read does not concern merely something called our
literary taste, but that it affects directly, though only amongst many other influences, the whole of what we are, is best elicited, I think, by a conscientious
examination of the history of our individual literary education. Consider the
adolescent reading of any person with some literary sensibility. Everyone, I
believe, who is at all sensible to the seductions of poetry, can remember some
moment in youth when he or she was completely carried away by the work of
one poet. Very likely he was carried away by several poets, one after the other.
The reason for this passing infatuation is not merely that our sensibility to
poetry is keener in adolescence than in maturity. What happens is a kind of
inundation, of invasion of the undeveloped personality by the stronger personality of the poet. The same thing may happen at a later age to persons who have
not done much reading. One author takes complete possession of us for a time;
then another; and finally they begin to affect each other in our mind. We weigh
one against another; we see that each has qualities absent from others, and qualities incompatible with the qualities of others: we begin to be, in fact, critical;
and it is our growing critical power which protects us from excessive possession
by any one literary personality. The good critic—and we should all try to be critics, and not leave criticism to the fellows who write reviews in the papers—is the
man who, to a keen and abiding sensibility, joins wide and increasingly discrim-
inating reading. Wide reading is not valuable as a kind of hoarding, an accumulation of knowledge, or what sometimes is meant by the term "a well-stocked
mind." It is valuable because in the process of being affected by one powerful

personality after another, we cease to be dominated by any one, or by any small number. The very different views of life, cohabiting in our minds, affect each other, and our own personality asserts itself and gives each a place in some arrangement peculiar to ourself.

It is simply not true that works of fiction, prose or verse, that is to say works depicting the actions, thoughts and words and passions of imaginary human beings, *directly* extend our knowledge of life. Direct knowledge of life is knowledge directly in relation to ourselves, it is our knowledge of *how* people behave in general, of *what* they are like in general, in so far as that part of life in which we ourselves have participated gives us material for generalization. Knowledge of life obtained through fiction is only possible by another stage of self-consciousness. That is to say, it can only be a knowledge of other people's knowledge of life, not of life itself. So far as we are taken up with the happenings in any novel in the same way in which we are taken up with what happens under our eyes, we are acquiring at least as much falsehood as truth. But when we are developed enough to say: "This is the view of life of a person who was a good observer within his limits, Dickens, or Thackeray, or George Eliot, or Balzac; but he looked at it in a different way from me, because he was a different man; he even selected rather different things to look at, or the same things in a different order of importance, because he was a different man; so what I am looking at is the world as seen by a particular mind"—then we are in a position to gain something from reading fiction. We are learning something about life from these authors direct, just as we learn something from the reading of history direct; but these authors are only really helping us when we can see, and allow for, their differences from ourselves.

A man who has lived in many places is not likely to be deceived by the local errors of his native village; the scholar has lived in many times and is therefore to some degree immune from the great cataract of nonsense that pours from the press and the microphone of his own age.

—C. S. LEWIS, "Learning in War-Time"

Now what we get, as we gradually grow up and read more and more, and read a greater diversity of authors, is a variety of views of life. But what people commonly assume, I suspect, is that we gain this experience of other men's views of life only by "improving reading." This, it is supposed, is a reward we get by applying ourselves to Shakespeare, and Dante, and Goethe, and Emerson, and Carlyle, and dozens of other respectable writers. The rest of our reading for amusement is merely killing time. But I incline to come to the alarming conclusion that it is just the literature that we read for "amusement," or "purely for pleasure" that may have the greatest and least suspected influence upon us. It is the literature which we read with the least effort that can have the easiest and most insidious influence upon us. Hence it is that the influence of popular novelists, and of popular plays of contemporary life, requires to be scrutinized most closely. And it is chiefly contemporary literature that the majority of people ever read in this attitude of "purely for pleasure," of pure passivity.

The relation to my subject of what I have been saying should now be a little more apparent. Though we may read literature merely for pleasure, of "entertainment" or of "aesthetic enjoyment," this reading never affects simply a sort of special sense: it affects our moral and religious existence. And I say that while individual modern writers of eminence can be improving, contemporary literature as a whole tends to be degrading. And that even the effect of the better writers, in an age like ours, may be degrading to some readers; for we must remember that what a writer does to people is not necessarily what he intends to do. It may be only what people are capable of having done to them. People exercise an unconscious selection in being influenced. A writer like D. H. Lawrence may be in his effect either beneficial or pernicious. I am not sure that I have not had some pernicious influence myself.

At this point I anticipate a rejoinder from the liberal-minded, from all those who are convinced that if everybody says what he thinks, and does what he likes, things will somehow, by some automatic compensation and adjustment, come right in the end. "Let everything be tried," they say, "and if it is a mistake, then we shall learn by experience." This argument might have some value, if we were always the same generation upon earth; or if, as we know to be not the case, people ever learned much from the experience of their elders. These liberals are convinced that only by what is called unrestrained individualism will truth ever emerge. Ideas, views of life, they think, issue distinct from independent heads, and in consequence of their knocking violently against each other, the fittest survive, and truth rises triumphant. Anyone who dissents from this view must be either a mediaevalist, wishful only to set back the clock, or else a fascist, and probably both.

> *Most of all, perhaps, we need intimate knowledge of the past. Not that the past has any magic about it, but because…we need something to set against the present, to remind us that the basic assumptions have been quite different in different periods and that much which seems certain to the uneducated is merely temporary fashion.*
> —C. S. LEWIS, "Learning in War-Time"

If the mass of contemporary authors were really individualists, every one of them inspired Blakes, each with his separate vision, and if the mass of the contemporary public were really a mass of *individuals* there might be something to be said for this attitude. But this is not, and never has been, and never will be. It is not only that the reading individual today (or at any day) is not enough an individual to be able to absorb all the "views of life" of all the authors pressed upon us by the publishers' advertisements and the reviewers, and to be able to arrive at wisdom by considering one against another. It is that the contemporary authors are not individuals enough either. It is not that the world of separate individuals of the liberal democrat is undesirable; it is simply that this world does not exist. For the reader of contemporary literature is not, like the reader of the established great literature of all time, exposing himself to the influence of divers and contradictory personalities; he is exposing himself to a mass movement of writers who, each of them, think that they have something individually to offer, but are really all working together in the same direction. And there never was a time, I believe, when the reading public was so large, or so helplessly exposed to the influences of its own time. There never was a time, I believe, when those who read at all, read so many more books by living authors than books by dead authors; there never was a time so completely parochial, so shut off from the past. There may be too many publishers; there are certainly too many books published; and the journals ever incite the reader to "keep up" with what is being published. Individualistic democracy has come to high tide: and it is more difficult today to be an individual than it ever was before.

Within itself, modern literature has perfectly valid distinctions of good and bad, better and worse; and I do not wish to suggest that I confound Mr. Bernard

Shaw with Mr. Noel Coward, Mrs. Woolf with Miss Mannin. On the other hand, I should like it to be clear that I am not defending a "high"-brow against a "low"-brow literature. What I do wish to affirm is that the whole of modern literature is corrupted by what I call Secularism, that it is simply unaware of, simply cannot understand the meaning of, the primacy of the supernatural over the natural life: of something which I assume to be our primary concern.

The journey homewards. Coming home. That's what it's all about. The journey to the coming of the Kingdom. That's probably the chief difference between the Christian and the secular artist—the purpose of the work, be it story or music or painting, is to further the coming of the kingdom, to make us aware of our status as children of God, and to turn our feet toward home.

—MADELEINE L'ENGLE, *Walking on Water*

I do not want to give the impression that I have delivered a mere fretful jeremiad against contemporary literature. Assuming a common attitude between my readers, or some of my readers, and myself, the question is not so much, what is to be done about it? as, how should we behave towards it?

I have suggested that the liberal attitude towards literature will not work. Even if the writers who make their attempt to impose their "view of life" upon us were really distinct individuals, even if we as readers were distinct individuals, what would be the result? It would be, surely, that each reader would be impressed, in his reading, merely by what he was previously prepared to be impressed by; he would follow the "line of least resistance," and there would be no assurance that he would be made a better man. For literary judgment we need to be acutely aware of two things at once: of "what we like," and of "what we *ought* to like." Few people are honest enough to know either. The first means knowing what we really feel: very few know that. The second involves understanding our shortcomings; for we do not really know what we ought to like unless we also know why we ought to like it, which involves knowing why we don't yet like it. It is not enough to understand what we ought to be, unless we know what we are; and we do not understand what we are, unless we know what we ought to be. The two forms of self-consciousness, knowing what we are and what we ought to be, must go together.

It is our business, as readers of literature, to know what we like. It is our business, as Christians, *as well as* readers of literature, to know what we ought to like. It is our business as honest men, not to assume that whatever we like is what we ought to like. And the last thing I would wish for would be the existence of two literatures, one for Christian consumption and the other for the pagan world. What I believe to be incumbent upon all Christians is the duty of maintaining consciously certain standards and criteria of criticism over and above those applied by the rest of the world; and that by these criteria and standards everything that we read must be tested. We must remember that the greater part of our current reading matter is written for us by people who have no real belief in a supernatural order, though some of it may be written by people with individual notions of a supernatural order which are not ours. And the greater part of our reading matter is coming to be written by people who not only have no such belief, but are even ignorant of the fact that there are still people in the world so "backward" or so "eccentric" as to continue to believe. So long as we are conscious of the gulf fixed between ourselves and the greater part of contemporary literature, we are more or less protected from being harmed by it, and are in a position to extract from it what good it has to offer us.

There are a very large number of people in the world today who believe that all ills are fundamentally economic. Some believe that various specific economic changes alone would be enough to set the world right; others demand more or less drastic changes in the social as well, changes chiefly of two opposed types. These changes demanded, and in some places carried out, are alike in one respect, that they hold the assumptions of what I call Secularism: they concern themselves only with changes of a temporal, material, and external nature; they concern themselves with morals only of a collective nature. In an exposition of one such new faith I read the following words:

"In our morality the one single test of any moral question is whether it impedes or destroys in any way the power of the individual to serve the State. [The individual] must answer the questions: 'Does this action injure the nation? Does it injure other members of the nation? Does it injure my ability to serve the nation?' And if the answer is clear on all those questions, the individual has absolute liberty to do as he will."

Now I do not deny that this is a kind of morality, and that it is capable of great good within limits; but I think that we should all repudiate a morality which had no higher ideal to set before us than that. It represents, of course, one of the violent reactions we are witnessing, against the view that the community is solely for the benefit of the individual; but it is equally a gospel of this world, and of this world alone. My complaint against modern literature is of the same kind. It is not that modern literature is in the ordinary sense "immoral" or even "amoral"; and in any case to prefer that charge would not be enough. It is simply that it repudiates, or is wholly ignorant of, our most fundamental and important beliefs; and that in consequence its tendency is to encourage its readers to get what they can out of life while it lasts, to miss no "experience" that presents itself, and to sacrifice themselves, if they make any sacrifice at all, only for the sake of tangible benefits to others in this world either now or in the future. We shall certainly continue to read the best of its kind, of what our time provides; but we must tirelessly criticize it according to our own principles, and not merely according to the principles admitted by the writers and by the critics who discuss it in the public press.

Authors, Authority, and the Humble Reader

Peter J. Leithart

Jean-Francois Lyotard has said that postmodernism is essentially a suspicion of metanarratives, those "master theories" like Marxism, Darwinianism, or Freudianism that claim to explain everything. Postmodern skepticism challenges not only these modern stories, however, but goes further in forswearing meta-narratives entirely. There is, for the postmodernist, no single, all-embracing story. There can be no talk about a "center" or "direction" to history, a fixed order for the world, or a worldview that is absolutely true. In place of truth there are truths, and in place of a single story is a lush garden teeming with delight-fully contradictory narratives. Let a thousand flowers bloom.

Though Lyotard's characterization is true enough, with respect to literary theory postmodernism is just as essentially the triumph of the reader, which corresponds to the so-called "death of the author." Though postmodern the-ory is wildly profuse, most species share certain basic commitments: creative reading has been elevated to the level of creative writing, criticism to the level of the original work, and the reader has begun to dominate the literary exchange. In the early part of the twentieth century, modernism shifted atten-tion from the author and his biography to the text as a literary object, and

---

PETER J. LEITHART *is a Fellow in Literature and Theology at New St. Andrews College, Moscow, Idaho. An ordained Presbyterian pastor, he has contributed articles to various publications and has written a number of books on literature, including* Heroes of the City of Man: A Christian Guide to Select Ancient Literature; Brightest Heaven of Invention: A Christian Guide to Six Shakespeare Plays; *and (most recently)* Ascent to Love: An Introduction to Dante's Divine Comedy *(Canon Press, 2001).*

postmodernism has finished the job by wrenching the text completely from its author's grasp.

When postmodern theorists speak of the "death of the author," they do not, of course, deny that some human being is responsible for putting the words on the page. They do not believe that books magically materialize from nothing. What they are challenging is the "authority" of the "author." In this respect, postmodernism represents a massive shift from earlier ideas of books and reading. Throughout the middle ages, for example, critics operated according to what A. J. Minnis has described as a "literary theory centered on the concepts of *auctor* [author] and *auctoritas* [authority]." For medieval literary scholars, the author was "an authority, someone to be believed and imitated." Anyone can scribble words on a page, but to call someone an *auctor* was "an accolade."

To receive this accolade, a work had to exhibit both "intrinsic worth" and "authenticity." Worth was measured by conformity with scriptural teaching, and "to be 'authentic,' a saying or a piece of writing had to be the genuine production of a named *auctor*." Works of doubtful origin, or "apocryphal" works, had a much lower degree of authority than works that were recognized as "authentic." Though Minnis does not list it as a separate criterion of *auctoritas,* antiquity was also an important element in establishing who was and who was not considered an *auctor:* "No 'modern' writer could decently be called an *auctor,*" either because the ancients "had by nature greater mental powers" or because they "applied themselves more diligently to study."

Given this theory of authorship, reading could not be anything but an act of humility—homage to the *auctoritas* of an *auctor.* This medieval insight should be a truism: simply by picking up a book, opening it, and following the words that someone else has written, a reader is subjecting himself to the author. In ages of confusion, however, truisms must be *argued,* and it is, especially in our postmodern climate, important to emphasize it once again. Though this conception of reading was applied in the medieval world to nonfiction as well as fictional writing, I wish to examine several implications for the modern reader of fiction.

ENTERING FICTIONAL WORLDS

Works of fiction present a world to us. In some sorts of fiction, like fantasy or science fiction, the world of the novel is a world quite completely different from the world of our experience. In many cases, of course, the world presented is much like our own world. Paris and London were really cities in the late eighteenth century, the Bastille really did fall, severed heads really were mounted on pikes and paraded through the streets of Paris—these are not figments of Dickens's imagination. But even the novel that strives for historical accuracy invites us to enter a world different from our world. Danton and Robespierre really existed, but Lucy Manette and Sidney Carton did not, and the world of *A Tale of Two Cities* is different from ours precisely because it is a world peopled by the likes of Sidney Carton and Lucy Manette.

No matter what the distance between the real and the fictional worlds, reading intelligently requires a humble acceptance of the world of the novel. It is a poor reader, and a proud one, who throws aside *A Tale of Two Cities* with the sneering complaint that "It's unrealistic. Sidney Carton never went to the guillotine." A "suspension of disbelief" is elementary to reading fiction, but it is rarely recognized as an act of humility. In part, that is due to the dour connotations that "humility" has in contemporary usage, but here those connotations are completely out of place. As G. K. Chesterton said, humility makes us small, and that means that everything around us becomes large and astounding and magnificent. Humility before the world that the author presents means that we allow him to set the rules, but it also gives reading an element of play. Across the centuries, Dickens says to us, "I'll pretend Jerry Cruncher was real if you will." By opening the book and beginning to read, we are saying, "Let me play too." To read well, we must become as little children.

The reader must…lay aside his own opinions and predilections and, as Coleridge put it, "listen like a three years' child"—till the time comes for him to step out of the charmed circle and back into his own world.

—CAROLINE GORDON, *How to Read a Novel*

Humility before the author is not only a matter of the minimal "let's pretend" acceptance of his world. It also includes following the contours of plot, imagery, and character by which a work of fiction progresses. It means paying attention to what the author thinks is important, and noticing how he signals that it is important. It means paying attention to the metaphors, analogies, and symbols that the author is using to explain the significance of his story. When

Dickens brings us into his parlor game of *A Tale of Two Cities* and entitles the first part of his narrative "Recalled to Life," he is telling us how to think about the opening chapters that tell about Dr. Manette's release from the Bastille: it is a rebirth, a resurrection. Many chapters later, Dickens's story ends with Sidney Carton, a ne'er-do-well lawyer, deciding to take the place of a man who has been condemned to death. Carton's death is triumphant self-sacrifice, and he goes to the guillotine meditating on John 11:25. Seeing the connection between Dr. Manette's "resurrection" at the beginning of the book and Carton's hope for resurrection at the end, we are supposed to recognize that the whole novel moves forward by a series of resurrections (including the macabre "resurrections" associated with Jerry Cruncher's grave robbing). We may not want the emphasis placed where the author has placed it, we may believe the characters unbelievable, we may think of better ways to construct or resolve the plot, we may think his symbols are forced or intrusive. There will be time for such criticism, but unless we first receive what the author has given us, our criticisms will be confused at best.

PATIENCE AND READING

Some readers have a well-trained eye for such things, but learning the contours of a fictional world or the intricacies of an author's methods always takes time. Robert Penn Warren commented that the most "intuitive and immediate" reading of a poem will likely not come at the first reading, but rather at the tenth or even the fiftieth reading. To grasp the whole, one must, he speculated, be able not only to remember the beginning of the poem, but remember its end; one must be able to "remember forward." Patience, in short, is an essential quality of a good reader, and this too is an act of humility.

Readers may fail to listen carefully to catch the author's tone of voice, rushing to judgment without asking whether the author means to be deathly serious, sentimental, satirical, or whatever. A recent example is so absurd that it parodies itself. Near the beginning of the 2000 school year, black parents at a Catholic school in Louisiana complained about the "racist" language and stories of Georgia writer Flannery O'Connor. It would be a mistake to charge these parents with a pathetic misreading of O'Connor. It would be a mistake because the parents had not read the stories at all. Their opposition was apparently based on a few titles and passages. Too frequently, Christians are guilty of equal absurdities.

Harry Potter creator J. K. Rowling has been quoted all over the Internet as saying that she is happy that her books have produced a surge in children's involvement in Satanism. This quotation has been used as evidence that the Potter books are infernal propaganda. The original source of the quotation, however, was a story from a satirical electronic magazine. For anyone who took a moment to check the original source, and took another moment to ask about the tone of the article, it was clear that the author was mocking hysterical responses to Rowling's books. It must be a delicious irony to the article's author that the satire has become fuel for even more hysteria.

Though they may be harsh opponents of postmodernism, readers who took the Rowling quote at face value are as domineering and prideful in their reading practices as any deconstructionist. But how was one to know that the Rowling quotation was a fake? The text did not come with a label "Satire." The author expected the readers to recognize the clues and read in submission to them. Quick and ignorant judgments such as these are not only an embarrassment that often makes Christians, quite rightly, objects of ridicule. Far worse, these misreadings signal an appalling lack of Christian character. Patience before the text is not merely a readerly virtue. It is a fruit of the Spirit.

> *However far [the reader] may go, the author has gone farther. Whatever connections he may establish among the different parts of the book...he has a guarantee, namely, that they have been expressly willed.... The creator has preceded him along the way.... A gentle force accompanies us and supports us from the first page to the last.*
>
> —JEAN-PAUL SARTRE, *What Is Literature?*

Patience is necessary not only to learn the contours of a particular work, but also to learn how literature works. Flannery O'Connor noted in one of her essays that some works of fiction should be commended only to mature readers. She acknowledges that works should be judged according to their "total effect," not by isolated passages. A book may have sexual content, for example, and not be pornographic or immoral. O'Connor wisely goes on to say that an immature reader lacks the tools and literary maturity to feel the "total effect." Immature readers will not be able to integrate passages that arouse passion into the total experience of reading a book. They may return again and again to the sexy passages to reexperience the original titillation, without ever realizing that the sexy passages are in a book that challenges cheap sex. Only long exposure to literature develops the skills necessary to recognize what a particular book or author is up to. O'Connor ended the essay by protesting that high school reading should not be selected by what the students wish to read: "Their tastes should not be consulted; they are being formed."

THE ETHICS OF READING

This is not to say that no ethical or moral judgments can be made concerning a work of fiction. T. S. Eliot famously said that the Christian reader must offer a judgment of a moral and theological kind "over and above" aesthetic standards. Though I agree with Eliot to the extent that theological and moral criteria must enter into any Christian judgment of literature, I disagree insofar as he considers this a separate critical task. I dispute his idea that moral standards are "over and above" artistic ones. Separating aesthetic and ethical judgment is an example of the "dissociation of sensibility," the disconnection between emotion and reason, that Eliot elsewhere decries.

One might wish to suggest that Melville, say, is an extraordinary stylist and rhetorician, but a wicked theologian. But the theology is so interwoven with the style that *Moby Dick* is, as Melville himself said, perhaps not altogether seriously, a "wicked book," celebrating Ahab's doomed assault on the whiteness that lies back of the world. The rhetorical skill of Milton's Satan is deceit as much as his temptation of Eve, and the smooth words of the adulteress in Proverbs are not praised for their lyricism because the smoothness is part of the danger, part of her amorality. "Excellent speech is not fitting for a fool," Proverbs 17:7 (NASB) says, and the word "fitting" means "comely" or "lovely." This is an aesthetic judgment; the disparity between style and substance, the use of high speech for a low purpose, makes the work not merely ethically but aesthetically repellent. Melville is not to be admired for his style and abhorred for his theology; we are not to judge a work good at a "literary" level, and then pass on to judge it pernicious at a "moral" or "theological" level. Melville is to be abhorred because he employed his gifts in an act of rebellion. I am a great admirer of Melville, but I admire him in the way that I admire a powerful and highly skilled enemy.

For some time, literary scholars have been reluctant to pass ethical judgments on the works they study. This is an oddity, for these are men and women who devote their lives to the study of literature, and we might be forgiven for taking this as evidence that they believe they are enriching students' lives by teaching them to read well. But if lives can be enriched by reading, it is certainly a fair question whether lives might also be spoiled. No doubt there are many reasons for this strange reluctance to judge literature ethically, but surely one of the chief among them is the notion that art is a zone sealed off from real life. Whatever the academy assumes, this is a separation that a Christian simply cannot accept. Though fiction creates its own world, the book also is an objective presence in our world; the word becomes flesh and dwells among us, and the question must be asked whether this incarnate word is doing mischief or good.

Moral standards…are as relevant to literature as they are to life itself.… If the subject matter of literary art is the full range of human values, then ethical principles are always relevant.… If literature itself is an evaluation of experience, both explicitly and by implication, then any adequate judgment of the art must measure the evaluation by the critic's own moral standards.

—KEITH MCKEAN, *The Moral Measure of Literature*

Ethical judgment of fiction is exceedingly complex, and I will focus here on only a few aspects. In general, I want to focus on how fiction molds the character of readers, rather than on the possibilities of passing judgment on the characters within a fictional work itself. In this connection, Wayne Booth has helpfully distinguished between the ethical issues involved in the *act* of reading and the ethical issues involved in the *consequences* of reading. As Booth points out, during the process of reading, the author through the book is promoting a particular "pattern of desire." A story encourages us to respond with a variety of emotions to the characters and their situations. Readers hope that Darcy will propose to Elizabeth Bennet again, fear that the White Witch has triumphed over Aslan, and regard Kafka's Gregor Samsa with an odd mixture of pity and laughter following his unexpected metamorphosis into a giant insect.

But such emotions can be rightly or wrongly directed. I have frequently had the experience of rooting for the protagonist in a movie, only to realize once the thrill was over that I had been rooting for a thief to escape, a murderer to get off, a wife successfully to betray her (inevitably oafish) husband so that she can be with her (gorgeous, if raffish) true love. This point about the shaping of desire is made in an exceedingly subtle way at the beginning of Dante's *Inferno,* where Dante encounters Francesca da Rimini in what is perhaps the best-known encounter in the whole *Comedy.* Francesca was murdered by her jealous husband, who caught his wife in an adulterous affair with his own brother. In the *Comedy,* she sings a hymn to tragic love, and Dante, in pity, ends the canto in a swoon. Most readers join Dante in his sympathy; after all, Francesca's marriage was purely one of political convenience and she found true love only in the arms of her brother-in-law. But for the poet Dante (as opposed to the pilgrim Dante, the character in the story), Francesca is not to be pitied. She is in hell, and justly so, and pitying those who justly suffer is, in the later words of Virgil, an act of "impiety" by one who attempts to "bend the divine will to his own." Dante uses Francesca to expose the reader's failure of piety and true pity, a failure that Dante hopes to correct through his own hymn to love, the *Comedy* itself.

As Booth points out, it is simply undeniable that fiction's manipulations of our desires have permanent effects in shaping our character:

> Our culture is full of stories about the fatal malleability of readers who somehow haven't heard the news that good readers are supposed to maintain their distance. One heard of the poet Infante attempting suicide on an airplane, so depressed was he by his travel reading of Malcolm Lowry's *Under the Volcano* (1947). One *knows* youngsters who first tried drugs after reading Kerouac's *On the Road* or listening to the Beatles' "Lucy in the Sky with Diamonds." Except when reading the most advanced literary journals, one hears accounts everywhere of "How my life was changed by reading X, Y, or Z."

Booth suggests that critics' refusal to acknowledge the relation of literature and life has roots in modern conceptions of the self, in which the self is an unchanging essence, impervious to outside influence, that must be "discovered" rather than trained. Rather, we should conceive the self as a project still under construction, a project that can come to wonderful consummation or be reduced to ruins. And we should realize that the self is shaped not only and not mainly by our sheer will power, but by our encounters with the world and with others, above all, with God. Many factors affect the outcome of this project, but the *auctors* we choose to submit ourselves to is one important factor.

MIMESIS AND METAPHOR

There are many mysteries in trying to unravel how reading shapes the self, and only two issues will be treated briefly here: mimesis and metaphor. Mimesis or imitation is one of the fundamental realities in the formation of the self. Children learn language, manners, gestures, parenting (!), and a host of other habits and passions from their parents, without either parents or children putting much conscious effort into it. And the dance of mimesis does not end with childhood: Disciples become like masters, soldiers are molded by their commander, and college basketball players (and many flabby former players) aspire to "be like Mike." It is absurd to suggest that fictional characters, whom most readers know more intimately than they know their own parents, do not have a similar effect. Earlier critics took it for granted that literature, an imitation of life, presents models for imitation to the reader. As Samuel Johnson put it, "If the power of example is so great, as to take possession of the memory by a kind of violence, and produce effects almost without the intervention of the will, care ought to be taken that the best examples only should be exhibited." This is one-sided, for a fiction can also function as a cautionary tale, presenting a bad model as a warning against certain kinds of conduct. At least, however, Johnson recognized that fictional characters are models offered for imitation.

Metaphor is equally inherent in human life and thought. Arguably, all seeing is "seeing as" (and the fact that this comes from Kant doesn't make it wrong). So long as the shadowy shape in the headlights cannot be given a name and a form, I feel I cannot really see it, even if my retinas and corneas and pupils are all working properly. Only when I can say, "Oh, it's a deer" do I sense that I have perceived the thing. Features that were obscure before now become clear: That white patch is a tail, and I can almost begin to count the points of his rack.

Perceptions are shaped by the names we assign. That is not the same as metaphor, but the operation of metaphor is similar. Metaphor invites us to "see as"—to see X as if it were Y. Like the act of assigning the name "deer" to the shaped darkness ahead of me, seeing X as if it were Y reveals unnoticed features of Y, and perhaps also of X. This kind of "seeing as" is the stock-in-trade of poetry, and gives support to poetry's sometimes inflated claims to be able to provide insight into the nature of the world. Poets name the world in unusual ways, and help us to experience it afresh.

In fiction, metaphor is extended to character and story, and this kind of extended metaphor shapes the reader by shaping his self-perceptions. Metaphor embraces mimesis, and we begin to "see ourselves as." We imagine ourselves embarked on a pilgrimage to the Celestial City, and start sniffing around for Vanity Fairs and Pliables. Or, we see our own courtship as a "taming of the shrew" or "much ado about nothing." Or, we hear of a compassionate foreigner who cared for a man fallen among thieves, and go and do likewise. We seek meaning in life by seeking to discern a narrative shape, and the stories we read provide metaphorical models for understanding the story that God is telling with us.

Examining reading from this ethical angle helps us to see what can be distinctive about a Christian reader's approach to fiction. To be sure, Christian reading is not only about passing ethical judgments; it is also, as I have been insisting, about humbly and patiently learning the world that is the work. But Christian humility demands ethical-aesthetic judgments, because Christian humility is ultimately humility before God. Humility before God means agreeing with His judgments. No reader, of course, has a red phone to heaven, nor is there an inerrant and infallible Index of Forbidden Books. Yet God has passed judgment on certain things, and it would be remarkable arrogance for a Christian to disagree. We know that books are bad if they pattern our desires to hope for anonymous sex, if they encourage imitation of characters who scorn God, if they invite us to see the world as a cosmic toilet.

And I could not doubt that the sub-Christian or anti-Christian values implicit in most literature did actually infect many readers.... I do not say that the sympathetic reading of literature must produce such results, but that it may and often does.... For some, [culture] is a good beginning. For others it is not; culture is not everyone's road into Jerusalem, and from some it is a road out.

—C. S. LEWIS, "Christianity and Culture"

Once ethical criteria are brought into play, the question of whether a book should be read at all must be addressed. Frenzied cries of censorship should not deter anyone from pursuing the question. Given the important role that humility plays in reading, one key sets of questions to ask is, "Do I wish to submit to this author? Is the pattern of desire that this book encourages healthy or unhealthy? Does the writer present models that may be imitated, or negative models as warnings? Will my involvement with the world and its Creator be enriched by seeing the world as the author wishes me to see it? Will my learning my way around his fictional world improve me or set me back?"

This is not to say that every book read must have a direct positive effect on the formation of Christian character. Ancient classics and modern fiction, read with care and attention, can form a Christian mind in significant though less direct ways. Anyone who shapes his life by the example of Achilles or Odysseus is, as Dante knew, on his way to hell. But exploring the pattern of desire in Homeric epic (basically, hope of glory *versus* fear of shame) can help us to understand the ancient mind, and help us to appreciate more deeply the difference that the gospel has made.

HUMBLE CREATIVITY

All this bowing and scraping: I seem to have substituted a death of the reader for a postmodern death of the author. Instead of sovereign readers listening to no one, I have suggested sovereign authors talking to a blank slate. There seems to be little for the reader to do but repeat the masters, glossing here and there at the margins perhaps, but essentially functioning as an empty receptacle waiting to be filled. Nothing, it seems, could be further from postmodern "free play" than this.

But this objection arises from a peculiarly modern notion that free creativity is fundamentally incompatible with submission to authority. In this respect, postmodernism is, as many have pointed out, simply a form of hypermodernism, a straightforward modernism that throws off the last pretense of humility before an *auctor*. For the Christian mind, however, this opposition is nonsensical. On the contrary, humility is the only possible starting point for creativity. Man cannot produce anything that is absolutely *ex nihilo,* and attempting to do so is of the essence of original sin. Pride is never creative, except of Pandaemonium.

Though not creative as God is creative, humans are creative beings. And creativity in every art presupposes a recognition of the qualities and contours of the materials being used. A sculptor must submit not only to the characteristics of marble, but to the peculiar shape and pattern of *this piece* of marble. A sculptor who says, "Damn the marble, I'm going to do what I'm going to do" is headed for a brief and disastrous career. Painters must submit to the realities of their paints and canvases, the play of light and color. Composers must bow before the physics of sound, must acknowledge the range and tone of their chosen instruments, must follow the pathway set out by a particular key. Poets and novelists who refuse to accept language as a *given,* as something they inherit rather than create on their own, will have few readers.

Reading is not, of course, creative in the same sense as writing or composing or painting. Yet it is creative in much the same way that performance of a piece of music is creative. Pianists and violinists, like the composer, are artists, and like all artists they must recognize the *auctoritas* of the material that has come from the hand of the *auctor.* In the case of a musical performer, the material is the pre-existing composition. That composition "limits" the creativity of the performer; if he is going to play *this* Bach fugue, he must play *these* notes, count out *this* rhythm, maintain *this* pace. If his performance of Bach reminds his audience of Philip Glass or Schoenberg, something has gone badly wrong with his performance. But once he acknowledges and bows before the contours of the piece he is playing, the notes on the page are not an "obstacle" to his creative expression, but the only possible means for a creative performance. Likewise with reading. Reading is no more simply "receptive" than performing a piece of music. Reading is a creative act, but it is genuinely creative only to the degree that the reader creates in submission to the creator, only if the reader "plays the notes" that have been written by the "composer." If it is to be genuinely artful, reading must bow before the materials of the art.

The reader, viewer, listener, usually grossly underestimates his importance. If a reader cannot create a book along with the writer, the book will never come to life. Creative involvement: that's the basic difference between reading a book and watching TV.

—MADELEINE L'ENGLE, *Walking on Water*

Creative reading does not, then, mean a free for all. There is a difference between discovering richnesses of meaning in a text and what Umberto Eco calls interpretive "drift," in which words can mean anything at all. Words are public property, and a writer using a word "foresees" that readers will draw certain meanings from it. Suppose we come across the phrase "a field of green grass." That, at least, foresees the meaning of a literal field. Beyond that, deciding what the words "foresaw" requires that we know something of the author and his setting and the context of the work in which the phrase appears. A late twentieth-century drama concerned with inner city gangs might use "a field of green grass" as a coded message about the availability of marijuana. The same phrase in a medieval text could not plausibly bear that meaning, but if it appeared in a dream allegory, it might have Edenic resonances. Humility before the text means entering the text and the world that it creates, and coming to know your way around. Once you become familiar with the hallways, floor plan, and general layout, you may be able to find hidden passageways. But it would be illegitimate—not to mention impolite—to create hidden passageways in a work before you learned your way around.

Let me offer an example, sticking with the "green grass" image, this time as it is found in Mark 6:39. At the superficial level, Mark is giving us a little detail concerning the location of Jesus' miracle of feeding the five thousand; the people who gather to hear Jesus "sit down in groups on the green grass." But reading the whole story (verses 30-43) makes us begin to suspect that something else is going on. When Jesus suggests that the disciples feed the people, after all, they complain that the "place is desolate." This may mean nothing more than that the place is unpopulated, but it still strikes an odd note to find a patch of green grass, large enough for several thousand people (verse 44), in the midst of a "desolate place." Quite literally, Jesus has led His listeners to "lie down in green pastures."

My echo of Psalm 23 is deliberate, but can we say that it is a legitimate reading of Mark's text? Several factors suggest that the answer is yes. When Jesus first sees the people, "He felt compassion for them because they were like sheep without a shepherd" (verse 34, NASB). Recognizing their need for "shepherding," Jesus "began to teach them many things." Thus, the whole story begins with Jesus identified as a faithful Shepherd to His people. Further, the immediately preceding story is about Herod's murder of John the Baptist. Instead of acting as a good shepherd who guides and feeds His flock, Herod is like the evil shepherds condemned in Ezekiel 34, one who feeds *on* his flock, preeminently on the Baptist himself, whose head is presented to the predatory Herod during a feast, on a plate! Once we have entered the room of the text, we find stairways that connect one story to the next, hallways that connect details of the text to a Davidic Psalm written a millennium before, and we learn to make our way creatively through the text.

THE HUMBLE SHALL BE EXALTED

The division of labor between writer and reader varies from writer to writer. Some writers cannot tell you enough; they mark out every link in a chain of associations with neon, and keep telling the reader how to respond to what has been going on. Others leave the reader to do his fair share. Among the latter, no writer in English is more skilled than Jane Austen. Austen is not completely passive; she tells us what to think at crucial moments. But she has an astonishing ability to convince the attentive and humble reader to "cocreate" the story with her.

Since the artist must entrust to another the job of carrying out what he has begun…all literary work is an appeal…. The writer appeals to the reader's freedom to collaborate in the production of the work…. The author's whole art is bent on obliging me to create *what he* discloses.

—JEAN-PAUL SARTRE, *What Is Literature?*

When I discuss *Pride and Prejudice* with my literature students, I ask them to close their books and describe the setting for the first chapter: Where are Mr. and Mrs. Bennet during their conversation? What is Mr. Bennet doing? Invariably, the students have answers: The Bennets are in their sitting room, Mr. Bennet is trying to read a book, and Mrs. Bennet is interrupting his reading with news of eligible bachelors moving to the area. In fact, not a single word of the chapter tells us about the setting; there is nothing about a sitting room, no mention of Mr. Bennet's book, and even Mr. Bennet's reluctance to enter the conversation has to be inferred from his initial silence.

Perhaps my students have been influenced by memories of the BBC television production of Austen's novel, and perhaps they have projected scenes from later in the book back into the first chapter. Perhaps. For my money, this exercise points more emphatically to the genius of Jane Austen. Like a caricaturist, Austen creates two recognizable and believable characters with a few strokes of the pen, and, more miraculously, she creates a setting without ever breathing a word about it. It is as if the setting and character emerge from the white space between the lines, as if Austen has performed an act of *creatio ex nihilo.*

For Austen's magic to work, however, she is dependent on the complicity of the reader, and it is not a given that all readers will be complicit. Someone could respond to my students: "You've got it all wrong. There is no setting described. We cannot know that they are in the sitting room. There is no book in Mr. Bennet's hand. You're reading into the text things that aren't there. Stick with the text!" Or, more simply, "green grass is green grass is green grass."

That sounds perfectly humble, but I think it is not. Humility demands that we submit to the rules of the game that the writer presents, and in Austen's case one of the rules of the game is that the reader is being treated like an adult who does not need everything spelled out for him. What I am urging as "creative reading" is not a domineering reader who masters the text and ignores the author. The text is not up for grabs, for there is much that no competent reading can deny: Mr. and Mrs. Bennet are married, they have several unmarried daughters, some eligible bachelors have just moved to the neighborhood, Mrs. Bennet is hysterical and Mr. Bennet is scornful, and so on. A reader must follow the pathways laid out by the text.

But, especially with an author such as Austen, this act of humility is not the end of the story. Having paid close attention to Austen's subtle clues, the imaginative reader can know far more about the characters and settings than is said. Having learned the way around the Bennet marriage, the reader can draw inferences that are not explicitly stated. Having humbled himself before the author, the reader shall, quite properly, be exalted.

Works Cited

Booth, Wayne. *The Company We Keep: An Ethics of Fiction.* Berkeley: University of California Press, 1988.

Eco, Umberto. *The Limits of Interpretation.* Bloomington: Indiana University Press, 1990.

Eliot, T. S. "Religion and Literature" in *Selected Prose of T. S. Eliot.* London: Faber and Faber, 1975.

"Harry Potter Books Spark Rise in Satanism Among Children," article found at http://www.theonion.com.

Lyotard, Jean-Francois. *The Postmodern Condition: A Report on Knowledge.* Trans. Geoff Bennington and Brian Massumi. Minneapolis: University of Minnesota Press, 1984.

Minnis, A. J. *Medieval Theory of Authorship: Scholastic Literary Attitudes in the Later Middle Ages.* London: Scolar Press, 1984.

O'Connor, Flannery. "Fiction Is a Subject with a History—It Should Be Taught That Way," in *Collected Works.* New York: Library of America, 1988.

Warren, Robert Penn. *Selected Essays.* New York: Alfred A. Knopf, 1966.

Viewpoint: C. S. Lewis

The Few and the Many:
Good Readers and Bad

Already in our schooldays some of us were making our first responses to good literature. Others, and these the majority, were reading, at school, *The Captain*, and, at home, short-lived novels from the circulating library. But it was apparent then that the majority did not "like" their fare in the way we "liked" ours. It is apparent still. The differences leap to the eye.

In the first place, the majority never read anything twice. The sure mark of the unliterary man is that he considers "I've read it already" to be a conclusive argument against reading a work.... Those who read great works, on the other hand, will read the same work ten, twenty or thirty times during the course of their life.

Secondly, the majority, though they are sometimes frequent readers, do not set much store by reading. They turn to it as a last resource. They abandon it with alacrity as soon as any alternative pastime turns up. It is kept for railway journeys, illnesses, odd moments of enforced solitude.... But literary people are always looking for leisure and silence in which to read and do so with their whole attention. When they are denied such attentive and undisturbed reading even for a few days they feel impoverished.

Thirdly, the first reading of some literary work is often, to the literary, an experience so momentous that only experiences of love, religion, or bereavement can furnish a standard of comparison. Their whole consciousness is changed. They have become what they were not before. But there is no sign of anything like this among the other sort of readers. When they have finished the story or the novel, nothing much, or nothing at all, seems to have happened to them.

Finally, and as a natural result of their different behaviour in reading, what they have read is constantly and prominently present to the mind of the few, but not to that of the many. The former mouth over their favourite lines and stanzas in solitude. Scenes and characters from books provide them with a sort of iconography by which they interpret or sum up their own experience. They talk to one another about books, often and at length. The latter seldom think or talk of their reading....

Our youngest [child] once said: "I can divide our town up in two—those who know Mole and Rat and Badger, and those who don't." Those who have broken fairy-bread with Kenneth Grahame have this feeling.
— RUTH SAWYER, *The Way of the Storyteller*

Though I shall concern myself almost entirely with literature, it is worth noting that the same difference of attitude is displayed about the other arts and about natural beauty.... Some buy pictures because the walls "look so bare without them"; and after the pictures have been in the house for a week they become practically invisible to them. But there are a few who feed on a great picture for years.... The approving comments which those who buy pictures make on them are all of one sort: "That's the loveliest face I ever saw"—"Notice the old man's Bible on the table"—"You can see they're all listening"—"What a beautiful old house!"... This attitude, which was once my own, might almost be defined as "using" pictures....

Real appreciation demands the opposite process. We must not let loose our own subjectivity upon the pictures and make them its vehicles. We must begin by laying aside as completely as we can all our own preconceptions, interests, and associations. We must make room for Botticelli's *Mars and Venus,* or Cimabue's *Crucifixion,* by emptying out our own. After the negative effort, the positive. We must use our eyes. We must look, and go on looking, till we have certainly seen exactly what is there. We sit down before the picture in order to have something done to us, not that we may do things with it. The first demand any work of any art makes upon us is surrender. Look. Listen. Receive. Get yourself out of the way....

The distinction can hardly be better expressed than by saying that the many *use* art and the few *receive* it. The many behave in this like a man who talks when he should listen or gives when he should take. I do not mean by this that the right spectator is passive. His also is an imaginative activity; but an obedient one. He seems passive at first because he is making sure of his orders....

Reading teaches receptivity, Keats's negative capability. It teaches us to receive, in stillness and attentiveness, a voice possessed temporarily, on loan.... And as we grow accustomed to receiving a book in stillness and attentiveness, so we can grow to receive the world, also possessed temporarily.

—LYNNE S. SCHWARTZ, "True Confessions of a Reader"

As the first demand of the picture is "Look," the first demand of the music is "Listen." The composer may begin by giving out a "tune" which you could whistle. But the question is not whether you particularly like that tune. Wait. Attend. See what he is going to make of it....

In general the parallel between the popular uses of music and of pictures is close enough. Both consist of "using" rather than "receiving." Both rush hastily forward to do things with the work of art instead of waiting for it to do something to them. As a result, a very great deal that is really visible on the canvas or audible in the performance is ignored; ignored because it cannot be so "used."

—*An Experiment in Criticism*
Cambridge: Cambridge University Press, 1961

Viewpoint: Sven Birkerts

Reading as a State of Being

Reading...is not really a place so much as a state or a condition. How, then, shall we characterize it? What is it that separate reading acts share that lies beyond the local disturbance of the setting, characters, and narrative particulars of any given book? Is there a fundamental and identifiably constant condition that one returns to over and over, one different from all other conditions, from being asleep, from being high, from daydreaming?

I think there is—certainly for me. But years of working in bookstores have convinced me that it's there for others as well, not just a specific inner state, but a need to keep getting back to it. They know it and they seek it. I study people in the aisles of bookstores all the time. I see them standing in place with their necks tilted at a 45-degree angle, looking not for a specific book, but for a book they can trust to do the job. They want plot and character, sure, but what they really want is a vehicle that will bear them off to the reading state.

In this condition, when all is clear and right...I feel a connectedness that cannot be duplicated (unless, possibly, in the act of writing when *that* is going well). For me, the reading state brings on an inside limberness, a sense of being for once in accord with time.... When I am at the finest pitch of reading, I feel as if the whole of my life—past as well as unknown future—were somehow available to me. Not in terms of any high-definition particulars...but as an object of contemplation....

The elsewhere state of being while reading was once—in childhood—a momentous discovery. The first arrival was so stunning, so happy, that I wanted nothing more than a guarantee of return. Escape? Of course. But that does not end the discussion. Here was also the finding of a lens that would give me a different orientation to what was already, though only nascently, the project of my life. Through reading I could reposition the contents of that life along the coordinate axes of urgency and purpose. These two qualities not only determined, or informed, the actions of whatever characters I was reading about, but they exerted pressure on my own life so long as I was bathed in the energies of the book....

Do you love, as we do, a world complete? Oh, we know perfectly well that all our worlds are in process and none is really complete. We are referring not so much to a phenomenon as to a feeling.... Often it is literature that delivers the feeling—as when Sigrid Undset gives us what seems to be the whole of the Middle Ages, felt and understood, or when Jane Austen entrusts to our keeping the entire social world of late eighteenth-century country houses. Sometimes a mystery story, with its precise form and limitations, may fill the bill. At other times, a memoir or even a photograph may yield the experience. But always the immensity of human longing finds, however momentarily, an adequate object, and one tastes...a throbbing satisfaction that can only be called peace.

—SUSAN AND THOMAS CAHILL, "A World Complete"

If anything has changed about my reading over the years, it is that I value the state a book puts me in more than I value the specific contents. Indeed, I often find that a novel, even a well-written and compelling novel, can become a blur to me soon after I've finished it. I recollect perfectly the feeling of reading it, the mood I occupied, but I am less sure about the narrative details. It is almost as if the book were...a ladder, to be climbed and then discarded after it has served its purpose.

I would guess that most adults who are now devoted readers began at a young age, and that they formed a good part of their essential selves through interaction with books. That is, they somehow founded their own inwardness, the more reflective component of their self, in the space that reading opened up. The space is implicit in the act of reading....

The time of reading—the time defined by the author's language resonating in the self—is not the world's time, but the soul's.... The energies which otherwise tend to stream outward through a thousand channels of distraction are marshalled by the cadences of the prose; they are brought into focus by the fact that it is an ulterior, and entirely new, world that the reader has entered.

—"The Woman in the Garden"
Agni 35 (1992): 72-74

REFLECTIONS ON
THE JOY OF READING

When I take up a work that I have read before (the oftener the better) I know what I have to expect. The satisfaction is not lessened by being anticipated.... In reading a book which is an old favorite with me...I not only have the pleasure of imagination and of a critical relish of the work, but the pleasures of memory added to it.... They are landmarks and guides in our journey through life. They are pegs and loops on which we can hang up, or from which we can take down, at pleasure, the wardrobe of a moral imagination, the relics of our best affections, the tokens and records of our happiest hours. They are "for thought and remembrance"! They...transport us, not over half the globe, but (which is better) over half of our lives, at a word's notice.

—William Hazlitt, "On Reading Old Books"

All books are divisible into two classes—the books of the hour, and the books of all time. Mark this distinction: it is not one of the quality only...; it is a distinction of species. There are good books for the hour, and good ones for all time.

—John Ruskin, "Of Kings' Treasuries"

I give hearty and humble thanks for the safe return of this book, which having endured the perils of my friend's bookcase and the bookcases of my friend's friends, now returns to me in reasonably good condition. I give hearty and humble thanks that my friend did not see fit to give this book to his infant for a plaything.... When I loaned this book, I deemed it as lost; I was resigned to the business of the long parting; I never thought to look upon its pages again. But now that my book has come back to me, I rejoice and am exceedingly glad! Bring hither the fatted morocco and let us rebind the volume and set it on the shelf of honor, for this my book was lent and is returned again. Presently, therefore, I may return some of the books I myself have borrowed.

—Christopher Morley, "On the Return of a Book Lent to a Friend"

I have always imagined that Paradise will be a kind of library.

—Jorge Luis Borge

Books are the windows through which the soul looks out. A home without books is like a room without windows.

—Henry Ward Beecher, "Books Are the Windows of the Soul"

Some books are to be tasted, others to be swallowed, and some few to be chewed and digested; that is, some books are to be read only in parts; others to be read, but not curiously; and some few to be read wholly, and with diligence and attention.

—Francis Bacon, "Of Studies"

It is a good rule, after reading a new book, never to allow yourself another new one till you have read an old one in between…. Not, of course, that there is any magic about the past. People were no cleverer then than they are now; they made as many mistakes as we. But not the *same* mistakes.

—C. S. Lewis, "On the Reading of Old Books"

Anybody who remembers a favourite fairy-story will have a strong sense of its original solidity and richness and even definite detail; and will be surprised, if he re-reads it in later life, to find how few and bald were the words which his own imagination made not only vivid but varied.

—G. K. Chesterton, "Fiction as Food"

We read books to find out who we are.... A person who had never listened to nor read a tale or myth or parable or story, would remain ignorant of his own emotional and spiritual heights and depths, would not know quite fully what it is to be human.

—Ursula La Guin, *The Language of the Night*

How beautiful to a genuine lover of reading are the sullied leaves, and worn-out appearance...of an old 'circulating Library' Tom Jones, or Vicar of Wakefield!... How they speak of the thousand thumbs that have turned over their pages with delight!...Who would have them a whit less soiled?

—Charles Lamb, "On Reading Old Books"

We read primarily to discover ourself—above all, perhaps, to discover what St. Augustine refers to as the dark corners of the heart.

—Simon Lesser, *Fiction and the Unconscious*

One constant and immediate effect may be said to characterize our reading experience: an enlarged sense of being more self-critical and at the same time compassionate.

—Epifania San Juan, *James Joyce and the Craft of Fiction*

For myself not only are the old ideas of the contents of the work brought back to my mind in all their vividness but...the place where I sat to read the volume, the day when I got it, the feeling of the air, the fields, the sky—those places, those times, those persons, and those feelings....

—William Hazlitt, "On Reading Old Books"

Books which we have first read in odd places always retain their charm, whether read or neglected.

—Thomas Wentworth Higginson, "Books Unread"

∽

The necessary, though not sufficient condition for a competent reader of poetry remains what it has always been—a keen eye for the obvious.
                    —M. H. Abrams, "Five Types of *Lycidas*"

∽

When we read the poem, or see the play or picture or hear the music, it is as though a light were turned on inside us. We say: "Ah! I recognise that! That is something which I obscurely felt to be going on in and about me, but I didn't know what it was and couldn't express it. But now that the artist has made its image—imaged it forth—for me, I can possess and take hold of it and make it my own, and turn it into a source of knowledge and strength."
                    —Dorothy Sayers, "Towards a Christian Aesthetic"

∽

One of our most ordinary reactions to a good piece of literary art is expressed in the formula, "This is what I always felt and thought, but have never been able to put clearly into words, even for myself."
                    —Aldous Huxley, "Tragedy and the Whole Truth"

∽

Why are we reading, if not in the hope of beauty laid bare, life heightened and its deepest mystery probed? Can the writer isolate and vivify all in experience that most deeply engages our intellects and our hearts? Can the writer renew our hope for literary forms? Why are we reading if not in hope that the writer will magnify and dramatize our days, will illuminate and inspire us with wisdom, courage, and the possibility of meaningfulness, and will press upon our minds the deepest mysteries, so we may feel again their majesty and power?
                    —Annie Dillard, *The Writing Life*

∽

We don't want to feel *less* when we have finished a book; we want to feel that new possibilities of being have been opened to us.

—Madeleine L'Engle, *Walking on Water*

~

Since no one will have sufficient time for all the greatest poets, I suggest the preferential choice of one. He need not exclude the rest, but one should have right of way over the rest to your attention and study. And this is a choice that you must make for yourself. Whatever else you read, adopt one of the greatest poets as your own for life, one with whom habitual companionship and deepening acquaintance become a more and more abundant source of refreshment and strength, a confirmation of spiritual truth, an elevation to a more comprehensive view of life…. Every recourse to him brings forth new thought, new feeling, new appreciation, new aspects of things familiar.

—Charles G. Osgood, "Your Poet," in *Poetry as a Means of Grace*

~

The good reader is one who has imagination, memory, a dictionary, and some artistic sense…. Since the master artist used his imagination in creating his book, it is natural and fair that the consumer of a book should use his imagination too.

—Vladimir Nabokov, "Good Readers and Good Writers"

~

Reading is a creative art…. The meaning received is created by the imagination from the symbols, and that imagination must first be educated—as the artist himself was educated—in the use and meaning of a symbolic system. The reader may believe that he is completely receptive and uncritical, he may and should attempt to expose himself to an experience without prejudice, but in fact he is performing a highly active and complex creative act. The reason he does not notice it is because most of it takes place in the subconscious.

—Joyce Cary, *Art and Reality*

It should not be forgotten that at one time or another we are both spectators and actors in the fiction which engages us. Most of the time we are both simultaneously, but there are wide shifts in the extent to which are involved and at various points...we are merely spectators.... It is the knowledge that the world of fiction is a world of make-believe which emboldens us to plunge into it as participants.

—Simon Lesser, *Fiction and the Unconscious*

The writer expresses what he knows by affecting the reader; the reader knows what is expressed by being receptive to effects. The medium of this process is language.

—David Lodge, *Language of Fiction*

Part Six

State of the Art: Success and Failure in Current Christian Fiction and Poetry

We are in the middle of a resurgence of literary activity among evangelical Christians. Indeed, the appetite for "Christian fiction" seems nearly insatiable, and the number of aspiring Christian poets is larger than ever.

In this ferment of activity, the pressing need is to know what criteria exist to differentiate between good and bad contemporary Christian fiction and poetry. The quest for reliable norms leads, in turn, to a consideration of how the classics (Christian and non-Christian) from the past relate to the current scene.

Through discussion and illustration, this unit will put forth norms by which to make enlightened sense of contemporary Christian fiction and poetry.

Christian Fiction:
Piety Is Not Enough

Richard Terrell

WHY STORIES?

Author Bob Briner, in his book *Roaring Lambs,* lamented the lack of hard-nosed critique of "contemporary Christian" fiction, suggesting that the Christian community was a bit easy on its own novelists (124). The acclaim accorded to various mediocre and poorly written novels of recent years, as well as the publication of a number of Christian "celebrity" novels, tends to support Briner's thesis. I will attempt to provide some of what he called for in the context of this essay. However, let us first face some preliminary questions. Given a Christian worldview, what is the significance of fiction as an art form? Should there be a specifically Christian fiction, and if so, why? What principles would guide it as unique and distinct from any other fiction? We may begin to examine these questions through a general consideration of the human condition.

Human beings enjoy stories, and storytelling is a universal human phenomenon, suggesting that storytelling is part of human nature itself. The encounter with story is significant to the extent that the mind experiences meaning. Whether they come to us through writing or film or theatrical production, stories will engage our interest and affirmation or bore and annoy us inasmuch as we perceive meaning or senselessness in the encounter.

RICHARD TERRELL *is Professor of Fine Arts and Humanities at Doane College in Crete, Nebraska. His involvement in the arts includes painting, theater performance, and church music. He is the author of* Resurrecting the Third Reich, *a Christian perspective on the Holocaust. He has authored articles and reviews for* Christianity and the Arts *and has been a longtime observer of the state of evangelical culture.*

The worldview of the Bible goes far in explaining the unique power of story-telling in human life. The Bible reveals that the universe in which we live is intelligible, that it has an origin, a purposeful development, and a final meaning and resolution. Humans, created in the image of God, act in ways that recapitulate on the level of space-time existence the character of the overall "big picture." Indeed, the biblical presentation of God and man is itself a narrative, a big story told through many smaller stories that comprise the whole. If God is a story-teller, then it simply makes sense that His creatures, made in the divine image, would act in similar fashion as a matter of course, as a natural and vital activity in the expression of creaturely life. Like our Creator, we create and tell stories. In writing and telling stories, we imitate our Creator and implicitly celebrate our origins.

What really happens is that the story-maker proves a successful "sub-creator." He makes a Secondary World which your mind can enter.
—J. R. R. TOLKIEN, "On Fairy-Tales"

The human creation of stories and our participation in them are activities of profound theological significance in which even unbelieving humanity shares in the nature of God's reality. Because this is so, storytelling has special significance in the life of people who acknowledge the truth of the Bible and its worldview. Madeleine L'Engle reflects: "I'm particularly grateful that I was allowed to read my Bible as I read my other books, to read it as story, that story which is a revelation of truth. People are sometimes kept from reading the Bible itself by what they are taught about it, and I'm grateful that I was able to read the Book with the same wonder and joy with which I read *The Ice Princess* or *The Tempest*" (60).

THE SPIRITUAL SIGNIFICANCE OF LITERATURE

Through fiction and literature, human beings energize the power inherent in the divine image to create new worlds or re-create the "real" world that we already know. Indeed, the way we interact with our own created stories recapitulates the temporal nature of the primary reality in which we live, for just as we exist in time we can only know a story in and through the expenditure of time. The art form of story, like music, comes alive in time, and as such it is a direct extension of our God-created reality itself. Story can build expectation, invite curiosity, warn, anticipate, surprise, disappoint, interrupt, and bring to resolution in ways that accord with the very physical and psychological mode of orientation that we have to the "real" reality we live in day by day. The unique power of fiction is rooted in the nature of the created order itself.

Russell Kirk, in *Enemies of the Permanent Things*, reflects on the significance of literature for human life. Literature is a key element in the development of humanity's moral imagination, and when that "imagination is enriched, a people find themselves capable of great things" (16). When it is impoverished, "they cannot act effectively even for their own survival, no matter how immense their material resources" (16). Literature, writes Kirk, "is meant to rouse and fortify the living, to renew the contract of eternal society" (72).

Literature…extends the range of vision, intellectual, moral, spiritual; it expands the compass of our sympathy; it sharpens our discernment; it corrects our appraisal of all things…. Literature, especially poetry, is probably our most powerful agent for rousing, sensitizing, and energizing our sense of beauty in all things.

—CHARLES G. OSGOOD, *Poetry as a Means of Grace*

In Kirk's analysis, literature does this through its attachment to "normative knowledge," or the knowledge of enduring standards which are made known to humanity through divine revelation and the insights of outstanding minds. Literary art, and all other art, is the "servant of enduring standards." Such service gives birth, now and again, to the "perceptions of genius" that see profoundly into the human condition and contribute to a heritage in which "[g]reat works of literature join us in an intellectual community" (33). Literature makes possible reflective thought, and the existence and use of literary media are vital to individual and social destiny. Indeed, the choices we make are potentially of great consequence. It is not merely coincidental, according to Kirk, that the literature of nihilism, pornography, and sensationalism arose in the wake of our civilization's post-Enlightenment disengagement from the "religious understanding of life." (41) Yet, the human need for story remains, in any case, and "if a small boy does not read *Treasure Island,* the odds are that he will read *Mad Ghoul Comics*" (45).

We will all read something—substantial or sensational, beautiful or debased, profound or trivial, hopeful or despairing, true or false—and in doing so will be shaped by it. Kirk's discussion helps us to see how the telling of story can be seen and should be seen as a Christian vocation and calling of the first order through which the artist may probe the great length, breadth, and depth of the human condition from the perspective of Christian understanding and biblical truth. What does such a project look like?

CHRISTIAN LITERATURE

The Bible's own narrative structure provides the very model for literary art of the highest order. Despite the conclusions of extreme and skeptical "higher" critics, the biblical narrative is coherent while maintaining a rich variety within that coherence. Its internal narratives express, through symbol and typology, the overall meaning of the whole. It touches upon every aspect of the human condition in all its glory and depravity. It encompasses the normal activities of daily life and the most fantastic visionary experiences. It is hopeful and tragic. Indeed, it is, in the words of Northrop Frye (affirming the judgment of William Blake), the "great code of art" (xvi).

Christian art is rooted in eternity, and Christian artists recognize that there is, in both the macrocosm and microcosm of nature and human affairs, an eternal purpose and meaning to things. This premise will inevitably inform our whole approach to artistic and literary expression. For the Christian writer and artist, universality is a possibility, and such matters as heritage and craft are fundamental concerns. Heritage is the linkage we have to an "artistic witness" antecedent to our own efforts, and craft informs us in regard to universality and durability. In today's atmosphere of "multicultural" parochialism, declining craftsmanship in the arts, and the dictates of "market forces," all artists and writers, no less those of Christian conviction and faith, are vulnerable to these eroding forces. Indeed, many of the shortcomings of contemporary Christian fiction works parallel those that are found in the broader cultural arena.

I will pursue this theme by posing a series of specific conceptual antitheses, beginning with a deeper exploration of the one implied above—the contrast of universality to parochialism. Here, the Christian vision of humanity is fundamental. Christian faith recognizes a unity to the human condition that transcends race, ethnic identities, or even ideological differences, and therefore embraces the possibility of writing stories that express universal experiences. The Christian writer, then, is not necessarily writing for specifically Christian readers (although he/she may choose to do so). In writing a human story, the writer tacitly admits the truth of the biblical vision of the singular, created humanity that we all share. Notable in this connection is the popularity of a writer like John Grisham, who explores themes of human depravity, redemption, and the hope of justice amidst the "boastful pride of life." Although a Christian may perceive Grisham's Southern Baptist orientation in his novels, his stories have a broader audience and appeal at a generally human level.

The efforts of the best poets and esthetic writers have been directed toward the universally human.

—Wolfgang Goethe, "World Literature"

The essential things in men are the things they hold in common, not the things they hold separately.

—G. K. Chesterton, "The Ethics of Elfland"

Against universality we may pose parochialism. Parochialism is a spirit that demands that we create only for the safely defined boundaries of our ethnic, ideological, or spiritual community. This is the spirit that animates certain extreme forms of "multiculturalism" today. Although such works may contribute to a group sense of cultural, racial, or religious esteem, they implicitly deny the biblical truth of humanity's universal relatedness to God's purpose and creation, and are likely to result in little of consequence beyond crass propaganda or cultural feel-goodism. Parochialism has been a problem in the evangelical, Christian Booksellers' Association (CBA) universe of fiction, contributing to a perception among many serious, committed Christian literary artists and their readers that the phrase "Christian fiction" identifies something narrow and artificial.

We may also contrast authenticity and contrivance. Here, we are dealing not only with content issues, but formal ones as well. Authenticity, however, is a very difficult concept to define. I would argue that it is best considered in relation to honesty, integration, and necessity. Conversely, contrivance identifies the lack of these qualities. Consider, for example, the use of profane speech in the scripts of two films—*Driving Miss Daisy* and *La Bamba.*

Driving Miss Daisy contains only a single episode of profane or blasphemous speech, and it occurs approximately halfway through the movie. In this sense, the film is "clean." *La Bamba,* on the other hand, is filled with profanity. In my judgment, however, *La Bamba* is the artistically superior work, judged from the standpoint of a Christian worldview. The single blasphemy in *Driving Miss Daisy* is out of harmony with the character who speaks it and also the overall script of the film itself. Indeed, the line seems thrown in for no other reason than to have an obligatory profanity for purposes of assigning a PG rating. It is not *honest.* In *La Bamba,* the character of Ritchie Valens's brother swears and curses throughout, but he does so because he is that type of character. The tragic story told in this movie is, in fact, a powerful "family values" drama.

Christian fiction may be particularly susceptible to the kind of flaw that distorts the integrity of *Driving Miss Daisy.* Consider a work of popular Christian fiction like Clint Kelly's *The Aryan,* vigorously promoted in Christian bookstores in the early '90s. The novel concerns the hero's attempt to undermine a latter-day aspirant to world leadership in the mold of Adolf Hitler. He is aided in his task by the new antichrist's mother. In a climactic scene, where the machinations of the villain are foiled and his plans are crashing around him, we find him whining to his mother about how he was never hugged by his father. This implausible dialogue reads as an artificial attempt to import some "family values" content into the story. But it simply seems untrue, false, and merely silly.

Other antitheses we may consider are those between truth and niceness and craft and sensation. A writer may approach a subject or narrative with language that is appropriate to the task or with language that is hostage to artificial criteria of value. Much of what we see in contemporary Christian popular fiction fails, in my estimation, to pass this test. The desire to avoid offending sensibilities in regard to dialogue and human situations often results in plastic, smoothed-over characters, and a holding back from the kind of writing that may evoke true inspiration or authentic villainy. Indeed, such fiction seems guided by an overriding necessity of avoidance, and creates a readership that reasons that so long as certain matters of speech and description are avoided, a novel is "good." Attempts to write honestly about the human condition, even in very mild ways, may cause an author trouble. In visiting a "family" Christian bookstore, for example, I purchased Stephen Lawhead's novel entitled *The Iron Lance.* The book carried a warning sticker, alerting the customer that some parts of the book might be "offensive" to some readers. Upon completing the book, I couldn't identify anything in it that could have offended any intelligent reader, except, perhaps, relatively mild description of the violence of medieval crusaders in Jerusalem. But when I reflect on the warning sticker attached to Lawhead's book, it becomes clear to me why such a Christian classic as Dostoevsky's *Crime and Punishment*, with its vivid description of an axe-murder, might never be sold in such a store.

All life, high and low, sordid and noble, vile and pure, is the province of art. Surely if the Bible is to be our standard we must admit that nothing lay outside the province of the inspired writers.... A Christian writer...cannot be a significant writer if his vision does not include the whole of human life, the depths of depravity as well as the heights of aspiration.

—JAMES WESLEY INGLES, "The Christian Novel and the Evangelical Dilemma"

Here we see how market considerations and the bookseller industry begin to dictate literary values and the process of writing itself. But, if everything is to be so nice, at what point does truth suffer? This problem has infected popular Christian fiction for many years, and although progress has been made, a comparative reading of "Christian" and "secular" novels of similar theme may be instructive. Compare, for example, two novels of World War II setting, Bodie Thoene's *Twilight of Courage* and Greg Iles's *The Black Cross*, and ask yourself which novel creates a genuine atmosphere of the moral, physical, intellectual, and spiritual dimensions and tensions of that great conflict. Thoene is a well-known evangelical writer, and her book was an award-winning novel in evangelical circles, whereas Iles is a "secular" writer. It is Iles's book, however, that is likely to arouse the reader's sense of indignation and horror as to what the Nazis were up to and grip him/her with vivid character portrayals. *Twilight of Courage* is an ultimately "nice" book of lightweight human interaction and scenarios, suitable for people whose cultural perspectives are formed almost exclusively by the environments of Christian bookstores.

Indeed, the most extreme instances of contrivance, parochialism, and niceness may be seen in Christian stories that feature conversion experiences. There is often little discernible difference between a character before and after conversion. The criterion of "cleanliness" demands that really bad aspects of character not be portrayed, although they may be mentioned in summary. So, there is likely to be little contrast communicated. This failing is seen in extreme form in the script for the evangelical film *Born Again,* based on Charles Colson's autobiographical account of his Watergate experiences. In the film, Colson is portrayed more or less as a basically good fellow who finds Christ. But, there is no convincing sense of the character's radical transformation. The same might be said for a neo-Nazi youth portrayed by Clint Kelly in *The Ayran.* In contrast, the convert in John Grisham's *The Testament* has strong credibility because the author has been frank about his character prior to his conversion to Christ.

Or consider the two characters Buck and Chloe in the Tim LaHaye/Jerry Jenkins Left Behind series that dominated not only evangelical but secular markets as well in the later '90s and early 2000s. Both characters have lived worldly lives prior to the Rapture, but subsequently receive Christ, fall in love, and get married. It turns out, however, that despite their worldly, God-rejecting lives prior to conversion, neither of them had ever had sexual relations with anyone, so they are virgins together as they marry. That is very "nice," and certainly it is a touch that protects the moral sensibilities of the authors' audience. But one may question its credibility, especially in the context of the rampant moral decay that characterizes the last days according to the dispensational eschatology that underlies the series' story line, as well as the characters' own alleged worldly behavior.

"Conversion stories" are often structured so as to provide for the presentation of sermonic discourses. This is very difficult ground, and can only be carried off successfully by master artists. George MacDonald did it very well in his novel *Thomas Wingfold, Curate* (republished by Bethany Press as *The Curate's Awakening* in 1985). Less masterful examples are such novels as Dave Hunt's *The Archon Conspiracy,* the contrived scripts for the popular evangelical *Thief in the Night* film series, or many of the products of World Wide Films, in which the stories always end up at a Billy Graham rally.

A CHALLENGING QUESTION

In developing this critique, I can hear an imaginary voice asking me a question. "Okay, you see stuff in contemporary Christian expression that you don't like. So then, what is your idea of a good book?"

A novel that I like very much is a work of popular fiction written by Ken Follett—*Pillars of the Earth,* a very stimulating, informative, and inspiring "secular market" book. I am indebted to my Christian friend John who discovered it and brought it to my attention. Follett's novel is set in the Middle Ages, and concerns the desire of a stonemason to build a great cathedral. The story reveals family rivalries and a church that faces its own tensions between the call of the gospel and the call of worldly power. The author, through characterization, dialogue, and vivid prose description, evokes a powerful sense of the brutish and dangerous life of the twelfth century. What is especially intriguing about Follett's story, however, is how the reader's sense of justice, and the desire to see it carried out, energizes the reading process. This is accomplished by the presentation of a vile and disgusting character whose fictional portrait reveals the essence of villainy—radical selfishness, crude speech and behavior, raging lust, and general disrespect for everything and everybody opposed to his own purposes. This portrait is played out amidst the themes of hope, beauty, and the quest for God that is seen in other primary characters who express a vision of courage and high purpose. The major contrast between good and evil is reflected in the minor characters as well, and the conflicts that animate their existence carry the reader forward toward a satisfying consolation and resolution.

Despite the explosion of interest in fiction among American evangelicals since 1987 (the year of publication of Frank Peretti's *This Present Darkness*), the most notable achievements in popular fiction and literature by Christian authors are still those written by people outside or transcendent of the evangelical CBA universe, authors like Frederick Buechner, Ron Hansen, Susan Howatch, Walter Wangerin, and Walker Percy among them, along with earlier writers like C. S. Lewis, Charles Williams, J. R. R. Tolkein, Lloyd C. Douglas, Henryk Sienkiewicz, and Taylor Caldwell. Indeed, with the exceptions of Lewis and Wangerin, most of these authors are likely to be among the missing in Christian bookstores, even though their major works may be considered classics of popular culture (for example, Douglas' *The Robe*, Sienkiewicz's *Quo Vadis*, or Caldwell's *Great Lion of God*). Their significance is that their works express a Christian worldview without becoming parochial, merely fit for a Christian readership. In Howatch's Church of England novels, for example, theological ideas are woven into stories of Anglican clergy in ways that, notwithstanding the church setting, have broad appeal as human dramas. Ron Hansen's *Mariette in Ecstasy* is a startlingly original novel in subject as well as in structure, and probes the mysterious relationship between sexual and spiritual experience and issues of spiritual discernment in a story that recalls the imagery of the biblical Song of

Songs or Lorenzo Bernini's sculpture of *The Ecstasy of St. Teresa*. Works like Howatch's and Hansen's, however, could not be written by authors tied to the CBA's universe of predictable content purity.

Christian writing may be found in some surprising places, sometimes in books that are not, on the surface anyway, obviously Christian in outlook. Consider, for example, Robert Girardi's *Vaporetto 13* (Delacorte Press, 1997). The novel is a haunting, macabre, and erotic story that concerns an American currency trader who, during a stay in Venice, encounters a mysterious woman named Caterina. Jack, the main character, is a lapsed Catholic whose view of life assumes the full panoply of modern secularist assumptions—"that God does not exist, that the universe in a meaningless, random place, that when people are dead, they stay dead" (191). He acts consistently with this worldview, and establishes a sexual relationship with Caterina, who introduces Jack to aspects of Venetian history through her own family descent and a saintly Venetian of past centuries named Paulo Sarpi.

Eventually Jack realizes that there is something very strange about Caterina and some of her friends. While following her through the mysterious avenues of nighttime Venice, he sees Caterina and her companions get onto a water bus (a *vaporetto*), number 13. But, there is no known vehicle with that number. Jack gets a friend to take him to the island destination of Vaporetto 13, and discovers to his horror that it is nothing but an old *ossario,* a dumping area for the bones of people previously buried on San Michele island but which have been cleared to make room for more recent burials.

Jack realizes that he has been in a relationship with the occasionally reanimated corpse of a seventeenth century aristocratic woman who exists among damned and wandering souls. The novel's conclusion, however, is a powerful affirmation of God's redemptive grace and the reality of moral absolutes. Jack, returning to Maine but haunted by his experience, seeks out a priest—Father McBride—in the hopes of understanding his experience. Is it really possible that such a thing could have happened? The priest responds:

> As good Christians, we must believe that the Lord in His ultimate wisdom can do many things that we might find incredible, and that might seem contrary to the laws of nature…. Contemplate these mysteries, if you will, Mr. Squire. But let me hasten to add, that if you are contemplating them in hopes of

reaching a rational understanding, then you are committing a very grave error indeed.... From here on out, I advise you to concern yourself with more earthly matters. (195)

The priest then urges Jack to take up parish responsibilities of confession and attendance at Mass, "because if, as you say, you pursued sexual relations with that Venetian woman outside the sanctity of marriage, it's still adultery plain and simple, even if she was dead when you did it. And adultery is a mortal sin. Do you understand?" (196).

One is left with the impression that Jack and Father McBride are going to enjoy not only a clergy-to-parishioner relationship and its spiritual authority, but a friendship as well. For the reader, Jack's promising move toward redemption and faith has power precisely because the author has genuinely exposed Jack's lost state. The sexual relationship with Caterina is itself a key symbol of his identity with death itself, but we finally see him moving from death to life. Girardi is a Catholic writer who admires the tradition of literary fiction evidenced in the work of Evelyn Waugh, Graham Greene, and Walker Percy. In *Vaporetto 13*, he crafts a story that blends romance, mystery, and horror that, while eschewing didacticism, surprises the reader through a confrontation with the moral vision that lies at the heart of the Christian worldview.

The Danger of Pious Evasion

Prudish evasiveness toward the body and the sexuality of human beings has long been a staple in Christian literature of the more narrowly defined genre. In 1981, James Wesley Ingles warned that explicitly Christian novelists seemed "almost as embarrassed in dealing with sex as is the non-Christian novelist in dealing with prayer" (342). But why, Ingles asked, should this area of life be turned over completely to non-Christian writers? "We cannot combat the pagan view of sex in our time by ignoring its significance in human experience" (342).

A reading of some leading evangelical fiction of the later '90s would suggest that not much has changed. In the immensely popular Left Behind series, when the character Buck meets the young heroine, Chloe, he is said to be powerfully impressed with her firm handshake! This is the only quality emphasized in relation to what Buck "likes in a woman" (*Left Behind* 364-365). In a later episode, after they are married, we find Buck returning from a harrowing escape from

Israel, having rescued a Bible-believing Israeli scholar. Surviving great danger, he returns to his wife. The narrative describing their reunion has all the emotional force of a mild concern over a late return from the grocery store. Eventually we find the young, healthy married couple lying in bed, "unable to sleep." They discuss (briefly) the moral question of conceiving a child during the tribulation, thereby hinting at the sexual act, but Chloe is "tired" and Buck is "on a different time zone." He decides to go to the church to check out the underground shelter that has been built there. Plaintively, Chloe pleads with him. "Oh, Buck! I've missed you. Can't you at least stay with me until *I* fall asleep?" (*Nicolae* 282).

This kind of narrative seems to be guided by avoidance, indeed a gnostic, heretical fear of physical reality and normal human desire. Another example may be found in the popular evangelical movie *China Cry*, sold in Christian bookstores as an "inspirational masterpiece." The scriptwriter seems embarrassed by the theme of young love, even though it is an important part of the story. Beyond its qualities of stilted acting, the film features a love scene that is simply dishonest to its subject. In the film, the young Chinese hero and heroine fall in love and get married. We see them on their wedding night in a scene that shows much movement under the bed covers. Then the covers are thrown back and we see the joyous newlyweds—in pajamas. Scenarios like this, whether they turn up in novels or film scripts, suggest a general rule that writers need to consider: If you can't deal with something honestly and with authentic humanity, then perhaps the story is better without it.

Can this sort of thing be what we mean by Christian art? If so, it is no wonder that many talented and creative artists are careful to avoid the "Christian" label for their work. Artistically corrupt novels, paintings, or theatrical productions can, of course, achieve great levels of popularity while ostensibly upholding standards of purity. But if the Christian world expects artists to work on their craft from the framework of a biblical worldview, can artistic corruption, even in the service of "purity," ever invite our accolades? Much more instructive to aspiring writers than the evangelical avoidance strategy is the earthy narrative of Frederick Buechner's *Godric,* where we find this account of an old man continuing to struggle with the loss both of physical strength and his sexual being:

How I rage at times to smite with these same fists I scarce can clench! How I long, when woods are green, to lark and leap on shanks grown dry as sticks! Let a maid

but pass my way with sport in her eye and her braid a-swinging, and I burn for her
although my wick's long since burnt out and in my heart's eye see her as the elders
saw Susanna at her bath—her belly pale and soft as whey, her pippins, her slender
limbs and thistledown. So ever and again young Godric's dreams well up to flood
old Godric's prayers, or prayers and dreams reach God in such a snarl he has to
comb the tangle out, and who knows which he counts more dear. (40)

THE CHRISTIAN WRITER'S OPPORTUNITY

If the Bible is the Christian writer's artistic model, then clearly the subject matter
of literature is virtually unlimited. History, the supernatural, ordinary human
life, the beautiful, the grotesque, redemption and damnation, the moral, the
immoral, the earthly and the cosmic, the triumphant and the tragic—all suggest
material infinitely pregnant with possibility to pursue the truths of God and the
human condition. Christian art expresses the nature of God's creation and is
informed by knowledge of God's mystery of creation, incarnation, and redemption. Keeping this mystery in mind leads inevitably to certain considerations of
artistic process itself, for, aside from subject matter concerns, the very approach
to creative labor in art can reflect our universal understandings and our theology,
whatever subjects may be in view. Indeed, the very character of God's created
order suggests some primary considerations of a Christian literary style.

Let us consider three fundamental principles in this regard. First, we recognize and acknowledge the subtle elements of reality. Secondly, we recognize that
not all things in the order of creation are religious. Third, we recognize a substantial lavishness in God's design.

When you write fiction you are speaking with *character and action, not*
about *character and action.*

> —FLANNERY O'CONNOR, "The Nature and Aim of Fiction"

The first principle brings into consideration a failing that has dogged evangelical artistic endeavors for many years, and that is what I choose to call the
"reign of the explicit." Enigma, nuance, evocation—qualities that engage a
reader's interest and invite an activity of mind—are often missing in the popular
arts of the evangelical world. This explicit approach does harm, in my assessment, to Frank Peretti's presentation of the angels and demons in his famous

"darkness" novels, and renders them boring and cartoonish rather than profound and mysterious presences. Yet, consider the nature of God's creation itself.
According to the Bible, what holds it all together and constitutes its meaning is
not anything that is explicit or obvious. Rather, it is the "word of His power." It
is God's will itself, not some kind of outward reality that a person can easily
identify. Likewise the spiritual warfare is in the unseen realm of the "principali-
ties and powers." The meaning of things in God's creation is underlying rather
than on the surface, a reality that invites reflection, meditation, searching,
curiosity. If, as the visual artist Leonard Baskin once observed, the making of
works of art is a human semblance to divinity, then the very way we go about
the process of making them can, and should, renew us re-creationally, according
to the nature of God's creative order itself. Walter Wangerin addressed this concern in an interview with W. Dale Brown:

> Only a small group of readers read at a level of subtlety, recognizing the literary
> qualities of the books they read.... We have ceased to acknowledge the com-
> plexity of literature. As a consequence, literature has lost its place.... We sell by
> category and classification, and because sales have taken over the literature
> industry, those who genuinely wish to write literature are embarrassed by it.
> I'm embarrassed for my publishers when I say I'm writing art because it makes
> them squirm.... Artistically, I do my best to tell the truth.... Much of this fic-
> tion produced these days is sedative. It benumbs us and reinforces stereotypes,
> doesn't move us to new levels. (50)

The most egregious validations of Wangerin's perspective may be seen in
books, movies, and visual arts that preach at the reader through doctrinal exposition. This is not, we must admit, a failing that is unique to evangelical arts, as
any reader of Ayn Rand's *Atlas Shrugged* or James Redfield's *The Celestine Prophecy*
will clearly see. Nevertheless, it is a profound temptation for writers and artists
who see their art as a means of reaching the lost or of edifying their spiritual
community. Yet, Russell Kirk's admonition is good advice to young, aspiring
writers of any worldview, Christian or otherwise: "The better the artist, one
almost may say, the more subtle the preacher. Inventive persuasion, not blunt
exhortation, commonly is the method of the literary champion of norms" (42).

The second principle stated above—not all things in creation are religious—invites the Christian writer to shelve anxiety about subject matter.

What, after all, is a Christian story? One set in biblical times? One that features conversion episodes and spiritual heroism? One that sedates the reader through insulation from troublesome or disturbing subjects, or that presumes its protective role vis-a-vis its audience by the smoothed-over presentation of those troublesome or disturbing subjects? Indeed, the whole of human life invites literary interpretation, from the grandest stage to the most intimate struggle, and even an outwardly secular story can establish and communicate biblical truths. One thinks, for example, of a novel like Boris Pasternak's *Dr. Zhivago*, a book that was dangerous to the regime of the Soviets for no other reason than it presented a vision of personal life apart from the false and worldly ideology of the State. Or consider Ron Hansen's *Atticus*. I doubt if anybody would think of this novel as an outwardly religious book. Yet, its story is supported throughout with the author's Christian understanding and sensibility, and its heart is family, redemption, reconciliation.

The sorry religious novel comes about when the writer supposes that because of his belief, he is somehow dispensed from the obligation to penetrate concrete reality. He will think that the eyes of the Church or of the Bible or of his particular theology have already done the seeing for him, and that his business is to rearrange this essential vision into satisfying patterns, getting himself as little dirty in the process as possible.... But the real novelist, the one with an instinct for what he is about, knows that he cannot approach the infinite directly, that he must penetrate the natural human world as it is.
—Flannery O'Connor, "Novelist and Believer"

EVOCATIVE LANGUAGE

Hansen's writing demonstrates a quality of language that exemplifies the third principle that I earlier labeled the "substantial lavishness of God's design." What, however, does this mean, and how does it relate to art?

By "substantial lavishness" I mean to identify a quality of reality whereby the system and meaning of things is supported in ways that seem to move beyond mere necessity or requirement. Whereas it is true that the colors, textures, odors, and sounds of our world can always be related to the survival function of living things, human beings who bear the *imago Dei* experience these things as beautiful or grotesque apart from utilitarian considerations. They are the occasions of aesthetic apprehension. Applying this principle to the arts, we note that the bare bones of a story's activity can be told through the driest forms of description. A statement like "Ellen was beautiful to look at," while instructive to the reader, leaves Ellen a remote abstraction, lacking humanity. There is no substance to the statement that invites us to be interested in Ellen. I have read evangelical novels, some of them by prominent authors, that proceed to present characters and situations in a similarly utilitarian manner. Yes, there is dialogue and description of events that move the story forward. What is often missing, however, is language that truly sets a mood, effectively evokes the ambience of the action, or suggests the actual substance of a character. In the LaHaye/Jenkins series, a female character who is the object of sexual temptation is simply described as "flat out gorgeous," and the charismatic Antichrist is noted to look like a "young Robert Redford." These bare, dry notations are essentially utilitarian statements that require little, if anything, from a reader and caused one reviewer of the series to note its "petrified" prose.

Consider, by way of contrast, the powerful description of a nun in Ron Hansen's *Mariette In Ecstasy:*

> Mother Saint-Raphael tugs her plain white nightgown up over her head. She is hugely overweight but her legs are slight as a goat's. Tightly sashed around her stomach just below the great green-veined bowls of her breasts are cuttings from the French garden's rosebushes, the dark thorns sticking into skin that is scarlet with infection. She gets into a gray habit, tying it with a sudden jerk. She winces and shuts her eyes. (5-6)

It is a brief passage, but it reveals much, not only about this particular character but also the whole context of convent life, especially when read in the overall narrative that creates the opening scenes of Hansen's novel. There is the tragic fact of aging, the irony of humble and worn flesh doggedly pursuing a spiritual vocation, the willingness to live with and accept pain, the burden and price of that pursuit. But there is more. Hansen clearly is a lover of words, and he gives us words that ring in their own right according to their own sounds and rhythmic structure. This makes this passage a literary embodiment of that larger reality of God's creation that manifests its own substantial lavishness. Hansen's art expresses reality, but it is not art-for-art's-sake either. Rather, his art expresses the deep humanity of his subject, playing the role of servant both to his story and to his reader.

I believe poets are…makers, craftsmen: it is given to the seer to see, but it is his responsibility to communicate what he sees, that they who cannot see may see, since we are "members one of another."
        —DENISE LEVERTOV, *The Poet in the World*

Attitude toward language itself distinguishes "literary fiction" and "literature" from mere "fiction." Fiction tells a story effectively while entertaining and engaging the imagination in temporary escape into the author's secondary world. Literature, on the other hand, is an evaluative concept assigned to works that invite reflection and a return path. There is something, a presence in the words, that calls one back for a closer look, that haunts or gathers us in beyond a mere temporary encounter. Our literary and fictional heritage abounds with such writing, which is found even in notable popular novels. Examples may be found in the opening scenarios of Chaim Potok's *The Promise*, Bram Stoker's description of vampiresses contemplating the possession of Jonathan Harker in *Dracula*, in Ayn Rand's vivid word-painting of the passing earth observed from a speeding train engine *(Atlas Shrugged)*, in Ron Hansen's presentation of a man's observance of a sundog in *Atticus*, or in Charles Williams' transportive narrative of the evil magician Simon in the third chapter of *All Hallows Eve*.

But this type of writing has been on a declining slope for many years, which suggests parallels between the general erosion of educational standards and an atrophying general literary culture. It is sobering to realize that the major fictional bestsellers of recent years have been the Harry Potter and Left Behind series, books of astonishing commercial success but virtually empty of literary value. More and more readers, Christians among them, desire things to come easy, and to the extent that they constitute the market, authors and publishers must take it all into account. The willingness to engage in intellectual work in regard to the act of reading is becoming a rare phenomenon. Yet readers who opt for the easily digested story carried by easily understood and identified characters, minus the poetics of descriptive, mood-enhancing language, miss out on much that is unique to the experience of reading itself. And authors who are under a requirement to meet the needs of those market realities may find their own creative labors in bondage.

When you can state the theme of a story, when you can separate it from the story itself, then you can be sure the story is not a very good one. The meaning of a story has to be embodied in it, has to be made concrete in it.... A story that is any good can't be reduced, it can only be expanded. A story is good when you continue to see more and more in it, and when it continues to escape you.

—FLANNERY O'CONNOR, "Writing Short Stories"

It would seem appropriate that Christian fiction especially should manifest a love of words and the power they have to evoke a sense of place and arouse the full range of emotions from sublime terror to radiant hope. For in the final analysis, the Christian literary artist is guided by the authority of one who is in essence the eternal Word. I am not advocating words-for-words'-sake, which is likely to accomplish nothing beyond mere affectation and a tiresome, self-conscious striving for literary effect. But I do mean to say that the writer can appeal, through words, to the imagination in all its sensuous, emotional, and moral capacities, seeking profundity and not mere sentimentality. But what is the difference?

SENTIMENT AND SENTIMENTALITY

Answering this question is to encounter the old saw about finding it impossible to define something but knowing it when you see it. Oscar Wilde once defined sentimentalism as the desire to enjoy a feeling without intending to pay for it. This is in contrast to true sentiment, which leads a reader or viewer to contemplate something deeper and more serious. Let us approach this contrast through a comparison of two passages from fictional works. In both passages we encounter a man reflecting upon the loss of his wife. One passage describes; the other, while shorter on description, evokes and invites. First, consider this passage from the LaHaye/Jenkins book *Left Behind*. The character, Rayford Steele, realizes that his wife has been carried away in the disappearances of the Rapture of the Church:

His throat tight, his eyes full, he noticed her wedding ring near the pillow, where she always supported her cheek with her hand. It was too much to bear, and he broke down. He gathered the ring into his palm and sat on the edge of the bed, his body racked with fatigue and grief. He put the ring in his jacket pocket and noticed the package she had mailed. Tearing it open, he found two of his favorite homemade cookies with hearts drawn on the top in chocolate.

What a sweet, sweet woman! he thought.… He climbed into the bed and lay facedown, gathering Irene's nightgown in his arms so he could smell her and imagine her close to him.

And Rayford cried himself to sleep. (75-76)

Fairness dictates that we not hold LaHaye and Jenkins accountable for a lack of literary subtlety, for their series does not aspire to achieve literary quality. The writing style seems contrived to maximize its potential for exploiting other media and markets (radio drama or film). Yet writing is an art form in its own right, and the greatest practitioners of fiction writing explore its unique capacities to address the humanity of a story's characters as well as to make contact with the experiences of readers. Here is another man, Richard Furnival, whose wife has been killed in a plane crash, contemplating her loss in Charles Williams' masterpiece *All Hallows' Eve:*

The most lasting quality of loss is its unexpectedness. No doubt he would know his own loss in the expected places and times—in streets and stations, in restaurants and theaters, in their own home. He expected that. What he also expected, and yet knew he could not by its nature expect, was his seizure by his own loss in places uniquely his—in his office while he read Norwegian minutes, in the Tube while he read the morning paper, at a bar while he drank with a friend. These habits had existed before he had known Lester, but they could not escape her. She had, remotely but certainly, and without her own knowledge, overruled all. Her entrance into all was absolute, and lacking her the entrance of the pain. (24)

REGARD FOR HERITAGE

The great American painter Jack Levine is well known for his exhortation that it is vital for an artist to "know what has been known." It is the same with writers, or any other artist. Artists and writers need to maintain contact with the out-standing works of the past. While evangelicals often criticize our society's cultural product, they need to credibly answer the question most likely to be asked: "What is *your* idea of a good movie, novel, etc.?" If evangelical Christians answer with citations of novels like *Left Behind* or movies like *The Omega Code* or *China Cry*, it should not surprise us that those perspectives will not be taken seriously by those deeply involved in the broader arenas of cultural controversy. We must, to borrow a phrase from Jack Levine, "know the great tradition and what was great about it, and build on it."

That tradition brought forth works that were, like the durable architecture of centuries past, rooted in acknowledged eternal realities of Creation—what Russell Kirk called the "normative values." These roots brought forth works of substance and universality, works that were both popular and profound. Aspiring writers of our time need to set aspirations beyond markets to see and command this heritage. Much of that heritage is itself the direct product of, or is heavily informed by, the action and presence of Christ in the world and the foundation that is the eternal Word. To consider and take hold of that heritage is to do one's work "as unto the Lord," and may constitute not only a creative process but an artist's obedience as well.

Works Cited

Briner, Bob. *Roaring Lambs: A Gentle Plan to Radically Change Our World.* Grand
    Rapids: Baker, 1993.

Brown, W. Dale. "Walter Wangerin Jr., Man of Letters." *Christianity and the Arts.*
    August-October 1997: 50-53.

Buechner, Frederick. *Godric.* San Francisco: Harper and Row, 1980.

Frye, Northrop. *The Great Code: The Bible and Literature.* New York: Harcourt Brace
    Jovanovich, 1982.

Girardi, Robert. *Vaporetto 13.* New York: Delacorte Press, 1997.

Hansen, Ron. *Mariette In Ecstasy.* New York: HarperCollins, 1991.

Ingles, James Wesley. "The Christian Novel and the Evangelical Dilemma." *The
    Christian Imagination: Essays On Literature and the Arts.* Ed. Leland Ryken.
    Grand Rapids: Baker, 1981. 337-345.

Kirk, Russell. *Enemies of the Permanent Things*. New Rochelle, New York: Arlington House, 1969.

LaHaye, Tim, and Jenkins, Jerry. *Left Behind*. Wheaton: Tyndale House, 1993.

———. *Nicolae*. Wheaton: Tyndale House, 1993.

L'Engle, Madeleine. *Walking On Water: Reflections on Faith and Art*. Wheaton: Harold Shaw, 1980.

Williams, Charles. *All Hallows Eve*. Grand Rapids: Eerdmans, 1981.

Confessions of a Poetry Editor

Robert Klein Engler

SOME PREMISES FOR POETRY

When it comes to texts, "All people love to edit." Yet when one works as an editor, he sometimes forgets how personal and arbitrary editorial decisions may be. Most editors try hard to be objective, but as anyone with experience in these matters knows, our heart masks our biases and prejudices very well. Nevertheless, I have been called upon more than once to justify what I select as good, Christian poetry to publish in *Christianity and the Arts* magazine, so, I am going to attempt here an apology for what my heart and mind tell me.

Here is what I believe in a few words; later I will elaborate on it. If there is going be a Christian poetry of worth in the twenty-first century, then this poetry must live on a high plateau and survive two pitfalls. On one side is the pitfall of pantheism, and on the other side is the pitfall of a radical spiritualism. The pitfall of pantheism is soft and mushy at the bottom, and everything disappears into it as if into a cloud. If a writer stumbles into this pit, all rules and standards are abandoned, and any honest expression of emotion is called a poem. On the other side, the pitfall of radical spiritualism is lined with sharp barbs and is as pointed as God's judgment without His mercy. For those who distrust art, the only literature worthwhile here is that which cuts away our own will so that we may accept the will of God. This is the sword that must cut away the vanity of the world and make us worthy for salvation, which is the bright light of the spirit.

ROBERT KLEIN ENGLER *lives in Chicago and New Orleans. He teaches at Roosevelt University. His poems and stories have appeared in* Borderlands, Hyphen, Christopher Street, The James White Review, American Letters and Commentary, Kansas Quarterly, *and elsewhere. He has received the Illinois Arts Council Literary Award for his poem "Flower Festival at Genzano," and he serves as poetry editor for* Christianity and the Arts.

Both of these pitfalls must be avoided by an artist working in the world today. The artist working today must strike the right balance between the body and the spirit. Yes, it requires grace to live above these two perils, and as I will attempt to show later, a biblical theology that accepts the created world as good and the Incarnation as the final proof of this is also necessary. These are what lift the artist up to do good work. It is for this art and grace that the Christian poet prays. This prayer can be answered by inspiration, education, and the gift of talent.

I will use the term *poetry* to refer to my chief area of concern, the reading and writing of the personal lyric. When I claim a poet or a poem is grounded in Christianity, or that a poet is a Christian poet, I am also saying the personal, lyric style of that poet is influenced by Christian belief and revelation. This Christian influence can either exist in the background, the way a skeleton of beams holds up a building while remaining hidden from view, or it can be out in the open, the way the girders of a bridge are an integral, evident part of the shape of the bridge. A personal, lyric poetry that does not consider Christian concerns also exists. That kind of poetry makes up the bulk of poetry written today.

If our lives are truly "hid with Christ in God," the astounding thing is that this hiddenness is revealed in all that we do and say and write. What we are is going to be visible in our art, no matter how secular (on the surface) the subject may be.

—MADELEINE L'ENGLE, *Walking on Water*

Poetry does not just happen. Like all human work, it is embedded in a social context. Religious poetry and poetry informed by a Christian perspective are no different from secular poetry in this regard. Although writing may be the most solitary of the arts, the finished product requires an audience. This audience of readers and listeners moves poetry from the private to the public arena. An audience is also the consequence of a social apparatus that publishes and distributes texts. The Christian poet needs a community to interpret and preserve his or her work just as any other poet does. Where Christian poetry differs from most other types of poetry is in its underpinnings. The unique view of the human condition that supports Christian poetry supports a literature that has universal concerns.

In poetry, as well as in other human concerns, there is a hierarchy of ability and understanding. Experience teaches us that some arts are more complex than others, and some people have better skills at making art than others. Furthermore, skills such as reading and writing must be developed by education and experience. Yet even with education and experience there is often disagreement on matters of taste. Some works are considered examples of excellence, and others are examples of decadence or a deterioration of tradition. In a society like ours, with democratic values and relativism in matters of life and style, we often have a tendency to overlook these facts of human existence.

So where does poetry come from? The kind of poetry we like is often justified by an artistic theory that includes our view of the world. One of the best answers to the question about the origins of poetry is given by the Chinese scholar James J. Y. Liu, who writes that "some poetry is the result of spontaneous expression that owes nothing to study, but in most cases natural talent needs to be enriched by study. However, without natural talent, no matter how hard one studies, one will not succeed as a poet. These ideas may not be original, but they are based on lifetime experience and confirm what previous poet-critics have said" (83).

The details of this world, no matter how harsh they may be, can be assembled into poetry and art. This is the mystery of faith and creation. This is assured us by the creation of the world in the book of Genesis (1:30-31). The fact that God blessed His creation and said that it was very good means that we are allowed to engage that creation and to take satisfaction in God's goodness as we wait the world to come. Furthermore, the Incarnation is the final seal placed upon God's creation. In the words of John's gospel, "And the Word became flesh and lived among us, and we have seen his glory, the glory as of a father's only son, full of grace and truth" (1:14, NRSV).

We need a poetry not of direct statement *but of* direct evocation: *a poetry of hieroglyphics, of embodiment, incarnation.*

—Denise Levertov, *The Poet in the World*

That the word became flesh means many things to various believers, but it can also mean that poets are not far removed from that very word which created and redeemed the world. The creation of the world and the salvation of the world are two poles of mystery over which the world hovers. It is this mystery that Christian poets attempt to fathom. It is because of this mystery that Christian poetry can aim toward excellence. By avoiding the pitfalls of denying the goodness of the world or losing oneself in a cloud of mysticism, Christian poetry can, on the one hand, live up to a standard of beauty and excellence, and on the other hand, engage life and the world. Let us see how this may be accomplished by three very different poets, John Keble, Charles Péguy, and Elizabeth Bishop.

THE RANGE OF GOOD CHRISTIAN POETRY

John Keble (1792–1866) was a poet and Anglican priest who became so famous as Chair of Poetry at Oxford that the university named a college after him. His series of poems in *The Christian Year* is still read and esteemed today by a small circle of admirers. Published in 1827, the volume contains poems for the Sundays and Feast Days of the church year. The book sold many copies and was highly effective in spreading Keble's devotional and theological views. To get a feel for the kind of poetry that Keble wrote—and that has always been prominent among practitioners of devotional poetry in the traditional style—we might note the opening verse of one of his most famous poems, which (like others of his poems) became a familiar hymn:

Sun of my soul, thou Savior dear,
It is not night if thou be near.
Oh, may no earthborn cloud arise
To hide thee from thy servant's eyes.

To Keble, poetry was in its essence simply religion. He argued that the best poets in every age had been those who have had the highest thoughts about God. In his most famous book, *The Christian Year,* Keble attempted to write poems that were liturgical and that celebrated the feasts of the church. This is exemplified by his poem "Twenty-second Sunday after Trinity," whose beginning sections I offer below.

What liberty so glad and gay,
As where the mountain boy,
Reckless of regions far away,
A prisoner lives in joy?

The dreary sounds of crowded earth,
The cries of camp or town,
Never untuned his lovely mirth,
Nor drew his visions down.

The snow-clad peeks of rosy light
That meet his morning view,
The thwarting cliffs that bound his sight,
They bound his fancy too.

Keble's devotional poetry may not be to everyone's taste these days. It may strike some as mechanical at worst, and far removed from our postindustrial time at best. Nevertheless, if one wishes to write like this, using form, meter, and rhyme, then one needs to learn from Keble and his poems (his thoughts on poetry were expressed in his Latin *Lectures on Poetry* [1939–1841]).

For a more modern example of a poem that engages the world and reaches for the spirit, I offer the example of a poem by Charles Péguy. Péguy is not widely known outside religious circles or his native France. Most readers in the United States know of the Christian poetry of Charles Péguy (1873–1914) through the English rendering of his French book *Basic Verities* by Ann and Julian Green, or Julian Green's translation of *God Speaks*. At first reading, Péguy's poetry might seem odd and unusual, for some of it deals with themes related to war and nationalism. Many are surprised to find out that Péguy died fighting in the First World War. Furthermore, his poetry is almost a complete contrast to that of Keble's because of Péguy's plain, almost prose language. Yet this plain way of writing also delivers to us "a world in a grain of sand." Paradoxically, Péguy's plain style is related to Keble's ornate style in that one of the sources of Péguy's inspiration was, like Keble's, liturgical. He was a careful reader of the prayer book that the French call their *paroissien,* which contains much spiritual wealth stored up since the early days of Christianity. Péguy's poetry also has a beautiful emotional quality and, as his translators maintain, "it bears the stamp of genius and has its origin in the depths of a truly religious heart." Péguy was a man who believed in putting faith into action. He also held strong views about freedom and justice and remarked once, "Short of genius, a rich man cannot imagine poverty." Consider Péguy's celebrated poem "Blessed Are":

Blessed Are

Blessed are those who died for carnal earth.
Provided it was in a just war.
Blessed are those who died for a plot of ground.
Blessed are those who died a solemn death.

Blessed are those who died in great battles.
Stretched out on the ground in the face of God.
Blessed are those who died on a final high place,
Amid all the pomp of grandiose funerals.

Blessed are those who died for carnal cities.
For they are the body of the city of God.
Blessed are those who died for their hearth and their fire,
And the lowly honors of their father's house.

For such is the image and such the beginning
The body and shadow of the house of God.
Blessed are those who died in that embrace,
In honor's clasp and the earth's avowal.

For honor's clasp in the beginning
And the first draught of eternal avowal.
Blessed are those who died in this crushing down,
In the accomplishment of this earthly vow.

For earth's vow is the beginning
And the first draught of faithfulness.
Blessed are those who died in that coronation,
In that obedience and that humility.

Blessed are those who died, for they have returned
Into primeval clay and primeval earth.
Blessed are those who died in a just war.
Blessed is the wheat that is ripe and the wheat that is gathered in sheaves.

Péguy is a poet who is not afraid to engage the reader. He does this by being
both moral and dramatic. We may disagree with the stance he initially takes, but

after the poem's masterful accumulation of detail, the final line of the poem is as convincing for many as a syllogism. This is an argument for faith that proceeds, not as theology, but as art.

The mystery of faith takes many forms. Sometimes those forms may even be unintentional. Let us look at the poem "Filling Station," by the American poet Elizabeth Bishop (1911–1979). We can use it as an example of a contemporary poem that establishes a change of direction, a movement from the sentiment of death to a sentiment of life, and in so doing lives on that high plateau that I argue is the place of art.

Filling Station

Oh, but it is dirty!
—this little filling station,
oil-soaked, oil-permeated
to a disturbing, over-all
black translucency.
Be careful with that match!

Father wears a dirty,
oil-soaked monkey suit
that cuts him under the arms,
and several quick and saucy
and greasy sons assist him
(it's a family filling station),
all quite thoroughly dirty.

Do they live in the station?
It has a cement porch
behind the pumps, and on it
a set of crushed and grease-
impregnated wickerwork:
on the wicker sofa
a dirty dog, quite comfy.

Some comic books provide
the only note of color—

of certain color. They lie
upon a big dim doily
draping a taboret
(part of a set), beside
a big hirsute begonia.

Why the extraneous plant?
Why the taboret?
Why, oh why, the doily?
(Embroidered in a daisy stitch
with marguerites, I think,
and heavy with gray crochet.)

Somebody embroidered the doily.
Somebody waters the plant,
or oils it, maybe. Somebody
arranges the rows of cans
so that they softly say:
ESSO—SO—SO
to high-strung automobiles.
Somebody loves us all.

Notice how Bishop makes use of details from this world in her poem. There are comic books, a hirsute begonia, and the embroidered doily. Yet this is not a random use of this and that. "Somebody arranges the rows of cans." She draws on time the way Keble uses time to document the holy days of the year, and she draws on place the way Péguy uses place to remind us that men and women are part of the earth. In the end, there is an order that pervades the dirty filling station, just as in this world, with its grease and grime, there is an order as well. What is that order? How odd to say it: It is the order of love. In Bishop's poetry, "Somebody loves us all." These words may seem trite to the cynical or unconvincing to the philosopher, but the art of her poetry adds for me the convincing touch, a touch that ever so lightly rests in this world of time and place and leads to that conclusion. In a very important way, good poetry is always a poetry of time and place. All three of the poets I cited write with a sense of time and a sense of place. God chose a people and in time a man from that people to bring salvation into the world. In a sense, a poetry that fails is a poetry that is "timeless" and "nowhere."

We cannot say from just this one poem that Elizabeth Bishop was a Christian, nor do we need to, for remember, this poem is a work of art and not a theological treatise. We do learn, however, that she expressed a belief in life and love. I think we could say the same thing about Elizabeth Bishop as Kathleen Norris said of Denise Levertov: They "believed that the discipline of writing was a preparation for the discipline of belief." Yet certainly there are those who are beginning to practice the discipline of writing and may be yet strong in their faith. Is there anything I can offer them as an editor besides the examples above about why some poems succeed and others fail?

SUGGESTIONS OF A POETRY EDITOR

As I hinted earlier, Christian poems commonly fail in two ways. First, they slip into the pitfall of mush and the failure of standards. Second, they slide into the pitfall of the sword and fail to engage life and the world. Such poems are cut loose to float in airy nothing without a name. These are the ways in which *any* poem can fail. If we remember that poetry is an art with a high and serious purpose, and actually believe, contrary to postmodern thinking, that there are still high and serious purposes, then we have to recognize that there are standards for all the arts. Poetry is no different in this regard. A poem is just not simply an expression of emotion. There are standards of diction, meter, rhyme, and form that make a work of words a work of art. Simple and honest expressions of emotion that do not consider the standards of art are not poetry. When Sally dropped the plate with her pie while rushing to answer the phone, she said, "Damn!" That word was an honest expression of emotion, but it is not in my view a poem. Those poems that are cut loose to get lost in the spirit usually do so by being formalistic, that is to say, they repeat the wisdom of the past, but not the struggle that gave rise to that wisdom. In the end, poems that fail as poems either get lost in the body or the spirit and do not strike the balance that art requires.

The kinds of poetry that invariably cross the desk of an editor may also be categorized by the economic situation of the writer. There are basically two categories: the well-to-do and the financially limited. It takes time and money to write, and more money to duplicate and send out a manuscript. Most of the poems I get from the well-to-do are poor poems, however. Just because someone is gifted with wealth and can afford to attend poetry writing workshops in Santa Fe, New Mexico, does not mean they are also gifted with a poetic vision or a poetic voice. The well-to-do often write three kinds of poems—the compulsory travel poem, the nature poem, and the "look at sensitive me poem." The financially limited usually write lilting greeting card verse or rhyming prayers, or they talk about their chronic diseases or costly operations. I imagine that many of them reside in small towns; while this is not necessarily a liability (witness the example of Emily Dickinson), there is an evident parochialism in the writing.

[The poem's] "message" was not there at the beginning (otherwise the poet could simply say the message and would have no reason to create the poem); if the poem has a "message" now, it is in any case inseparable from the process, the body of awareness, the incarnated poem…. Most poems (modern poems especially) begin not with ideas but with things and their relationships. Imagination (image-making) begins its work with surfaces, with what the senses are in contact with. Art is fed by the experience…of the everyday world.

—ROD JELLEMA, "Poems Should Stay across the Street from the Church"

Most writers who send in their work seem to have no understanding of the direction poetry took in the twentieth century, nor do they seem to have been influenced by the sensibility of modernism. This is probably the chief reason that their poems fail. In spite of that, I hardly ever see a traditionally crafted sonnet, nor do people follow the guidelines we print in our ad in *Poets and Writers Magazine*, where we list our theme issues. Why would someone send us poems about Adam's fall from grace when the next issue is on women mystical saints? Advances in technology have not improved poetry writing either. The computer seems to have just made the output of bad poems increase.

All of this output makes me wonder at the great mill of words that is grinding away in this vast country and the desire so many have to be heard, or even just to have their name heard. What to do about that need? Unfortunately, I end up rejecting the lot. The hard truth is that any magazine, even a Christian arts magazine, has to reject most of what it gets. If we are in the publishing business, we are also in the rejection business. The difficulty that this poses is how to reject people's poems and yet not hurt their feelings. For the most part, this is impossible. Poets by definition are a sensitive lot. Usually the bad poets are also the most sensitive to rejection.

As an editor and critic, I can offer suggestions to new poets so that their submissions stand a chance of being accepted. I propose here ten rules that might profitably be followed before anyone submits a poem to a magazine, especially a magazine that publishes Christian poetry.

1. *Don't rewrite the Bible.* Too often writers think that because they are retelling a biblical story they are writing religious poetry. This is hardly the case. Furthermore, isn't it better for us to read the Bible story in its original instead of some poem about it? We also get a lot of poems that take a biblical character or event for their subject or starting point. Most of them are bad. They are bad because they are derivative. Usually the original biblical story is much more engaging. What makes the occasional poem in this genre succeed? The same thing that makes any poem succeed—heightened language and engaging imagery, or as Coleridge put it, "The best words in the best order." This does not mean we cannot use the Bible as a source of inspiration and as a guide in our writing. As a matter of fact, all the techniques, both literary and theological, that have been developed to understand and interpret the Bible, especially those that encourage us to make a close reading of the text, can be applied to our own writing as well. Just what exactly does a text mean and how does it effect that meaning? This is a good question to ask about a poem, too. If only poets would read their poems closely and compare them to other literature, we would see an improvement in what is sent to many magazines.

2. *Don't write doggerel.* If we can learn anything from modernism, it is that good poems do not have to rhyme.

3. *Don't butcher rhyme and meter.* If you are going to use these artistic devices, use them well or not at all.

4. *Don't overlook the importance of imagery and metaphor.* This is probably the most important advice to follow. Aristotle said, "But the

greatest thing of all by far is to be master of metaphor. It is the one thing that cannot be learned from others; and it is also a sign of original genius, because a good metaphor implies the intuitive perception of the similarities in dissimilarities." A teacher once assigned a class to write a poem about the miracle of water being changed to wine at the marriage feast at Cana. While most students wrote poems of sophisticated meter and rhyme, one student wrote this memorable short verse: "The simple water blushed / seeing its creator near." This is the kind of imagery I look for in poems submitted to *Christianity and the Arts* magazine.

5. *Don't use the automatic "center line" command in your word processor.* This is self explanatory. Been there! Done that! Over it!

6. *Include your name, address, etc., on all poetry submissions.* This protects your work from getting lost or being mixed up with the work of others.

7. *Include a self-addressed stamped envelope with all your correspondence and submissions.* Little magazines have little budgets and cannot afford to return material if you do not include sufficient postage.

8. *Don't write Holy Land travel poems.*

9. *Don't forsake the Spirit for fame and popularity.* Listen, read, study, and be patient, then write.

10. *Don't despair.* Poetry does not save the world. Believe me, if you adhere to these suggestions, you will not need to meditate in the desert around Taos, New Mexico, nor will you need to read silly books on Zen and writing that are so popular nowadays.

THE SUCCESSFUL CHRISTIAN POEM

If we go swimming in the sea of language, an odd thing may happen. We may come out sometimes at a loss for words. It is as if words were everywhere, but none is fit to say. Nevertheless, that loss of words may signify that we are also lost in this world for the sake of the world to come. We all know that love may sometimes render us speechless. Likewise, a great love fundamentally alters the soul. Successful Christian poetry is a human poetry of this world that simultaneously expresses the world of the spirit. This is the kind of poetry I look for to pass on to my editor-in-chief. Such poetry comes in the mail as a gift. And why shouldn't it? The Spirit moves where it will.

I need not supply examples of bad poems. They can be found in the best anthology of bad poems I have seen—in a book entitled *Very Bad Poetry*, by Kathryn and Ross Petras. The examples of dreadful poems range from the "Ode on the Mammoth Cheese" by James Mcintyre, through bad poems written in baby talk to what the editors consider the worst poem ever written in English, "A Tragedy" by Theophile Marzials. The reader is even offered introductions to the poems and humorous commentary. Instead of duplicating these examples, I can offer as a positive example one of the good poems we decided to publish in the summer 1999 issue of *Christianity and the Arts*. Here is a poem that engages the world, a poem that is rooted to life by details of time and place, and that reaches for the spirit by affirming acts of charity. Yet even in regard to this example, there is room for varying degrees of taste and judgment.

And He Shall Give His Angels Charge Over You
Sharon Singleton

The waitress stands over me at 6:00 a.m. with pad
and pen. She recites her litany with weary kindness;
she says orange juice, coffee, two eggs over easy,
says whole wheat toast, marmalade, each word
a wafer I take from her hands and eat.

I stand before the white robed technician, my blouse
draped around my hips. She gently cups my breasts
in her hand, guides me between the cold steel wings
of the machine. It will aim its radiant eye to uncover
whatever mystery might be hidden there.

The beautician holds my head in her hands,
tips it backward over the white chalice of the sink,
sluices warm water through my hair again and again,
smoothing the wings of my emptiness with her fingers
until I am loosened and released.

On a transcontinental train I once met a woman who told me that because Jesus had suffered and died for our sins, there was no need for us to suffer anymore. She said that if things get too bad we can always commit suicide. This sounded so singular and easy to me. I did not want to argue with her, but all of us sitting at the table were drawn into her neurosis, and the meal ended badly. Somehow, today, I feel that a poem like Sharon Singleton's is a good argument against what my fellow passenger had to offer. Not only when things get unbearably bad, but even in our everyday life, there are those who commit small acts of mercy. They are the ones who help us by smoothing the wings of our emptiness until we are "loosened and released." This is the story Singleton tells in her poem, and she does so by rooting her tale in time and space and by using the details of everyday life. Here is a deeply religious poem that, except for the title, makes little use of stock religious expression or even religious diction. It takes the high road between radical spiritualism and mushy sentimentalism. I tried to be objective when I read this piece. Needless to say, it was to my liking. I recommended it to my editor-in-chief. This is how poems get published in *Christianity and the Arts* magazine.

I do not think we should expect contemporary Christian poets to be candidates for beatification. Nor should we expect them to be mystics. The tradition from which a Spanish poet like Saint John of the Cross emerges is no longer accessible in modern America. At best, the Christian poet will be a martyr, a martyr in the original sense of the word as witness. The Christian poet of our time, immersed in a culture that is materialistic, must simply be a witness to the hope of life everlasting. If poetry does not offer this witness, then maybe criticism will.

Sometimes it seems that we are living in an age where our criticism is more interesting than our poetry. Is it too obvious to say life encompasses many gifts? One may be a critic, the other a poet. One may be blessed to bring life into the world, while another is equally blessed by preserving and advancing the life already here, even if it is but a faint spark. Perhaps it is a spark from the celestial fire, a small part of the divine flame, that we look for in all good poetry. Those who happen to be fortunate to receive the gift of fire are the ones we call poets. They may also be the ones who are blessed and burdened at the same time. How are we to give light without heat? How are we to make pure without burning away? Those poems that achieve an embodied revelation, those poems that seem to us a kind of pure light held by words, are the ones we come to cherish. All else will pass away, as the old heaven and the old earth will pass away.

————————

Works Cited

Bishop, Elizabeth. "The Filling Station." *The Complete Poems, 1927-1929*. New York: Farrar, Straus, Giroux, 1979.

Keble, John. "Twenty-second Sunday after Trinity." *The Christian Year: Thoughts in Verse for the Sundays and Holy Days*. Oxford: Oxford University Press, 1827.

Liu, James J. Y. *Language—Paradox—Poetics: A Chinese Perspective*. Princeton: Princeton University Press, 1988.

Péguy, Charles. "Blessed Are." *Basic Verities*. Trans. Ann and Julian Green. New York: Pantheon Books, 1943.

Petras, Kathryn and Ross, eds. *Very Bad Poetry*. New York: Vintage Books, 1997.

Poets and Writers Magazine (72 Spring St., New York, N.Y., 10012).

The Aesthetic Poverty of Evangelicalism

I want to base what I have to say on three facts which I think indisputable. The first is that the Bible belongs to literature; that is, it is a piece of art.... The second indisputable fact is that...the Bible is an imaginative book.... The third indisputable fact is that the greatest artist of all, the greatest imaginer of all, is the one who appears at the opening of Genesis....

Now when we look from these three facts to contemporary evangelical Christianity, we find a great oddity. The people who spend the most time with the Bible are in large numbers the foes of art and the sworn foes of imagination. And I grow in the feeling that these people have quite an astonishing indifference to the created world. Evangelicals hear the great "I am" of God, but they are far less aware of the "I am" of his handiwork. Furthermore, when evangelicals dare attempt any art form it is generally done badly.

As to the evangelicals' skittishness toward imagination, I have looked into the Scriptures and I cannot find such a prejudice there. One prominent evangelical holds that the triad of truth-goodness-beauty is Greek in origin, and the Hebrew concept is only that of the true and the holy. I doubt it. I doubt it primarily because of the glorious beauty I see every day in God's handiwork, but I also doubt it from looking at Scripture. The Revised Standard Version shows ninety uses of the words *beauteous, beautiful, beautify,* and *beauty* (the King James Version uses seventy-six of these words), and overwhelmingly in a favorable sense. I see no esthetic difference between God's word and his creative work. Even if his world were purely a functional one, the bee and the flower around which it buzzes would be equally glorious, equally fantastic, equally miraculous.

How can it be that with a God who created birds and the blue of the sky and who before the foundation of the world wrought out a salvation more romantic than Cinderella, with a Christ who encompasses the highest heaven and deepest hell, with the very hairs of our heads numbered, with God closer than hands and feet, Christians often turn out to have an unenviable corner on the unimaginative and the commonplace?...

Evangelical Christians have had one of the purest of motives and one of the worst of outcomes. The motive is never to mislead by the smallest fraction of an iota in the precise nature of salvation, to live it and state it in its utter purity. But the unhappy outcome has too often been to elevate the cliché. The motive is that the gospel shall not be misunderstood, not sullied, not changed in jot or tittle. The outcome has often been merely the reactionary, static, and hackneyed....

There is a simplicity which diminishes and a simplicity which enlarges, and evangelicals have too often chosen the wrong one. The first is that of the cliché—simplicity with mind and heart removed. The other is that of art. The first falsifies by its exclusions; the second encompasses. The first silently denies the multiplicity and grandeur of creation, salvation, and indeed all things. The second symbolizes and celebrates them. The first tries to take the danger out of Christianity and with the danger often removes the actuality. The second suggests the creative and sovereign God of the universe with whom there are no impossibilities. The contrast suggests that *not* to imagine is what is sinful. The symbol, the figure, the image, the parable—in short, the artistic method—so pungent in the Lord's teaching and acting, are often noteworthy for their absence in ours. Is this not a case of humanism far more reprehensible than the sort of humanism we often decry?...

Our excuse for our esthetic failure has often been that we must be about the Lord's business, the assumption being that the Lord's business is never esthetic.

—"The Aesthetic Poverty of Evangelism"
Christian Herald, March 1969

Part Seven

Realism

Considered in terms of type of content, literature exists on a continuum with realism at one pole and fantasy at the other. Realism aims to give us a replica of the known world. Fantasy whisks us away to an alternate world. Readers of literature, including Christian readers, are rather evenly divided as to their preferences in the matter.

Of course all literature involves a selectivity and adherence to literary conventions that makes it different from actual living and the empirical world around us. But within that artifice, realism aims to reproduce the texture of life as we know it, eschewing anything that violates the standards of plausibility. Realism is both an aesthetic (a philosophy regarding what literature is) and a set of techniques. The purpose of this unit is to make the best possible case for realism as a type of literature.

While realism is not alone in the literary portrayal of evil, it is the arena within which the issue of evil is most obviously confronted. It is appropriate, therefore, to place the consideration of the portrayal of evil in literature in this unit of the book.

When a Spider Is Only a Spider

James Schaap

It's five in the morning, there's nothing moving in the house besides me and the cat, and I'm not even all that sure about me. I toss some coffee into the basket of our machine, close it up tightly, hit the *on* button, and reach for my toast, when I see him, a quarter-sized spider who emerges shockingly from some unseen crack between the kitchen sink and countertop. I've never been partial to arachnophobia; my bones don't immediately chill. But I do wake up rather quickly, struck by the sudden and astonishing reality that the two of us—our cat and I—are not alone at this half-darkened hour in the kitchen.

I wasn't shocked by the reality of there being unseen worlds in our kitchen, worlds our cat knows far better than I. So I was neither deathly afraid of him nor shocked by his residency somewhere beneath our sink. Yet, a half-hour later, here I am, a floor away in the basement, telling multiple yous about him. I suppose what prompts my storytelling is the fact that this morning, the visit of the spider is far more interesting than the texture of my toast or the sound of percolating coffee.

But why should I call his appearance a *visit?* When other spiders ask him where he lives, he likely gives the same address I do. My guess is he's not a recent immigrant; after all, it's summer and most beasts presently lurking outside our screens feel no particular urge to gain entrance to this house or any other at this time of year. His visit was likely not just a visit. The two of us just happened to cross paths. It's likely he was as shocked as I was, and his behavior, in fact,

JAMES CALVIN SCHAAP *is a novelist, short story writer, and essayist. He lives on the eastern edge of the Great Plains, where he teaches literature and writing at Dordt College, Sioux Center, Iowa. His fiction is rooted in the ethno-religious milieu in which he lives—a small town, Dutch Reformed world. His novel* Romy's Place *was nominated for the 2000 Christy Award in contemporary Christian fiction.*

suggests as much. First, he crinkled those long legs and went into a stall, mistaking himself for a possum; then, he shot off at a speed likely far beyond the posted limits of the blue highway between kitchen sink and window. In a flash he was gone. My coffee wasn't even perked.

Fiction keeps its audience by retaining the world as its subject matter. People like the world.… When the arts abandon the world as their subject matter, people abandon the arts.

—ANNIE DILLARD, *Living by Fiction*

What just happened in the kitchen, and what's happening as the letters emerge on the screen before me, as well as what's going on as your mind translates the inky shapes marching along in the line on this page, is what happens every time someone deliberately attempts to record very real human experience. If I've entertained you at all so far, then I've already accomplished something of the first objective of good writing: I've kept your mind off the goings-on at the office, the crankiness of your joints, or the creeping jenny in the flower bed. "No great novel can be written about a flea," Melville once said, "but a great writer can make a flea take wing." This spider of mine—I'd like to think that you've already met him too.

If the spider incident has made you smile, I'd like to believe that your reaction is directly attributable to the quality of my writing, but there's undoubtedly more to it. For a moment at least, I've tried to bring you directly into the Schaap's kitchen; but it would be only a half-truth to say that world isn't already familiar to you, since my serendipitous meeting with a local spider may well have brought you back to a similar meeting, not at our house, of course, but yours. It's not simply my manipulation of the materials of the story that kept your attention; just as substantial to your interest is the good possibility of your having experienced a similar early-morning face-off. "Been there," people say, "done that."

ROMANTICISM, NATURALISM, AND REALISM

Just for a moment, let's revisit the story by way of literature's three traditional ways of recording such incidents—romanticism, naturalism, and realism. Let me try to offer a textbook definition of *realism* before saying a few words in its defense. Here's the story.

Outside, night. Inside, man (or woman), half-asleep, brews a cup of coffee. Before his (or her) bleary eyes a spider emerges, sits still for a moment, then scuttles away. Man (or woman), startled, is no longer tired.

Rising action, complication, climax, denouement. All the rudimentary stuff is there. We've got ourselves a story.

If I were a textbook romanticist, someone given to interpret the day-to-day and moment-to-moment events of our lives in the luminescent glow of a much higher reality, I'd likely tell the story not so much to entertain as to enlighten. Romanticism, broadly speaking, always seeks the higher light, and that's not difficult for someone like me, Sunday School-trained to ferret out gospel truth from God's own narrative, so that the story of Daniel becomes an object lesson for undergoing our own fiery trials.

In fact, a fine seventeenth-century Calvinist writer has already taken his albeit poetic turn with a spider. Edward Taylor, a New England Puritan preacher, created something of a masterpiece out of the story of a wasp's final seconds in a spider's sticky web. "Upon a Spider Catching a Fly" is a story of sheer malevolence, really. The wasp is webbed; the spider's eight therapeutic fingers gently calm its victim, lest the wasp, Taylor says, wreak havoc on his sinewy snare. Once he's steadied his victim, the spider has lunch: "Whereas the silly fly, / Caught by its leg, / Thou by the throat took'st hastily, / And 'hind the head / Bite dead."

Now Taylor's ample Calvinist psyche gave him little choice but to make additional meaning from what he'd seen. He saw much more to this spider's lunch than a spider's lunch.

"Thus," Taylor says, "this fray seems thus to us," and proceeds in the final stanzas to offer a conventional Puritan take on the events—as you can imagine, the devil is the spider and we are the helpless wasp, although by virtue of our fallen character we're not exactly innocent; after all, we've wandered into the spider's sticky entrails ourselves.

By *romanticism* here I'm not referring to *romance*—wind-tossed ringlets of hair dangling over ample cleavage and pressed up against pecs to die for—nor nineteenth-century *romanticism*, a movement in the arts which had its own unique agenda. What I mean is far less genre than propensity: the writer's desire to make meaning out of the things of our lives by using them to point toward ideas and ideals. To Taylor, the engagement of the spider and the wasp was important not simply because it happened, but because the event pointed unmistakably at the whole course of human experience.

Romanticism and naturalism are hardly kissing cousins, even though they share more than they'd care to admit. *Naturalism* usually refers to a specific movement in nineteenth-century American literature, something born, in part, out of Darwinian ideas and often defined as the application of the principles of scientific determinism to fiction. Naturally, I suppose, naturalists would disdain Taylor's lofty visions of the spider and the wasp, largely because they would prefer to draw their visions of reality from the netherworld of impulses human beings share with their animal ancestors.

Were an advocate of literary naturalism to write the saga of this morning's incident with the spider, he or she likely would have featured the bumbler, me, who really did nothing at all during the entire encounter, largely because in the face of such a phenomenon I was rendered numb and powerless. This spider, arising from the seamy underworld of loose fitting cabinet joints, shocked me into momentary paralysis by forcing me to confront a something *which was there*, but a something I had considered tightly and safely controlled.

I don't know a naturalist who's toyed with a spider, but most naturalist writers, it seems, toy with their subjects, whether human or not. For years I've used Theodore Dreiser's *Sister Carrie* in an introductory American novel course; almost to a person, my students dislike him, and it is because of Dreiser's intrusiveness. All writers are puppeteers of their characters after a fashion, but Dreiser forces the reader to note the strings. My students growl because he's explaining his characters' actions and reactions, generally treating the reader as patronizingly as he does George Hurstwood, or Carrie Meeber herself.

I like *Sister Carrie* more than they do, but I understand their reactions. They stem from a weakness it is possible to attribute to most naturalistic writers: In their supposed objectivity as scientific naturalists, they tend to stand so aloof from their poor and misguided characters that, at least by contemporary standards, we come to trust neither them nor the characters they create.

Here's the irony: Naturalists really aren't much different from romanticists. Although a naturalist's vision of truth comes from an entirely different worldview than, say Edward Taylor, both Taylor's form of romanticism and Dreiser's form of naturalism are committed to a similar proposition—that a spider is not just a spider. For both, the characters and action of any story tend to point toward another reality, although those realities lie in wholly different directions.

Enter, the realists. Realists, via the textbook, are those who give their undying support, not to various visions or versions of our common experience, but to the experience of life itself. To realists, a spider *is* only a spider. For a realistic writer to render the story of this morning's encounter, there would be only one reason to tell the story: to tell the truth about what happened. Realists—again, by definition—are those who seem most concerned with fidelity to what's real in what they write.

So here's the story, *realistically:* I got up, put on the coffee, was suddenly shocked by the appearance of a spider emerging from somewhere I didn't see. He scurried off.

That's the story—the whole story.

Fiction is about everything human and we are made out of dust, and if you scorn getting yourself dusty, then you shouldn't try to write fiction.
—FLANNERY O'CONNOR, "The Nature and Aim of Fiction"

Would that life were textbook theory, but, just for a moment, let's get real. Take Walt Whitman, who had his own meeting with a spider. It's possible to cast the poet Whitman as a textbook realist; after all, his abiding principle was to create a new and vividly real American poetry by way of a poetic line in tune with the cadences of American speech. He despised all adopted poetic conventions and forms, felt them unsuitable to the glorious new culture emerging in the nation. He intended to create a new poetic style that belonged to the people, entirely and substantially real. Whitman wanted to get it right.

It's possible, in other words, to call Whitman a *realist*. In fact, I think he'd rather like the description. Now, have a look at his poem "Noiseless, Patient Spider."

A noiseless, patient spider
I mark'd where on a little promontory it stood isolated,
Mark'd how to explore the vacant vast surrounding,
It launch'd forth filament, filament, filament, out of itself,
Ever unreeling them, ever tirelessly speeding them.

The first stanza includes the personal pronoun, so Whitman himself is not conspicuously absent; but the stanza is little more than a description of the spider. Then the second half of the poem:

And you O my soul where you stand,
Surrounded, detached, in measureless oceans of space,
Ceaselessly musing, venturing, throwing, seeking the spheres to connect them
Till the bridge you will need be form'd, till the ductile anchor hold,
Till the gossamer thread you fling catch somewhere, O my soul.

Whitman's spider may be nothing but a spider, but the arachnidic observations he makes are the occasion for an idea which finally is greater than the spider itself. The substance certainly wouldn't suit Edward Taylor's Puritan romanticism, since what Whitman feels reveals much more of doubt than faith. A doctrinaire naturalist might be more comfortable with the poem, given that the author's revelation of his own loosened moorings suggests a human being very much unsure of himself. Nonetheless, to Whitman, in his most famous spider poem, a spider is not just a spider. Thus, the realist, by textbook definition we've been establishing, is not a realist. Realism is a propensity, not a genre.

Throughout its long history all over the world, lyric poetry has been less fanciful than fiction. A book of lyric poems is most often a collation of interpreted facts. Poetry's materials, its characters, objects, and events, its landscapes and cities, its mornings and afternoons, are far more likely to have been actual than fabricated. This means that poetry has been able to function quite directly as human interpretation of the raw, loose universe.

—ANNIE DILLARD, *Living by Fiction*

If realism were to be viable as a specific genre, there would be no need for the imagination. How about this?—click on a tape, capture the dialogue of a midafternoon tea, type it up, and submit it for publication. That kind of realism—slavish commitment to reality—will almost always fail by way of its own banality. It's been tried, I'm sure, but such attempts at literal realism offer scant appeal for anyone other than the speakers whose voices register.

Even documentary films require editing. As I write, the hottest television programs of the season are what some call "reality TV." Put a dozen people into a blender and turn on the camera. But even those shows require editing, the conscious attempt to shape materials so that focus and timing and narrative drive create viewer interest.

Murder confessions can make good stories, but it's unlikely that a murderer's confession alone will ever make great literature. Anyone who's ever picked up a pen knows that each word she chooses emerges from a process of selection. Any writer who believes that fidelity to life in certain situations simply requires a trainload of vulgarity and profanity is ignoring the truth of the writing process—specifically, that we choose each word we write. That doesn't mean, of course, that vulgarity and profanity cannot be the language of story. It only means, *realistically*, that we transcribe very little in the writing process. We choose.

If realism, as a genre, exists only as experiment, that doesn't mean there are not realistic propensities in writing. It's arguable, I suppose, but the name most frequently associated with literary realism may well be that of novelist Honoré de Balzac, who, for the sake of realism, made it a mission to record endless details of his French culture, yet fashioned plots that overflow with sensational coincidences. In his case, fidelity to actuality ended with the details.

However, whenever a writer strives for fidelity to actuality in human experience, something of the realistic impulse exists. That impulse is very much in evidence, for instance, in the young Kate Chopin, whose early stories of the bayou ("Caline," "A Visit to Avoyelles," and "Madame Celestine's Divorce" are examples) clearly suggest the themes of her masterwork, *The Awakening*, but seem far more concerned with their Louisiana settings than theme, documenting as they do the exotic flavors of a Creole culture. Her bayou stories are as attentive to the exacting detail of that world as some pre-Raphaelite painter might have been.

Yet something else happened in the writing of *The Awakening*, her classic novel about the emotional isolation of a woman in that same Creole society. This is the way she explained it in *Book News,* July, 1899, in response to her many (and angry) critics:

> Having a group of people at my disposal, I thought it might be entertaining (to myself) to throw them together and see what would happen. I never dreamed of Mrs. Pontellier making such a mess of things and working out her

own damnation as she did. If I had the slightest intimation of such a thing, I would have excluded her from the company. But when I found out what she was up to, the play was half over, and it was then too late.

The Awakening features the same attention to Creole culture that characterizes her early stories. But the strength of Kate Chopin's realism in *The Awakening* transcends anything she'd done before, because with Edna Pontellier—if we believe her own description of the writing of the novel—she stumbled onto realities readers ever since have found strikingly accurate, something that emerges not from local color, but from the desperation of her protagonist, Edna Pontellier. The realism of *The Awakening* is, of course, psychological realism, fidelity to actuality of what readers themselves feel, by way of their own experience, to be true. The novel is known to readers around the world, not because it features Creole high society, but because Edna Pontellier's situation and her reactions to that situation resonate with the lives and the imagined lives of many thousands of readers. The novel's power and popularity emerge from its being psychologically real.

It seems obvious to say it, but realism, the desire to achieve fidelity to life itself, as we feel it to be true, can achieve great things when it touches upon what Faulkner called "the verities of the human heart," desires, impulses, situations, choices which we all feel and face and make, but not often without some memorable hesitation and/or anxiety. We are all remarkably alike when it comes to some of those very basic human dilemmas, the kind that cost us. I've often told my writing students that an odd paradox emerges from the evaluation of good writing—that which is most personal is, strangely enough, most universal.

So long as people wish to explore the truth about themselves, novels are likely to be written.... Don't think you read novels in order to be moved by imaginary circumstances. You read them...in order to find yourself.
                    —ALAN PRYCE-JONES, "Plagued by the Nature of Truth"

Being real means touching on a universal humanity of shared experiences— joys and sorrows that are, regardless of gender or race, shared in the human story. Any writer is most real when what she writes comes off the page, not just as vividly imagined narrative but as something at least a cousin to what readers themselves have, at least in part, realized or experienced. Substantial, powerful, and edifying literature succeeds, at least in part, because we know it to be true on the basis of our own lives, our own human experience.

That, presently, we live in a time when the belief in such a communion of human spirits is eschewed goes without saying. Theoretically, of course, the ruling hegemony would have us believe that there is no such thing as shared human experience, since we all are segmented, somewhat like dissimilarly sized grapefruit chunks within the sour rind of human experience.

Maybe. But maybe not. Years ago, I was blessed with an unusual student in an introduction to college writing class—a fifty-something, Cuban-American woman, whose thinning hair was colored a deeply burnished mahogany as dramatic as her eye-liner.

When it came time to assign the narrative essay, I anticipated reading her assignment, sure that it would spin a yarn unlike any other I would read. When that essay came in, however, I learned a lesson. The story she wanted to tell had nothing to do with Cuba, or communism, or political repression. It was about sitting on a beach (presumably, but not revealed as, Cuba) where she watched her children play in the surf. I have no doubt that she could have spun the kind of exotic tale I expected, but she chose instead to tell a story about worrying about what her children might be. It was about motherhood, about caring for one's own.

Postmodernists may theorize as they'd like, but I believe certain songs play in all of our hearts and souls, songs that arise from longings and hurts, joys and concerns that belong to all of us in the human family. All of us worry about those we love. For that matter, all of us have encountered a spider when we really weren't expecting it.

We recognize the realistic impulse, I believe, when we recognize ourselves in narrative or exposition. That old definition may be vague, but it is certainly not off-base: Realism is fidelity to the actuality of human experience.

CONNECTING WITH WHAT IS REAL

A story. A year ago, when teaching an Elderhostel program, I read a poem by Stanley Wiersma titled "Last Visit in Three Voices," in which the narrator tells the story of his aged father's death. The audience that morning was sizable and attentive, not a one all that much younger than the aged father in the poem.

"Last Visit" has much to savor, much to invoke tears. But when the class was dismissed, one man came up, waited patiently until others had made their comments, then pointed at me, straight in the eye. "I like tomatoes sliced on bread with sugar," he said, winking. Then he walked away.

I honestly had no idea what he meant. Later, I looked at the text again. The old man is complaining about hospital food: "…they cut tomatoes into wedges for salads.… I like tomatoes sliced on bread with sugar." That's what the poem says.

And that's exactly what he told me: "I like tomatoes sliced on bread with sugar." All he wanted me to know is that when he heard that one particular line, some machine in his mind went "bing, bing, bing" and turned up a straight line of tomato sandwich icons. That poem had made a connection, even if it may not have been the connection the poet was trying to create. One feels the realistic impulse, I believe, when the reader somehow understands that the story or its ingredients authenticate what he or she knows to be true.

[The novelist's] aim is…to understand the deeper, hidden meaning of events.… The realist, if he is an artist, will seek not to give us a banal photography of life but a vision of it that is fuller, sharper, more convincing than reality itself.

—GUY DE MAUPASSANT, preface to *Pierre et Jean*

One of my most treasured reviews came from a farmer in rural Minnesota who had just heard me read a story in the fellowship hall of his church, a story about a hog farmer and his wife surviving a blizzard. That he liked what he'd heard was evident in the almost stunned look on his face as he reached for my hand. "You know, Mr. Schaap," he said, "you write about real people." That's all he said, but I understood he meant it as the most generous compliment he could muster. And I knew why. That retired farmer had found a hook in my story from which he could hang his own seed cap. In the fiction, he really did "experience" the story, in part because he could so easily identify his own experience within. Somewhere through the narrative, almost shockingly, he'd come to feel he was hearing his own story.

Perhaps that story, "The Privacy of Storm," will serve to illustrate something of the way the realistic writer operates, at least the realist in me. My story began with a real story. A friend of mine once told me about a young wife from

Florida, a newlywed, who, with her husband, lived just up the road outside of a small town not far from here. One night, in a violent snowstorm, she called, full of excitement, because her husband, who worked in town, was going to buck the drifts to try to make it home. They'd made an arrangement, she said; he would call from farmhouses along the way to be sure she knew he was fine. What the young Floridian didn't understand is that, out here where I live, violent snowstorms can be killers.

The critic is interested in the novel; the novelist is interested in his neighbors.

—ANNIE DILLARD, *Living by Fiction*

What followed was a series of excruciatingly tender conversations, all of them carried on a thin copper wire. The young Floridian, sealed up against the cold in her house trailer, would call my friends, her neighbors, every time her husband would report. She thought the whole affair was thrilling; all the while, they didn't know whether they dared to tell her the truth about her husband's very real danger.

Those telephone conversations fascinated me, strung as they were between innocence and experience; it was those conversations that prompted me to try to tell the story on paper. I didn't know those newlyweds; but I knew *newlywedism*. What's more, my own life has taught me all I need to know about the difficulties we all face balancing between the reckless optimism of youth and the measured sensibility of maturity. I wanted to tell the story that arose from my friend's narrative, but was born from my own experience and imagination.

But somewhere in that story, "The Privacy of Storm," that Minnesota farmer found himself. For the realistic writer, that kind of discovery on the part of the reader is not only a joy but an attribute of the finished work. Such close identification helps the reader ease into the willing suspension of disbelief and thereby, I believe, experience one of the grandest blessings of story—the opportunity to become beneficially lost, as John Gardner would say, in the narrative dream.

REALISM AND FANTASY

In the community of writers in which I operate, the world of writers and readers who are believers, for the most part *realism* is often defined by what it's not;

simply stated, it's not fantasy. None of us, after all, live in a world of hobbits (J. R. R. Tolkien), none of us really knows what goes on in the hearts of whales (Robert Siegel), and no one I know has ever witnessed, firsthand, the cosmic battles of a barnyard (Walt Wangerin). Nonetheless, add up the readers of the heretofore mentioned, throw in the myriad additional devotees of C. S. Lewis, Madeline L'Engle, Steven R. Lawhead, and a host of others, and one can account for a goodly number of Christian bookstore sales slips in the last several decades.

This morning's encounter with a spider, created by a fantasy writer, might go something like this. Our protagonist, bleary eyed, rises with the sun, puts on the coffee, and suddenly notices a spider emerge from some unknown spot in the geography of his kitchen. The spider, shocked by the grotesque, human monster in front of him, feigns death. Then, obviously unsuccessful and with nowhere to turn, he begs for grace. "Schaap," he says to me, "I've just lost my wife and children in the storm." We're off on a tale.

Far be it from me to forswear fantasy as some kind of lesser narrative art than realism. In the first place, there is no question that, in order to achieve story-telling's necessary ends, I'd have to create that spider's grief with such fidelity to the actuality of human experience that the reader would, in a moment, totally abandon skepticism about grief-stricken arachnids. I'd have to use every weapon in my realistic arsenal to create the same degree of identification tomatoes-and-sugar-on-toast achieved with the man who discovered his own experience in the poem I read. Simply enough, I'd have to spin a terrific yarn about the humanity of spiders. What I'm saying is, fantasy won't succeed without realism.

So let's put this rumor to sleep. The requirements for achievement in the field of literature—whether fantasy or realism—are much the same: Both require some of the attention implied by that old word *verisimilitude,* a word my little dictionary defines simply as "the appearance or semblance of truth." Readers must somehow identify with questing hobbits or heroic roosters before the flea can take wing. Fantasy requires realism.

Differences do exist, of course, between fantasy and realism, in the limited way we are now discussing differences. While the conveyance to imagined worlds is likely much the same (verisimilitude), and the end is undoubtedly similar (to tell a whoppin' good story), the givens of fantasy and realism are drawn from different worlds. Fantasy, usually, is set where none of us have been; realism, often enough, grows from worlds we all have known—or will.

To ask which is better is as silly as to wonder about which is most "Christian," if we can use that word as an adjective at all. From my point of view, the propensity toward realism is likely a predilection. The longer I write, the more I find myself agreeing with Flannery O'Connor, who used to say that we can choose what we'd like to write, but we can't choose what we can write well.

One need only to read my own titles to guess what it is that draws me to write. How about the following list? *Things We Couldn't Say, The Privacy of Storm, In the Silence There Are Ghosts, Still Life, The Secrets of Barneveld Calvary.* You can guess, perhaps, why I like Hawthorne. I'm nearly obsessed—I sometimes wish it weren't so—by secret sin. What am I hiding? I'll ask my analyst. We can choose what we write, but I don't know that I have a choice in what it is I do well.

There are always two kinds of art. One faces, grips, and wrestles with life. The other runs away from, or at least discreetly evades it. There is no disgrace in such a flight into worlds of fancy free.... Shakespeare was just as praiseworthy for creating "Twelfth Night" and its Illyria, so exquisitely hazy, so sweetly musical, so "high fantastica," as for grappling with all the urgent, actual, and ugly problems of being and of doing in "Hamlet." Incidentally, he wrote both plays, the best of his fantasies and the best of his tragedies, within a year or so. That surely gives a hint to us now. Art's splendor, as well as its utility, lies in its infinite variety. Our writers can be simultaneously the servants of reality and romance.

—IVOR BROWN, "And Why Not Write of Daffodils?"

Perhaps it's the Calvinist in me, but I believe a kind of foreordination operates the choice between realism and fantasy as well. Some of us are simply drawn to one, some to the other. Some love to create worlds where spiders grieve; some prefer our fictional grief to be human. Which is the better fruit—apples or oranges?

Years ago, I remember my son's fascination with Tolkien. I'm not sure how often he read *The Hobbit,* but I began to think that with a few more rounds at the dog-eared pages of the edition I bought him, he could simply put it on the shelf and tell the story by heart. Anyway, in the middle of that phase of his reading life, he once asked me why I didn't write things like *The Hobbit.* After observing his tenacity, I wondered myself.

The only answer I could come up with was this: Rather like Bartleby, I preferred not to. I never had a Tolkien or Lewis or L'Engle phase in my life. My interest in literature arose from my reading of a very realistic novel by a writer named Frederic Manfred, a man who lived, at the time, right down the road from where I attended college (and where I teach today). In a little-known novel titled *The Secret Place*, he brought me directly into a world I knew very well, a Dutch Reformed world, so that, at eighteen years old, I found tomatoes-and-sugar-on-toast. I suppose I've been a victim of the limitations of that experience ever since.

But if that's true, I can live with it, because to me spiders are interesting in and of themselves—and so are our stunned reactions to their untimely appearances. I've always been far more interested in the here and now than in yesterday or tomorrow or some meticulously fashioned time warp.

THE REALISTIC TALE

So, for better or for worse, how does this penchant for realism really work? Let me, once again, tell you a story.

Years ago, somewhere in the rural American South, a young preacher introduced his all-white Baptist church to the possibility of racial integration when a black family began to attend. Integration, at that time, was something touted only by a renegade preacher named Martin Luther King; it wasn't something sought by most white Southerners. This young preacher, however, was idealistic; and when the membership of that black family became a question for congregational approval, he told the people in his church that if they voted no, he had no reason to continue in their pulpit, for every last tenet of the gospel would be denied by their prejudice, by what he likely thought of as their sinful hate. His speech, a man who witnessed it told me, was unforgettable.

The congregation voted. The African-American family was denied membership.

The man who told me this story lost track of him and the church, but years later he heard that the young pastor, no longer so young certainly, and likely not as idealistic as he once might have been, ended his own life. That young pastor, whom my friend had admired so much throughout his life for his courageous stand, killed himself.

For whatever reason, the stories of this world are, to me at least, far more fascinating than the stories of some other. Why, I ask myself, would this man, this courageous, religious man, this man who looked in the face of sin and pleaded for righteousness, this man who was so right about what he saw and felt around—why would this man eventually kill himself? What could lead that man to the despair that leads to utter hopelessness?

The realist in me would love to write that story, to discover for myself what might have happened by undertaking a relentless pursuit of the elements I know—his powerful faith, his courage, and his ultimate despair. I'd like to answer for myself, imaginatively, what can make a man, a believer, fall to dire hopelessness. I would like to write that novel, if for no other reason than to pursue something I find very mysterious—and make sense of it. I suppose I could do that same investigation with red squirrels who give up hope, with defeated plow horses, or extraterrestrials; but I'd much prefer the feel of real life—not only to tell the story, but to read it myself.

What keeps me from writing that novel? Oddly enough, realism. I am well aware the best of writers are entirely capable of moving into arenas far from their own experience; that, for instance, *Sophie's Choice,* with some prudent editing, could well be the finest novel of the Holocaust, despite the fact that William Styron is neither a survivor nor Jewish. I know the great writers can move from setting to setting without missing a beat.

The only reason for the existence of a novel is that it does attempt to represent life.... The air of reality (solidity of specification) seems to me to be the supreme virtue of a novel—the merit on which all its other merits...depend.... [Other aspects of a novel] owe their effect to the success with which the author has produced the illusion of life.

—HENRY JAMES, "The Art of Fiction"

In spite of this, I fear a Midwesterner like myself could not handle the time-and-place givens prerequisite to making the story take wing. My telling it would make me look like the carpetbagger I'd be. Instead, I'd attempt to remove it from its setting in the American South. I'd have to create a powerfully difficult issue for some small-town Protestant preacher in the upper Midwest, an issue

296 THE CHRISTIAN IMAGINATION

over which he, or she, would have to take up Jeremiah's hectoring, because—realistically—the racial conflict simply would not play as well in rural Wisconsin as rural Alabama. I'd have to set the story here, where I know how people think and how the late afternoon sky opens reassuringly after a storm. To pursue the mystery of that story, I have to believe I can, first of all, achieve fidelity to actuality of time and place.

To a writer, what are the advantages of that kind of realism? I'm not sure there are any, actually. The success of Harry Potter and anything by Stephen King make it painfully clear that much of the reading public often prefers other worlds to our own. Should a census be undertaken, I am quite sure there would be more fantasy writers than realistic writers among believers who are novelists. Why? In part, I'm sure, sheer escape, arguably the most important ingredient in storytelling of any kind ("once upon a time..."). Fantasy offers escape more readily and more fully, I believe.

Second, at least among Christian readers, there is already an existing interest in and allegiance to another world than the one we inhabit, not only a fascination with John's Isle of Patmos dream sequences, but also a distaste and even a fear of the perils of this world of flesh and sin. Fantasy offers a template for a worldview already in place in many believers' minds, while realism only drops us back into the real world, an arena we, by some theologies, spend a lifetime escaping. "This world is not my home," we used to sing; "I'm just a passin' through." For some reason, writing about this world may well remind believing readers of a world they would rather forget or shun.

I don't believe writing in one genre is, in any sense, easier than the other. However, realism leads us toward the known, as opposed to the only imagined. In the real world, most men or women who smack their fingers with hammers say words that some Christians don't like to see on a page. A purely imagined world may offer freer playgrounds because fantasy's opportunities for sheer speculation are certainly more bountiful. We all know, in a way, this world; we can only dream of others.

That doesn't mean that fantasy writers keep us away from life's dark corners. They don't. Nonetheless, for a reader, despair may be easier to take in a hobbit than in a young preacher who, in a well-told story, comes painfully to resemble some revered relative.

WHAT BRINGS US TOGETHER

But there's one more side road we need to take here, and once again it's Flannery O'Connor who points directions. "People without hope," she said, "don't write novels." What she meant, I believe, is quite simple. The arduous work of creating life by way of words—whether it's fantasy or realism or anything else—is a task undertaken because the writer wants badly to gather the sometimes disparate strands of our lives together into narrative structure that has a beginning and an end. Writers—all of them—try to make sense of life itself, even if, like Poe, for instance, they see human madness as divinest sense.

And for that reason, all of us writers and readers are family. What we're after is order and meaning and some semblance of truth. A bearded man cusses out a flight attendant; a woman finds something strong in a heart she'd given up on; we know a place the sun shines only when it moves between towering office buildings: every writer I know attempts to juggle an exotic mixture of image, anecdote, and character, in order to make sense. And making meaning, O'Connor suggests, is a job not undertaken by the hopeless.

I think that she'd say that to all writers—things have meaning. Only in the seconds and minutes of our chronological lives is a spider, really, just a spider.

So what do we make of this morning's confrontation? I'm a realist; I think my arachnid buddy is worth a story all by himself, without hanging some additional transcendent thematic baggage on his surprise emergence or his speedy getaway. But I'm also a storyteller and something of a liar. If you've stayed with me for all this time, you've spent a century longer reading about him than he spent aboveboard on our kitchen counter. I'd like to tell you that, to me, a realist, a spider is only a spider, but his sudden appearance this morning has been the very real occasion of some peculiar flights of fantasy.

Somewhere beneath the sink right now, this eight-legged intruder is likely sitting in a barber chair, a circle of friends around him, telling them of his morning meeting with a monster. I hope it's entertaining. I bet it is—but if I'm going to write that conversation, it better be real.

I say, let him make of me what he will. More power to him. Just get it right.

Three Faces of Evil: Christian Writers and the Portrayal of Moral Evil

Susan Wise Bauer

My mother was a literate woman who prized books. She got me a library card as soon as I began to read and set me loose in the stacks. We took laundry baskets to the library so that we could carry all our books home. But each week, as she handed me my card, she repeated the same motto: *Whatever is true, whatever is noble, whatever is right, whatever is pure, whatever is lovely, whatever is admirable—if anything is excellent or praiseworthy—think about these things.*

This put a decided crimp in my book selection, even in the juvenile section. Pictures of vampires or ghosts? Not true and certainly not lovely. *Alexander's Terrible, Horrible, No Good, Very Bad Day?* Less than noble. Judy Blume? Certainly not. I carefully censored my own reading, lining everything up against the Philippians standard (and rereading *Little Women* again and again).

But evil pervades literature. For a child with an overactive conscience, I seem to have acquired a remarkably malevolent adult library. The holdall shelf beside my bed contains a dozen different portrayals of badness: Elie Wiesel's *Night*, *The Strange Case of Dr. Jekyll and Mr. Hyde*, *The Mayor of Casterbridge*, *Crime and Punishment*, Caleb Carr's serial-killer novel *The Angel of Darkness*, *Wise Blood*, Barbara Kingsolver's *The Poisonwood Bible*, and (hidden under *Wise*

SUSAN WISE BAUER *teaches American literature at the College of William and Mary in Virginia. She is a contributing editor to* Books and Culture *and the author of two novels. She is also coauthor of* The Well-Trained Mind *(W. W. Norton, 1999).*

Blood, because I'm embarrassed to be reading them) Stephen King's double-pack of horror novels, *Desperation* and the pseudonymous *The Regulators.* My night-time reading stands as testimony to Simone Weil's famous observation that imaginary evil is romantic, varied, and full of charm, while imaginary good is tiresome and flat.

There is nothing in our experience, however trivial, worldly, or even evil, which cannot be thought about christianly.
—HARRY BLAMIRES, *The Christian Mind*

The books on my shelf all deal with *moral* evil—the cruelty and corruption of men and women. Philosophers tell us that other kinds of evil exist: the physical evil of sickness, accident, and disease; and metaphysical evil, which causes catastrophe and decay. But moral evil, the wickedness we inflict on each other, is most troubling for the storyteller. Tales of physical and metaphysical evil can ultimately become stories of goodness, as the victims exercise strength, faith, and compassion in response to the difficulties they face. But how can descriptions of moral evil be anything but destructive for readers? What good can come from a careful chronicling of murder, and abuse, or a faithful investigation of the twisted thought paths of a serial killer?

Great good, if that investigation is done with a full understanding of what moral evil involves: willing capitulation to a transcendent evil that cannot be explained away in psychological terms.

EVIL, OR SIMPLY "OTHER?"

The devil is dead in America. He's been tottering for years, but Elaine Pagels erected his tombstone in 1995 with *The Origin of Satan.* Satan, Pagels declared, was the embodiment of the early Christians' desire to see themselves as righteous and their opponents (the "Other") as demonic. "Within the ancient world," Pagels writes, "so far as I know, it is only Essenes and Christians who escalate conflict with their opponents to the level of cosmic warfare." Pagels accuses Jesus himself of identifying his enemies with Satan, and the gospel writer John of turning those enemies into an identifiable ethnic group: the Jews. When Jesus and John decided to make the Jews a "symbol of human evil," Pagels concludes, centuries of Christians followed them in hating those who were different: Jews, heretics of all varieties, independent women, homosexuals, and all variety of "sinners" became "demonic," sons and daughters of Satan.

"Demonizing" is destructive, of course. You should strive to understand those who are "other" instead of labeling them as Satan-filled. The morally evil are recast as the "different"; a quest for understanding replaces the rush to judgment. The very use of the word *evil* implies that you refuse to enter into the experience of another, misunderstood person, or ethnic group, or sexual preference, stigmatizing them instead as allied with transcendent wickedness that can't be redeemed.

It's little surprise that this idea of otherness has usurped the place once held by transcendent evil. Our age speaks with the vocabulary of Freud; and religion, Freud theorized, was a childish and immature way to explain reality, and a society that clings to religious explanations is a sick society. "A turning-away from religion," he wrote, "is bound to occur with the fatal inevitability of a process of growth." A turning-away from God is part of this growth—but so is a parallel rejection of Satan and the transcendent evil he represents. Faced with evil, the mature civilization first asks: Is it truly evil, or is it just...different? And if the "difference" (a tendency to molest children, say) threatens social order, can we understand how the difference arose?

There is undoubtedly a great deal of fiction which sidesteps, minimizes, or sugar-coats the disagreeable. But so far are such evasions from the essential purpose of narrative art that we intuitively assign a low value to work of this character.... Among stories whose artistic authenticity cannot be questioned we give the highest place precisely to those works which ignore no aspect of man's nature, which confront the most disagreeable aspects of life deliberately and unflinchingly.

—SIMON LESSER, *Fiction and the Unconscious*

What does this have to do with the moral evil of literature? Novelists investigate human nature, laying bare its flaws and compulsions. The mind of the child killer or terrorist is fair game. But when the mind of a serial murderer or rapist is explained to us *solely* in terms of psychology, evil is reduced to difference—to mere otherness. Caleb Carr's hero in *The Angel of Darkness* and its prequel, *The Alienist,* is a nineteenth-century psychologist. He tracks a series of horrific murders so that he can explain the deaths in terms of the science of the mind. "You're a *man*," the child murderess in *The Angel of Darkness* shouts at the good Doctor. "What *man* could understand what my life has been like—why I've had to make the choices I have? Do you think I *wanted* any of this? It wasn't my fault that it happened!"

Serial-killer novels that are content to explain evil by dissecting the psychology of the perpetrator—or that lovingly describe the dismemberment of a victim so that we, too, can understand the joy of the kill—try to open the mind of evil to us, so that we can understand. We may put down the book thinking: *The killer is not so very different from me.* But this is a very far remove from: *There, but for the grace of God, go I.*

GRIMM'S FAIRY TALES FOR GROWNUPS

How can moral evil be more responsibly portrayed? Horror writer Dean Koontz, in describing his serial-killer novel *Intensity*, objects to the psychologizing of evil. Part of the thrust of his book, he argues, comes

> out of the Freudian theory that has led us to believe that virtually anybody can be understood or rehabilitated. But this isn't true. We put ourselves at risk when we accept that there is no such thing as real evil in the world, that it's really one degree or another of dysfunction and that it can all be treated.

Horror novels work against this Freudian obsession, reminding us that evil is not just a matter of twisted neural pathways. In his book *The Death of Satan*, Andrew Delbanco suggests that the popularity of horror novels is "a response to our panic over the loss of a language for speaking about evil":

> A gulf has opened up in our culture between the visibility of evil and the intellectual resources available for coping with it.... The repertoire of evil has never been richer. Yet never have our resources been so weak. We have no language for connecting our inner lives with the horrors that pass before our eyes in the outer world.... We certainly no longer have a conception of evil as a distributed entity with an ontological essence of its own, as what some philosophers call "presence." Yet something that feels like this force still invades our experience, and we still discover in ourselves the capacity to inflict it on others.

THE DEVIL HAS DIED IN AMERICA, BUT HIS GHOST LINGERS ON

So does Stephen King offer us a more responsible story of evil than Caleb Carr? In King's universe, evil is more than Otherness. Supernatural forces lurk in gloomy corners. Demons are real, waiting at every turn. There's no psychologizing here.

Great literature must treat evil, sometimes in a base and repulsive form…as do the Christian Scriptures.
—ROLAND M. FRYE, *Perspective on Man: Literature and the Christian Tradition*

In *Desperation*, which King calls "the best story I've written in probably ten or fifteen years," Tak—the demon *du jour*—has been trapped underground in a copper mine for centuries. When a strip-mining company opens its imprisoning shaft, Tak immediately escapes and possesses one of the inhabitants of a nearby town.

The life of a roaming demon is not as easy as you might suppose, and Tak has two sizable problems. Its superhuman energy wears out the bodies of its human hosts in short order, forcing it to jump ship as its present body disintegrates in typical King style. ("Cat got your tongue?" is not a figure of speech in this book.) Furthermore, Tak has to feed itself by killing off the surplus players—those who aren't useful host material—and feasting on the psychic energy thus released. An assortment of happy Nevada campers, traveling through the bare and sunny desert, find themselves sucked into battle with this creature, sized up as either habitation or hors d'oeuvre.

The Regulators treats us to the same set of characters, including the demon Tak, plopped down in the sleepy little hamlet of Wentworth, Ohio, and acting out an entirely different scenario. This time, Tak escapes from the Nevada copper mine and attaches himself to the consciousness of an autistic child named Seth, who happens to be driving by with his vacationing family. The family goes home, unaware of the hitchhiking parasite. But back in Wentworth, Tak is bored. Trapped by the limitations of his host, Tak slowly turns the town into a reproduction of Seth's imaginary universe, complete with giant avenging play-action figures armed with automatics. After three-quarters of the town is dead, Seth kills himself to save the survivors, thus effectively disembodying the demon. Have a nice day.

Any reasonable person, you might think, would flee all this grimness as quickly as possible. Or at least quit driving through Nevada on vacation. But King's public willingly forks over close to thirty dollars for his hardbacks, seven bucks per movie. King's Web site records thousands of hits daily. Bookstores where he appears in person brace for a torrent of fans. Loyal readers turn on their reading lights and stay up all night with Tak, deserting the real world in favor of a realm where moral evil is real, threatening—and transcendent, caused by the demon who inhabits his human hosts.

Why this passion for supernatural explanations of moral evil? In *The End of Education*, Neil Postman argues that we cannot live without a narration—a story that "tells of origins and envisions a future, a story that constructs ideals, prescribes rules of conduct, provides a source of authority, and above all, gives a sense of continuity and purpose." We tell ourselves stories that explain where we are, why we exist, why the world works the way it does. A good story tells us why we love, and why we hate. A good story explains why some people sacrifice their lives, while others destroy and mutilate.

The Christian story served this purpose well, with its narrative of a transcendent God and a personified Evil. But for twentieth-century Americans, the Christian story has been largely overwritten by snappier narratives. Postman offers the stories of inductive science, technology, and consumerism as examples. Each story offers us a purpose for living—the pursuit of knowledge, the mastery of the physical world, the accumulation of wealth.

The central theme found in Flannery O'Connor's writing is the redemption of man; but, since her talent inclines her toward the portrayal of sin, she shows the effects of the redemption (i.e., grace) in a negative manner. She reflects the beauty of virtue by showing the ugliness of its absence.

—JAMES F. FARNHAM, tribute to Flannery O'Connor
in *Flannery O'Connor: A Memorial*, ed. J. J. Quinn

None of these stories, though, offers a satisfying explanation for the evil that we inflict on each other. Ignorance, psychological trauma, poverty, and disenfranchisement—all of them fall silent in the face of Bosnia, Rwanda, Nazi Germany, or even Susan Smith, who murdered her two small boys by rolling her car into a lake with the children strapped safely into their car seats. We simply cannot account for these atrocities: *Time*'s cover article on the death of Smith's toddlers concludes that Smith was sexually abused, abandoned, depressed, and suicidal, but the headline trumpets the unanswered question, "How Could She Do It?" The same query confronts us as we view the corpses sprawled on Bosnian streets, floating down Rwandan rivers, stacked in heaps at the gas chambers.

Stephen King offers the answer: Transcendent evil exists and stalks the earth. In a 1992 *Writer's Digest* interview, King described his writing process as "like walking through a desert and all at once, poking up through the hardpan, I see the top of a chimney. I know there's a house down there, and I'm pretty sure that I can dig it up if I want. That's how I feel. It's like the stories are already there."

The innate human knowledge that Evil exists—malignancy with personality, a force that wishes us harm—keeps poking up through the neat narrative landscape of the twentieth century. Like our everyday lives, King's books don't look like hell at first glance. His characters are normal folks, going about their regular business. *Desperation* begins with its cast of assorted vacationers driving blamelessly through the Nevada desert; *The Regulators* opens with two children buying candy at the 7-Eleven, while the sounds of Little Leaguers at bat chunk happily over the hill. It's a world like Caleb Carr's, where evil is a matter for therapy, not exorcism. But there's something wrong in the cheerful suburb. A dark shadow bobs into view behind the ten-year-old batter's shoulder; a horrible creature whisks out of sight as he turns his head to look.

Americans read King for the same reason that a four-year-old asks to hear the "real" Hansel and Gretel, the one where the witch bakes in her own oven: We already know that evil is real, and we want to see it defeated. A good fairy tale serves this purpose for a toddler. Children are born knowing perfectly well that evil exists. Not even the most gently reared child escapes nightmares of the Thing Under the Bed. My middle son, carefully protected from television scariness by the vigilance of a resident grandmother, had his first nightmare at age three: a monster who came in the window and cut up his favorite blanket with giant scissors—a three-year-old's version of Tak, the evil force that descends to wipe away our security and destroy our carefully ordered lives. Gail Caldwell of the *Boston Globe* writes,

Most of us get acquainted with such fears by an early age; if we are fortunate, we have a chance to corral some of them within the sheltered realm of fantasy:

through some form of narrative where the ghouls disappear with the words "the end"—thus ensuring a frisson of danger while one is still safely ensconced in feet pajamas and a toast-like bed.

Children can go happily to sleep as soon as the witch dies. But adults, living in a world where a killer can snatch a twelve-year-old from her living room during a slumber party, where a hijacked jet can destroy a tower full of thousands of unsuspecting people, need a Grimm for grownups—a narrative that not only explains the presence of evil but offers a triumph over it.

Flannery O'Connor wrote of her own work, "I want to be certain that the Devil gets identified as the Devil and not simply taken for this or that psychological tendency." King—lacking both O'Connor's literary artistry and her solid theological underpinnings—nevertheless fulfills this exact function. The evildoers in *Desperation* are possessed by Tak, and the death that results originates in the mind of Tak. This devil is no mere metaphor.

RANDOM EVIL AND GUILTLESS EVILDOERS

King's picture of moral evil may represent an advance on purely psychological portrayals, but he still hasn't quite gotten it right. Evil in King's world is real and transcendent, but it is also (apparently) patternless. What terrifies us most is violence that descends without purpose, the serial killer who picks my bedroom window through a process of eeny-meeny-miney-mo. Both *Desperation* and *The Regulators* center on this kind of random evil. The travelers through the Nevada desert stumble on the one town where a demon is roaming around looking for victims to devour. In *The Regulators,* the autistic child who unwittingly serves as a channel for demonic power simply happens to pass by the mine where the demon lived. And even the demon chooses his victims without reason. The five-year-old girl in *Desperation* dies casually, for no reason, while her brother survives; who lives and who dies in *The Regulators* depends on who happens to be walking down the street when the giant action-figures-come-to-life cruise by with their automatic weapons. As in life, there is no guarantee that the character you like is going to survive.

At first glance, King's plots may seem the fictional counterpart of Harold Kushner's pop cosmology. Kushner writes that "some things happen for no reason." Evil is truly random, just as you've always feared. And this is the most frightening monster of all. If evil—as Rabbi Kushner explains—is simply a matter of "pockets of chaos" that stand outside God's creative and regulative power, there is no defense against it.

The serious writer has always taken the flaw in human nature for his starting point, usually the flaw in an otherwise admirable character. Drama usually bases itself on the bedrock of original sin, whether the writer thinks in theological terms or not.

—FLANNERY O'CONNOR, *Mystery and Manners*

King, lacking anything that resembles a coherent theology, doesn't even try to locate the purpose of evil. But he supplies us with an alternative method of mastering it by giving evil a personality. And this is the first step toward containing it. A personality can be appeased, wheedled with, defeated through an act of the will.

In *Desperation* and *The Regulators,* King satisfies all our yearnings. Don't want to believe that terrific evil has its source simply in the human soul? You're quite right; evil is supernatural. Can't live with a supernatural evil that strikes without reason? Don't worry. You're not defenseless; the Evil has personality, which makes it vulnerable to human wiles.

In both novels, Tak is conquered by human ingenuity. The small hero of *The Regulators* outwits the demon through a trick. In an echo of Christ's temptation in the desert, the dissolute hero of *Desperation* rejects Tak's offers of success, money, and wisdom and plunges into the mine shaft strapped with high explosives. (Why this should destroy a disembodied demon is anyone's guess, but it seems to work.) This is perhaps the most seductive element of King's narrative. Real and overwhelming evil is defeated, not by a transcendent God, but by a self-sacrificial act of the human will.

As in *Desperation,* the self-sacrifice is often performed by one of King's less admirable characters. King's recent novels have no bad people in them. People are just people; petty, self-absorbed, stupid, unadmirable, but not wicked. Wickedness comes from the supernatural powers that inhabit them. King's heroes aren't even necessarily on the good side. In *Insomnia,* the narrator explains that "nice moral questions as who was working for the good and who was working for the bad" aren't really the point. The hero fights evil because "the important thing was not to let the bullies kick sand in your face. Not to be led by the nose." In *Desperation*, this scrappy, human independence is overlaid by the presence of God. King describes *Desperation* as a "deeply Christian book," which will startle anyone who has actually read it; God is present, but he's an undemanding fellow who assigns the job of overcoming Tak to his human creations, and then desperately hopes they can pull it off. In fact, he is much like Rabbi Kushner's God—creative, good, well-meaning, but limited. The real heroes are King's characters, all of them pure at heart despite their flaws, all of them capable of nobility, all of them capable of defeating monsters.

Face to face with the reality of evil, the American public is reassured by King's fairy tales. The Thing Under the Bed is real. King doesn't tell you to go back to sleep and stop being silly; he equips you with an AK-47 and tells you that you're perfectly capable of blowing the monsters away. But King manages to recognize pure evil while absolving humanity in general of any particular impulse toward monstrosity. This concurrent distancing of ourselves from The Thing while recognizing that it may be as close as the nearest closet seems to comfort us. We read about *Desperation*'s serial killers and recognize them as creatures that might indeed exist in our safe comfortable world. But after all, those folks were possessed by Tak. Once again, we are spared any uncomfortable recognition of the possibility that there, but for the grace of God, go I.

The most tremendous indictments of evil-doing were written in the Jacobean English of the Authorized Version of the Bible and nobody ever will improve on that as a vehicle of righteous indignation.

—IVOR BROWN, "And Why Not Write of Daffodils?"

There is no guilt in King's world, which is why Audrey Wyler can serve as demonized murderer in *Desperation* and as sacrificial heroine in *The Regulators*. King absolves humanity of any responsibility for evil. Evil is real, but entirely transcendent, visiting Earth (as it were) from outer space. Evil is real, but we are all its victims.

But in the end, the comforting fantasy of King's novels turns out to be less satisfying than we think. King's answer to the most troubling question about evil—why do reasonably moral people sometimes choose it?—lies entirely in demonic possession. He seems to want to preserve the basic humanity of his characters. Of course, none of them would do such horrible things of their own free will. When given free will, they always choose to defeat the monster through self-sacrifice.

But this construction, paradoxically, destroys the very humanity King tries to save. Seth and Audrey Wyler and the demented police officer Collie Entragian are forced into evil against their will, possessed and turned into manslayers through a quirk of fate. King solves the problem of evil by removing any choice from his murderers. And so they become less than human, losing control of their own souls.

In the end, the Christian story yields more comfort. Orthodoxy may insist on responsibility, guilt, and the lake of fire, but it also offers choice. We aren't promised that we will never fall victim to a serial killer. But we are assured that we won't be transformed into serial killers against our will.

THE WILLING SURRENDER TO EVIL

Psychological explanations with no transcendent evil, transcendent evil without any human responsibility: The responsible portrayal of evil walks directly between Carr and King, and the multitude of novelists they represent. A true picture of evil retells the story of the Fall, so that we do not forget evil's double side: It is both human and transcendent, both demonic and psychological. Satan does walk the earth, but he goes only where he is welcomed.

Robert Louis Stevenson's Dr. Jekyll is in full control of himself when he begins his search for a potion that will separate the two parts of his nature—the good and the evil. But he finds the experience sweet; as Mr. Hyde, purely evil, he knows himself "to be more wicked, tenfold more wicked, sold a slave to my original evil; and the thought, in that moment, braced and delighted me like wine. I stretched out my hands exulting in the freshness of these sensations." Dr. Jekyll *chooses* to transform himself into Mr. Hyde again and again. Only this willing and repeated surrender allows Mr. Hyde to finally overcome Dr. Jekyll's remaining good. At the end, Dr. Jekyll is as helpless to resist Hyde as any of Tak's victims; he mourns, "I became, in my own person a creature eaten up and emptied by fever, languidly weak both in body and mind…a soul boiling with causeless hatreds, and a body that seemed not strong enough to contain the raging energies of life." But Jekyll, unlike Tak's unwilling hosts, opened the door himself.

Stevenson knew his Bible; this is how the evildoers of Scripture are portrayed, as ordinary men and women who, for whatever psychological reasons, open the door to transcendent evil—and willingly leave it cracked. Saul broods over David's popularity, and an evil spirit enters his spear-arm. Judas turns his back on Christ, and Satan enters his soul. Cain yields to jealousy, and the evil crouching at his door springs onto his back. Eve, indulging her wish for independence, holds out her hand, and the serpent twines around it.

The Christian novelist is distinguished from his pagan colleagues by recognizing sin as sin. According to his heritage he sees it not as sickness or an accident of environment, but as a responsible choice of offense against God which involves his eternal future.

—FLANNERY O'CONNOR, *Mystery and Manners*

This portrayal of evil need not involve Jekyll-and-Hyde transformations, or actual demons clinging to their victims' heads in Peretti-like fashion. Flannery O'Connor's Hazel Motes, founding his Church of Truth Without Jesus Christ Crucified, rejects God and then spirals into madness; Dostoevsky's Raskolnikov commits a crime of the intellect and finds himself possessed by guilt.

Yet Christian writers should be wary of dismissing more obvious supernatural elements as sensationalistic. King's books are pulp novels, scorned by critics partly because the knowledge of supernatural evil poking up to do us harm is considered lower class. The more prestigious literary publications stick to psychological evil, insisting that only the ignorant crowds believe in the supernatural. Fantasy is a mass-market genre; realism is literary. This decree of taste is rooted in a basic misunderstanding of existence as encompassing only the physical, the psychological, the explicable.

Art is Biblically Christian when the Devil cannot stand it. If the Devil can stand it or would hand out reproductions, then there is no Biblical Christian character to it.... The Devil cannot stand exposure of sin as sin, dirty, devastating misery for me; it unmasks him.

—CALVIN SEERVELD, *A Christian Critique of Art*

Christian writers have a double challenge: to return the transcendence of evil to their work, by showing its relationship to human psychology without tipping their work into the fantasy ghetto, and simultaneously to challenge the idea that the presence of supernatural elements in a book immediately removes its resemblance to reality. Asked about the grotesque elements in her fiction, Flannery O'Connor answered:

> The novelist with Christian concerns will find in modern life distortions which are repugnant to him, and his problem will be to make these appear as distortions to an audience which is used to seeing them as natural: and he may well be forced to take ever more violent means to get his vision across to this hostile audience. When you can assume that your audience holds the same beliefs you do, you can relax and use more normal means of talking to it; when you have to assume that it does not, then you have to make your vision apparent by shock—to the hard of hearing you shout, and for the almost-blind you draw large and startling figures.

The lack of transcendent evil in literary fiction is a distortion of reality. It may be necessary for the Christian novelist to draw the presence of the demonic large and startling, so that it can be seen.

Christian readers and writers have a long tradition on which to lean. In this century, fantasy masters J. R. R. Tolkien and C. S. Lewis have painted evil in just this way. Tolkien's Ring of Power represents the evil, which we first put on because we choose to—and then are unable to rid ourselves of. The Ring swallows Gollum, transforming him from an innocent hobbitlike creature into a demonic goblin. But Gollum's fall begins with his willingness to gaze at, and then covet, the beautiful golden circle. His first surrender to the Ring's magic is voluntary; only as he continues to indulge in its use does he become enslaved. Bilbo Baggins, hero of *The Hobbit*, and Frodo, his young heir in *The Lord of the Rings*, almost suffer the same fate. They are preserved from possession only by the intervention of Gandalf, the wizard and guide who serves as Tolkien's Christ-figure (not only in his ability to offer grace, but in his "death" and "resurrection"). Lewis, working in a different mode, gives us Professor Weston, who visits Perelandra with scientific intent, but allows his ambitions and cravings to slowly overtake him until he becomes the Un-man, possessed by a Force that he has summoned but can no longer control.

Lewis and Tolkien follow in a rich tradition: Marlowe's Faustus is a medieval Gollum, chasing after knowledge and power, in full control of himself—until the play's end. Faced with damnation, he discovers that he has passed, without knowing it, the point of repentance. He has lost the capacity to cry out for grace; he can only look, helpless, at the mercy which could have once been his. And Milton gives us a Satan who is himself in the grip of a compulsion which he created and to which he yielded. Setting himself and his army against God, Satan is "hurled headlong flaming from th'ethereal sky," into the fiery gulf where he squats at the beginning of *Paradise Lost.* Now he is devoured by the lust for revenge. His companions warn him that his attacks on man will only serve to advance God's providential causes, but Satan refuses to listen. "Hail horrors!" he spits back:

> ...hail
> Infernal world, and thou profoundest Hell
> Receive thy new possessor: one who brings
> A mind not to be changed by place or time.
> The mind is its own place, and in itself
> Can make a Heavn' of Hell, a Hell of Heav'n.

He is insane with hatred: He nursed it, and now it has overwhelmed him, the possessor possessed.

Christian writers, then, become (in the words of the great science fiction writer Orson Scott Card, a devout Mormon) "lovers of good and students of evil." Their evildoers should reenact the great and true story of the Fall, showing a willingness to yield to the transcendent evil that ultimately overcomes them. And their portrayals of evil should point, without apology, toward the reality of a transcendent realm where evil exists—along with the good that will ultimately defeat it.

Viewpoint: John Ciardi

The Writer's Facts

"You have to give them something to write about," Robert Frost once said in discussing his classroom principles. His own poems are full of stunning examples of the central truth that good writers deal in information, and that even the lofty (if they are lofty) acreages of poetry are sown to fact. Consider the opening lines of "Mending Wall."... It contains as much specific information about stone walls as one could hope to find in a Department of Agriculture pamphlet. Frost states his passion for the *things* of the world both in example and in precept. "The fact is the sweetest dream the labor knows," he writes in "The Mowing."...

Even so mystical a poet as Gerard Manley Hopkins...is gorgeously given to the fact of the thing. Consider: "and blue-bleak embers, ah my dear, / Fall, gall themselves, and gash gold-vermilion" (*i.e.,* "Coal embers in a grate, their outside surfaces burned out and blue-bleak, sift down, fall through the grate, strike the surface below or the side of the grate, and are gashed opening to reveal the gold-vermilion fire still glowing at their core").

The writer of fiction deals with his facts in a different way, but it will not do to say that he is more bound to fact than is the poet: he simply is not required to keep his facts under poetic compression; keep hard to them he still must. Consider Melville's passion for the details of whaling; or DeFoe's for the details of criminality, of ransoming an English merchant captured by a French ship, or of Robinson Crusoe's carpentry. The passion for fact was powerful enough in these masters to lure them into shattering the pace of their own best fiction, and to do so time and time again. And who is to say that a person reading for more than amusement, a person passionate to touch the writer's mind in his writing, has any real objection to having the pace so shattered? All those self-blooming, lovingly-managed, chunky, touchable facts!

For a writer is a person who must know something better than anyone else does, be it so little as his own goldfish or so much as himself. True, he is not required to know any one specific thing. Not at least until he begins to write about it. But once he has chosen to write about X then he is responsible for knowing everything the writing needs to know about X....

Poetry and fiction, like all the arts, are a way of perceiving and of understanding the world. Good writing is as positive a search for truth as is any part of science, and it deals with kinds of truth that must forever be beyond science. The writer must learn, necessarily of himself and within himself, that his subject is the nature of reality, that good writing always increases the amount of human knowledge available.

—"What Every Writer Must Learn"
The Saturday Review, 15 December 1956

Viewpoint: Larry Woiwode

The Superiority of Realism to Fantasy

From the time that the Law and then Christ established a standard for measuring the reality of truth, I believe that every writer has been striving for (besides accuracy and clarity) a substantiality of detail that causes the reader to say, "This is *true*." This sort of accuracy is easy to blur if you're writing about Saturn. All writing is imaginative, as any writer who has worked at it realizes; the question is which world do you wish to exercise your imagination in?...

When a writer like John Gardner talks about the "great lie" of fiction, he doesn't mean the writer is perpetrating a lie in order to pull the wool over a reader's eyes, but that the reader is able to enter a fictional world so fully he takes the metaphor constructed of words to be a reality as substantial as the one in which he just dropped that book to the floor.... Accuracy occurs when proper weight is given through the metaphor of words to an act or process or object within that reality. Truth is reality in all its precision and fullness....

The tradition in fiction that attempts to portray this world as it exists (and would have been a bore to previous generations, according to Lewis) is largely the Christian tradition. Its power is that the best of its characters bear the breathing reality of members of the household of God. We couldn't otherwise meet these people and extend the hospitality of our hearts to them in the edification that builds up the Church in love....

Now it was precisely the "earthly" realistic note which Christianity introduced into Western literature.

— AMOS N. WILDER, *Theology and Modern Literature*

"Suspension of disbelief" is not only an awful Coleridgian jawbreaker but a binary confusion you never have to wonder about when you feel another person take your hand. Characters in the best fiction enter your life with that directness, and the more they conform to the image of Christ, the more they provide a means for a young man, for instance, to walk at the side of a father he never had. And with those characters who don't conform to Him, since they aren't actual people who can do us physical harm but metaphors for people and the states we sometimes find ourselves in, we can always walk the extra mile along their way and learn from them before bidding them good-bye....

What do [children] learn from fantasy—which is not necessarily a child's choice of genre but the one adults choose for them? Is it a better genre? Can they translate what those bears and lions are up to in a way that could be called, generously, even imaginatively, constructive? In realistic fiction they could learn how to start a car, but would they steal one? At least the discussion could be brought up. In realistic fiction they could learn to honor their parents, not a vague concept of honor transmitted from the stars....

I regret to report that...you will probably find the most resistance to reexamining imaginative writing, which includes science fiction and fantasy, within the Christian community. That community seems to want to live in an ideological never-never land, in which it takes at least two transpositions—translating fantasy into a recognizable truth and then attempting to transpose that translation into the life we know—to bring the fiction home. If you look at the genre's lifeline (any Christian publishing house's life of fiction), you are forced to come to the conclusion that members of the modern church want to be drawn out of the life they're to attend to, or dumbed-down, if not deceived.

But I also sense a fragrance of hope for contemporary writing, and Christian fiction in particular. In recent years I've seen students grow more interested in accuracy, in the many-layered dimensions of reality, and in the importance of people over recycled Big Ideas.

—*Acts: The Word Set Free*
© 1993 by Larry Woiwode
Reprinted by permission of HarperCollins Publishers, Inc.

Part Eight

Myth and Fantasy

While realism and fantasy together comprise the realm of literature, they are separate provinces, having their own local rules and customs. Like realism, myth and fantasy have their own enthusiasts, their own "apology," their own aesthetic (philosophy), and their own methodology. And while there is no necessary quarrel between realism and fantasy, so that readers can relish both of them equally, most readers have a temperamental preference for one of them, just as writers do.

The purpose of the essays and excerpts in this unit is to place myth and fantasy in the best possible light (just as the previous unit did for realism). Contributors to this unit address the following questions specifically:

- What are the differentiating traits of myth and fantasy?
- What are the particular excellences of myth and fantasy as literary forms?
- How do myth and fantasy relate to the Christian faith?

The Gospel As Fairy Tale

Frederick Buechner

THE UNIVERSALITY OF FAIRY TALES

Once upon a time there was a great wizard who lived in a far country. Once upon a time, in a deep forest, there was a poor woodchopper and his wife. Once upon a time a deep sleep fell upon all the inhabitants of the palace, and spiders spun their webs like silver curtains across all the windows and in the throne room, where once the king held court, birds flew in to build their nests and red squirrels came in to store their acorns because in all the place there was no man left awake to hinder them. *Once upon a time,* which is to say at a time beyond time, or at a different kind of time altogether from the kind the clock measures, or at a time that is no time at all because it is without beginning and without end. *There was* a wizard, a woodchopper, a king, which is to say that if you are to believe that *there was,* you have to give up other beliefs you believe in including the belief that *there was not* because there could not be such creatures as these. *A far country, a deep forest, a palace,* which is to say that if you care to enter these places for yourself, you must be willing to enter them in some measure as a child because it takes a child to believe in the possibility at least that such places exist instead of dismissing them out-of-hand as impossible.

Once upon a time there was a child named Lucy, who was playing hide-and-seek with some other children in an old house. It was her turn to be It, and

FREDERICK BUECHNER *is widely known as an author and speaker on literary and religious topics. His writing extends across an impressive range and includes fiction (the Bebb books), theology, biblical criticism, autobiography, and literary criticism. The following excerpt is taken from Buechner's book* Telling the Truth: The Gospel As Tragedy, Comedy, and Fairy Tale *(Harper-Collins, 1977). Copyright © 1977 by Frederick Buechner. Reprinted by permission of Harper-Collins Publishers, Inc.*

finding herself in a room where there was no furniture except for a big old-fashioned wardrobe, and hearing the sound of the others clattering down the corridor in search of her, she stepped into the wardrobe to hide. There were clothes hanging in it and mothballs on the floor, and as she moved farther in toward the back of it, she could feel the clothes brushing against her face and arms and could hear the sound of the mothballs under her feet.…

Or in George MacDonald's tale *Fantastes* the hero, Anodos, is awakened by the sound of water and opens his eyes to find that a clear brook is running through his bedroom. The carpet has turned to grass that bends and sways in the light breeze and the furniture is all entwined with ivy. The curtains of his bed have become the branches of a great tree whose leaves are dappling him with shadow. The tree is at the edge of a dense forest, and there are faint traces of a footpath much overgrown with grass and moss leading into it. Or Alice, drowsing by the fire with her cat, notices that the looking glass over the mantel has a curious look to it so she climbs up on the mantel to see, and sure enough the glass starts to melt away like a bright, silvery mist, and she steps through it. Or a farmhouse is caught up in a cyclone and whirled up higher and higher into the stormy sky until finally it comes to rest again and the child inside opens the door onto the Land of Oz.

All the elements of the fairy tale are waiting within us: the quest; the younger son; the true princess; the benevolent brothers (or sisters); the witch, or wizard; the wise old woman; beasts and monsters; the happy ending.
—MADELEINE L'ENGLE, *The Rock That Is Higher*

As far as I know, there has never been an age that has not produced fairy tales. It doesn't seem to matter what is going on at the time. It can be a time of war or peace, of feast or famine. It can be Calvin's Geneva or Calvin Coolidge's U.S.A. No matter what's up politically, economically, religiously, artistically, people always seem to go on telling these stories, many of them stories that have been around for so long that it is as impossible to be sure when they first started as it is to be sure when if ever they will finally end. Different as they are from each other, they seem to have certain features in common, and since more than any other kind of literary form I can think of they come not necessarily from literary people but just from people generally, the way dreams come, there seems reason to believe that if nothing else, they have something to tell us about the kind of things we keep on dreaming century after century, in good times and bad. We keep on telling them to our children and remembering them so well out of our own childhood, that we don't have to look them up and read them out of books most of the time but can simply dredge them up out of ourselves because to one degree or another they have become part of who we are. For my own tastes, it is both more difficult and less interesting to try to explain what fairy tales mean—as a psychologist or a mythologist might—than it is simply to look at them for what they contain. Like the world of dreams or the world of memory, the world of the fairy tale is one of the worlds where most of us have at one time or another lived whether we read fairy tales as children or read them still or not because Cinderella and the Sleeping Beauty are part of the air we breathe, and my inclination is to approach their world not as some kind of archaeologist, trying to excavate and analyze, but simply as a tourist guide, trying only to describe some of the principal sights to be seen.

RECURRENT MOTIFS

To start with, the stories that do not just tell us about the world of the fairy tale in and of itself but tell us something about where it is located and how to reach it seem to agree that it is not as far away as we might think and under the right circumstances not really all that hard to get to. The house where the children are playing hide-and-seek is an ordinary house just as the tent where Abraham and Sarah laughed until the tears ran down their cheeks was an ordinary tent. The young man Anodos woke up in his bedroom just as he'd awakened there hundreds of times before, and there was nothing particularly unusual about the time and place where Alice curled up beside the fire with her cat, Dinah, any more than there was anything particularly unusual about Alice herself living in Victorian London or about Dorothy Gale living in turn-of-the-century Kansas or about the cyclone that came twisting across the prairie as cyclones had often come before and come still. The fairy-tale world that they all stepped into was very different from the world they normally lived in and very different, too, from the ordinary world of who they were inside themselves, their inner worlds, but the point seems to be that they did not have to go a great distance to enter it any more than you have to go a great distance to enter the world of dreams—you just have to go to sleep—or the world of memory—you just have to cast your mind's eye backward and let it float up out of the past.

It might be more accurate to say that the world of the fairy tale found them, and found them in the midst of their everyday lives in the everyday world. It is as if the world of the fairy tale impinges on the ordinary world the way the dimension of depth impinges on the two-dimensional surface of a plane, so that there is no point on the plane—a Victorian sitting room or a Kansas farm—that can't become an entrance to it. You enter the extraordinary by way of the ordinary. Something you have seen a thousand times you suddenly see as if for the first time like the looking glass over the mantel or the curtains of the bed. Furthermore, even the fairy tales that do not describe the actual passing from one world to the other as such tell about people who though they come in more exotic guise than most of us—poor woodchoppers and fair maidens—are people more or less like ourselves who suddenly, usually without warning, find themselves on the dim frontier. A bankrupt merchant picks a rose for his beautiful daughter and suddenly hears the terrible voice of a beast at his side. A brother and a sister lost in the wood come unexpectedly on a house made of gingerbread. Cinderella, who lives in a loneliness and despair all too familiar, is visited by an old woman who changes a pumpkin into a golden coach. In each case, a strange world opens up when it chooses to open up, and when they enter it things happen that in the inner world of who they are and the outer world of where they ordinarily live their lives couldn't possibly happen.

What distinguishes the fairy-tale world from the other world of fiction?
First of all, the most obvious: its universality. The same plots appear again
and again; it is only the physical environment that is changed; for the fairy
tale is…simple [and] sparsely told.

—ERIK CHRISTIAN HAUGAARD, "Portrait of a Poet: Hans Christian Andersen and His Fairy Tales," in *The Openhearted Audience*, ed. Virginia Haviland

---

And what is it like, this world itself, once they have entered it? Maybe the first thing to say is that it is a world full of darkness and danger and ambiguity. Almost the first thing that Lucy's brother Edmund sees when he too steps through the wardrobe into Narnia is a sleigh being pulled through the deep snow by reindeer and seated in the sleigh, wrapped in furs, a queen with a face white as death who holds the whole land under her icy sway. There are fierce dragons that guard the treasure and wicked fairies who show up at royal christenings. To take the wrong turning of the path is to risk being lost in the forest forever, and an awful price has to be paid for choosing the wrong casket or the wrong door. It is a world of dark and dangerous quest where the suitors compete for the hand of the king's daughter with death to the losers, or the young prince searches for the princess who has slept for a hundred years, or the scarecrow, the tinman, and the lion travel many a mile in search of the wizard who will make them whole, and all of them encounter on their way great perils that are all the more perilous because they are seldom seen for what they are. That is another mark of the fairy-tale world. The beautiful queen is really a witch in disguise, and to open the lid of the golden casket is to be doomed. Not only does evil come disguised in the world of the fairy tale but often good does too. Who could guess that the little gray man asking for bread is a great magician who holds in his hands the power of life and death? One thinks again of *King Lear,* which is itself a kind of fairy tale with the two wicked sisters and the one good one, and like the three rings or the three caskets, the three speeches each must make about how they love the old king, their father. In the world of *King Lear* it is the wicked ones like Goneril and Regan who go about in gorgeous robes, and the good ones, the compassionate and innocent ones, who wander disguised in a fool's motley or the rags of beggars and madmen.

Beasts talk and flowers come alive and lobsters quadrille in the world of the fairy tale, and nothing is apt to be what it seems. And if this is true of the creatures that the hero meets on his quest, it is true also of the hero himself who at any moment may be changed into a beast or a stone or a king or have his heart turned to ice. Maybe above all they are tales about transformation where all creatures are revealed in the end as what they truly are—the ugly duckling becomes a great white swan, the frog is revealed to be a prince, and the beautiful but wicked queen is unmasked at last in all her ugliness. They are tales of transformation where the ones who live happily ever after, as by no means everybody does in fairy tales, are transformed into what they have it in them at their best to be.

The Beast falls sick for love of Beauty and lies dying in his garden when she abandons him until she returns out of compassion and says that for all his ugliness she loves him and will marry him, and no sooner has she kissed him on his glistening snout than he himself becomes beautiful with royal blood in his veins. In "The Happy Hypocrite" Max Beerbohm tells about a regency rake named Lord George Hell, debauched and profligate, who falls in love with a saintly girl, and, in order to win her love, covers his bloated features with the mask of a saint. The girl is deceived and becomes his bride, and they live together happily until a wicked lady from Lord George Hell's wicked past turns up to expose him for the scoundrel she knows him to be and challenges him to take off his mask. So sadly, having no choice, he takes it off, and lo and behold beneath the saint's mask is the face of the saint he has become by wearing it in love. The scarecrow gets his brain from the great and terrible Oz, the lion his courage, the tinman his heart. Even in Hans Christian Andersen's "The Steadfast Tin Soldier," one of the darkest of his tales, the theme of the transformed hero is repeated. With only one leg to stand on and battered by his misadventures, the tin soldier remains so steadfast in his love for the paper doll that even after the little boy hurls him in the stove and the flames have melted him, what the servant girl finds in the ashes is a piece of tin in the shape of a heart. For better or worse, in the world of the fairy tale transformations are completed, and one thinks of the angel in the book of Revelation who gives to each a white stone with a new name written on it which is the true and hidden name that he was named with even from the foundations of the world.

He does not despise real woods because he has read of enchanted woods: the reading makes all real woods a little enchanted.

—C. S. LEWIS, "On Three Ways of Writing for Children"

To moralize or allegorize these tales or to explain them as having to do with sexual awakening or the successful resolution of Oedipal conflicts is not so much to go too far with them as it is not to go far enough because beneath whatever with varying degrees of success they can be shown to mean, and beneath the specific events and adventures they describe, what gives them their real power and meaning is the world they evoke. It is a world of magic and mystery, of deep darkness and flickering starlight. It is a world where terrible things happen and wonderful things too. It is a world where goodness is pitted against evil, love against hate, order against chaos, in a great struggle where often it is hard to be sure who belongs to which side because appearances are endlessly deceptive. Yet for all its confusion and wildness, it is a world where the battle goes ultimately to the good, who live happily ever after, and where in the long run everybody, good and evil alike, becomes known by his true name.

GLIMPSES OF JOY

It is perhaps this aspect of the fairy tale that gives it its greatest power over us, this sense we have that in that world, as distinct from ours, the marvelous and impossible thing truly happens. No one speaks of this quality more eloquently than one of the great modern masters of the fairy tale, J. R. R. Tolkien. He writes that the fairy tale

> …does not deny the existence of…sorrow and failure: the possibility of these is necessary to the joy of the deliverance; it denies (in the face of much evidence, if you will) universal final defeat…, giving a fleeting glimpse of Joy, Joy beyond the walls of the world, poignant as grief.
>
> It is the mark of the good fairy-story, of the higher or more complete kind, that however wild its events, however fantastic or terrible the adventures, it can give to child or man that hears it, when the "turn" comes, a catch of the breath, a beat and lifting of the heart, near to (or indeed accompanied by) tears, as keen as that given by any form of literary art.

Good and evil meet and do battle in the fairy-tale world much as they meet and do battle in our world, but in fairy tales the good live happily ever after. That is the major difference. So great is the power of magic that even the less-than-good live happily ever after. It is the beast who becomes beautiful, the cowardly lion who becomes brave, the wicked sisters with their big feet and fancy ways who repent in the end and are forgiven. It is really two impossible things that happen because happiness is not only inevitable, it is also endless. Joy happens, to use Tolkien's word, and the fairy tale where it happens is not a world where everything is sweetness and light. It is not Disney Land where everything is kept spotless and all the garbage is trundled away through underground passages beneath the sunny streets. On the contrary, the world where this Joy happens is as full of darkness as our own world, and that is why when it happens it is as poignant as grief and can bring tears to our eyes. It can bring tears to our eyes because it might so easily not have happened, and because there are the wicked ones to whom it does not happen, and just because there are some to whom it does not happen, it happens in a world where those who live happily ever after must do so in a world where though happiness is both inevitable and endless, darkness persists because happiness is not universal. Dark spells can still be cast and bad witches prosper. In Tolkien's *The Lord of the Rings,* it is true that in the destruction of the demonic ring a great evil is destroyed, but the universal triumph of good is still only a hobbit's dream, and the golden age of elves and dwarfs is fated to be followed by the tragic age of men. Yet the tears that come to our eyes at the joy of the fairy tale are nevertheless essentially joyous tears because what we have caught a glimpse of, however fleeting, is Joy itself, the triumph if not of goodness, at least of hope. And I do not think it is entirely fanciful to say that it is not only in fairy tales that we have glimpsed it.

You wake up on a winter morning and pull up the shade, and what lay there the evening before is no longer there—the sodden gray yard, the dog droppings, the tire tracks in the frozen mud, the broken lawn chair you forgot to take in last fall. All this has disappeared overnight, and what you look out on is not the snow of Narnia but the snow of home, which is no less shimmering and white as it falls. The earth is covered with it, and it is falling still in silence so deep that you can hear its silence. It is snow to be shoveled, to make driving even worse than usual, snow to be joked about and cursed at, but unless the child in you is entirely dead, it is snow, too, that can make the heart beat faster when it catches you by surprise that way, before your defenses are up. It is snow that can awaken memories of things more wonderful than anything you ever knew or dreamed.

And actually fairy-stories deal largely, or (the better ones) mainly, with simple things...made all the more luminous by their setting.... It was in fairy-stories that I first divined the potency of the words, and the wonder of the things, such as stone, and wood, and iron; tree and grass; house and fire; bread and wine.

—J. R. R. TOLKIEN, "On Fairy-Stories"

If you still have something more than just eyes to see with, the world can give you these glimpses as well as fairy tales can—the smell of rain, the dazzle of sun on white clapboard with the shadows of ferns and wash on the line, the wildness of a winter storm when in the house the flame of a candle doesn't even flicker. The world can give us such glimpses, and dreams can too sometimes— the dreams you wake up from without being quite able to remember them yet with the knowledge that you are somehow the better for having dreamed them, dreams that erase old hurts and failures and start a kind of healing, dreams where the old man who had his last birthday all those summers ago is alive and well still. He is wearing a paper hat and nods at you as if you had met only yesterday, and his death turns out to have had no more substance to it than the smoke from his fifty-cent cigar....

Here and there and not just in books we catch glimpses of a world of once upon a time and they lived happily ever after, of a world where there is a wizard to give courage and a heart, an angel with a white stone that has written on it our true and secret name, and it is so easy to dismiss it all that it is hardly worth bothering to do. It is sentimentality. It is wishful thinking. It is escapism. It is dodging the issue and whistling in the dark and childish. And amen we have to say to the whole cheerless litany because there is not one of us who does not know it by heart and because there is not one of us either who does not know that all these things are part of the truth of it. But if the world of the fairy tale and our glimpses of it here and there are only a dream, they are one of the most haunting and powerful dreams that the world has ever dreamed and no world more than our twentieth-century one.

THE UNQUENCHABLE LONGING

We do our twenty minutes of meditation a day in the hope that, properly stilled, our minds will stop just reflecting back to us the confusion and multiplicity of our world but will turn to a silvery mist like Alice's looking glass that we can step through into a world where the beauty that sleeps in us will come awake at last. We send scientific expeditions to Loch Ness because if the dark and monstrous side of fairy tales can be proved to exist, who can be sure that the blessed side doesn't exist, too? I suspect that the whole obsession of our time with the monstrous in general—with the occult and the demonic, with exorcism and black magic and the great white shark—is at its heart only the shadow side of our longing for the beatific, and we are like the knight in Ingmar Bergman's film

The Seventh Seal, who tells the young witch about to be burned at the stake that he wants to meet the devil her master, and when she asks him why, he says, "I want to ask him about God. He, if anyone, must know."...

At the close of his career, after the period of the great tragedies, Shakespeare turned to something much closer to true fairy tales. He wrote *Cymbeline,* where innocence is vindicated and old enemies reconciled, and *The Winter's Tale,* where the dead queen turns out not to be dead at all, the lost child, Perdita, restored to those who love her. And he wrote *The Tempest* itself, where the same great storm of the world that drowned the Franciscan nuns aboard the *Deutschland* and lashed old Lear to madness and stung Job in his despair is stilled by Prospero's magic; and justice is done, and lovers reunited, and the kingdom restored to its rightful king so that in a way it is the beautiful dream of Caliban that turns out to be real and the storm of the world with all its cloud-capped towers and gorgeous palaces and solemn temples that turns out to be the insubstantial pageant that fades into thin air and leaves not a rack behind.

Like the last self-portraits of Rembrandt, where the ravaged old face of the painter smiles out of the shadows, it is as if at the end of his career Shakespeare comes out on the far side of the tragic vision of *Lear* and *Macbeth* and speaks into the night a golden word too absurd perhaps to be anything but true, the laughter of things beyond the tears of things.

Shakespeare had always favoured old tales—the venerable casket story and the tale of Lear.... Fairy tales, romance and adventure appeal to us, not just because they are different from our ordinary experience but because they present in easily assimilable form an essential element of that experience, the shrouding mystery of life and the tremulous human desire for an unseen glory.

—S. L. BETHELL, *The Winter's Tale: A Study*

The biographer of Henry Ward Beecher tells us that on his travels he often carried with him a pocketful of precious stones. People would give them to him, or jewelers, knowing his taste, would lend them to him, and he would take them out and look at them and hand them around at the places he went. Garnets and cat's eyes and pearls, sometimes even sapphires and emeralds, he called them his "unfading flowers" and "loved to watch the colors come and go in their cryptic depths as a child might." Looking at one of them once, he said that he felt "as if there were a soul back of it looking through the rays of light flashing over it and in every way it seemed a thing of life."

I wonder if there is any real doubt what it was that he saw in them or what the world was whose light gleamed up at him out of their glittering depths. "Thou hast been in Eden, the garden of God," the Lord says to Ezekiel. "Every precious stone was thy covering, the sardius, topaz, and the diamond, the beryl, the onyx and the jasper, the sapphire, the emerald, the carbuncle and the gold...thou wast upon the holy mountain of God; thou hast walked up and down in the midst of the stones of fire" (Ezek. 28:13-14). In cathedrals and temples, on high altars where the host is enshrined, there are always jewels like the ones the old preacher carried around in his pocket or if not jewels, then stained glass turned to jewels by the sun's shining through it or the fire of candles as jewels that waver and live. They are there because in their depth and brilliance they speak of joy and beauty and holiness beyond the walls of the world. They speak to us of the world of the Gospel as itself the world of the fairy tale.

THE GOSPEL AS FAIRY TALE

Like the fairy-tale world, the world of the Gospel is a world of darkness, and many of the great scenes take place at night. The child is born at night. He had his first meal in the dark at his mother's breast, and he had his last meal in the dark too, the blinds drawn and everybody straining to catch the first sound of heavy footsteps on the stair, the first glint of steel in the shadowy doorway. In the garden he could hardly see the face that leaned forward to kiss him, and from the sixth hour to the ninth hour the sun went out like a match so he died in the same darkness that he was born in and rose in it, too, or almost dark, the sun just barely up as it was just barely up again when only a few feet off shore, as they were hauling their empty nets in over the gunnels, they saw him once more standing there barefoot in the sand near the flickering garnets of a charcoal fire.

In the world of the fairy tale, the wicked sisters are dressed as if for a Palm Beach wedding, and in the world of the Gospel it is the killjoys, the phonies, the nitpickers, the holier-than-thous, the loveless and cheerless and irrelevant who more often than not wear the fancy clothes and go riding around in sleek little European jobs marked Pharisee, Corps Diplomatique, Legislature, Clergy. It is the ravening wolves who wear sheep's clothing. And the good ones, the potentially good anyway, the ones who stand a chance of being saved by God because they know they don't stand a chance of being saved by anybody else? They go around looking like the town whore, the village drunk, the crook from the IRS, because that is who they are. When Jesus is asked who is the greatest in the kingdom of Heaven, he reaches into the crowd and pulls out a child with a cheek full of bubble gum and eyes full of whatever a child's eyes are full of and says unless you can become like that, don't bother to ask.

And as for the king of the kingdom himself, whoever would recognize him? He has no form or comeliness. His clothes are what he picked up at a rummage sale. He hasn't shaved for weeks. He smells of mortality. We have romanticized his raggedness so long that we can catch echoes only of the way it must have scandalized his time in the horrified question of the Baptist's disciples, "Are *you* he who is to come?" (Matt. 11:13); in Pilate's "Are you the king of the Jews?" (Matt. 27:11) you with pants that don't fit and a split lip; in the black comedy of the sign they nailed over his head where the joke was written out in three languages so nobody would miss the laugh.

But the whole point of the fairy tale of the Gospel is, of course, that he is the king in spite of everything. The frog turns out to be the prince, the ugly duckling the swan, the little gray man who asks for bread the great magician with the power of life and death in his hands, and though the steadfast tin soldier falls into the flames, his love turns out to be fireproof. There is no less danger and darkness in the Gospel than there is in the Brothers Grimm, but beyond and above all there is the joy of it, this tale of a light breaking into the world that not even the darkness can overcome.

The world of the fairy tale, fantasy, myth, is inimical to the secular world, and in total opposition to it, for it is interested not in limited laboratory proofs, but in truth. When I was a child, reading Hans Christian Andersen's tales, reading about Joseph and his coat of many colours and his infuriating bragging about his dreams, reading The Selfish Giant *and* The Book of Jonah, *these diverse stories spoke to me in the same language, and I knew, intuitively, that they belonged to the same world. For the world of the Bible…is the world of Story.*

—MADELEINE L'ENGLE, *Walking on Water*

That is the Gospel, this meeting of darkness and light and the final victory of light. That is the fairy tale of the Gospel with, of course, the one crucial difference from all other fairy tales, which is that the claim made for it is that it is true, that it not only happened once upon a time but has kept on happening ever since and is happening still. To preach the Gospel in its original power and mystery is to claim in whatever way the preacher finds it possible to claim it that once upon a time is this time, now, and here is the dark wood that the light gleams at the heart of like a jewel, and the ones who are to live happily ever after are...all who labor and are heavy laden, the poor naked wretches wheresoever they be.

Pilate lets the cigarette smoke drift out of his mouth to screen him a little from the figure before him. Sarah tries to disguise her first choke of laughter as a cough by covering her mouth with her apron, and Job sits at the table with his head in his arms so that he won't have to face the empty chairs of his children. Poor old Beecher's hand slips, and a bead of blood swells on his upper lip as he stares at his reflection in the shaving mirror thinking about the lectures that he should have gotten together months before and about little Lib Tilton, his old friend's wife, and about the small chamois bag in his pocket with an uncut topaz in it, some pearls, a cat's eye. The preacher holds a knot of black gown in his fist to keep from tripping as he mounts the steps to the pulpit, and the high-school math teacher makes a sharp crease with his thumbnail down the center of his order of service. Once upon a time is their time, all of them. They are the ones to live happily everafter. "The joy beyond the walls of the world more poignant than grief" breaks through the walls of the world, and like Rumpelstiltskin, evil is defeated by being named for what it is, and the world itself receives the true and holy name by which the master magician calls it to himself....

Thanks to the MGM movie, everybody knows the story. The tinman, the lion, the scarecrow, and the child travel many a long mile of yellow-brick road in search of the great wizard who they believe will be able to grant them their hearts' desire: the tinman a heart, the lion courage, the scarecrow a brain, the child a way to get home. After many a perilous adventure, they finally reach the Emerald City, where the wizard lives, and in a devastating audience in which he appears to them variously as a beautiful lady, a terrible beast, a great ball of fire, he tells them that he will do nothing for them until they first destroy the wicked witch and bring him back her broomstick to prove that they have done it. They are almost destroyed themselves in the process, but somehow they manage to bring it off, and when they return with the broomstick to claim their reward, the wizard grants them a second audience. It is a great tragicomic scene. Again the wizard appears to them in all his glory, but instead of granting them their wish, he puts them off and so great is their indignation and disillusion that there is a scuffle in the course of which a screen is knocked over, and there behind the screen is the wizard himself, who turns out to be not a beautiful lady or a terrible beast or a ball of fire, but only a little bald man with a wrinkled face.

Only when they did not see the wizard for what he really was did he appear majestic and beautiful. Only when they did not understand his true nature did they bow down before him as great mystery and power. The Emerald City itself turns out to have looked as if made of emeralds only because they were looking at it through spectacles made of emerald-colored glass. His magic turns out to have been only a series of illusions he worked from behind his screen. In other words, their faith in his power to do anything for them that they could not do for themselves is revealed to be groundless. "You are a very bad man," Dorothy says, and the wizard's answer is, "Oh, no, my dear. I'm really a very good man, but, I'm a very bad wizard." So the great and terrible Oz is only a human being like Dorothy herself, and the only good he can do for them is a human good. He cannot give them anything that they do not already have, and that is the meaning of the gifts he then distributes among them.

I'm never surprised when I discover that one of my favourite science fiction writers is Christian, because to think about worlds in other galaxies, other modes of being, is a theological enterprise.
—MADELEINE L'ENGLE, *Walking on Water*

The silk heart stuffed with sawdust that he gives the tinman, the pins and needles he stuffs inside the scarecrow's head, the drink out of a saucer that he serves up to the lion, are only talismans of the heart, the brains, the courage that they have already acquired by their conscientious pursuit of them and their defeat of the wicked witch. By bringing out in them the best that they are, their faith proves to have been an end in itself and not a means to an unimaginably greater end. Like a skilled psychotherapist, the wizard helps them to an inner adjustment that makes them better equipped to deal with the world as it is, but he is not able to open up for them or inside of them a world of transcendence and joy because although he is a very good man, he is not really a wizard at all. Like people who have been successfully psychoanalyzed, they are all dressed up but with no place to go except where they have always been. The only best for them is the best they can do for themselves and for each other. As for Dorothy, the wizard fails her entirely when the balloon he plans to take her back to Kansas in takes off prematurely without her, but the story of how the good witch, Glinda, deals with her bears the same meaning. Glinda tells her that although Dorothy didn't know it, the silver shoes that she has worn from the start could have taken her home at any point on her way, so that, like her three friends, she has had it in her own power all along to achieve her goal. L. Frank Baum entitles the chapter of *The Wizard of Oz* in which all this is described "The Magic Art of the Great Humbug," and they are very sad and eloquent and suggestive words.

The Wizard of Oz is the fairy tale dehumbugged, and the good news it bears is the good news that hard and conscientious effort and a little help from our friends pay off in the end, and faith is its own reward. The most important thing to have faith in is ourselves, and that is also the chief magic. Insofar as they receive their hearts' desire, Dorothy and her friends, it is essentially a do-it-yourself operation, and the joy of it is not beyond the walls of the world but within the walls of the world. The book was published in the year 1900, and maybe it is not stretching things too far to say that in a way it foreshadows something of what became of the fairy tale of the Gospel in the century it ushered in. The magic and the mystery fade. Like the Emerald City, the city whose gates are pearl and whose walls are adorned with jasper and onyx and sapphire turns out to be too good to be true for all except those who see it through stained glass; and just as for Dorothy home is finally not the Land of Oz, where all things are possible, but Kansas, where never yet has a camel managed to squeeze through the eye of a needle, so for us home is not that country that Gideon and Barak, Samson and Jeptha, glimpsed from afar, but rather just home, just here, where there are few surprises. As for the one who promises to save the world, he is in the richest sense a good man to be sure, but like the little bald man behind the screen, when you come right down to it not all that much of a wizard. His goodness, his love, his simple eloquence, touch our hearts and illumine our darkness across the centuries, but for all of that, both we and our world remain basically untransformed. Though he is wizard enough to set us dreaming sometimes of a world of joy more poignant than grief, we tend to believe in our hearts that, however holy and precious, it is only a dream.

Myth: Flight to Reality

Thomas Howard

Toward a Definition of Myth

Let me begin with the premise that when we speak of "myth" we don't mean something that is untrue. The important thing about myth is not that it involves an event that never occurred on this planet, or out of it, for that matter. The stories of Zeus and Odysseus are not myths by virtue of the fact that they didn't happen. On the contrary, they are myths at least partly because they occurred in a realm that is beyond the reach of the geographers' and historians' tools.

The question of whether or not they occurred somewhere around a place we know geographically as the Aegean or the Baltic, or so many years before Pericles, is irrelevant. The question about myth is not whether the tales it tells have happened in our history or prehistory. There is probably no one alive today who would insist that they have occurred in that way.

But on the other hand, the people (nearly everybody, in effect) who blithely assume that of course these things didn't happen may be whistling in the dark. How do *they* know? Unless you are a doctrinaire materialist and live in a tiny universe whose limits are determined by microscopes, telescopes, and measurements like 186,000 miles a second, you will always wonder what's going on just outside your lens frame. A Christian, especially, living as he does in a huge universe all ringing with the footfalls of hurrying seraphim, cherubim, archangels, angels, men, and devils, will never be too peremptory concerning what creatures

THOMAS HOWARD *is an author, lecturer, and teacher. He is currently a professor of English at St. John's Seminary. Howard's books fall chiefly into the categories of literary criticism, autobiography, and Catholic apologetics. The Inklings are one of his specialties, and he is well known as a defender of myth as a literary form. The following essay was originally delivered as an address at a literary conference at Wheaton College.*

aren't in on the traffic. He can only demur and say, "Elves? I don't know much about them. I've never come across one (worse luck)."

The question about the myths is, rather, How true do they ring? Does such and such a tale or set of tales suppose a world that convinces us by its own integrity, that is, its fidelity to its own laws? Is the fabric of that world whole and tough? Or is it tattered? Does it hold together by some binding energy that is really at work in it? Or must it be basted together by pins and threads borrowed from some other world?

Perhaps it's here that we come upon the rather elusive clues to what makes myth different from other kinds of tales. We can say that myth represents a world created by the imagination. For one thing, there is a sense in which real myth must be large. You can't have a myth with only one incident, or one or two characters in it. The individual episodes form part of a whole landscape. Myth, moreover, has to do with a whole world, not necessarily a world of any particular geography or chronology. You can have an imagined geography (utopia or Lilliput) and not have what we call real myth. Or you can have our geography (Parnassus or Olympus) and yet have real myth.

Fantasy, of course, starts out with an advantage: arresting strangeness.

—J. R. R. TOLKIEN, "On Fairy-Stories"

What seems to be required is that there be a world, a whole world, that is remote from us and at the same time rooted in our world. We don't want our myths taking place in 1929, or even 1066, nor do we want them to occur in East Lansing or Gary, Indiana. If they did, they would have a distressing tendency to keep draining into the dry sand of history or contemporaneity. But on the other hand, remote and entire in themselves as they must be, we do want them to be in some sense rooted in our world, that is, in our understanding of experience. We don't want them to be crowded or spoiled by the immediate world, but we do want them to ring bells that our ears can hear.

THE MEANING OF MYTH

The whole poetic or artistic or mythic phenomenon that we find when we look at the history of human imagination represents, I think, the search for perfection. Now you can give this perfection a hundred names—truth, beauty, goodness, wholeness, bliss, repose, order, form, the eternal, and so on, depending on what you want to stress at the moment. There's no word in human language that will name it adequately. Let's call it *perfection* here. We all have imaginings of it (some poets would urge that we have memories of it). Perfection hounds us remorselessly. It is what stands over against every experience we have of nostalgia, frustration, and desire. We find sooner or later all the data of our experience to be faulted—our bodies, our minds, our wills, our relationships, our landscapes, our states, our institutions, our programs.

Politics, medicine, ecology, and jurisprudence are our efforts to repair the damage. Most of what we do, starting with brushing our teeth in the morning, would be seen by the angels as a waste of time, since they don't know what it is to be almost wholly occupied with shoring things up. When we've been allowed to take time from our plowing and fighting and brushing our teeth, we have tried to say something about perfection and our experience of the discrepancy that we feel between ourselves and perfection. We want tranquility and we find tumult. We want permanence and we find decay. We want order and we find havoc. We want health and we find sickness. We want strength and we find weakness. We want beauty and we find horror.

But we neither can nor will settle for this state of affairs. We are driven by who knows what—maybe it's the Holy Ghost—to complain about this discrepancy, to oppose it, and to transcend it. We write about our experience, and we sing about it, and we reenact it because we think that somehow if we can stand off from it and get a look at it, we can get ahold of it once more. We signal our awareness of perfection by making something approximating perfection out of our experience—something true, beautiful, good, and incorruptible. Myth is one version of this effort.

DISTANCE AND IDENTITY IN MYTH

I do not think the words *art* and *myth* are synonymous, but perhaps myth stands at the pinnacle of the narrative art. In it you will find more or less perfectly manifested what is implicit in all art: distance from the immediate but identity of substance. Myth stands off from our experience, but it *is about* our experience.

Perhaps a distinction needs to be made here. We should speak of *high myth* when we are talking about those great tales that come out of the Mediterranean and the North, since the loose term *myth* can refer also to the controlling atmosphere or set of ideas or pool of presuppositions that govern an era. The twentieth century, for example, operates within a secularist myth. The Middle Ages operated inside a Christian one. And so forth.

We who hobnob with hobbits and tell tall tales about little green men are quite used to being dismissed as mere entertainers, or sternly disapproved as escapists. But I think that perhaps the categories are changing, like the times. Sophisticated readers are accepting the fact that an improbable and unmanageable world is going to produce an improbable and hypothetical art. At this point, realism is perhaps the least adequate means of understanding or portraying the incredible realities of our existence. A scientist who creates a monster in his laboratory; a librarian in the library of Babel; a wizard unable to cast a spell; a space ship having trouble in getting to Alpha Centauri: all these may be precise and profound metaphors of the human condition. The fantasist, whether he uses the ancient archetypes of myth and legend or the younger ones of science and technology, may be talking as seriously as any sociologist—and a good deal more directly—about human life as it is lived, and as it might be lived, and as it ought to be lived.

—URSULA LE GUIN, National Book Award Acceptance Speech

You get in high myth a fairly pure example of what art is about: distance and identity. Perhaps this is why you used to have frames around paintings. Such and such a scene or person or event was "in there," and you, the viewer, had leisure to regard it and contemplate it. You were free from any entanglement. By the same token, when you read one of the older novels you can look at the experience being described precisely because you aren't called upon to sort it out. Of course, part of the genius of the whole thing is that you *do* get involved. But it is an involvement that is not cluttered by having to attend to a thousand trifling details. You are free to get a grip on things exactly because you are at a remove from them.

By the same token, if we move the world of myth away from the immediate, out of the twentieth century or the nineteenth or the eighteenth or the tenth, out of our calendar completely, we disengage it from the fuss of our world, and by thus setting it free from our time, we set ourselves free with respect to it. For time may be *the* tragic dimension of human experience. It is the agent and vehicle of change and decay and death. If we can get free from time, we can approach bliss. This is why poetry and the promise of paradise are so attractive to us. They all offer an escape from time. And the escape seems to be an escape *from* the unreal, from the transitory and evanescent, *to* the solid and immutable, that is, the real.

"Once upon a time" is no time.… In reality…it means "at all times, in all places." It is a declaration, announcing that what you are now going to hear is the truth.
—ERIK CHRISTIAN HAUGAARD, "Portrait of a Poet: Hans Christian Andersen and His Fairy Tales," in *The Openhearted Audience*, ed. Virginia Haviland

So we need distance, probably both chronological and geographical. We like the formula, "Once upon a time in a far off land." That's the best opening for a story—there's no question about it. For at that point we can settle in. There's no danger of any clutter and intrusion from the immediate world. If we sat down to read a story that began "At eleven o'clock on the morning of Friday, October 16, 1970, in the living room at 210 East Seminary in Wheaton, Illinois, an old crone began to stir her brew," we'd say, "Wait! Stop! It won't work. It's no good." The trouble is that we know that room. It's too defenseless against the postman and plumber and electrician, and we don't want them in our midst.

THE FATE OF MYTH IN THE MODERN WORLD
Of course, it will be observed here that most of the writing that engages our attention now is realistic in this way. Isn't *this* art and therefore a form of myth? What about Updike and Saul Bellow and all the fiction that gets published now, to say nothing of cinema and theater? The whole avalanche of contemporary imagery tumbles out of our living rooms and kitchens, and bathrooms and bedrooms. What about all this? Can't things be local and contemporary?

It may be here that we come upon the trouble that the mythmakers and storytellers have nowadays, and indeed the trouble with the whole era. For they have to make their images out of what their world is made of. There has to be some identity of substance between what they make and what we know, so that we can recognize it. And it turns out that the stuff our world is made of won't shape up into high myth. Oh, you can make something out of it—cigarette ashes and tiny situations—but you can't get anything huge and wonderful and breathtaking and beautiful.

Why not? Because the world that gave birth to the high myths—to those huge worlds of story that are remote from us but terrifyingly close—that world has disappeared. It has disappeared under our interdict. For we have decided (sometime in the Renaissance it was and we finished the job in the eighteenth century) to recreate the world. It's a very small one now, limited as it is by microscopes and telescopes and computers, and asphalt parking lots at MacDonald's hamburger stands. And it's a horror. It is, above all, boring, for mystery has fled from it. We have announced to anyone who cares to listen—and somehow one imagines that the angels and elves aren't all that enthralled by the information— that we can explain everything. We know what our forefathers never guessed: that if you take things apart you can explain them and thus master them. And we're dead right. You certainly can master them. The only difficulty is that the thing you've got the mastery of is a pile of pieces all taken apart. We haven't found the spells (since we don't believe in spells) to put them back together again. We're in the position of all the king's men in "Humpty Dumpty."

[Shakespeare's] universe was not the neatly depressing universe of psychological determinism; he found room for the two poles of natural and supernatural between which humanity is poised; for providence and guidance, miracle, mysterious prompting to good or evil.... The Winter's Tale expresses this universe more clearly than would a story derived from contemporary Jacobean life, since it makes obvious on the plane of recognisable events what is usually concealed by the familiarity of routine existence.
—S. L. BETHELL, *The Winter's Tale: A Study*

By the eighteenth century the myth became sovereign that the analytic and rational capacity is absolutely adequate for unscrambling the mystery of the universe. Somewhere in the process the gods fled. The irony is that in the very effort of modern art to disentangle human experience from the transcendent, human experience turned to ashes. In painting and sculpture the focus is on less and less, until indeed there is *less* there than meets the eye. We are told that we must no longer ask what a work of art *means,* since all that matters is that it *is.*

The problem of the modern writer is obvious. He can't make bricks without straw. He can't make a rope out of sand. He can't create heroes and evoke courage and nobility and courtesy out of the materials that his world furnishes him. He may feel that what we have now is the truth of the matter.

On the other hand, the modern writer may be unhappy with the way things are. He may, like Francois Mauriac or Flannery O'Connor or Tolkien, think that the time is out of joint, that what we have is most emphatically *not* the way things are, in which case he can try various things. He can try to find tiny pieces in the pile that is left of the world in the twentieth century—pieces which, if put together in a certain way or held up to a certain light, may bring back an old memory that once upon a time it wasn't broken like that. Or, like Flannery O'Connor, the storyteller can hail us, shout at us with frightening images to try to remind us that what we've made is not, in fact, very satisfactory. Or, like Tolkien, the mythmaker can step away from things and hold up for us some unabashedly ancient shapes, since he can find nothing at hand that will suit his purpose. When we have entered Tolkien's remote world we find that it is a true one, and therefore true of ours.

But apart from a few plucky spirits like this, what are the mythmakers giving us? You wonder whether the poets and artists are really fulfilling their ancient office, which is to see further than the rest of us, to see the mysteries and bear witness somehow to what they see in an imagery drawn from our world.

THE NECESSITY OF MYTH

If we believe that the pile of broken pieces is a late and false creation, and that the world the old bards knew was, in fact, the world where our real life lies, then it must be confessed that, reactionary as it sounds, a return is indicated. At least some sort of return. Remember that not all returns are bad. A return to health after sickness, a return to shore after a voyage, a return to home after estrangement, to liberty after prison—these are salutary returns. Let's have no cant about reactionism.

The chances of a writer finding inside the modern world an imagery that will suggest the big, real, whole world are slim. The writer will have eventually to lift his sights away from the shards and catch once more the vision that was born in olden days when an imagery of heroes and elves and gods was alive. He'll have to search for it with all his heart, and he will, if he looks hard enough, find at least something. He'll find that, despite the cold and lethal myth that holds the whole world in a frosty sovereignty, there are pockets of warmth and life. The old vision, the vision that was affirmed in the high myths, *is* kept alive and nourished in the households of good and humble people everywhere. And (we wish it were true) in the church. At least it is still celebrated in the church, for we still sing *Kyrie* and *Gloria* and *Sanctus,* and break bread and pour wine, and call them the body and blood of God.

> *Fairy-stories offer also, in a peculiar degree or mode, these things: Fantasy, Recovery, Escape, Consolation, all things of which children have, as a rule, less need than older people.... Recovery (which includes return and renewal of health) is a re-gaining—regaining of a clear view.... We need...to clean our windows; so that the things seen clearly may be freed from the drab blur of triteness or familiarity.*
>
> —J. R. R. TOLKIEN, "On Fairy-Stories"

The human spirit at its best is impatient with the small and local and fragmented. It demands images of greatness and wholeness. The world of the imagination that I have called myth is a repository of such images—images of courage and glory and mystery and romance and deity and heroism. Excursions into that world are never a flight away *from* reality; they are, rather, a flight *to* reality.

The Well at the World's End: Poetry, Fantasy, and the Limits of the Expressible

Robert Siegel

In his essay "On Stories," C. S. Lewis asks two rhetorical questions about *The Well at the World's End*, by William Morris: "*The Well at the World's End*—can a man write a story to that title? Can he find a series of events following one another in time which will really catch and fix and bring home to us all that we grasp at on merely hearing the six words?" Lewis concludes that no story can live up to the promise of a title as good as this one, and then he continues,

> If Story fails in that way does not life commit the same blunder? In real life, as in a story, something must happen. That is just the trouble. We grasp at a state and find only a succession of events in which the state is never quite embodied.... In life and art both, as it seems to me, we are always trying to catch in our net of successive moments something that is not successive. Whether in real life there is any doctor who can teach us how to do it, so that at last either the meshes will become fine enough to hold the bird, or we be so changed that we can throw our nets away and follow the bird to its own country, is not a question for this essay. But I think it is sometimes done—or very, very nearly done—in stories. I believe the effort to be well worth making.

ROBERT SIEGEL *is Professor Emeritus of English at the University of Wisconsin-Milwaukee. He is the author of seven books of poetry and fantasy fiction, including* In a Pig's Eye *and the* Whalesong *trilogy. His work has received awards from a number of sources, including* Poetry, *the* Ingram Merrill Foundation, *and* The National Endowment for the Arts.

In this rich and complex passage, Lewis suggests that one reason we read stories is that they can create in us a state of mind beyond the mere succession of events that make up the plot. He adds that we desire the same in life—a state of thought and feeling beyond the mere sequence of events we experience in time, though we need that "net of successive moments" to try to catch the bird at all. Whatever rare bird this state is (and I suspect it is a bird ultimately beyond description), in story one may glimpse it, feel the brush of its wing, or for a moment, hold it in one's hand.

What Lewis describes here with an arrestingly beautiful metaphor is an example of the *inexpressible* in literature—something that can be partly "expressed" only by figurative language, by metaphor, symbol, or other form of parabolic utterance. Although, as Lewis implies, all story points to the inexpressible (and to story I would add all forms of literature, music, and art), it is particularly characteristic of fantasy and poetry. Both are fundamentally metaphoric and symbolic; in Robert Frost's words, they say "one thing in terms of another." More frequently than realistic fiction or drama, they attempt to express the ineffable, touching upon the realms of myth and ultimate meanings.

But this is only a matter of degree. I would be the first to confess that there is an atmosphere, a quality, in Dickens's novels that one could wish to hover in forever. And I've never seen a Shakespeare play without feeling at some point an atmosphere of pregnant language on the stage, a logos inviting us to some richer, elusive reality lurking behind the gorgeous tapestry of language. I believe this is the case because every work of art is in itself a metaphor, a symbol, for something else, and insofar as it reflects life, it will also reflect the mystery behind life.

LANGUAGE AND THE IMAGINATION

The nature of all language is metaphoric in the sense that it refers beyond itself to something else. Exactly what it refers to is a source of endless debate among philosophers of language. I take exception to those who see language as a self-consistent system of symbols that refers only to itself and has no substantial relation to the exterior world. As Wordsworth said about similar systems in his own day, this one leads to "a universe of death." Words consist of a sound and marks on a page and would remain only that if they did not stand for—signify— meaning. And the meaning exists in the minds of both speaker and listener—

though never quite the same meaning, which we know to our endless frustration and fascination. I'm convinced, too, that a word is a symbol pointing to more than "a thought," because involved in and finally inseparable from thought is the whole warp and woof of the universe. As Coleridge said, a word is somewhere "between a thought and a thing." The word *oak* refers to your or my thought of it, certainly, but also to the living tree that suggested it. A word is a part of the world of which we are conscious, as well as a part of our consciousness of the world. As such, it both unites us to and conceals from us what it represents. But this has to do with the nature of the language-making mind and imagination, as we shall see later.

Meanwhile, let us note that metaphor (and therefore literature) is seminally present in the nature of language itself. When we examine it, we notice that many if not most words are figurative in their origins, that words develop out of metaphors. We explain new things in terms of old. The poet Robert Wallace points out that we get the word *verse* from the Latin past participle *versus,* meaning "having turned"; as a noun it came to mean "the turning of the plow," hence "furrow," and later "row" or "line." Lines of verse are metaphorically plowed furrows. We cover our automobile engines with a hood in America, but with a bonnet in England. The word *insult* originally meant "to leap upon" an enemy. The process continues today. As the poet Wallace notes, we do not have a common name for the little hammock of skin between the thumb and forefinger, unlike the bridge of the nose, or the ball of the foot.

More obviously, artful or poetic language is metaphoric or parabolic, saying one thing in terms of another. The phrase *parabolic utterance* covers all those kinds of speech or writing where we say one thing in terms of another—from parable through simile, metaphor, allegory, and symbol. (*Parable* itself comes from *parabola,* the curve we know from geometry or the path of a ball in the air. It literally means "to throw beside.") Parabolic utterance—what Owen Barfield calls "other-saying"—is the heart of poetic language, though every now and then some group of scientific precisians or literary minimalists will try to strip language of it—an impossible task.

To understand more completely the metaphoric nature of language, we need to look at the imagination. The most suggestive definition of imagination is the famous one of Coleridge, which also tells us much about the nature of mind:

The Primary Imagination I hold to be the living Power and prime Agent of all human Perception, and as a repetition in the finite mind of the eternal act of creation in the infinite I AM. The Secondary Imagination I consider as an echo of the former, co-existing with the conscious will, yet still as identical with the primary in the *kind* of its agency, and differing only in *degree,* and in the *mode* of its operation. It dissolves, diffuses, dissipates, in order to recreate; or where this process is rendered impossible, yet still at all events it struggles to idealize and to unify.

Consciousness itself, Coleridge says, is an act of imagination, a creative act that mirrors that of a Creator. Basically he is saying that the mind "half perceives and half creates" the world, to use Wordsworth's phrase from "Tintern Abbey." Owen Barfield spent a good part of his life explaining how this works—how what we think of as reality, our waking consciousness, is partly objective and partly what we create. By the time we are four or five, he explains, we have constructed our conscious world through a process he calls *figuration.* For example, mother, father, the family cat, and much else by now has a distinct appearance combined in our mind with a name and all sorts of feelings and experiences. Unconsciously, metaphor is there from the beginning. For instance, we may identify thunder with aspects of our father's voice or the smell of lilacs with our mother's presence in a room. When we begin school and are taught to think about our world, our consciousness of it grows ever more complex, as do our language skills. (See Barfield's *Saving the Appearances* and *What Coleridge Thought* for a full elaboration of these ideas.)

My point here is that the words we learn, such as *green* or *cat* or *butterfly,* our imaginations naturally make part of what they represent. They are symbols, or metaphors, which represent our total experience of, and awareness of, cat, green, and butterfly. The term for butterfly, in whatever language, whether *papillon, farfala,* or *cho-cho-san,* in addition to the individual's experience of the animal carries the freight of a whole language and its culture as well. So our consciousness, what we refer to as "the real world," is partly a continuing imaginative construct, to which language provides the metaphoric keys. This is true not only of our ordinary experience and the arts, but also of the sciences, as many modern physicists have argued.

This view of metaphor and symbol as constructive of consciousness differs from the widely held view that metaphor is basically fictitious or fictive, playing with the elements of an objective real world that is independent of it. One version of this view is expressed by Roger Cardinal in the intriguing first two chapters of his *Figures of Reality: A Perspective on the Poetic Imagination,* where he discusses the fictive nature of metaphor and the imagination. For Cardinal, fantastic images in Rimbaud, such as "carriages racing across the highways of the sky," or "a drawing-room in the depths of a lake," provide pleasure *because* they are unreal. The problem I have with Cardinal's view is not with the pleasure he derives from this contrast, but rather his identifying only the everyday, actual world as "real." The world of the work of art may also be called real—though of a different order of reality. In fact, it can be said that the story of Prince Hamlet recounted in Shakespeare's play is in many people's experience more real than an ordinary trip to the local convenience store to pick up a quart of milk. Though the second takes place in the actual world, and the first in a fictional, most, I think, would agree that the story presented by the play has the greater reality. Furthermore, the empirical physical world that we often think of as the only real one appears phantasmal and insubstantial when examined by subatomic physicists or astrophysicists in terms of quantum theory and relativity.

People are always asking—who invented the myths? And do you think they are true? Well, true? What is true? As far as I am concerned it doesn't matter tuppence if the incidents in the myths never happened. That does not make them any less true, for, indeed, in one way or another, they're happening all the time. You only have to open a newspaper to find them crowding into it. Life itself continually reenacts them.

—P. L. TRAVERS, "Only Connect,"
in *The Openhearted Audience,* ed. Virginia Haviland

The artistic imagination, what Coleridge calls the "Secondary Imagination," is in essence the same as the primary, except that it is exercised by the will: "It dissolves, diffuses, dissipates, in order to recreate…it struggles to idealize and to unify." The artistic imagination can, for instance, choose the color blue from the sky and the ball of our sun and imagine a solar system where sunlight is blue.

It can take Cleopatra out of shadowy ancient history and imagine her speaking immortal Elizabethan English. The power of the artistic imagination, in the context of Coleridge's definition of consciousness, is reflective of godlike power, of the Creator's "eternal act of creation in the infinite I AM." J. R. R. Tolkien echoes this analogy in his term "subcreation," the capacity for which is, he says, perhaps the most important way in which we resemble our Creator.

POETRY

The imagination is constructive of reality, and metaphor and symbol are the means to creating and discovering new knowledge in all literary forms, but especially in poetry and fantasy. It is worthwhile to take a closer look at how metaphoric language achieves this. Some might say that in the form of simile, metaphor merely points out likeness, as in Byron's well-known song, "She Walks in Beauty":

> She walks in beauty like the night
> Of cloudless climes and starry skies,

But the simile is more complex than this. The likeness also underscores the difference: she walks "like the night," and the distance between the terms *woman* and *night* is stunning, even when the second is a warm, starry night in Italy. After all, this night sky opens out into the cosmos. The second two lines make the simile clearer, but the difference is still before us:

> And all that's good of dark and bright,
> Meet in her aspect and her eyes.

We see her dark eyes shining, as the simile implies, but the word *aspect* gives her appearance an astrological import. She awes the speaker like the night sky; her beauty has a kind of cosmic power. In this simile, as in all metaphor, we first notice the similarity, then the difference, and by a process of the mind's moving back and forth between the terms, a third thing is created that is neither woman nor night, an archetypal or mythic figure like that of Artemis, goddess of the moon, who has the force of both woman and night. In the pure form of metaphor, without *like* or *as,* the fusion of the terms is more immediate, as in

Sidney's "With how sad steps, O Moon, thou climb'st the skies, / How silently, and with how wan a face." Here we have a combined lover and moon, something different from both an earthly lover and a pale moon. The fusion creates a new thing entirely, which has not existed in our world before, a figure, like Byron's night/lady, of some mythic force. Still, while asking us to combine the terms, the metaphor draws our attention to the difference as well. The distance between the terms makes for a dynamic tension, a sublime vagueness which opens out into mystery.

In much modern and postmodern poetry, the two terms of the metaphor are shockingly different, as in the well-known beginning of Eliot's "The Love Song of J. Alfred Prufrock:"

Let us go then, you and I,
When the evening is spread out against the sky
Like a patient etherized upon a table.

The distance between the terms is what we first notice here, but soon the mind notes the similarity between a cloudy sunset and a patient wrapped in sheets and bleeding, unconscious. Last, the terms fuse into a third thing that is both and neither, the sunset/patient. The mind travels back and forth between fusion and difference and in that space may be said to experience something else, the "je ne sais quoi" in all poetry, the mysterious imageless toward which the metaphor points. (In this particular case we may find the metaphor disturbing, reflective as it is of Prufrock's state of mind.)

With the symbol, matters become more complex, the mystery increases, because a symbol stands for more than one thing. A symbol is a metaphor with an indefinite, perhaps infinite, number of second terms. No interpretation of the symbol exhausts it or the work it appears in. As we know, the white whale Moby Dick lives, despite our critical attempts to harpoon him. None of the meanings we find in a reading of a symbol is adequate to it, though each is revealing. A true symbol is finally inexhaustible.

Like the metaphor, the symbol both reveals and conceals. In *Eyes of Light,* the Benedictine monk Henri Le Saux points out that from time immemorial the chief symbol of the spiritual world for the Hindu has been the sun:

The Sun was considered as the symbol of this luminous world, and its already so brilliant face that it turns toward us is the sign of the sun's other face…the one that it turns towards the eternal. The sun was the 'golden gateway' that opens on the Real, the golden cup that at one and the same time contains and conceals the True, the supreme object of the soul's desire.

Every symbol and metaphor has these twin aspects of revelation and concealment.

Largely because of metaphor and symbol, poetry brings us new knowledge. It brings us truth that cannot be discovered by more utilitarian language. This is the symbolic and prophetic side of poetry, that found in much of Blake, in Coleridge's "Kubla Khan," or Rilke's *Duino Elegies*. Poetry in its prophetic mode helps us to glimpse truths otherwise unknowable. It enables us to represent to ourselves what Barfield calls the "unrepresented," the Kantian *ding an sich,* those unknowable aspects of the universe beyond the categories of space and time, of our senses and our reason—truths metaphysical, theological, mystical. Metaphor and symbol afford the only way we have of expressing the inexpressible, the inner workings of the universe, even on the physical plane.

Myth can enter poetry as that dominant theme each writer has below the surface of the majority of his works; as allusion to, and incorporation of, specific known myths, the shared myths of his culture or borrowed from other accessible cultures; or by the invention of new fictions which (whether or not they pertain to that writer's dominant theme) attain mythic stature in the culture (perhaps because they turn out to be new versions of archetypal stories).

—DENISE LEVERTOV, *The Poet in the World*

Blake's "Tyger" is one of these prophetic, mythic kinds of poems. Many explications seem to miss its startling visual and visionary character, caught initially in the phrase "burning bright" and the hypnotic rhythm:

Tyger, tyger burning bright
In the forest of the night,
What immortal hand or eye
Could frame thy fearful symmetry?

It moves through alarming and glorious images that, despite allusions to Milton and the Scriptures, defy complete explanation:

When the stars threw down their spears,
And water'd heaven with their tears,
Did He smile His work to see?
Did He who made the lamb make thee?

The poem presents the problem of evil without affording answers. But the visionary atmosphere may propel us toward an intuition that resists paraphrase.

Perhaps more than any other kind of poetry, the haiku, arising from the tradition of Zen Buddhism, illustrates this principle strikingly and with great simplicity. The whole point of a haiku is by images and metaphor to point to what is finally inexpressible. Consider this one:

My barn burned down
last night—now I can
see the moon.

One may chuckle ruefully with the speaker, thinking, "Well, with the barn gone, it's some compensation that it no longer blocks the moonrise;" or reflect (as Thoreau might), "Too busy with things, he now has time to contemplate nature." But surely the force of this haiku is not in these discursive, if true, observations. In reading it, there is a sudden break, where barn is replaced by moon. One feels it in the sense of a weight lifted and sight restored. There's an indefinable freedom and expansion of the soul that comes.

This, I believe is the ultimate direction and goal of poetry, metaphor, and symbol—to express what is inexpressible, to fuse together what still remains separate. Coleridge celebrated what he called the "coadunating" power of the imagination to draw disparate things together and felt that this was the imagination's chief work. It is also where literature touches upon ultimate things, including myth and mystery.

FANTASY

Like poetry, fantasy is a cardinal form of other-saying. Often the whole story serves as a suggestive metaphor or symbol for which the other term or terms are not clear. What makes fantasy, like poetry, so apt a form for this is its freedom from the strictures of realism. In fantasy things happen that we assume are impossible in the actual world, such as a wolf impersonating a grandmother or a child passing through a wardrobe into another universe. This freedom allows the author to be especially sensitive to the suggestions of the unconscious or subconscious mind, which, while active in all works of the imagination, may be of particular use to the fantasy writer, as to the poet.

Art...is not to be judged by any external standard of resemblance.... She has flowers that no forest knows of, birds that no woodland possesses.... She can work miracles at her will, and when she calls monsters from the deep they come. She can bid the almond-tree blossom in winter, and send the snow upon the ripe cornfield.

—OSCAR WILDE, "The Decay of Lying"

Just as it provides the imagery of our dreams, often symbolic, so does the unconscious provide much of the imagery of fantasy—since the writer is not preoccupied with holding a mirror up to nature or the actual world. So often is this the case that it is fair to say that almost all fantasy is about our interior lives, psychological or spiritual. As Lewis says, in fantasy "the insides are on the outside." The unconscious is rich in archetypal patterns and figures, in symbols of universal significance for the psyche and spirit, and it is wise for the writer to pay attention to it. Of course, the unconscious contains all sorts of material, not all of it benign. But in this connection, it is wise to remember that toads may turn out to be princes in disguise. Also, the writer should avoid trying to impose her convictions upon the material offered by the fantastic imagination. To do so often results in the wooden and artificial, or the thinly transparent allegory. It is better to concentrate on the story and allow one's deepest concerns to come out indirectly, as they invariably will. If one writes as well as he can, taking the story seriously, his deepest convictions will live in the work, however unapparent on the surface.

When fantasy touches upon ultimate questions, matters of origin and destiny, of transformation between (and including) birth and death, it can create literary myth. Although any fantasy writer by imitating one of the forms of myth can be said to create "myth," I prefer to reserve this word for the most profound works of fantasy—those that strike the reader, in C. S. Lewis's phrase, as "a real though unfocussed gleam of divine truth falling on human imagination." Upholding this high standard elsewhere, Lewis claims that genuine myth "arouses in us sensations we have never had before, never anticipated having, as though we had broken out of our normal mode of consciousness and 'possess joys not promised to our birth.'"

In its longer, more ambitious forms, fantasy tries to pronounce this world, or several worlds, in terms of another—as do Narnia and Middle Earth. Or perhaps it tries to express unimaginable worlds in terms we can yet imagine, as do both *The Divine Comedy* and *Paradise Lost*. States of mind and heart, or the world of the spirit, are notoriously hard to represent except in terms of parabolic utterance: "There was a man who had two sons…," "A sower went out to sow…," or,

I saw Eternity the other night
Like a ring of pure and endless light.

No matter how many meanings we may pull out of these fecund symbols, no explanation is ever adequate to the whole, none ever diminishes the radiance of the original. What they are about is finally inexpressible, though we may use their terms like a net to catch it. For, as Lewis says, it is not a definable second term to the metaphor, another interpretation of the symbol, we are primarily after. We are after something like a state of being, which the story provides us if only temporarily. We are trying to catch in a net of successive moments something that is not successive at all. Meanwhile there has been an intense moment when the images fused and faded, an experience similar to Coleridge's description of the sublime:

The grandest efforts of poetry are where the imagination is called forth, not to produce a distinct form, but a strong working of the mind, still offering what is still repelled, and again creating what is again rejected; the result being what the poet wishes to impress, namely, the substitution of a sublime feeling of the unimaginable for a mere image.

I believe one may associate this experience with what Lewis in his autobiography points to with the word *Sehnsucht,* the untranslatable German word that mingles the English words *desire* and *yearning*. The experience was stimulated in him as a boy by the sight of a flowering currant bush, among other things, but could never be identified with the thing that prompted it. As a man, he referred to the experience of this most desirable state of joy as the "tracks" that an ineffable "It" leaves in the psyche, and he found it in works of myth and fantasy.

Myth...deals with impossibles and preternaturals.... [It] is not only grave but awe-inspiring. We feel it to be numinous. It is as if something of great moment had been communicated to us.

—C. S. LEWIS, "On Myth"

For many of us a similar experience lies behind our interest in fantasy literature and poetry. The net of words may hold the bird momentarily, but the net is not the bird. The story is like the finger that points to the moon, and not to be confused with the moon itself, as oriental masters say. Many of us have encountered people who have had similar experiences reading Tolkien's *Lord of the Rings* or Lewis's *Perelandra*. Often they have experienced something profound while reading these fantasies, but are at a loss to describe it. All they seem to know is that they were part of the music while the music lasted. The fantasy has become a primary symbol, one that cannot be translated into other terms. The word *red* is such; it refers beyond itself to an experience we can know only by having. Red is red is red: One cannot explain the color to a person blind from birth.

The very images that help us on our way eventually must be abandoned, for the reality is greater than any of them. We recall that Thomas Aquinas toward the end of his life had an experience compared to which all he had written was "straw." St. Augustine himself, once caught in sensuous meshes, in love with all the various things of this world, used them to propel himself toward the ineffable, where the images themselves are abandoned to return paradoxically in a transfigured form:

But what do I love when I love my God?...not the brilliance of earthly light;...not the sweet melody of harmony and song; not the fragrance of flowers, perfumes, and spices; not manna or honey; not limbs such as the body delights to embrace.... And yet, when I love him, it is true that I love a light of a certain kind, a voice, a perfume, a food, an embrace; but they are of the kind that I love in my inner self.

A classic formula of this experience, possibly that of the fifth-century pseudo-Dionysius, is quoted by Charles Williams: "Neither is this Thou; yet this also is Thou." At the very point of the abandonment of images lies the fulfillment of images. In Lewis's terms, the meshes indeed grow fine enough to hold the bird before the reader discards it and follows the bird to its own country. I want to stress the paradox here. The image is in a profound sense actually not abandoned.

At the end of Ransom's mystical vision of the Great Dance in *Perelandra* occur three wonderful sentences:

For...the whole solid figure of these enamoured and inter-animated circlings was suddenly revealed as the mere superficies of a far vaster pattern in four dimensions, and that figure as the boundary of yet others in other worlds: till suddenly as the movement grew yet swifter, the interweaving yet more ecstatic, the relevance of all to all yet more intense, as dimension was added to dimension and that part of him which could reason and remember was dropped farther and farther behind that part of him which saw, even then, at the very zenith of complexity, complexity was eaten up and faded, as a thin white cloud fades into the hard blue burning of the sky, and a simplicity beyond all comprehension, ancient and young as spring, illimitable, pellucid, drew him with cords of infinite desire into its own stillness. He went up into such a quietness, a privacy, and a freshness that at the very moment when he stood farthest from our ordinary mode of being he had the sense of stripping off encumbrances and awaking from trance, and coming to himself. With a gesture of relaxation he looked about him.

For Ransom, the complexity of eternity is resolved in the simplicity of an ordinary waking to recognizable images, to "a sober certainty of waking bliss." After the blinding vision of white noon, St. John of the Cross claims, the seer returns to the knowledge of the evening, where the world is seen in sharp, if glowing, outline. The abandonment of images is followed by a return to them.

That which for Lewis is the most valuable experience arising out of story is analogous to the religious quest for the ultimate, or the absolute. At the very least it is the esthetic experience of the sublime, which for the romantics and several of the Inklings was the threshold of revelation. Though fantasy has much else to offer, its strongest attraction for us may lie in its power to take us out of our skins—away from the small, limited, half-life that is our ordinary consciousness—and to give us an experience of a larger, more complete life, in which we hear the music of the turning spheres.

Viewpoint: Miriam Hendrix

Why Fantasy Appeals

In recent years we have seen people who are more familiar with the geography of Tolkien's Middle Earth than with that of their own country or state; we have known adults who would rather reflect on Christian truth in Lewis's Narnia books than read his or anyone else's theological works. I would like to suggest three reasons for this popularity, though they are by no means the only ones.

First, the secondary worlds of fantasy provide a sense of completeness that is missing in more realistic fiction. The virtues of this completeness are two: the pleasure of a travelogue, and the possibility of enchantment. One virtue derives from concrete detail, and the other from the insubstantiality of atmosphere. Both are to be found distinctively in fantasy.

Each of the fantasy worlds exists independently of our world. As a result, each has its own geography, citizens, and customs. Anyone who has ever pored over a copy of *National Geographic* will know the experience. Disparities of climate, dress, and custom between the fantasy world and our world are cause for curiosity and speculation.

You either have a taste for such things or you don't. If you do, the worlds of fantasy literature have a significant advantage over merely foreign places in our own world, transmitted to us by photographs. No photograph confines our mental pictures of Mirkwood, Cair Paravel, or Prydain. But they are no less immediate for that.

At the opposite pole from this descriptive concreteness, yet equally characteristic of fantasy, is the atmosphere of enchantment, the wind blowing from the realm of faerie. It is compounded of mystery, enigma, and magic. The desire is all, in this atmosphere. Remoteness is the essence of the enchantment of fantasy. Only at a distance can a dragon remain the heraldic creature of enamel-bright scales, wicked claws, and fiery mouth.

If the sense of completeness, with its attendant pleasures of travelogue and enchantment, is one reason for the popularity of children's fantasy, an even stronger reason is its ability to set us free. Reading fantasy feels like a holiday. Tolkien discusses at length the escape offered by fantasy. The kind of freedom I have in mind has to do with problems and their solutions.

I desired dragons with a profound desire. Of course, I in my timid body did not wish to have them in the neighbourhood, intruding into my relatively safe world.

—J. R. R. TOLKIEN, "On Fairy-Stories"

Both the problems and the solutions in fantasy narratives are remote from us, and once again their very remoteness is a pleasure. We praise great fiction, and properly so, for an action that exemplifies universal problems of the human condition. We all have reason enough to know the "temptations common to man." But for that very reason we can turn with enjoyment, in fantasy, to the spectacle of a protagonist who meets, not an alienated society of the consequences of flawed vision or his own inadequacies, but a wizard or a giant or a land gripped by evil enchantment.

Jungian critics would see the struggle between heroes and monsters in fantasy as archetypes of the struggle between good and evil forces within us. One great pleasure we receive from fantasy comes from the opportunity it gives us to align ourselves so completely with what is good against what is unequivocally evil. Nevertheless, there is a pleasure inherent simply in the great disparity between those worlds and ours, and part of that pleasure comes from a temporary withdrawal from our own kinds of problems.

Of course, the disparaging epithet "escapist" is always easy to attach to literature of fantasy. Tolkien objects to this kind of criticism by insisting that escape is a perfectly admirable and mature thing to do in our circumstances. For we really are imprisoned in an ugly, depersonalized, and barren world, he says; the only sensible thing to do about imprisonment is to try to escape.

I would add a further objection to "escapist" criticism: escape from the external appearances of the modern world, or even from the psychological introspection of modern fiction, is not necessarily an evasion of the moral ambiguities of human life. It is true that appearances in fantasy literature conform far more closely to the reality they represent than is the case in our world; that is, evil in fantasy is usually easily identifiable by its ugliness and open malice, whereas evil in our world is often more subtle and hard to define. But it is easy to exaggerate the complexity of evil and good in our own time and world as a means of excusing a half-hearted struggle for what we know to be right against what we know to be wrong. "How shall a man judge what to do in such times?" asks a character in *The Lord of the Rings*. "As he ever has judged," comes the reply. "Good and ill have not changed."

Fairyland is nothing but the sunny country of common sense.
—G. K. Chesterton, "The Ethics of Elfland"

I think, too, that critics who sneer at the stories of fantasy do so frequently because of their assumptions about the nature of the universe. If supernatural intervention in our natural world is a lie, a baseless myth formulated by primitive peoples to help them face their hostile environment, then it follows that books that depend upon magic or enchantment for the defeat of evil will appear to be fanciful and cowardly in the extreme. Christians, who do not share those anti-supernatural assumptions (and some non-Christians who wish they did not), may judge the stories very differently. Not that magic swords or enchanted castles are any more believable for Christians than for non-Christians; it is just that the idea of a miracle is not, to them, an offense.

A third pleasure fantasy offers is its moral framework. Certainly no one would want to compare the modest productions of children's fantasy writers with the gifted writing of serious modern authors. But many of them do offer, in addition to their other pleasurable qualities, the virtue of a supernatural moral framework unavailable in almost any other worthwhile contemporary literature. Lewis's world of Narnia is overarched by a supernatural order that combines wonder and enchantment with clear, luminous reflections of Christian truth. MacDonald's books, too, combine the atmosphere of faerie with Christianity. The supernatural in Tolkien's Middle Earth, while not specifically Christian, has many of the same qualities as the others.

Beyond the presence of the supernatural in these books, goodness itself is admirable, lovely, and heroic. It is no easy task to create a hero both good and likable, but the fantasy writers accomplish it repeatedly. In literary worlds where goodness is made desirable and where order and meaning derive from a morally absolute supernature, the Christian can momentarily relax his vigilance and free his attention for the humble but refreshing pleasures of nature, friendship, and adventure. Perhaps more significantly, an unbeliever can feel he is a stranger in a gracious place, and wish he were at home.

—"Flight to Fantasy"
Christianity Today, 13 September 1974

Viewpoint: G. K. Chesterton

The Religious Meaning of Myth

All the best critics agree that all the greatest poets, in pagan Hellas for example, had an attitude towards their gods which is quite queer and puzzling to men in the Christian era.... Sometimes it would seem that the Greeks believed above all things in reverence, only they had nobody to revere. But the point of the puzzle is this: that all this vagueness and variation arise from the fact that the whole thing began in fancy and in dreaming; and that there are no rules of architecture for a castle in the clouds.

This is the mighty and branching tree called mythology which ramifies round the whole world, whose remote branches under separate skies bear like coloured birds the costly idols of Asia and the half-baked fetishes of Africa and the fairy kings and princesses of the folk-tales of the forest, and buried amid vines and olives the Lares of the Latins, and carried on the clouds of Olympus the buoyant supremacy of the gods of Greece. These are the myths: and he who has no sympathy with myths has no sympathy with men. But he who has most sympathy with myths will most fully realise that they are not and never were a religion, in the sense that Christianity or even Islam is a religion. They satisfy some of the needs satisfied by a religion; and notably the need for doing certain things at certain dates; the need of the twin ideas of festivity and formality. But though they provide a man with a calendar they do not provide him with a creed. A man did not stand up and say "I believe in Jupiter and Juno and Neptune," etc., as he stands up and says "I believe in God the Father Almighty" and the rest of the Apostles' creed.... Polytheism fades away at its fringes into fairy-tales or barbaric memories; it is not a thing like monotheism as held by serious monotheists. Again it does satisfy the need to cry out on some uplifted name or some noble memory in moments that are themselves noble and uplifted; such as the birth of a child or the saving of a city.... Finally it did satisfy, or rather it partially satisfied, a thing very deep in humanity indeed; the idea of surrendering something as the portion of the unknown powers; of pouring out wine upon the ground, of throwing a ring into the sea; in a word, of sacrifice.... Where that gesture of surrender is most magnificent, as among the great Greeks, there is really much more idea that the man will be the better for losing the ox than that the god will be the better for getting it....

The resemblance between [pagan] myths and the Christian truth is no more accidental than the resemblance between...a historical fact and the somewhat garbled version of it which lives in popular report.

—C. S. LEWIS, *Reflections on the Psalms*

The pagan...feels the presence of powers about which he guesses and invents. St. Paul said that the Greeks had one altar to an unknown god. But in truth all their gods were unknown gods.... The substance of all such paganism may be summarised thus. It is an attempt to reach the divine reality through the imagination alone; in its own field reason does not restrain it at all.... The rivers of mythology and philosophy run parallel and do not mingle till they meet in the sea of Christendom. Simple secularists still talk as if the Church had introduced a sort of schism between reason and religion. The truth is that the Church was actually the first thing that ever tried to combine reason and religion. There had never before been any such union of the priests and the philosophers. Mythology, then, sought God through the imagination; or sought truth by means of beauty....

We therefore feel throughout the whole of paganism a curious double feeling of trust and distrust. When the man makes the gesture of salutation and of sacrifice, when he pours out the libation or lifts up the sword, he knows he is doing a worthy and a virile thing. He knows he is doing one of the things for which a man was made. His imaginative experiment is therefore justified. But precisely because it began with imagination, there is to the end something of mockery in it, and especially the object of it. The mockery, in the more intense moments of the intellect, becomes the almost intolerable irony of Greek tragedy....

In a word, mythology is a *search;* it is something that combines a recurrent desire with a recurrent doubt, mixing a most hungry sincerity in the idea of seeking for a place with a most dark and deep and mysterious levity about all the places found. So far could the lonely imagination lead, and we must turn later to the lonely reason. Nowhere along this road did the two ever travel together.

God...sent the human race what I call good dreams. I mean those queer stories scattered all through the heathen religions about a god who dies and comes to life again and, by his death, has somehow given new life to men.

—C. S. LEWIS, *Mere Christianity*

That is where all these things differed from religion.... They differed from the reality not in what they looked like but in what they were. A picture may look like a landscape; it may look in every detail exactly like a landscape. The only detail in which it differs is that it is not a landscape.... Anyone who has felt and fed on the atmosphere of these myths will know what I mean, when I say that in one sense they did not really profess to be realties. The pagans had dreams about realities.... We may truly call these foreshadowings; so long as we remember that foreshadowings are shadows.... These things were something *like* the real thing; and to say that they were like is to say that they were different.

—"Man and Mythologies"
The Everlasting Man

Viewpoint: J. R. R. Tolkien

The Consolation of the Happy Ending

The "consolation" of fairy-stories has another aspect than the imaginative satisfaction of ancient desires. Far more important is the consolation of the Happy
Ending. Almost I would venture to assert that all complete fairy-stories must
have it. At least I would say that Tragedy is the true form of Drama, its highest
function; but the opposite is true of fairy-story. Since we do not appear to possess a word that expresses this opposite—I will call it *Eucatastrophe*. The *eucata-
strophic* tale is the true form of fairy-tale, and its highest function.

The consolation of fairy-stories, the joy of the happy ending: or more correctly of the good catastrophe, the sudden joyous "turn" (for there is one true
end to any fairy-tale): this joy, which is one of the things which fairy stories can
produce supremely well, is not essentially "escapist", nor "fugitive". In its fairy-
tale—or otherworld—setting, it is a sudden and miraculous grace: never to be
counted on to recur. It does not deny the existence of *dyscatastrophe,* of sorrow
and failure: the possibility of these is necessary to the joy of deliverance; it denies
(in the face of much evidence, if you will) universal final defeat and in so far is
evangelium, giving a fleeting glimpse of Joy, Joy beyond the walls of the world,
poignant as grief.

It is the mark of a good fairy-story, of the higher or more complete kind,
that however wild its events, however fantastic or terrible the adventures, it can
give to child or man that hears, when the "turn" comes, a catch of the breath, a
beat and lifting of the heart, near to (or indeed accompanied by) tears, as keen as
that given by any form of literary art, and having a peculiar quality....

I would venture to say that approaching the Christian Story from this direction, it has long been my feeling (a joyous feeling) that God redeemed the corrupt making-creatures, men, in a way fitting to this aspect, as to others, of their
strange nature. The Gospels contain a fairy-story, or a story of a larger kind
which embraces all the essence of fairy-stories. They contain many marvels—

peculiarly artistic, beautiful, and moving: mythical in their perfect, self-contained significance; and at the same time powerfully symbolic and allegorical; and among the marvels is the greatest and most complete conceivable eucatastrophe. The Birth of Christ is the eucatastrophe of Man's history. The Resurrection is the eucatastrophe of the story of the Incarnation. The story begins and ends in joy. It has pre-eminently the "inner consistency of reality." There is no tale ever told that men would rather find was true, and none which so many sceptical men have accepted as true on its own merits....

It is not difficult to imagine the peculiar excitement and joy that one would feel, if any specially beautiful fairy-story were found to be "primarily" true, its narrative to be history, without thereby necessarily losing the mythical or allegorical significance that it had possessed.... The Christian joy, the *Gloria*, is...pre-eminently (infinitely, if our capacity were not finite) high and joyous. Because this story is supreme; and it is true. Art has been verified. God is the Lord, of angels, and of men—and of elves. Legend and History have met and fused.

But in God's kingdom the presence of the greatest does not depress the small. Redeemed Man is still man. Story, fantasy, still go on, and should go on. The Evangelium has not abrogated legends; it has hallowed them, especially the "happy ending".

—"On Fairy-Stories"
Essays Presented to Charles Williams
Oxford: Oxford University Press, 1947

Part Nine

Poetry

P oetry has always appealed to only a minority of the population. This is not, however, a mark against it. Many of the most worthwhile things in life appeal to the few rather than the many. For those who have developed a taste for poetry, what Kenneth Koch said in a book on the pleasures of reading and writing poetry rings true: "Read in the right way, poetry is a rich source of pleasure, knowledge, and experience. Not knowing poetry is an impoverishment of life such as not knowing music or painting would be, or not traveling." Owen Barfield, in his book *Poetic Diction,* speaks of how the very element of strangeness in poetry is so powerful in the lives of some people that "it binds [them] to their libraries for a lifetime."

Reaching back to the psalms of the Bible, religious poetry has held a special place in the lives of Christians. This is not to say that Christians should relish only devotional poetry dealing with the specifically spiritual dimension of life. All of life is the subject that should engage Christian poets. Yet the religious lyric holds a special place in the affections of Christians. A particular branch of religious lyric is the hymn. The section that follows addresses the Christian as poet and the poet as hymn writer.

On Poets and Poetry

Jeanne Murray Walker

Poetry is, perhaps, the most puzzling of literary forms. Most poets I know admit that they can't produce it upon demand. In fact, they often claim that it arrives from another source. From where? The Greeks liked to say poetry flowed from Mount Olympus, but Milton and Spenser gave God credit, and many poets after Coleridge have pointed to the Unconscious.

If we can't agree about where poetry comes from, maybe we can define it by what it does. A poem like "The Rime of the Ancient Mariner" tells a story. Then there are sonnets, such as those by Sidney, which don't tell stories, but make arguments. Furthermore, in many good poems, such as "My Last Duchess," we hear a voice and almost feel that a performance is going on. Ah! we say, but they're all in form! It must be rhyme and meter that define poetry! But what about the work of Wallace Stevens and Nancy Willard and most poets who've written since 1950? It's not so easy to pin down what a poem does.

Then what on earth *is* poetry?

POETRY AS A DIALECT

Paul Valery claimed that poetry is a kind of language. The trouble is, that term is already taken to mean French and English and Swahili. So I want to change Valery's definition slightly to suggest that poetry is a *dialect.*

Language is a tool. Using it we give directions to the store, warn about

---

JEANNE MURRAY WALKER, *professor at the University of Delaware, is the author of numerous essays and plays, as well as five volumes of poetry, the latest of which is* Gaining Time. *Among her many awards are an NEA Fellowship and a Pew Fellowship in The Arts. She leads workshops around the country in both script and poetry writing, and she lectures frequently at universities, churches, and conferences on spirituality and writing.*

computer viruses, and announce the news *I love you.* By contrast, poetry appears less concerned with practical communication. It seems to arise out of silence and to disappear into silence. And while it is present, it behaves as if a disruptive child had gotten hold of the word processor, wreaking havoc on normal word order and creating rhythmic patterns that focus attention on themselves. It repeats sounds for effect. It forces decent nouns and adjectives into positions in sentences they never imagined. And it makes claims that are, on the face of it, outrageous— *Love is a house where I have taken up abode.* As a dialect, poetry appears to be impractical.

Poetry is an art of Language; certain combinations of words can produce an emotion that others do not produce, and which we shall call poetry.... *In short, it is a* language within a language.

—PAUL VALÉRY, "Poetry, Language and Thought"

But oddly, a good poem is often the shortest and most powerful way to make a point. (This essay would be shorter if it were a poem.) Take, for example, the irony and knock-your-socks-off grief Elizabeth Bishop was able to convey in less than twenty lines:

One Art

The art of losing isn't hard to master;
so many things seem filled with the intent
to be lost that their loss is no disaster.

Lose something every day. Accept the fluster
of lost door keys, the hour badly spent.
The art of losing isn't hard to master.

Then practice losing farther, losing faster:
places, and names, and where it was you meant
to travel. None of these will bring disaster.

I lost my mother's watch. And look! my last, or
next-to-last, of three loved houses went.
The art of losing isn't hard to master.

I lost two cities, lovely ones. And, vaster,
some realms I owned, two rivers, a continent.
I miss them, but it wasn't a disaster.

—Even losing you (the joking voice, a gesture
I love) I shan't have lied. It's evident
the art of losing's not too hard to master
though it might look like (*Write* it!) like disaster.

Any novice can see that Bishop is speaking a strange dialect of English. "One Art" is a villanelle. For starters, in a villanelle, nine of the required nineteen lines must be repeated word for word (Bishop cheats a bit here) without boring the reader. Furthermore, the poet must rhyme every first and third line while also rhyming all the second lines. In addition, the poem must keep a strict beat ticking and the line length is determined by counting those beats. Performing these feats, Bishop still manages to sound like a friend giving advice. In fact, repeated lines, rhyme, meter, and voice—the recipe for a villanelle sounds like a form of madness. If such demands were made on ordinary speakers, conversation would come to a halt and silence would descend on the land.

But maybe Bishop's poem conveys so forcefully the depth of her loss precisely *because*—as poets have learned—certain kinds of convoluted dialect arouse emotions in the reader. Around the beginning of the nineteenth century, Wordsworth wrote that poetry is "emotion recollected in tranquility," and though that definition seems incomplete now, it gets right the main point, which is that poetry conveys emotion, not pragmatic information. Milton said that poems ought to be simple, sensuous, and passionate so they can convey emotion in a way that moves the reader.

A poet is, before anything else, a person who is passionately in love with language.

—W. H. AUDEN, "Squares and Oblongs"

It seems strange, perhaps, that poetry, which is about emotion, should be more artificial than any other literary form. It would seem that great emotion would demand great honesty. Take down the fences, gang, and go anywhere you want! In fact, much contemporary poetry *has* departed from the prefabricated

forms such as sonnets and villanelles and ballads and sestinas that have characterized poetry through its history. But the finest recent poetry still employs—
albeit not so predictably—the formal strategies that have always characterized
poetry, because those strategies move readers.

Too often poetry is thought to be impossibly far apart from ordinary
human existence. Anyone's mind is a teeming gallery of sensations and
memories.... We all know the taste of things sweet or bland or sour,
we all have known rage, we all feel the passion to recall even a painful
past. A rich confusion of awareness underlies all human feeling, and
the language for it surges all around us. The poet reaches into that
rich confusion toward the wellspring of the surging speech of life. He
must, through language alone, catch a tone, a perception, a quality of
sensation and arrange a whole poem round the impulse of energy so
captured.

—M. L. ROSENTHAL. *Poetry and the Common Life*

RHYME AND RHYTHM

A reader doesn't have to know the poet's strategies in order to be delighted by
poetry, but being aware of them increases the pleasure. After all, tennis players
probably enjoy watching Wimbledon more than people who don't know the
rules. It's more fun if you can guess why your man's going to the net, which may
also allow you to predict the next move of his opponent. In the same way, I love
to watch a poet set up a rhythm and then break it to get an effect. I love to
watch a metaphor gathering steam. I love to guess what it will turn into next.
Such guessing depends on form. If there's no net and any number of players are
allowed to hit the ball, who wants to watch?

Perhaps the most primitive element of poetic form is rhythm. All of us,
when we were babies in the womb, felt content hearing the heartbeat of our
mothers. No wonder many of us are comforted by the repetitive, hissing pulse of
the ocean. Not surprisingly, words in regular English express rhythm, alternating
stressed and unstressed syllables. Poets organize these stresses into a system. The
basic unit of the system is called a *foot*. The most common foot in English is the

iambic foot, which I always remember by recalling what day it is: To*day.* The second syllable of that word gets the stress. Very simply, To*day* is an iambic foot. Five To*days* form an iambic line.

Why is iambic the most common foot in English poetry? Because it is the most common foot in English. Our language is basically iambic. So most poets, like most other speakers of English, use mainly iambic feet when they talk to the bank teller and scold their children. They just don't notice, because they aren't paying attention to it.

Our love of rhythm and meter is rooted even deeper in us than our love for musical repetition. It is related to the beat of our hearts, the pulse of our blood, the intake and outflow of air from our lungs. Everything that we do naturally and gracefully we do rhythmically.... So native is rhythm to us that we read it, when we can, into the mechanical world around us. Our clocks go tick-tick-tick-tick, but we hear them go tick-tock, tick-tock in an endless trochaic. The click of the railway wheels beneath us patterns itself into a tune in our heads. There is a strong appeal for us in language that is rhythmical.

—LAUREN PERRINE, *Sound and Sense*

No poem, even a poem so maniacally organized as Bishop's "One Art," uses absolutely metrically perfect iambic pentameter lines. For the reader, that would be like medieval water torture. *Drip. Drip. Drip. Drip.* No! As soon as we get the pattern, we want to see it varied. So the best formal poems first establish a clear beat and then, within the confines of that beat, create a rhythm, which is where the music of the poem lives. To see a master at work, first establishing a meter, then creating rhythmic dives and swoops, now pulling back and then rushing forward, look at a Shakespearean sonnet.

There are many other kinds of metrical feet in English poetry, and they can be combined in various ways to create lines. The five stress line is a favorite of English poets, but some poets like W. H. Auden and Theodore Roethke used lines with as few stresses as three. It is probably because nursery rhymes have short lines that when we read one of these adult poems we feel ourselves entering a world of lost simplicity.

The lines of most poetry until about the middle of the last century ended in rhyme. The shorter the rhymed line, the more firmly the rhyme gets hammered home. *Jack and JILL / went up the HILL.* For the last fifty years, poetry in this country has moved away from such rhythmic certainty and such pointed end-rhymes, perhaps because the last two World Wars stripped people of their sense that things fit together in a pattern. Then came the free-to-be-you-and-me sixties and seventies, when many cultural restraints were tossed out, which helped to finish off end-rhyme. Although there has been a passionate move back to form among some younger poets (for whom the sonnet, for instance, seems to be a radical new discovery), many readers still feel instinctively suspicious of poems that slam closed with two end rhymes in a row (called a closed couplet).

But good poets have always adored the music in language, and most of them have simply moved from a jingle at the end of the line to less noticeable kinds of harmony within the line. Poets have at their disposal a wonderful supply of sound tricks. There is assonance, for example, which is the repetition of vowel sounds (wonder, done / seamy, beat / rake, acorn) and alliteration, which is the repetition of consonant sounds (the snide sparrow sings on the sill; wheel in when you want to whine). Poets can devise lines whose words move up the vowel ladder (man, moan, moon, mine, main, mean). Richard Wilbur does something like this in the first lines of his brilliant poem "Love Calls Us to the Things of This World": "Eyes open to the cry of pulleys." Combine the many sound strategies of poetry with rhythmic patterns and line breaks (pauses within sentences that mark the end of lines), and you have a dizzying universe of musical possibilities.

Most of the time when I sit down to write a poem I am thinking about such matters of craftsmanship as form and meter and the antics of words. If the poem emerges as one with an implicit or explicit religious dimension, O.K. If not, O.K.... My first obligation is to take my craft seriously.
—CHAD WALSH, "The Wary Witness of the Poets"

If you want to be able to take pleasure in assonance and alliteration, it's not a bad idea to train your ear. When I teach poetry writing, I sometimes ask my students to make up a sound chart of words with off rhymes (imperfectly matching sound-alike words) across the top line and full rhymes (traditional nursery-rhyme like rhymes) descending from them in columns. Here's a start on one possible paradigm:

man	moan	moon	mine	main	mean
ban	bone	croon	brine	bane	bean
can	crone	boon	dine	crane	keen

The next step, after finishing the chart, is to write a poem using as many of these words as possible and as few *other* words. What comes out of this experiment is hardly ever orderly English sentences, but the verse is often surprisingly touching in the way chamber music can be touching.

There are great poets to whom music sang so powerfully that it lured them further and further away from the syntax of practical English. Take a look at the beginning of "Fern Hill" by Dylan Thomas:

Now as I was young and easy under the apple boughs
About the lilting house and happy as the grass was green,
The night above the dingle starry,
Time let me hail and climb
Golden in the heydays of his eyes,

To relax into Thomas's opulent diction and syntax, to let it carry you wherever it wants, can be a great vacation from the tyrannical business of everyday language. Enjoying a poem like this can send us back to regular English with an ear honed to better hear its music.

WORDS AND TRUTH

Poetry is built of the same words and sentences such as the very English I'm using to write this essay. This seems quite amazing to me, that human beings have taken snippets of *language*—the word *losing*, for example, with all its practical uses—to make art. Unlike words, colors (such as orange) and sounds (such as A flat) don't have predetermined, conventional meanings (although there used to be an iconography of colors and once upon a time the church banned certain chord resolutions!). But who would ever mistake a painting of a landscape in the National Gallery with the Connecticut River Valley? No one would be enraged to discover that you can't actually hear Aaron Copeland's *Appalachian Spring* in Appalachia. And yet I suspect readers often confuse the dialect of poetry with the language of English because poetry is built out of what the reader recognizes as apparently familiar words, phrases, and sentences.

I think that throughout history poets have gotten it in the neck more often than other artists because they use words (which are routinely evaluated for their truth and falsehood) instead of oils, for example, or alternating sound and silence. Plato—so massive and so early a thinker—attacked poets (by which he meant writers of fiction/scripts, scripts/poetry) for lying. That he should have done so is enough to give one pause. There's no point in denying that poets make things up. But think for a minute about a painter. There is a sense in which he lies too. On the canvas, if he wants to make a landscape appear "real," he has to paint a lake smaller in order to make it appear farther away. But in fact, everything on his canvas *is exactly the same distance from the viewer* because the canvas exists in two dimensions, not three.

In other words, artists *have to* pass off one thing as another. It is this trickery Plato objected to. Thousands of years later, when Plato's arguments were renewed by the Puritans, who censored poets for lying, Sir Philip Sidney made the point that they had to lie in order to tell the truth more fully. Sidney's point seems to have been that poets invent hypothetical events in order to approximate probability more closely. Dostoevsky described *Don Quixote* as a novel in which truth is saved by a lie. Picasso said that art is a lie that makes us realize truth and that the artist must know how to convince others of the truthfulness of his lies.

Reading poetry gives experiences there is no other way to have. It gives them quickly, suddenly, just about whenever we want.
                                        —KENNETH KOCH, *Making Your Own Days:*
                                        The Pleasures of Reading and Writing Poetry

---

That is why poetry, like other arts, really shouldn't be thought of as either true or false. Poetry is representative. It either *represents* with fidelity or it doesn't. Like other artists, poets can't avoid using deception to make the truth clear. The narrator may tell as personal experience events that didn't actually happen. He may choose a word mainly because of its sound or rhythm. He may create a character who never lived or make an argument in order to reveal its stupidity. In poetry he is simply not bound by the truth requirements he uses in his private life.

And I think that's why reading poetry can suddenly make us see English in a new way. Think of the way English gets used every day by hundreds of millions of people. Like everyone else, I often pick up English like a wrench to turn a bolt and then toss it away to rust in the rain. Then I read a brilliant poem. The disruptions caused by sound, rhythm, metaphor, the odd use of words, the order of the sentences—force me to see possibilities in English. I remember how, after looking at one of Turner's late paintings, I saw fog and realized I had never really noticed it before. So a poem can make me see English once more. No wonder we pick up the best phrases from our poets for general use. From them we learn strategies for argument and metaphor. So the little dialect of poetry keeps quietly rehabilitating the big, practical English language.

METAPHOR

As I have already admitted, to me perhaps the most profound difference between the language of poetry and English itself is that in poetry the agenda is not a practical one. Poems aren't written to convince you to march for peace or to buy underwear from Target. They're hypothetical. They pass readers through experience. They exist in the world of *As If.* No poem goes on very long without tilting its hand to show this. Poetry is radically nonsurface, antimaterialistic, and nonliteral because at its heart lies metaphor. And metaphor is subversive.

Metaphor is the Renaissance term used to cover more than two hundred rhetorical figures that create different kinds of comparisons. Comparisons these days tend to be divided into two categories. What we now call metaphor is the strongest form of comparison because it suppresses the notion of *like* or *as*.

The formulation of a metaphor is that of an equation, X=Y. Say, *the sun is a thumbtack in the sky.* But at the risk of belaboring the obvious, the sun is not like a thumbtack in most senses. It cannot be held in your hand, for example, and if it could, it wouldn't feel metallic. So X is also *utterly different from* Y.

The first term—the sun—let's call it the X—is the given. The second term—a thumbtack—the Y—is supposed to explain X. But Y doesn't just explain. It argues. If the sun is like a thumbtack, that's one kind of day. If the sun is like a yellow M&M, that's altogether different. You'd better be right about it. It can't be both.

In fact, it isn't quite enough to say that the Y argues. It does more than that. It sets off a little explosion in the reader, whose mind has to jump the broken circuit from X to Y. When reading a metaphor, for a fleeting moment you see the two terms as married and you understand the truth, which is a third thing beyond either of the two terms.

Poetry provides the one permissible way of saying one thing and meaning another.... We like to talk in parables and in hints and in indirections.

—ROBERT FROST, "Education by Poetry"

I think of this spark as the transcendent going off in a human mind. God doesn't live *in* images, as the first commandment is at pains to inform us. And as most of us realized from sad experience, the human impulse to worship *things* leads to disappointment. But we need images to think with, even about God. So we have been given this gift: Moving *between* the two terms of the metaphor, we can glimpse the third thing, which isn't available in either of the two terms. Metaphor ignites the sensible world to make us experience meaning that can't be apprehended by our senses.

The other well-known form of comparison, the one that uses *like* or *as* is called simile: *The sun, like a thumbtack, pierces the sky.* Now the violence is at one remove. The writer is not making the absurd claim that the sun *is* a thumbtack, only that the sun at the moment seems to be like one. Simile is both less drastic and less powerful than metaphor because it compromises with reason and admits that the equation is only apparent, not actual.

Although a lot of people think of poetry as "nice" and "beautiful," there's nothing ornamental about it. The fierce engine of metaphor was built to pull a heavy load. Look at Emily Dickinson's poem "Because I Could Not Stop for Death:"

Because I could not stop for Death
He kindly stopped for me—
The Carriage held but just Ourselves—
And Immortality.

We slowly drove—He knew no haste
And I had put away
My labor and my leisure too,
For His Civility—

We passed the School, where Children strove
At Recess—in the Ring—
We passed the Fields of Gazing Grain—
We passed the Setting Sun—

Or rather—He passed Us—
The Dews drew quivering and chill—
For only Gossamer, my Gown—
My Tippet—only Tulle—

We paused before a House that seemed
A swelling of the Ground—
The Roof was scarcely visible—
The Cornice—in the Ground—

Since then—'tis Centuries—and yet
Feels shorter than the Day
I first surmised the Horses' Heads
Were toward Eternity.

A gallant but headstrong carriage driver sweeps us away. The Action of Death = The Action of a Carriage Driver. The equation is surprising, but Dickinson details the equation with such vividness that I, for one, never once think about getting off. In fact, by the end of the poem I can almost believe she is speaking from beyond the grave. It is metaphor that allows Emily Dickinson to make such a powerful argument about death.

Metaphor arrives in a lot of different forms. Here are some examples:

- The Y can go on at some length. *Each day is an empty pail I fill and carry to the kitchen.* The whole phrase after pail is the Y part of the comparison.
- X can *act* like Y without being called Y: *I unlock her handcuffs with a stem of grass.* We know the grass is a key, though the comparison doesn't spell that out.

- A metaphor can be buried in an adjective that modifies X: *By midnight, the carnal rain has swamped us.* The rain has a body.
- The Y can appear in a prepositional phrase*: There he stands on the verandah of Mozart's Third Concerto.* The Concerto suddenly becomes a house with a porch.
- The Y can be missing entirely. *I have never worn any shoes but those in which to bring fire.* The shoes suggest a whole way of life which, from the speaker's birth gave him no choice but to bring humans fire.
- The Y can be personified by the X. *Midnight, with his hangdog face, is on the prowl again.* A time of night shows up as a man.

VOICE

What helps persuade me as a reader to buy the paradox of metaphor is not only the aptness of the equation, but also the personal voice of the poet. I remember clearly the first time I felt poetry to reach out and drag me into its circle. I was about twenty years old, and I had just fallen in love and I was reading John Donne for the first time. The first lines of "The Sun Rising" just about lassoed me out of my chair in the library:

Busy old fool, unruly sun,
Why dost thou thus
Through windows, and through curtains call on us?

I understood the irritation of dawn coming too early, though I had never thought about it as a literary topic. When, from three hundred years away, I heard Donne screaming insults at the sun, I liked him so much that I would have followed him anywhere. Since then, I have often been held rapt by the voice of a good poet. Listen to Mary Oliver in "One or Two Things":

Isn't it plain the sheets of moss, except that
they have no tongues, could lecture
all day if they wanted about
spiritual patience?

And here's Stephen Dunn in "After the Argument":

Whoever spoke first would lose something,
that was the stupid
unspoken rule.

Each of these openings surprises me. In each I feel called by an immediate, intelligent friend. In each I am immediately ushered into a very particular, apparently *unliterary* place. It's all very well for a poet to master metaphor and rhythm and sound, but if he doesn't have a voice that can make the reader care about what he's saying, he might as well give up.

BAD POETRY

In fact, maybe the most obvious clue to bad poetry is that it usually sounds as if it's being spoken by some arcane poet-in-the-sky instead of by the odd and fascinating person next to us. Usually, too, in a bad poem, the metaphor is clichéd, which means it's been around too long. Like fish, when metaphors get old, they go bad. Think, for instance, of people "having a whale of a good time." Think of how love can "go south," making a person who is already "on edge" finally "go round the bend," more than likely in the difficult "dog days of summer" and end up on "the junk heap of life." These clichés have lost so much energy through overuse that it's easy to forget that they are metaphor. But they (and their many brothers) still put in cameo appearances in bad new poems. Add to the reader's misery that in a bad poem the verbs tend to be passive and there are no specific details, and the rhyme, if there is any, is forced.

Some bad poetry is devotional verse, but devotional verse is by no means the only kind of bad poetry. Have you taken a look at the cards in the Hallmark store lately? Have you read the tormented verse of adolescents who listen to popular songs on the radio? And yet this bad poetry often gives us the feeling that it's telling the truth. Why? Maybe because it sounds familiar. Because it uses the clichés of religious and/or emotional life. Clichés don't offend anyone, by the way, since they're the agreed-upon daily traffic of the language. It can take work to recognize bad poetry.

I would add another category of bad poems: those that are not marked by a struggle with the medium of language. They are English gussied up to look like poetry. Some such poems are written in order to argue some dogma: Marxism, Christianity, the superiority of a breath freshener. There is poetry and there is dogma. Both have their place. But they have very different personalities. If I start a poem with dogma rather than a metaphor, say, or a dramatic voice, it usually goes bad, even if I try to fix it by using a lot of metaphor. I don't mean that any poem with an idea in it is bad. Not at all. I mean that a poem seems to include its own fossil record of how it was conceived. I find that I can't cheat on this score. If I *start* with an idea, if I don't have to struggle to get there, the poem is likely to sound idea-driven and polemical. Other poets have told me that this is true for them as well.

That is the terrifying challenge of poetry. Can I think out the logic of images?

—STEPHEN SPENDER, "The Making of a Poem"

Then what is the relationship between poetry and truth? I think the point of all the arts, including poetry, is to tell the truth about what it is to be human. For this, those of us who make art, finally, are responsible to God. But the question of truth in a poem is not so easy to settle. A poem is not a brief. It is meant to be an experience. So any proposition within the borders of a poem changes meaning if it is wrenched out and quoted. This point is easier to make about a script. I remember how shocked I was when I realized that Polonius is actually an old windbag and Shakespeare wrote "This above all, unto thine own self be true," and all the lines of gorgeous poetry that follow it to make Polonius look pompous. Polonius always speaks majestically. As Gertrude points out, he needs more matter and less art. And yet I hear people quote those speeches as if Shakespeare had meant them straight.

The irony or humor with which something is said is part of its meaning. Rip a stud from the wall of a house and it might be useful for something, but it has lost its meaning as a support. Every sentence in a poem helps to hold the poem up. The point is, it's wrong to read a poem as if it were a list of propositions. And it's wrong to ask poetry to supply us with such a list, since poetry, like other arts, *represents* rather than argues. Beyond this, I am very skeptical toward anyone who tells me that he knows some piece of art or another doesn't conform to the truth and therefore should be banished. Human experience is very broad, and truth is wider than the universe. Even when I die, I will know only a very small percentage of it. And so will everyone else.

I myself believe that the ultimate purpose of our creation is to know and love God, but there are a practically infinite number of interesting things going on in the universe, and it seems to me that they are all fair game for writers. I believe that the art for arts' sake movement, for example, which led to confessional poetry, is heartbreakingly and awfully mistaken. Art is wonderful, but it cannot save us and it cannot be the whole point. And yet I do not believe that the point of art is to spread the gospel either. Take a look at the variety and subtlety of what God has created: giraffes, hedgehogs, the dawn, the mind-boggling world of a cell, the Milky Way. He is not didactic. He has a sense of humor. And He must be fascinated by His whole creation.

Maybe it will be useful to contrast truth in poetry with the truth of the creed. I repeat the creed every Sunday, and when I do, I try to be mindful that men and women were tortured and died to defend it—not merely to secure its *ideas,* but to defend its very *words.* In that way, the creed is the opposite of cliché. It *needs* to be passed down from generation to generation exactly as it is. Christ has died. Christ has risen. Christ will come again. Saying that for me is like coloring in the lines once a week because I desperately need to be reminded where the lines are.

Poetry is not eloquence or decoration or a nice way of saying things. It is a way of seeing, a way of discovering perceptions, moments of awareness that were not there before. The poem is the body of a different kind of "knowing," a kind of awareness that the conscious intellect by itself cannot get to…. Poems expand consciousness, deepen human awareness…. The poem is a thousand times closer to the concerto or the painting than it is to the sermon, speech, article, editorial, or discussion.

—ROD JELLEMA, "Poems Should Stay Across the Street from the Church"

By contrast, consider the wildly various music and painting and poems that creed has inspired. Who could have predicted this marvelous graffiti on the wall of Christianity? The Sistine Chapel ceiling, the Madonnas of Raphael, the ethereal pieces of Palestrina, the great masses of Bach, the Mozart *Requiem,* the Medieval cathedrals, *Paradise Lost, The Four Quartets*—such brilliance and variety boggles the mind. I am one of those who fervently hopes the list is To Be Continued. Our mandate is to make the truth new for each new age.

And that brings us to the question: What is Christian art? Many of the Christian works in the list you just read were commissioned by Princes or Popes who specified what they wanted. And some of the artists seem to have been much less enthusiastic Christians than their patrons. Can a non-Christian make Christian art? I don't know. Is explicitly Christian art the only kind we can call Christian? What if it is written for money? Is all art that is made by Christians Christian art? Do Christians always have to make art that refers to the great religious truths? Of course, it would seem that all Christians must *sometimes* write about the Christian experience, since that, for them, is part of what it means to be human. Can these same Christian artists make art that *isn't* obviously Christian? These questions have become vexed. I fear they are often divisive.

Surely all truth is God's truth. Suffering can be redemptive. That is one of our great Easter truths. And yet Aeschylus has one of his characters observe something very similar in *The Oresteia,* and it is borne out by the plot of the play. Think of the truths in the inestimable work of Shakespeare. Was he a Christian? The jury is still out. But how amazingly truthful his plays feel when we experience them! Consider Carriavagio. And what about Shostakovich? Ponder hundreds of other brilliant artists. What moves you? Who speaks to you? That artist has told great human truths, and we would be immeasurably poorer if we did not have his work.

ONE WRITER WRITING, ONE READER READING

Like most other poets, I can't explain how I write poetry. No wonder. It requires performing all the aspects of poetry I have talked about plus a number that I haven't had space to mention—all at once—playing all the instruments in the orchestra at the same time. But then, we all do things every day that are veiled in mystery. Can you explain how, after passing your eyes over these words, you formed the idea you now have in your mind?

I hasten to add that I do whatever I can to light the rocket. I read like a maniac—poems, novels, plays, journalism, nonfiction prose—anything. And for many years I have scrutinized good poems. Duty doesn't drive me to do this. Love does. It's rather like finding a coat so attractive that you want to turn it inside out to see how it was made.

Generally for me a poem comes in a whoosh. Typed cleanly on the paper, it feels immense and splendid, like the creation must have seemed on the first morning of the world. I'm happy as a new mother—until I go back to look at it several days later. Then the work begins. I see it with the cold, beady eyes of a critic. I find fault with it. I consider throwing it away. Sometimes I do. But usually I begin the slow process of revision which can take from several months to five or six years. Crazy as it sounds, I love to revise. It gives me another chance. It's like saying, *Wait! That's not what I meant at all. Let me take another stab at it!* Paper and ink are endlessly forgiving. I thank God for these second chances, which sometimes become fifteenth chances and ninety-seventh chances. It is humbling and redemptive, the process of rewriting.

> *The ideal experience of reading a poem is, in many respects, close to the experience of writing it: one goes through uncertainty, flashes of perception, small satisfactions, puzzlement, understanding, surprise.*
> —KENNETH KOCH, *Making Your Own Days:*
> *The Pleasures of Reading and Writing Poetry*

Why go to all this trouble over a poem? I'm not sure. I hear the lines, and if they aren't right, I can't leave them alone. But why? I will admit that as long as I can remember, language has seemed as vast and impossible to scale as a sheer rock wall, and in its presence I have always felt uniquely and disastrously inarticulate. Maybe that's why language has such power to bewitch. It is such a challenge.

But more interesting and perhaps more common to other writers is the fact that I have the sense that someone is waiting for the poem. For one thing, I know some people who will read whatever I write. For them the poem needs to be immediate, as Adrian Rich suggested, scrawled for instant distribution. But I can't believe, as many of my friends do, that we are trapped in Now and that current readers are the only readers. I also imagine readers like the ones Renaissance poets wrote for, the generations who will be born later. (They were right. For them those future generations are *us*.) And since I believe in life after death—whatever it may be like, I take seriously the words in Hebrews, that we are compassed "by such a great cloud of witnesses" (12:1). It is certainly bracing to imagine that John Donne, for example, might have some idea what is going on in contemporary poetry, or my father perhaps, who died when I was thirteen. Instantly the stakes go up.

I am frequently asked what I write about. This is a question that can reduce a grown-up poet to a gibbering child. I suspect it is so difficult to answer because writers who choose their own topics—as opposed to writers who are hired guns—don't *know* what they write about. It has been said that fiction writers keep writing the same novel over and over because they are trying to find an answer to something and if they ever got it, they would stop. That must be true for poets as well. In fact, even the questions are hidden, questions powerful enough to drive a person through years of writing with few rewards. On the other hand, when I read my work, I do have some strange sense of what it's about—although it may have seemed to be about something quite different when I was writing it. My work seems to be constantly ripping aside the veil of the mundane to find mystery. Appearances are deceiving precisely because we don't know we're being deceived. Our miscalculations leave us vulnerable to one rude awakening after another. In a way we can't usually imagine, the world teems with grace. This is funny, I think. It is, surely, the ultimate comedy.

In the end, maybe, writing poetry is for me a particularly loud or tall form of reading. I write poetry because it is my way of knowing the world. I try to tell the truth about what I know. But I also read and write poetry because I am having a love affair with the form. Poetry is an expression of hope. It is play. A lifetime is too short to exhaust its possibilities.

The Poet as Hymn Writer

Timothy Dudley-Smith

When A. E. Housman, in his Leslie Stephen Lecture of 9 May 1933, was asked by an American to define poetry, he replied that he "could no more define poetry than a terrier can define a rat," though he surmised that "we both recognize the object by the symptoms which it provokes in us" (46). In commenting further on his own creation of poetry, Housman called it "a secretion" (47). Since I first read these words—I think as a schoolboy—I have known what he was talking about. There was a time when I was writing and publishing occasional poems. They were almost all on Christian themes, and kindly friends would sometimes urge me to try my hand at hymns. I knew, however, that what "came to me" in my verses was very different from what would make a hymn. I recall only one effort at hymn writing during this era, and it falls far short of any standard of technical competence.

I did not think of myself, therefore, as having in any way the gifts of a hymn writer when in May 1961 I jotted down a set of verses that began, "Tell out, my soul, the greatness of the Lord." I was reading a review copy of the *New English Bible New Testament,* in which that line appears exactly as I have put it above. I saw in it the first line of a poem and speedily wrote the rest. I cannot now recall how it came to the hands of the editors of the *Anglican Hymn Book,* then in the early stages of compilation. But the editors told me that they would like to use it as a hymn and asked me to try my hand at a hymn text on the theme of home. So followed "Lord, who left the highest heaven," and later (unsought by the editors, but on a favorite text of Scripture) "Christ be my leader." Since then, I have written few lines intended as poetry instead of hymns. Faced with this

TIMOTHY DUDLEY-SMITH *is one of the best-known contemporary hymn writers. A retired Anglican Bishop, he has had a varied career as preacher, editor, and author (including, most recently, the biography of John Stott). His hymns are published and sung around the world.*

turnaround in my own experience, I have naturally reflected on the relationship of hymns to poetry. Many other hymn writers have done the same.

HYMNS AS POETRY: THE VERDICT OF THE MASTERS

John Wesley addresses the subject in the preface to *A Collection of Hymns for the Use of the People Called Methodists* (preface dated 1779). Writing with the hymns of his brother Charles as well as his own in mind, Wesley theorizes,

> May I be permitted to add a few words with regard to the *poetry*? Then I will speak to those who are judges thereof, with all freedom and unreserve. To these I may say, without offence, 1. In these hymns there is no doggerel; no botches; nothing put in to patch up the rhyme; no feeble expletives. 2. Here is nothing turgid or bombast, on the one hand, or low and creeping, on the other. 3. Here are no *cant* expressions; no words without meaning.... We talk common sense, both in prose and verse, and use no word but in a fixed and determinative sense. 4. Here are, allow me to say, both the purity, the strength, and the elegance of the English language; and, at the same time, the utmost simplicity and plainness, suited to every capacity. (iv)

Although Wesley's familiarity with the leading English poets of his own day and the past is well attested (Bett), Wesley nonetheless asserts later in his preface that for the hymn writer "the spirit of piety" is "of infinitely more moment than the spirit of poetry," adding that "when Poetry thus keeps its place, as the handmaid of Piety, it shall attain, not a poor perishable wreath, but a crown that fadeth not away" (v).

Writing thirty years before Wesley, Isaac Watts, in the preface to his *Hymns and Spiritual Songs,* gives some indication of the restraint under which he labored in the writing of what he called his "compositions." Watts contrasts his metrical psalms to his hymns, "whose form is of mere human composure." Regarding these hymns Watts writes,

> If there be any poems in the book that are capable of giving delight to persons of a more refined taste and polite education, perhaps they may be found in this part: but except they lay aside the humour of criticism, and enter into a devout frame, every ode here already despairs of pleasing. I confess myself to have

been too often tempted away from the more spiritual designs I proposed, by some gay and flowery expressions that gratified the fancy; the bright images too often prevailed above the fire of divine affection; and the light exceeded the heat: yet, I hope, in many of them the reader will find, that devotion dictates the song, and the head and hand were nothing but interpreters and secretaries to the heart. (112)

Not only Watts and Wesley, but John Newton also, in the preface to his *Olney Hymns* (1779), discusses this relationship of hymns to poetry, and his viewpoint is similar to that of his predecessors:

There is a stile and manner suited to the composition of hymns, which may be more successfully, or at least more easily attained by a versifier, than by a poet. They should be *Hymns,* not *Odes,* if designed for public worship, and for the use of plain people. Perspicuity, simplicity and ease, should be chiefly attended to: and the imagery and coloring of poetry, if admitted at all, should be indulged very sparingly, and with great judgment.... It behooved me to do my best. But though I would not offend readers of taste by a wilful coarseness and negligence, I do not write professedly for them. If the Lord, whom I serve, has been pleased to favor me with that mediocrity of talent, which may qualify me for usefulness to the weak and the poor of his flock, without quite disgusting persons of superior discernment, I have reason to be satisfied. (vii-viii)

If Newton here gives the impression that a hymn is a poem by a writer of only mediocre talent, that is certainly mistaken, and equally certainly not his meaning. He is concerned to point out—to warn the reader and disarm the critic—that the two are not quite the same.

I myself believe hymns can best be considered as a very particular kind of poetry—what Erik Routley has called "lyric under a vow of renunciation" (19). Such renunciation extends to both theme and style. J. R. Watson believes that "narrowness of subject and a limitation of figurative language is a pointer to the difference between a hymn and poem" (12). He adds,

The first demand of a hymn is that it must be singable, and in this are comprised a number of characteristics. It has to be rhythmically stable, understandable in the time it takes to sing the words, and doctrinally sound. Because of this the imagery of a hymn is limited by its needs to refer to orthodox belief, and by its need to avoid ambiguity. Above all, perhaps, a hymn needs to mean something while a poem *is* something, means itself; the greatest hymns attain to this condition of poetry, but they start from a different place.... (12)

Not everyone agrees with the dominant tradition that views hymns as a very particular kind of poetry. Bernard Lord Manning, for example, will have none of it. He writes, "To say of any hymn it is 'not poetry' or it is 'poor poetry' is to say nothing. A hymn—a good hymn—is not necessarily poetry of any sort, good or bad: just as poetry, good or bad, is not necessarily a hymn.... Hymns do not form a subdivision of poetry. They are a distinct kind of composition" (109). Perhaps Manning is looking over his shoulder at those poor hymns which he valiantly defends as hymns, while deprecating them by every other canon of taste. C. S. Lewis might say that what he personally desired in church services were fewer, better, and shorter hymns, but especially fewer (Babbage 73), but Manning boldly defends even the halt and the lame of the hymnbook: "Reverence is due to hymns as to any other sacred object. The hymn that revolts me, if it has been a means of grace to Christian men, I must respect as I should respect a Communion cup, however scratched its surface, however vulgar its decoration" (109).

Hymns are sung by those people who share certain things: Bible-reading, doctrine, common prayer, and moral precept.
    —J. R. WATSON, *The English Hymn: A Critical and Historical Study*

What we have, in short, is an inherent tension of hymns between ordinary poetic criteria and the religious aims of the hymn. On one side we have Archbishop Benson claiming that "a great many of our hymns are nonsense, sheer nonsense, irritating nonsense, if you regard them simply as literature, and yet they undoubtedly awaken the conscience and raise the soul to God. It is a great puzzle, the badness of most really effective and stirring hymns" (592). On the other side we have the sentiment of Christopher Driver that hymns possess "technical achievements of a high order. They attempt the difficult task of mar rying verse to theology and clothing religious sentiment in decent and singable language" (340).

VOWS OF RENUNCIATION

A hymn accepts a number of very severe limitations, found together in no other class of poetry. First, there is the limitation of theme, which Samuel Johnson stigmatized with the description "paucity of topicks" resulting in "perpetual repetition" (310). The hymn's narrow range of subject matter can lead to sacrificing quality to quantity and producing an overabundance of hymns. For hymn writers, "more" can easily mean "worse." To mint fresh phrases for old truths is not an everyday affair, and the old phrases always lie about one's path, clamoring for inclusion. Unconscious plagiarism, whether of oneself or of another, is a constant hazard. In the search for "inevitability," something that "sounds right," it is all too possible that a phrase or a line will sound right because one has heard or used it before.

Alongside the limitation of theme, if not indeed part of it, is the fact that a hymn is written (or, at least, chosen by an editor for inclusion) with an *aim* in view. For a hymn to serve its defined purpose (edifying, unifying, glorifying), it also needs, in the words of Bernard Lord Manning, to be "combining personal experience with a presentation of historic events and doctrines" (138). A hymn must not only express sentiments with which the generality of worshipers can identify in their own spiritual experience, but it must do so in words they can understand (even if not necessarily, in my view, exhaust at a first reading) and sing to music.

There is a simplicity which diminishes and a simplicity which enlarges.
—CLYDE S. KILBY, "Christian Imagination"

Is there in truth no beauty?…Nor let them punish me with loss of rhyme, /
Who plainly say, My God, My King.
—GEORGE HERBERT, "Jordan (1)"

This, in turn, requires the metrical discipline, foreign to English verse, of working by strict meter rather than by the stress that gives spring and life to so much of our poetry. In particular, there must be euphony in the choice of dominant sounds, especially in the consonants, to prevent a polysyllabic phrase (over which the reader of a poem might linger with enjoyment) from becoming a mere mouthful of gabble in the singing of a hymn to strict time.

Along with meter, most hymns seem to me to require rhyme. To be sure, some manage very well without it, as does a large class of poetry. But we would be the poorer without a rhyming hymnbook for at least two reasons. The first brings me back to the concept of inevitability, the sense of fulfillment and satisfaction that rhyme helps to convey—the knowledge that what is being said is most fittingly and conclusively said in this particular way. The second reason has to do with craftsmanship—the fusing of sound and meaning until the form of expression most aptly conveys the thing expressed. Certainly a true poet does not need rhyme, as a true painter does not need representational form. But as I am suspicious of the abstracts done by an artist who cannot draw, so I am suspicious of certain overly facile lyric poems (or hymns) which evade the difficulties and the rewards of handling rhyme.

But the heart of the distinction between hymns and poetry lies, to my mind, not in the presentation or style—rhyme, meter, smoothness, regularity, rhythm—vital though these must be. It is nearer to those words of J. R. Watson that a hymn must mean something, where a poem "is something," means "itself" (12). A poem therefore can particularize the experience of an individual's response to some event in a way that can attract the reader, even though he or she may know nothing of the experience or reject the response. In such poetry we recognize a certain individual—or even more general truth—without necessarily identifying ourselves with it. It is enough for the poem to be a work of art.

In its own way, a hymn also needs to be a work of art. A good hymn should exist (as, in Manning's comparison, a communion cup exists) in its own right as the product of craftsmanship and the artist's ear and eye. But it must also be a vehicle for the congregational worship of God, expressing for the worshipers sentiments which they can honestly acknowledge and share, providing a form which, at best, finds fitter words for their devotion and aspiration than they might find themselves.

Jane Austen has a fictional character say, when asked what she is reading, "Oh! it is only a novel," adding, "Only some work in which the greatest powers of the mind are displayed, in which the most thorough knowledge of human nature, the happiest delineation of its variety, the liveliest effusions of wit and humour, are conveyed to the world in the best-chosen language" (*Northanger Abbey*, chapter 5). May we not say something of the same of the best of our inheritance of hymnody? "Only a hymn," the critics say. To which George Sampson gives us this reply: "If [Charles Wesley's] hymns had been addressed to Pan or Apollo or some other heathen figure, or if they were written in some foreign tongue, how loud the praise would be! But, alas, he addressed the Christian Deity in English, and his poems are dismissed as mere hymns" (219).

Samuel Johnson said of the hymns of Isaac Watts that "the sanctity of the matter rejects the ornaments of figurative diction" (310). One reason why hymns must renounce overly elaborate figures is that they must stand the test of repetition. Few poems—but many hymns—arrive at such familiarity that, without intending it, we know them by heart. To retain and renew freshness and depth of meaning under such circumstances is not achieved by recondite, elaborate, or fanciful imagery.

The good hymn is the hymn that passes two tests. One is simple to apply; as a piece of craftsmanship in literature it must be without blemish. It must not offend against the rules of grammar, syntax, or scansion.... To judge a hymn on this test is tolerably easy; either the author has split an infinitive, or left a hanging participle, or written nonsense, or he has not.

The other test is more difficult for the author to pass and for the critic to judge. It is necessary that when written the hymn shall do, precisely and in full, the thing it was designed to do. A hymn is designed to be a congregational act of praise. If therefore it is not the kind of thing a congregation can sing, being more suitable for personal devotion, it fails; and if it is not praise, that is, addressed to God and dealing with the things of God, it fails. Furthermore, if it distracts the congregation from the act of worship by obscurity, by irrelevance, or by seductive language or music, it fails.

—ERIC ROUTLEY, *Hymns and Human Life*

Other renunciations include metrical freedom, individualism, and the attributing of the sentiments of the poem to another *persona*. A wide variety of worshipers must be capable of making a hymn's sentiments their own. Some of these renunciations do mean, of course, that good hymns can be written by those who lack some essential for the making of a poet. But balancing this, hymn writers must have particular qualities theological and mystical, in religious experience and in a certain craftsmanship, that many a poet lacks.

To illustrate the craftsmanship of a good hymn, consider the skill with which so many of our best hymns say what they have to say complete within the line. Charles Wesley is again a supreme example:

> He breaks the power of cancelled sin,
> He sets the prisoner free:
> His blood can make the foulest clean,
> His blood availed for me.

It is a skill to be found, certainly, in other poets besides the hymn writers. But that it is not a general characteristic of lyric poetry is amply demonstrated by a dip into most anthologies. It is a further example of the constraints, the renunciations, under which the hymn writer begins his or her task.

THE HYMNS OF ZION

"The hymn is never a piece of private poetry," writes Arthur Pollard, adding,

> nor is its appeal limited to a narrow group. It is directed at a wide audience, differing vastly in background, education and sensibility. Furthermore, this audience must be able to share in the thoughts and emotions evoked by the hymn. That is one reason why the good hymn can never be a product of narrow sectarianism. (8)

Yet the hymn is often the vehicle of private experiences and emotions. I do not mean the purely personal variations that are adapted from time to time but the personal association of individual hymns. William Bright's communion hymn "And now, O Father, mindful of the love..." has been to me an aid to devotion over the years, even if my theological understanding of the author's sacramental language may differ from his own. The poetry of hymns can leap theological barriers.

Perhaps the final word can come from a poet, not himself a believer, who bears testimony to the enduring influence of hymns which may be doubtful poetry but good religion. D. H. Lawrence, in a newspaper article published two years before his death, claimed that "the hymns which I learned as a child and never forgot mean to me almost more than the finest poetry, and they have for me a more permanent value" (6). Against such testimony, hymns do not need to press their claim to any special place within the ranks of poetry or literature. They have glory enough of their own.

It is odd how hymns can trigger off memories of the past more strongly than visual scenes or smells.... If as a child I disliked the sermon, I loved the hymns, and this affection has remained with me. The soaring triumph of the processional Easter hymns, the celebration of All Saints' Day, with the hymn "For All the Saints,"...and the plangent melancholy of the evening hymns, particularly "The Day Thou Gavest, Lord, Has Ended," sung while the church windows darkened and the mind moved forward to the walk through the churchyard between the gleaming tombstones in the evening dusk. Some of my early religious memories are of the hymns.... Some of them still have the power to move me to tears.

—P. D. JAMES, *Time to Be in Earnest*

Works Cited

Babbage, Stuart. "To the Royal Air Force." *C. S. Lewis: Speaker and Teacher.* Ed. Carolyn Keefe. Grand Rapids: Zondervan, 1971. 65-76.

Benson, A. C. *Edward White Benson, Archbishop of Canterbury.* Vol. I. London: Macmillan, 1899.

Bett, Henry. *The Hymns of Methodism in Their Literary Relations.* London: Epworth, 1920.

Driver, Christopher. "Poetry and Hymns." *Congregational Quarterly.* October 1957: 333-340.

Housman, A. E. *The Name and Nature of Poetry.* New York: Macmillan, 1933.

Johnson, Samuel. "Watts." *Lives of the Poets.* Ed. George B. Hill. Vol. 3. New York: Octagon, 1967.

Lawrence, D. H. *Selected Literary Criticism.* Ed. Anthony Beal. London: Heinemann, 1955.

Manning, Bernard Lord. *The Hymns of Wesley and Watts.* London: Epworth, 1942.

Newton, John. "Preface." *Olney Hymns.* London: W. Oliver, 1779. v-xiii.

Pollard, Arthur. *English Hymns.* London: Longmans, Green and Company, 1960.

Routley, Erik. *Hymns Today and Tomorrow.* Nashville: Abingdon, 1964.

Sampson, George. *Seven Essays.* Cambridge: Cambridge University Press, 1947.

Watson, J. R. *The Victorian Hymn.* Durham: University of Durham, 1981.

Watts, Isaac. "Preface." *The Psalms of David…with Hymns and Spiritual Songs.* London: Samuel Bagster, [n. d.]. I1-III2.

Wesley, John. "Preface." *A Collection of Hymns for the Use of the People Called Methodists.* London: Wesleyan Conference Office, 1877. iii-vii.

Viewpoint: Wendell Berry

The Responsibility of the Poet

It has seemed to me increasingly that a poem—a good poem—exists at the center of a complex reminding.... Fundamentally, the existence of a poem reminds first its poet and then its readers of the technical means of poetry, which is to say its power as speech or song: the play of line against syntax and against stanza; the play of variation against form and against theme; the play of phrase against line, and of phrase against phrase within the line; the play of likenesses and differences of sounds; the play of statement with and against music; the play of rhyme against rhythm and as rhythm; the play of the poem as a made thing with and within and against the histories—personal and literary, national and local—that produce it.

A poem, that is, has the power to remind poet and reader alike of things they have read and heard.... Thus the art, so private in execution, is also communal and filial. It can only exist as a common ground between the poet and other poets and other people. Any poem worth the name is the product of a convocation.... Poetry can be written only because it has been written. As a new poem is made,...past voices are convoked—to be changed, little or much, by the addition of another voice.

A poem, too, may remind poet and reader alike of what is remembered or ought to be remembered—as in elegies, poems of history, love poems, celebrations of nature, poems of praise or worship, or poems as prayers. One of the functions of the music or formality of poetry is to make memorable....

By its formal integrity a poem reminds us of the formal integrity of other works, creatures, and structures of the world. The form of a good poem is, in a way perhaps not altogether explainable or demonstrable, an analogue of the forms of other things. By its form it alludes to other forms, evokes them, resonates with them, and so becomes a part of the system of analogies or harmonies by which we live. Thus the poet affirms and collaborates in the formality of the Creation. This, I think, is a matter of supreme, and mostly unacknowledged, importance.

A poem reminds us also of the spiritual elation that we call "inspiration" or "gift." Or perhaps we ought to say that it should do so, it should be humble enough to do so, because we know that no permanently valuable poem is made by the merely intentional manipulation of its scrutable components. Hence, it reminds us of love. It is amateur work, lover's work. What we now call "professionalism" is anathema to it.... The standards of love are inseparable from the process or system of reminding that I am talking about. This reminding, I think, must be our subject if we want to understand the responsibility of the poet.

—*What Are People For?*
San Francisco: North Point Press, 1990

Writing Hymns

My own insights into the dynamics of hymn writing come not from my being an author of hymn texts but as a composer of hymn tunes. In that capacity, I have observed hymn writers and worked with them. My collaborators have been preachers, and this is a fruitful starting point for my observations about how and why hymns come to be written.

Often the best hymn writers have been ministers who penned hymn texts to summarize and imprint the salient points of their sermons in the minds of congregants. Pastors, particularly those seasoned in the ministry and holding an intimate knowledge of the Word of God, are especially well suited to hymn writing, as a survey of Protestant hymnody verifies—from Luther to Gerhardt, Watts to Wesley, and Bonar to Boice. Biblical learning and a knowledge of great literature grant the hymn writer requisite subject matter, poetic models, and ample fare for allusion. Coupled with personal exposure to the joys and sorrows of life, such a background potentially supplies a suitable proportion of sound exegesis with empathetic human experience. This is not to say, however, that being a preacher is a requirement for being a hymn writer. Anyone with poetic talent who shares the experiences I have noted above can write hymns.

Whether preacher or poet, hymn writers find inspiration in the same places that all Christian poets do—in Scripture, in nature, in a life experience that prompts reflection upon spiritual neediness, or in an overpowering awareness of God's glory. Hymn writing can also be an act of Christian devotion. It both

PAUL S. JONES *is Organist and Music Director of historic Tenth Presbyterian Church, Philadelphia, Pennsylvania. He also serves as Artistic Director of the Csehy Summer School of Music, Langhorne, Pennsylvania. With the late James Montgomery Boice, he published* Hymns for a Modern Reformation *in October 2000. "Writing Humns" was written exclusively for this book.*

germinates and develops through study of the Bible, and it may, in fact, lead one to deeper levels of spiritual discovery.

As well as having a knowledge of Scripture and being situated within a Christian community, successful hymn writers understand the nature of their chosen genre. Great hymn texts serve the roles of praise, prayer, or proclamation. They often paraphrase a psalm, distill the teaching of a specific scriptural passage, or relate a doctrine or other spiritual truth by drawing on numerous biblical texts. Many hymns are filled with direct imperatives and encouragement to Christians. In most cases, regardless of topic, the consecutive stanzas follow a progression of thought or narrate a sequence of events. There are multiple formats for a hymn: In addition to doctrinal and ideational structures, hymns texts may follow a story line or develop as a personal testimony (where the challenge for a hymn writer is to avoid sentimentality, self-centeredness, and allowing personal experience rather than the Bible to become the basis of theological belief). Another generic trait of hymns is that they eschew subtlety, complexity, and density of poetic texture in favor of simplicity and directness. The goal of direct illumination necessitates a poem rich in meaning, not one cloaked in clever phraseology.

Hymn writers also understand the difference between a hymn and a poem. Not every good poem makes a good hymn, and not every good hymn meets the criterion of great poetry. Hymn poetry, for example, *should be limited to six strophes or fewer of consistent length* rather than taking a free form. *Four to six lines per stanza will be best managed,* and *each line should maintain parallel meter, rhythm, and stress with its corresponding line in other stanzas* so as to avoid an awkward rendering when sung. Strong and weak syllables should appropriately correspond to the musical beats, and this cannot occur if the hymn writer is inconsistent. Each hymn poet should *take into account the potential musical setting of the text.* When direct collaboration is not possible, the second party, be it author or composer, must observe the structure, rhythm, mood, and language (poetic or musical) of the first contributor and do everything possible to ensure a superior union of the two. Most hymn stanzas rhyme, and while there are numerous rhyme scheme options, and although good hymns exist that do not rhyme, *rhyming is preferable.*

A *consistent mood throughout the stanzas works best* because the music cannot be altered strophe by strophe, and the hymn will be stronger if its verbal and musical sentiments agree. A refrain, however, can provide opportunity for a change of spirit or direction if this is desired; it can also serve as a unifying element or summarizing message. Further, while a hymn text may contain metaphors or other figures of speech, *the primary goal should be the delivery of an identifiable message*—as is the aim of a well-crafted sermon. Hymn singing is a forum in which a broad public encounters Christian doctrine, so the poetry should permit the least educated to comprehend (although not necessarily at first reading) and likewise give the discerning mind something to ponder.

Despite the current popularity of "choruses," the church continues to need hymns written by preachers and poets who heed the command of Scripture to "sing to the Lord a new song." Choruses rarely rise to the beauty of form and depth of content that hymns do. Hymns make demands on the whole person—on the heart, soul, and mind, and they have special power to communicate memorable spiritual truth.

Since a hymn writer may not find an immediate audience, it may be helpful to know that while Charles Wesley wrote more than five thousand hymn texts, no modern hymnal contains more than twenty of these. Anyone who possesses a poetic gift should consider joining the company of men and women who have contributed to this repertory of Christian worship. As Martin Luther said in his foreword to the first edition of Johann Walter's *Geistliches Gesangbüchlein* of 1524, "Therefore, I too, with the help of others, have brought together some sacred songs, in order to make a good beginning and to give an incentive to those who can better carry on the Gospel and bring it to the people.... I therefore pray that every pious Christian will agree with this, and if God has given him equal or greater gifts, will lend his aid."

DEFINITIONS OF POETRY

The greatest thing by far is to have a command of metaphor,…an eye for resemblances.

—Aristotle

[Poets are] the antennae of the race.

—Ezra Pound

The rhythmic creation of beauty.

—Edgar Allan Poe

The spontaneous overflow of powerful feelings recollected in tranquillity.

—William Wordsworth

Simple, sensuous, and passionate.

—John Milton

Prose: words in their best order; poetry: the best words in the best order.

—Samuel Taylor Coleridge

The art of doing by means of words what the painter does by means of colors.

—Thomas Macaulay

The expression of the imagination.

—Percy Bysshe Shelley

The gaiety (joy) of language.

—Wallace Stevens

Speech framed to be heard for its own sake and interest even over and above its interest of meaning.

—Gerard Manley Hopkins

What ideas feel like.

—Karl Shapiro

No ideas but in things.

—W. C. Williams

The art that offers depth in a moment.

—Molly Peacock

Memorable speech.

—W. H. Auden

Perfection of form united with a significance of feeling.

—T. S. Eliot

A way of using words to say things which could not possibly be said in any other way, things which in a sense do not *exist* till they are born…in poetry.

—C. Day Lewis

Part Ten

Narrative

One of the most universal human impulses can be summed up in the four words, "Tell me a story." The interest in narrative is currently so high that the very concept of literature is equated in most people's minds with story. Narrative has become (perhaps it always was) the primary literary genre.

This unit provides answers to the following questions:

- What are the ingredients of successful stories?
- How do storytellers exploit these ingredients to produce optimum effects?
- What are the particular excellences of narrative as a literary form?
- What is the religious significance of narrative?

The human significance of stories has long been recognized. The religious significance of stories is currently a lively topic of discussion, and the essays and excerpts that follow are major contributions to those conversations.

In Praise of Stories

Daniel Taylor

Tell me a story.

In this century, and moment, of mania,
Tell me a story.

Make it a story of great distances, and starlight.

The name of the story will be Time,
But you must not pronounce its name.

Tell me a story of deep delight.

—Robert Penn Warren

Tell me a story.
These words make up the oldest invitation in the human experience. They are an invitation to participate in those things which make us human—an invitation to relationship, to joy and suffering, to good and evil, and ultimately to meaning for our lives. The first act of human civilization occurred when one person, with gestures and signs rather than words, conveyed to another person something that had just happened—and, perhaps with a look on her face, how she felt about it. That was the first story—and we have been telling each other stories ever since.

We are drawn to stories because our own life is a story and we are looking

DANIEL TAYLOR *is a professor of literature and writing at Bethel College (Minnesota) and the author of various books, including* Tell Me a Story *and* Before Their Time. *He is stylist for the* New Living Translation of the Bible *and writes fiction. He is a contributing editor for* Books and Culture, *and cofounder of The Legacy Center, an organization devoted to helping people identify and pass on their life experiences and core values.*

for help. Stories give us help in many ways. They tell us we are not alone, and that what has happened to us has happened first to others and that they made it through. They also help us see, however, that our own story is not big enough, that the world is larger and more varied than our limited experience. They help us be more fully human by stimulating and appealing to all that we are—mind, body, spirit. They help by calling us into relationship—with other people, with other places and times, with creation, and with God. They help by giving us courage to be the kinds of characters we should be in our own stories, and by making us laugh, empathize, and exercise judgment. But most of all, stories help us by telling us the truth, without which we cannot live.

Human beings require stories to give meaning to the facts of their existence. For example, ever since we can remember, all of us have been telling ourselves stories about ourselves, composing life-giving autobiographies of which we are the heroes and heroines. If our stories are coherent and plausible and have continuity, they will help us to understand why we are here, and what we need to pay attention to and what we may ignore. A story provides a structure for our perceptions; only through stories do facts assume any meaning whatsoever. This is why children everywhere ask, as soon as they have the command of language to do so, "Where did I come from?" and, shortly after, "What will happen when I die?" They require a story to give meaning to their existence. Without air, our cells die. Without a story, our selves die.

—NEIL POSTMAN, "Learning by Story"

Stories are not optional for human beings. It is not the case that some people like stories and seek them out, and other people do not. This is more or less true for other forms of literature—poems, plays, essays, and the like—but it is not true for narrative. We are all, without exception, drawn to stories, and it may have to do with the way the brain works. As our experience presents itself to us, the brain organizes the stream of perceptions in story form—making connections between things, seeking out a plot, searching for meaning and coherence, trying to decipher what actions and responses are required. As a result, we are as instinctively drawn to story as to water and food. The attraction requires no education or training or special inclination.

We are shaped by stories from our first moments of life, and even before. Stories tell us who we are, why we are here, and what will become of us. Whenever humans try to make sense of their experience, they create a story, and we use those stories to answer all the big questions of life. The stories come from everywhere—from family, church, school, and the culture at large. They so surround and inhabit us that we often don't recognize that they are stories at all, breathing them in and out as a fish breathes water.

But there is a special class of stories, sharing the same qualities as all stories, that we call literature. These are the consciously crafted stories that take various narrative forms: short fiction and the novel most obviously, but also literary nonfiction, drama, and essay. Even most poems tell us a story of some kind. We are drawn to the stories of literature for the same reasons as for story in general, with the added allure that these stories are told by master storytellers.

STORY AND COMMUNITY

Bloodless definitions are the opposite of story, but I will offer one nonetheless: *A story is the telling of the significant actions of characters over time.* Each element is important, both in the stories of literature and in those that shape our own lives. Remove or fail in any of these elements and you no longer have a story.

It is the *telling* aspect of story that first marks its humanity. A teller implies someone with something to say who believes that someone else, somewhere, wants to hear it. Many a story is sent out into the world as an act of faith. "Here is what has happened—to me or to those I love or to someone else. Here is what I think, what I feel, what I want, what I value, what I imagine. Does anyone care? Is anyone listening?" Also implied in the act of storytelling is the reciprocal question, "What about you? What is your story?"

Here, in this most basic element of telling, we discover the moral dimension that permeates every aspect of story. There are inescapable ethical implications in storytelling for both teller and listener. The teller promises, at the least, not to waste our time. We have only so many moments to live. We cannot afford to waste them on thin or foolish stories, much less on those that do us actual harm.

A story must, literally, be for our good, though good must be understood in the widest possible way. Stories don't necessarily make you a nicer or more ethical person—though many can; they draw out of you more of what makes you a feeling, giving, thinking, creating, laughing, curious human being. Not every story must improve us—stories are valuable on other scores—but we should be different and better because of the cumulative effect of the stories in our lives.

God made man because he loves stories.

—ELIE WIESEL, *The Gates of the Forest*

For this reason, we should pick our stories and storytellers carefully. This also explains why some stories are told and retold and others are not. Simply put, we return to the things we value. The stories of Homer and Sophocles and Dante and Shakespeare and Tolstoy and Dostoevsky keep being told, not because a few teachers persist in assigning them to hapless students, but because something in those stories still stirs and challenges the human heart and continues to speak to the human condition. And in our own time, new stories are being written that will be prized for as long as people tell stories, both because they also deal with timeless human issues and because they tell their stories in voices we have not heard before.

The stories we choose for ourselves define who we are. Every story defines a community—at the least a community of two, teller and listener, at the most the community of all humanity. A community, a family, is a group of people who share common stories. The health of any community depends directly on the health of the stories the community embraces. This places a great responsibility both on storytellers and on us as we choose our stories.

If the ethical responsibility of storytellers is to not waste our time, the responsibility of the audience is to listen with a predisposition toward belief. Belief includes belief in the absolute right of all people to tell their own story in their own words (even Adam and Eve, after they messed things up, got a chance to explain themselves). It also includes an initial empathy and desire to understand. Enemies listen to each other for the sole purpose of discovering better ways to destroy their opponent. A person in the community of storyteller and audience listens with compassion and the hope for common ground.

THE CRAFTING OF WORDS

Everyone has the ability to tell a story, especially his or her own story, but we rightfully have special expectations for the tellers of stories we call literature. The single most important thing that sets them apart from the rest of us is not their insight or their sensitivity or even their imagination—though they often excel in these things. That which most sets them apart, and makes us treasure them, is their mastery of language.

Writers carve language like a sculptor carves stone. They shape words into realities that compel belief and action. They listen not only to the rhythms of words but also to the silences between words. They understand that words do far more harm in the world than bombs and bullets, and more good than all the charities and humanitarian schemes put together.

Every episode, explanation, description, dialogue—ideally every sentence— must be pleasureable and interesting for its own sake.

—C. S. LEWIS, *An Experiment in Criticism*

Because they value words, writers use them sparingly. Even when they write at great length, they make sure that each word carries its weight. Economical writing does not mean short sentences; it means that every word, even in the page-long sentences of Henry James, knows its place and purpose. Such writing aspires to the condition of unaffected artfulness described by T. S. Eliot in "Little Gidding":

> every phrase
> And sentence…is right (where every word is at home,
> Taking its place to support the others,
> The word neither diffident nor ostentatious,
> An easy commerce of the old and the new,
> The common word exact without vulgarity,
> The formal word precise but not pedantic,
> The complete consort dancing together)….

Neither is economy the enemy of detail. Writers create an entire world for us, and the short story and novel build that world out of what one writer has called "authenticating detail." Such detail is a key to our willingness to believe in that which we have not previously experienced and even in what never happened. Does the place have the look and smell and feel of how such a place would be? Are the gestures and dialect and movement of a character so described that we believe the character exists? Are the details of description, individually and collectively, significant—that is, do they reveal as opposed to simply piling up?

The work of fiction is a smaller and more coherent world alongside the great world.... Fiction elicits an interpretation of the world by being itself a worldlike object for interpretation.

—ANNIE DILLARD, *Living by Fiction*

If the writer uses language skillfully, then the narrative creates for the reader what John Gardner called "a fictional dream." We enter into the world of the story and it becomes, for that time, the only world there is. Its adventures are our adventures, its hopes and fears our hopes and fears, the ones it cares about we care about. When the writer falters—through clumsiness or manipulation or cliché—the dream evaporates and the reader is back in his or her chair. We turn to stories—in fiction and elsewhere—because of the power of their dreams.

CHARACTER AND PLOT

The next two elements in our definition of story—the telling of the significant action of characters over time—focus on plot and character. The two must be discussed together because they cannot be separated, either in fiction or in life.

Character, in both spheres, is values in action. What we do reveals who we are, and who we are determines what we do. The central action in every valuable story is characters making choices. In choosing, or failing to choose, characters reveal who they are. In dealing with the consequences and implications of their choices, they define the action of the story. And a central reason that stories attract us is our fascination with watching characters make those choices and waiting to see what the consequences will be.

That fascination is rooted in our instinctive understanding that character is more important than personality. Personality is the concept developed by psychology when it realized that values are messy. Psychology wanted to be a science, and *oughts* and *shoulds* are notoriously difficult to measure. So it stripped out value judgments and replaced character traits (courage, honesty, loyalty) with personality traits (assertiveness, compulsiveness, self-esteem). Despite our culture's overwhelming preoccupation with mere personality, we hunger for a deeper exploration of the human struggle to act rightly. And so we seek out stories.

We are drawn to tales of fellow human beings facing choices that remind us of our own, or at the least prompt us to ask, "What would I do if...?" In that question lies not only our humanity, but also the potential for our own character to be formed by the characters in our stories. For while "What would I do?" hangs in the air, who we are is up for grabs. Answering the question does not simply entail *discovering* who we are, but allows us in part to *determine* who we are. Every powerful character we encounter in story is a challenge to our own character, and holds the possibility of changing us.

All Christianity concentrates on the man at the cross-roads. The vast and shallow philosophies...all talk about ages and evolution and ultimate developments. The true philosophy is concerned with the instant. Will a man take this road or that?—that is the only thing to think about, if you enjoy thinking.... The instant is really awful: and it is because our religion has intensely felt the instant, that it has in literature dealt much with battle and in theology dealt much with hell. It is full of danger, like a boy's book: it is at an immortal crisis. There is a great deal of real similarity between popular fiction and the religion of the western people.... Life (according to that faith) is very like a serial story in a magazine: life ends with the promise (or menace) "to be continued in our next."

—G. K. CHESTERTON, *Orthodoxy*

Consider Huck Finn. In *Adventures of Huckleberry Finn*, Mark Twain gives a character the greatest freedom that anyone can give to another—the freedom to tell his or her own story. One of the most important questions to ask of any narrative is, "Who is telling us this story and how does that affect what is being told?" Allowing Huck to tell his own story in his own words is the key to the power of the novel and the immortality of the character.

The process of character formation is, in fact, the central preoccupation of the story. Huck Finn, in the timeless pattern of so many stories, is adolescent innocence coming to terms with adult experience. He is faced with innumerable choices, many of them microcosms of the devastating choices facing Twain's society at that time, and, in different guises, facing human beings at any time.

How Huck responds to each choice is a reflection of his character in the literary and ethical as well as developmental senses. As he analyzes, agonizes, theorizes, and rationalizes, we get both an insight into who he already is and into what he is becoming. An early struggle over the ethics of stealing food while on the run is typical:

> Mornings, before daylight, I slipped in corn fields and borrowed a water-melon, or a mushmelon, or a punkin, or some new corn, or things of that kind. Pap always said it warn't no harm to borrow things, if you was meaning to pay them back, sometime; but the widow said it warn't anything but a soft name for stealing, and no decent body would do it. Jim said he reckoned the widow was partly right and pap was partly right; so the best way would be for us to pick out two or three things from the list and say we wouldn't borrow them any more—then he reckoned it wouldn't be no harm to borrow the others. So we talked it over all one night, drifting along down the river, trying to make up our minds whether to drop the watermelons, or the cantelopes, or the mushmelons, or what. But towards daylight we got it all settled satisfactory, and concluded to drop crabapples and p'simmons. I was glad the way it come out, too, because crabapples ain't ever good, and the p'simmons wouldn't be ripe for two or three months yet.

Our laughter at Huck's self-deceptive rationalizing does not prevent us from seeing his essential morality. He is trying hard to be a good person. If he doesn't quite measure up to the external standards for such a person, that gives us more comfort than concern, because we are all too aware of our own shortcomings.

There are more important things at stake in *Huckleberry Finn,* however, than watermelons and crab apples. At the center of the novel is the relationship between Huck and the runaway slave, Jim. Huck is a boy of his time (pre-Civil War America) struggling to break free of the inhumanity of that time—and all times. And it *is* a struggle. If it weren't, the story would not be valuable or of interest.

An action is a work organized so that it introduces characters about whose fates we are made to care....

—SHELDON SACKS, *Fiction and the Shape of Belief*

Huck constantly rehearses what he knows he is expected to do, as taught to him by society, and what he feels he ought to do, as he is learning from his personal experience with Jim. He comes down alternately on one side and then on the other. What finally tilts him in the right direction (and Twain and the reader both are sure there is a *right* direction) is his entanglement in the story of Jim's life.

The abstract law says Jim is a runaway slave and must be returned. Only Huck's growing awareness of Jim's humanity and pain allows Huck to question that public morality (think of the story of Christ and the woman caught in adultery). He must move from seeing Jim as a stereotype, a move Twain himself did not entirely achieve, to seeing him as an individual human being with a story:

> I went to sleep, and Jim didn't call when it was my turn. He often done that. When I waked up, just at day-break, he was setting there with his head down betwixt his knees, moaning and mourning to himself. I didn't take notice, nor let on. I knowed what it was about. He was thinking about his wife and his children, away up yonder, and he was low and homesick; because he hadn't ever been away from home before in his life; and I do believe he cared just as much for his people as white folks does for their'n. It don't seem natural, but I reckon it's so. He was often moaning and mourning that way, nights, when he judged I was asleep, and saying, "Po' little 'Lizabeth! po' little Johnny! its mighty hard; I spec' I ain't ever gwyne to see you no mo', no mo'!" He was a mighty good nigger, Jim was.

Yes, Jim is still "nigger" to Huck, a fact that has led some of late to reject *Huckleberry Finn* as a racist novel. But if Huck's (and Twain's) moral education is not complete, may that not raise in our minds the salutary thought that neither is our own? Which of us so perfectly lives up to our own moral vision that we can eagerly reach for the first stone? If Huck and Twain are alternately morally sensitive and morally obtuse, so are we all, and an awareness of that condition is one of the healthy outcomes possible from our encounter with characters like Huck and Jim.

The moral struggle within Huck Finn is not only an aspect of character in the novel; it is also the plot. We think of plot as the "what happens next" of narrative, but it is important to understand that the central things that happen in important stories don't happen *to* a character, but *within* a character. And if the story has drawn us into its fictional dream, they happen to us as well.

This is why significance is part of our definition of story—the telling of significant action. John Gardner says "accident without significance is boring." That is, randomness is incompatible with meaning and therefore finally not interesting to us—creatures who crave meaning like an addict craves cocaine. Story transforms the useless freedom of chaos into the invaluable freedom of responsibility, and it does so by insisting on the significance of choices.

[...stories in which] the deep significance of life reveals itself in its entirety.
                                        —CHARLES BAUDELAIRE, *Notebooks*

One can write a powerful story about the sense that life is random and meaningless, but it is part of the transforming magic of art that in making a story out of our feeling of meaninglessness we take the first step toward overcoming that very feeling. It is like writing a great poem about one's despair over not being able to write poetry anymore.

If randomness is incompatible with a meaningful plot, so is mere sequence. E. M. Forster made a famous observation about plot. "The king died and then the queen died" is, Forster says, merely a temporal sequence of events: "the chopped off length of the tapeworm of time." "The king died, then the queen died of grief" is a plot, what we are calling a story. All our interest in stories resides in "of grief." There lies human motivation, character, psychology, values, aspirations, and the like.

WHAT STORIES ARE ABOUT

If stories require telling, they also require something to tell. And not just any something, but something that eventually persuades us is worth the telling. Even skillful and detailed descriptions of objects, people, and actions do not necessarily make a story, any more than a security camera in a bank lobby necessarily creates a film. What is required are circumstances or events that matter.

What, then, matters? A brief answer is anything that reveals and explores our humanity. What matters, among other things, is a human encounter with and response to pain, happiness, evil, boredom, love, hate, grace, violence, goodness, greed, God, laughter, spite, and on and on. The fact is, we find ourselves and our fellow human beings endlessly fascinating. Every story we tell is about *us,* even those we stock with animals and aliens.

In fact, almost every story is ultimately about one thing—a person in trouble. The archetypal story goes as follows: Something is not right, we try to fix it, it gets worse, we almost fail, but we make it through. (And it usually happens in the singular—a person—because we can only get to know a very few people at a time.) Even those stories where the character doesn't make it through often leave us with the feeling that perhaps we will, in part because we have heard the story of the one who didn't and are wiser for it.

Only stories that recognize the inseparableness of plot and character matter to us in the long run. What we call plot-driven stories, which focus on events rather than on characters choosing, are always popular because they are always easy—intellectually and emotionally. They require little of us, and we are lazy enough to appreciate that. But the habitual enjoyment of such stories is actually a form of prostitution, offering momentary, superficial pleasure without the cost of commitment or human interaction. The great sin of most of the stories of popular culture—in film, television, novels, and the like—is not that they are violent or obscene or godless, but that they waste our time. Since I can hear only so many stories in my life, why settle for anything less than the best ones?

The writer…has to find some meaning in life before he gives it to us in a book…. All great writers have a theme, an idea of life profoundly felt and founded in some personal and compelling experience.

—JOYCE CARY, *Art and Reality*

And the best stories will always be about morality, about values, about how we should behave in the world. This is not a judgment based on piety or religious belief or a hyperactive conscience. It is a simple recognition of the nature of the human condition and the way story expresses that condition. I have argued that the essence of story is characters choosing. Because characters must choose (and refusing to choose is itself a choice), they are inherently valuing beings. Every choice implies an underlying value—a *because,* an *ought.* I do this and not that *because…*

This is why it is foolish to pretend that stories can be separated from morality, from notions of right and wrong, from ethical judgment—a separation that even many writers and critics have tried to maintain in the last hundred years. Stories cannot exist without characters making meaningful choices that have significant consequences. And in those choices and those consequences lie judgments of right and wrong, good and evil, desirable and undesirable, both on the part of characters and of readers. We have endless opinions about how things in this world *should* be, about what is fair and not fair, about who deserves a better fate and who is getting what they deserve. When stories no longer require moral judgments of their characters or of us, we will no longer value them. We will understand that they no longer offer us help for the judgments required of us in our own lives.

Consider again poor Huck Finn. He lives in a world not of his own making. He didn't invent slavery, he does not practice it, and he does not have the power to end it.

Or does he?

Huck's story changes forever when it gets mixed up with Jim's story. Huck the adolescent can never again be Huck the child. Whether by mere accident or larger design (is anything in a *story* ever really an accident?), Huck encounters Jim, the runaway slave. All Huck has ever wanted is to be free—of the Widow Douglas's insistent do-gooding, of Pap's elemental harshness. Now he is confronted with a man who also wants to be free, and whose freedom depends on him.

Huck doesn't want the job. Life has been fishing, caving, exploring wrecks, staying clear of obligations. He would like to stay with his beginnings, but stories insist on moving from beginnings to middles. And the middle of a story is, we say, the time of complication, when the implications inherent in a situation—that is, a character in a context faced with a choice—begin to make themselves felt. It is the inescapable nature of reality to move from beginnings to middles, from simplicity to complication, from innocence to experience. Because Huck's story has intersected Jim's, he must now make choices. He must now, whether he likes it or not, take on the conscious role of a character in his own story.

Huck finds he does, in fact, have the power to end slavery—at least in his own life and relationships. He can reject the arguments of slavery, can expose their illusory foundations in dehumanization, and he can purpose to be different—even if it means he will go to hell.

Huckleberry Finn *made my boyhood imaginable to me in a way that it otherwise would not have been.*

—WENDELL BERRY, *What Are People For?*

Of course Huck does not use the artificial language of academics—dehumanization, power, diversity, and so on. He is moved not by abstract logic but by Jim's story and by specific memories of their shared story together. Having written a letter to Jim's owner informing her of Jim's whereabouts, his initial feeling of having done the right thing gives way under the pressure of shared experience:

> I felt good and all washed clean of sin for the first time I had ever felt so in my life, and I knowed I could pray now. But I didn't do it straight off, but laid the paper down and set thinking—thinking how good it was all this happened so, and how near I come to being lost and going to hell. And went on thinking. And got to thinking over our trip down the river; and I see Jim before me, all the time in the day, and in the night-time, sometimes moonlight, sometimes storms, and we a floating along, talking, and singing, and laughing.

Huck engages in moral reasoning, "set thinking," to reassure himself that turning Jim in is the right thing. But he "went on thinking," literally thinks again, in a way that undermines his previous judgment. And that thinking is story thinking: "I see Jim before me…" And the Jim he sees is the Jim with whom he has a relationship and shared experiences that cannot be left out of his moral reasoning:

> But somehow I couldn't seem to strike no places to harden against him, but only the other kind. I'd see him standing my watch on top of his'n, stead of calling me, so I could go on sleeping; and see him how glad he was when I come back out of the fog; and when I come to him again in the swamp, up there where the feud was; and such-like times; and would always call me honey, and pet me, and do everything he could think of for me, and how good he always was; and at last I struck the time I saved him by telling the men we had small-pox aboard, and he was so grateful, and said I was the best friend old Jim ever had in the world, and the *only* one he's got now; and then I happened to see that paper.

It is crucial that Huck remembers not just what Jim has done for him, but what he has done for Jim. Huck's earlier decision and action on Jim's behalf began a momentum in the direction of righteousness that he cannot now undo. Past action shaped and directed future possibilities. Similarly, he is influenced not only by what he thinks of Jim, but what Jim thinks of him. Bearing the burden of being Jim's best and only friend, Huck must act in light of that relationship. He literally is not free to reason as an objective observer would be. (What others in our own story think and expect of us is an important factor in what we are and do.) Huck, in his reverie, *sees* Jim, and now he "happened to see that paper," and must choose between the two:

> It was a close place. I took it up, and held it in my hand. I was trembling, because I'd got to decide, forever, betwixt two things, and I knowed it. I studied a minute, sort of holding my breath, and then says to myself:
> "All right, then, I'll *go* to hell"—and tore it up.

All readers know that Huck has done the right thing and is not going to hell for doing it. The story has told them so, and there is no room for second opinions—neither authoritarian nor relativistic. This is the high point of the novel and of Huck's moral development, and the often noted decline in the long and unsatisfying conclusion to the narrative is evidence that writers, like the rest of us, sometimes lose track of the meaning of their stories.

STORIES NEED TIME (AND SO DO WE)

Stories cannot happen in an instant. They need the room—temporal, psychological, metaphysical—to unfold. And so our definition of story ends with the claim that stories relate action "over time." Because stories happen over time, there is the chance for change, on the part both of characters and of readers. This links stories to hope. Because characters can genuinely choose, things *can* be different than they presently are or seem doomed to become. And we, if we enter into the story and allow it to make its appeal, can be changed too. And sometimes we will be changed by the story of a character who refused to change.

If stories have beginnings and middles they must also, as Aristotle told us, have ends, even in a time such as ours that is suspicious of tidy and happy endings. Stories have ends in both senses of the word. End means cessation, the stopping of something, but it also means goal, the target at which something aims. In a curious way, the beginnings and middles of stories cannot be fully meaningful unless they end. The end is the final working out of all the latent potential of the beginning, and the consequences of choices in the middle. Without that working out, the story risks degenerating into mere sequence.

By truly choosing, a character both limits freedom and gives it value. Each choice limits subsequent possibilities in a way that increases the likelihood for significance, just as pruning a fruit tree limits possibilities for growth but encourages the eventual production of the best fruit. Each choice in the middle reduces the possible endings, but without those choices the end would have no meaning.

That middles affect ends is obvious, but ends can also affect and even shape middles. It seems curious that something that does not yet exist, the end, can influence that which already exists, the middle. But of course the end does exist before it comes into being. It exists in the latent possibilities of the givens of the beginning, and in the working out of those possibilities in the middle. The trajectory of a life—and its end—is created by choices made in the context of the beginning and middle.

The power of an imagined end, and it literally can only be imagined, lies in its ability to influence present choices. Most characters, in life and in fiction, have some notion, however hazy or unarticulated, of what would constitute a successful life for them. They have an idea of how they would like to "end up." That idea, that imagined end, can be as powerful as anything in the given of beginnings in determining the direction of our lives. Huck is able, based on the motivation of past experience, to imagine himself protecting Jim rather than turning him in, and therefore changes how he acts in the present.

Nations need stories, just as people do, to provide themselves with a sense of continuity, or identity. But a story does even more than that. Without stories as organizing frameworks we are swamped by the volume of our own experience, adrift in a sea of facts. Merely listing them cannot help us, because without some tale to guide us there is no limit to the list. A story gives us direction by providing a kind of theory about how the world works—and how it needs to work if we are to survive. Without such a theory, such a tale, people have no idea what to do with information. They cannot even tell what is information and what is not.

—NEIL POSTMAN, "Learning by Story"

We can do the same in our own stories, and one of the experiences that can motivate our actions is experience with the stories from literature. This seems far-fetched to some, especially those who make a dubious distinction between literature and the supposedly real world. Are we genuinely prepared to say that working in an office building or shopping in a mall is real, while reading Tolstoy is not? Which engages us most fully as thinking, feeling, believing, questioning creatures? Which best draws out our humanity? Which is most likely to change us? Which, then, is more real? A story is something that *happens to you*, as much as a car wreck or job promotion or falling in love.

We are all, in fact, the products of our stories, including the stories from literature. I believe, for instance, that my life took a slight but perceptible change in direction in my late teens from reading J. R. R. Tolkien's *The Lord of the Rings*. Trolls, elves, hobbits, wizards, dark forests, forest havens, caves, mountain strongholds, treachery, cowardice, courage, perseverance—what have these to do with being a teenager in California during the Vietnam War?

Nothing and everything. I found embodied in that fantasy what every teenager needs to find—especially one coming of age in the moral ambiguity of the late 1960s: that there is a difference between good and evil, that the distinction is usually clear enough to act on, that fighting for good is worthwhile even if one loses, that average, even unimpressive, people can do so, and, far-fetched as it may seem, that good eventually wins out in the end—though not without lingering wounds.

Even though there is a strong "what happens next" element in *The Lord of the Rings*, I was drawn not so much into the plot of the adventure as to the characters having the adventure. Maybe it is better to say that the testing of their character *was* the adventure for me—as I later realized it was for Tolkien as well. I discovered that I did not so much forget myself while reading the story as I found myself going along on the journey, dealing like the nonheroic, comfort loving hobbits with weariness, fear, uncertainty, and agonizing choices. With them I felt terror when confronted with undisguised evil and enormous gratefulness for unexpected good.

Tolkien's story gave me the courage to say to myself what I already felt to be true from my own experience—that good and evil are real, that it matters a great deal which one wins out in the world, and that the outcome depends on me. *The Lord of the Rings* is filled with unexceptional people—that is, hobbits, elves, and the like—called on to do exceptional things if good is going to survive in the world. Reading the story (and its predecessor, *The Hobbit*), reinforced in me a tremendous desire that good should win in the world and evil be defeated, and to do what I could to help—not least because it helped me see that evil was not only out there, but within me as well. I genuinely believe this story helped shape who I was and am. Its characters became a part of my character.

The literary, ethical, and psychosocial notions of character were all at work in this one experience with a story. It did me a service. It helped form my mind as well as my ethics at a time when both were up for grabs. When I later discovered sophistical thinkers who assured me that good and evil were not real categories but only subjective and transient points of view, I knew better. I lacked then the intellectual resources to articulate my disagreement, but I was armed with the holistic experience of a story that kept me from naively embracing what I now think is a widely influential but unliveable view of the world. The story served me then, and it continues to do so, not least when I read it last year to my youngest daughter. This is how it is with good stories—we want to share them with those we love.

MEANING IN STORIES

After air, food, and water, the thing we most need is that our lives mean something. Michael Edwards says, "We tell stories because we desire a world with a story." We desire that there be meaningful connections between things, that seemingly chaotic events are heading somewhere, that there is a link between what we do and what becomes of us, that it matters that we have been here.

Nothing answers that need so well as a true story. Story is a vessel for carrying meaning. It is the currency of human interchange, the net we cast to capture fugitive truths and the darting rabbits of emotion.

Humankind is addicted to stories. No matter our mood, in reverie or expectation, panic or peace, we can be found stringing together incidents, and unfolding episodes. We turn our pain into narrative so we can bear it; we turn our ecstasy into narrative so we can prolong it.... We tell our stories to live.

—JOHN SHEA, *Stories of God*

But what do we mean by a true story? How can we talk believably about truth in a relativistic world? In what helpful sense is a fictional story about a boy and a slave on a raft, or, worse yet, a story about hobbits and wizards, true? Here is the answer: Any story is true, fictional or otherwise, that testifies accurately to the human condition. Any story that does not is false, a waste of time, and potentially dangerous.

Truth is as varied as it is elusive. Most people associate truth with intellectual or rational truth, especially the truth of propositions and the scientific method. But there is also the truth of the keen observation and penetrating reflection. There are the truths of the emotions and of the spirit and of the imagination. These are not less important simply because they are less verifiable. (Few of the really important things in life can be proven beyond doubt.) These in fact are the truths that do most to shape our lives. And all these kinds of truths, including rational truth, are to be found in story.

In his speech written on the occasion of receiving the Nobel Prize for Literature, Alexander Solzhenitsyn rejects much of the received opinion about the relationship between literature and life. He argues that the main service the writer offers is to show us ourselves accurately and to expose lies, in his case the lies, among others, of totalitarianism and materialism. He sides with those who have always believed that words are stronger than tanks, that an accurate and sympathetic treatment of the human condition is, in itself, a moral act. And he finishes his speech by citing a Russian proverb that makes an amazing claim: "One word of truth outweighs the world." It is a claim that stands in stark contrast to a world that sees the key to a successful life in power, possessions, prestige, and pleasure. It is a claim, furthermore, that is rooted both in his Christian faith and in the long history of world literature.

But at the same time that we insist that meaning is at the heart of story, we must be clear where that meaning lies. It lies in the whole story or not at all. Meaning inhabits story like a morning mist envelops a pine forest—everywhere present, but nowhere tangible. Detach meaning from the story and both die.

Writers and readers each need to understand this. John Gardner advises writers, "The temptation to explain should almost always be resisted." When you start explaining, you stop storytelling. You become a pedagogue, not a novelist. Likewise, readers must not insist on little, detachable nuggets of truth from stories. A composer once played a very difficult piano piece and was asked what it meant. His answer was to sit down and play the piece again. Similarly, stories are incarnational. They say to us, "Do you want to know what love is, or courage or greed or petulance or laughter or compassion? Let me tell you a story." And the truth of that story will be found in every sentence, but in no one sentence by itself.

The great enemy of truth, and of stories generally, is cliché. Cliché is a form of fraud. It trades on the promise of story to provide us the true, the good, and the beautiful, and instead substitutes the platitude, the sentimental, and the cute. Clichés take many forms—of expression, of emotion, of thought, of character and action—and each of them is deadly to stories. Bad writers use them and bad readers insist on them.

When we support poor writing—and, worse yet, fail to support the best writing—we commit a moral offense. When we reward writers who tell us only conventional things in conventional ways we contribute to the decline of a civilization—and a kingdom of faith—which desperately needs good stories. We foolishly settle for stories—on the screen and on the page—which tickle us, instead of demanding those which interrogate us (likewise in our conversations and from our pulpits). We use feeble stories to kill time, when there are so many available that redeem the time.

We must insist, in a cynical age, that there is such a thing as a good story. We should identify and prize the good stories from the past, and we must fulfill our responsibility to tell new ones.

Is It Good Enough
for Children?

Madeleine L'Engle

Several years ago, when I was teaching a course on techniques of fiction, a young woman came up to me and said, "I do hope you're going to teach us something about writing for children, because that's why I'm taking this course."

"What have I been teaching you?" I asked her.

"Well—writing."

"Don't you write when you write for children?"

"Yes, but—isn't it different?"

No, I assured her, it isn't different. The techniques of fiction are the techniques of fiction, and they hold as true for Beatrix Potter as they do for Dostoevsky. But the idea that writing for children isn't the same as writing for adults is prevalent indeed, and usually goes along with the conviction that it isn't quite as good. If you're a good enough writer for adults, the implication is, of course, you don't write for children. You write for children only when you can't make it in the real world, because writing for children is easier.

Wrong, wrong, wrong!

I had written several regular trade novels before a publisher asked me to write about Swiss boarding school experiences. Nobody had told me that you

MADELEINE L'ENGLE *is perhaps the best-known contemporary writer of children's fiction. Among the famous titles in this genre are* A Wrinkle in Time *(winner of the Newbery Medal),* A Swiftly Tilting Planet, *(recipient of the American Book Award), and* A Wind in the Door. *She has also written voluminously on literature, the Christian life and faith, the Bible, and the craft of writing. She has conducted writing workshops around the world. "Is It Good Enough for Children?" originally appeared in* The Writer.

write differently when you write for children, so I wrote *Camilla*, which was reissued as a Young Adult novel, and then *Meet the Austins*. It's hard today for me to understand that this simple little book had a very hard time finding a publisher, because it's about a death, and how an ordinary family reacts to that death. Death at that time was taboo. Children weren't supposed to know about it. I had a couple of offers of publication if I'd take the death out. But the reaction of the family—children as well as the parents—to the death was the core of the book.

When as a writer I address myself to children's literature…I address myself to literature; and when I address myself to children I address myself to equals.

—IVAN SOUTHALL, "Sources and Responses,"

in *The Openhearted Audience*, ed. Virginia Haviland

Nowadays what we offer children makes *Meet the Austins* seem pale, and on the whole, I think that's just as well, because children know a lot more than most grown-ups give them credit for. *Meet the Austins* came out of my own family's experience with several deaths. To have tried to hide those deaths from our children would have been blind stupidity. All hiding does is to confuse children and add to their fears. It is not subject matter that should be taboo, but the way it is handled.

I think it possible that by confining your child to blameless stories of child life in which nothing at all alarming ever happens, you would fail to banish the terrors, and would succeed in banishing all that can ennoble them or make them endurable. For in the fairy tales, side by side with the terrible figures, we find the immemorial comforters and protectors, the radiant ones.

—C. S. LEWIS, "On Three Ways of Writing for Children"

A number of years ago—the first year I was actually making reasonable money from my writing—my sister-in-law was visiting us, and when my husband told her how much I had earned that year, she was impressed and commented, "And to think most people would have had to work so hard for that!"

Well, it is work, it's most certainly work; wonderful work, but work. Revision, revision, revision. Long hours spent not only in the actual writing, but in research. I think the best thing I learned in college was how to do research, so that I could go right on studying after I graduated.

Of course, it is not *only* work; it is work that makes the incomprehensible comprehensible. Leonard Bernstein said that for him music was cosmos in chaos. That is true for writing a story, too. Aristotle wrote that what is plausible and impossible is better than what is possible and implausible.

That means that story must be true, not necessarily factual, but true. This is not easy for a lot of people to understand. When I was a child, one of my teachers accused me of telling a story. She was not complimenting me on my fertile imagination; she was accusing me of telling a lie.

Fantasy is true, of course. It isn't factual, but it is true. Children know that. Adults know it too, and that is precisely why many of them are afraid of fantasy.

—URSULA LE GUIN, *The Language of the Night*

Facts are fine; we need facts. But story takes us to a world that is beyond facts, out on the other side of facts. And there is considerable fear of this world.

The writer Keith Miller told me of a young woman who was determined that her three pre-school children were going to grow up in the real world. She was not, she vowed, going to sully their minds with myth, fantasy, fairy tales. They were going to know the truth—and for truth, read fact—and the truth would make them free.

One Saturday, after a week of rain and sniffles, the sun came out, so she piled the children into her little red VW bug and took them to the Animal Farm. The parking lot was crowded, but a VW bug is small, and she managed to find a place for it. She and the children had a wonderful day, petting the animals, going on rides, enjoying the sunshine. Suddenly, she looked at her watch and found it was far later than she realized. She and the children ran to where the VW bug was parked, and to their horror, found the whole front end was bashed in.

Outraged, she took herself off to the ranger's office. As he saw her approach, he laughed and said, "I'll bet you're the lady with the red VW bug."

"It isn't funny," she snapped.

"Now, calm down, lady, and let me tell you what happened. You know the elephant your children had such fun riding? She's a circus-trained elephant, and she was trained to sit on a red bucket. When she saw your car, she just did what she was trained to do and sat on it. Your engine's in the back, so you can drive it home without any trouble. And don't worry. Our insurance will take care of it. Just go on home, and we'll get back to you on Monday."

Slightly mollified, she and the kids got into the car and took off. But she was later than ever, so when she saw what looked like a very minor accident on the road, she didn't stop, but drove on.

Shortly, the flashing light and the siren came along, and she was pulled over. "Lady, don't you know that in this state it's a crime to leave the scene of an accident?" the trooper asked.

"But I wasn't in an accident," she protested.

"I suppose your car came that way," she said, pointing to the bashed-in front.

"No. An elephant sat on it."

"Lady, would you mind blowing into this little balloon?

That taught her that facts alone are not enough; that facts, indeed, do not make up the whole truth. After that she read fairy tales to her children and encouraged them in their games of Make Believe and Let's Pretend.

Putting away childish things, surely, has nothing to do with putting away the child.... The child should go on inside you helping you to reach out to each new emotion, helping you to excite to each new encounter, helping you to delight unconditionally to each new experience of the senses.

—IVAN SOUTHALL, "Sources and Responses," in *The Openhearted Audience*, ed. Virginia Haviland

---

I learned very early that if I wanted to find out the truth, to find out why people did terrible things to each other, or sometimes wonderful things—why there was a war, why children are abused—I was more likely to find the truth in story than in the encyclopedia. Again and again I read *Emily of the New Moon*, by Lucy Maud Montgomery, because Emily's father was dying of diseased lungs, and so was mine. Emily wanted to be a writer, and so did I. Emily knew that there was more to the world than provable fact, and so did I. I read fairy tales, the myths of all nations, science fiction, the fantasies and family stories of E. Nesbitt. I read Jules Verne and H. G. Wells. And I read my parents' books, particularly those with lots of conversation in them. What was not in my frame of reference went right over my head.

We tend to find what we look for. If we look for dirt, we'll find dirt, whether it's there or not. A very nice letter I received from a reader said that she found *A Ring of Endless Light* very helpful to her in coming to terms with the death of a friend, but that another friend had asked her how it was that I used dirty words. I wrote back saying that I was not going to reread my book looking for dirty words, but that as far as I could remember, the only word in the book that could possibly be construed as dirty was *zuggy*, which I'd made up to avoid using dirty words. And wasn't looking for dirty words an ugly way to read a book?

One of my favorite books is Frances Hodgson Burnett's *The Secret Garden*. I read it one rainy weekend to a group of little girls, and a generation later to my granddaughters up in an old brass bed in the attic. Mary Lennox is a self-centered, spoiled-rotten little heroine, and I think we all recognize at least a little of ourselves in her. The secret garden is as much the garden of Mary's heart as it is the physical walled garden. By the end of the book, warmth and love and concern for others have come to Mary's heart, when Colin, the sick boy, is able to run again. And Dickon, the gardener's boy, looks at the beauty of the restored garden and says, "It's magic!" But "magic" is one of the key words that has become taboo to today's self-appointed censors, so, with complete disregard of content, they would add *The Secret Garden* to the pyre. I shudder. This attitude is extreme. It is also dangerous.

It comes down to the old question of separate standards, separate for adults and children. The only standard to be used in judging a children's book is: *Is it a good book?* Is it good enough for me? Because if a children's book is not good enough for all of us, it is not good enough for children.

Redemption in the Movies

Brian Godawa

ONLY A MOVIE?

"It's only a movie."

"You can't take it so seriously."

"All I want is to be entertained."

So say people who prefer not to analyze movies beyond their entertainment value. Many moviegoers want no more than to escape and have fun for two hours in another world. When challenged by cultural critics to discern the messages within the movies, they balk at such criticism as being too analytical. And many filmmakers mouth agreement with them.

Hollywood's motto is, "If you want to send a message, use Western Telegram," meaning that movies are for entertainment, not the transmission of propaganda or political, sociological, or religious views. No less a screenwriter icon than William Goldman (author of *Butch Cassidy and the Sundance Kid, The Princess Bride,* and *Misery*) has pronounced, "Movies are finally, centrally, crucially, primarily *only* about story" (emphasis in the original) (2).

Conventional wisdom notwithstanding, nothing could be a greater half-truth. While it is true that story is the foundation of movies, an examination of the craft and structure of storytelling reveals that the very drawing power of movies is not simply "good stories" in some undefinable sense, but because stories are about redemption. Redemption is the recovery of something lost or the

BRIAN GODAWA *has sixteen years of experience in marketing and advertising art direction, design, and copywriting. He is a member of Screenwriters Network in Los Angeles. He has taught screenwriting, and he speaks on the art of movie watching to community groups. Four of his screenplays have won multiple awards in screenplay competitions, and he wrote the screenplay for the movie,* To End All Wars. *His Web page is http://www.godawa.com.*

attainment of something needed. And one's view of redemption reflects one's values about the way people ought or ought not to live and behave in this world. The truth can perhaps be summed up in this revision of Goldman's statement: *Stories* are finally, centrally, crucially, primarily, *mostly* about redemption.

SUSPENSION OF DISBELIEF

We are all aware of the age-old question of whether art mirrors or influences society. In his book *Hollywood Versus America,* film critic and Hollywood bogeyman Michael Medved has convincingly documented that filmmakers both intend to influence and do influence the public through the values and characters they portray in television and film. His thoroughly documented book brings together statistics, studies, anecdotes, and examples to demonstrate that while movies may not singlehandedly cause destructive behavior in America, they certainly encourage and exacerbate it. In a broader sense, the cultural milieu created by entertainment often reinforces certain values over others, chiefly those which reflect the current fashion of the creative community. While calling for a return to the values that make America virtuous, Medved notes the hypocrisy of moviemakers who proclaim that movies do not influence belief or behavior while they charge hundreds of thousands of dollars for advertising and product placements in movies.

The thesis of this essay is that movies as an art form both reflect *and* influence society. An Oliver Stone film like *JFK* (or for that matter, any of Oliver Stone's films) may be obvious in its intent to influence people's political commitments, but it is no less a good story simply because it is propaganda. And by the same token, a lighthearted family comedy like *Liar, Liar* is not without its own message of redemption or social values simply because it is highly entertaining and funny.

While it is true that some movies may be more or less didactic than others, it is incumbent upon moviegoers to understand what they are consuming and the nature of their amusement. It is instructive to note that the word *amusement* means *without thought,* with its original meaning being *to delude or deceive.* Sadly, this is all too often what happens when the lights go down and the curtains go up. We suspend our disbelief and along with it our critical faculties.

By knowing something of the dynamics of storytelling, of its structure and nature, the average moviegoer might be less inclined to treat his or her moviegoing as mere entertainment and see it more for what it is: a means of communicating the storyteller's values and view of redemption. And this discernment need not spoil the fun of entertainment. It can deepen one's appreciation as well.

But I incline to come to the alarming conclusion that it is just the literature that we read for "amusement," or "purely for pleasure" that may have the greatest and least suspected influence upon us. It is the literature which we read with the least effort that can have the easiest and most insidious influence upon us. Hence it is that the influence of popular novelists, and of popular plays of contemporary life, requires to be scrutinized most closely.

—T. S. ELIOT, "Religion and Literature"

To Exploit or Not to Exploit: Isn't That the Question?

The dominant theme of cultural critics and media bashers is morality, especially the excessive preoccupation that many movies have with sex and violence. There is no need to recite the studies that have conclusively linked media consumption with degenerate social behavior or the statistics of the thousands of acts of violence, profanity, and reprobate sexuality that saturate the minds of Americans every year, indeed every week. While these facts are decidedly a part of the issue of influence, they have already been dealt with extensively by Medved and others. The part of the puzzle not typically addressed is the issue of context and the philosophy out of which the fascination with brutality and promiscuity pour forth. And it is perhaps here that the most damage or good can be done to the individual and collective psyche.

Accounts of sex and violence are not in and of themselves evil. It is the context of these misbehaviors and meanings given to them that primarily dictate their destructive nature. It is not so much the individual acts of violence portrayed in teen slasher series like *Friday the 13th* or *Nightmare on Elm Street* that make them detrimental to the minds of youth. It is that these acts exist within a nihilistic view of the world as survival of the fittest, with murder demythologized through diabolical detail, and the existential association of sex with death. The devaluing of human life is realized through *evil as entertainment*. On the other hand, a film like *Schindler's List* portrays graphic brutality with equal clarity, but its context creates a revulsion in the audience toward the inhumanity that is portrayed. We have similar extremities of violence, different contexts, and opposite results.

The ultimate source book of most sex and violence media watchdogs is the Bible. And it ought to be because without its definition of universal morality that transcends and restricts individual choice, we as a society have no absolute reference point of truth. We are left with nothing but a sea of relativity that logically results in the violence of personal wills in conflict, the ethical fruit of survival of the fittest. Without God and His Law that defines absolute right and wrong, there can be no ultimate value difference between the acts of Jeffrey Dahmer and the acts of Mother Teresa. Relative personal subjective feelings cannot translate into objective moral norms without an appeal to an absolute standard. It is the Bible alone that provides a rational meaningful standard to make moral judgments that transcend the arbitrariness of personal opinion.

But we must be careful in our appeal to the Good Book for justification of moral condemnation of story. For in its pages are detailed accounts and descriptions of every immoral act known to man. Just a cursory list of the atrocities depicted therein includes blasphemy (2 Kings 18:28–19:5), vulgar insults (1 Kings 12:10), sex orgies (Exodus 32:3-6), gang rape (Judges 19:22-25), prostitution (Genesis 38:12-19), adultery (Proverbs 5), incest (Genesis 19:31-36), Peeping Toms (2 Samuel 11:2), murder (Genesis 4:8), being shot in the forehead (1 Samuel 17:49), decapitation (1 Samuel 17:51), disemboweling (Judges 3:21-22), being burned alive by fire (Daniel 3:22), nuclear type annihilation of an entire city (Genesis 19:24), dismemberment (1 Samuel 15:32-33, RSV), cannibalism (2 Kings 6:28), genocide, infanticide (Matthew 2:16), suicide (Acts 1:18), masochism, satanic worship (1 Kings 18:25-28), bludgeoning of a thousand men (Judges 15:15-16), gouging out of eyes (Judges 16:21), destruction of public property (Judges 16:30-31), and the list goes on. There is even the dramatic enactment of proper sexuality. An entire book, the Song of Solomon, subtly but nonetheless distinctly, portrays the erotic visual stimulation, verbal seduction, and physical consummation of a married couple.

And for those who would justify these examples as mere historical recounting, there are the allegorical uses of beatings, murder, dismemberment, and torture that climax many of Jesus' own parables (Matthew 18:23-35; 21:33-43; 22:1-13; 24:45-51; 25:14-30). The Master Himself used mafia-style drowning and dismemberment to illustrate the seriousness of sin (Matthew 18:6, 18:8-9), as well as the destruction of private property as a fictional analogy of disobedience (Matthew 7:26).

As a religious book, the Bible does not escape from life. It uses the technique of realism to tell us something that we need to know, namely, the sinfulness of the human condition and the misery of a fallen world.

—LELAND RYKEN, *The Liberated Imagination*

Now what is to be made of all this sex and violence that runneth over the cup of the defining moral standard of Western civilization? Is this hypocrisy or self-contradiction? Does such ribald revelation of humanity's darker side justify exploitation of our prurient baser instinct? May it never be! Having laid down a rationale for the depiction of depravity, let us now qualify that rationale with its context. In all of the impropriety portrayed in the Bible, we see several elements that make it very different in nature from the lurid celebration of wickedness found in many movies of today. It is the difference between moral exhortation and immoral exploitation.

First, most biblical spectacle is historical journalistic reporting on the highest ground. Storytellers cannot stop the evil that people do, but they can use that evil against the perpetrators through eyewitness accounts and written testimony. The writers *expose* inhumanity for the purpose of moral instruction.

Secondly, though evil is depicted, it is not glorified through intimate detail. While the text does not avoid divulging David's adultery with Bathsheba or Shechem's rape of Dinah, it does avoid voyeuristic explorations of body crevices and private parts writhing in sexual ecstasy or pain. When David cuts off Goliath's head, we are not indulged in a slow motion closeup of the sword piercing the neck and the carotid artery spurting blood as the eyes pop and the flesh rips (violence as pornography). The literature of the written page or speaking voice allows for mystery and reticence that is difficult for the visual image to achieve. Not that movies cannot achieve such reticence: Witness the fade-out that once followed the kiss. Alfred Hitchcock was famous for his suspenseful moral tales devoid of cinematic gore, still among the finest films to watch.

Thirdly, in the Bible immoral deeds are always contextually presented as immoral. Sin leads to destruction, not to freedom unfettered by moral restraint. Jacob's deception leads to paranoia and backfires against him. Sodom and

Gomorrah lead to fire and brimstone. David's adultery leads to the loss of a son. This is a far cry from the propagandistic attempts of movies like *Philadelphia* and *The Scarlet Letter* to legitimize destructive sexual behavior as "alternate lifestyles" and portray their deviants as poor victims of puritanical oppression.

Lastly and most importantly, the Bible's portrayal of depravity is never dehumanizing. Evil itself is not glamorized as entertainment. There is always a call to redemption, the hope for a better humanity, not a nihilistic message of "Hey, this is real life, baby. Get used to it."

By contextual qualifications the greatest story ever told maintains its status as the supreme standard of behavior without compromising its honesty about the human condition.

THE NATURE OF STORY: MOVIES AS MYTH

As the context of movie sex and violence determines a movie's moral status, so the philosophy behind the film determines the worldview the movie espouses. And the philosophy or worldview is carried by the film much in the same way as myths of old would carry the values and beliefs of a society. Movies are the new myths of American culture. Their very storytelling structure embodies values and incarnates myths.

For a definition of *myth*, we can turn to Chris Vogler, educator of writers and student of famous mythologist Joseph Campbell:

> What is a myth? For our purposes a myth is not the untruth or fanciful exaggeration of popular expression. A myth, as Joseph Campbell was fond of saying, is a metaphor for a mystery beyond human comprehension. It is a comparison that helps us understand, by analogy, some aspect of our mysterious selves. A myth, in this way of thinking, is not an untruth but a way of reaching a profound truth. Then what is a story? A story is also a metaphor, *a model of some aspect of human behavior* (emphasis mine). (vii)

Since the beginning of time, the human race has used story to convey the meaning and purpose of life. Within its various forms (myth, fable, parable, allegory) and within its evolution from oral tradition to codification, storytelling has been the backbone of civilizations. It maintained ritual, systematized beliefs, and taught dogma. In essence, story incarnated the myths and values of a culture with the intent of perpetuating them. Moses' Pentateuch told the story of the redemption of the Hebrews (both mythical *and* historical); the Babylonian *Epic of Gilgamesh* told the heroic redemption of its principal character, Gilgamesh; Homer's epic *The Odyssey* narrated the redemptive journeys of Odysseus.

From the Greek tragedies of Euripides to the bawdy comedies of Shakespeare, both ancient and classical writers suffered no shame in telling a good story with the intention of proving a point or illustrating how they believed we ought to live in this world. Storytelling from its very inception was expected to be "more than entertainment." Through their craft, the first storytellers were expected to teach the culture how to live and behave in their world. The rejection of "messages" in movies as "preachy" or "propagandistic" is a recent phenomenon of the Cartesian dualistic worldview that results in the splitting of reality into secular/sacred distinctions. This view is the denial of man's holistic existence, a gnostic divorce of mind from body, meaning from behavior, as if a story about human beings relating to one another could exist in a vacuum without reference to values or meaningfulness.

> *That movies play an increasingly significant role in defining both ourselves and our society seems beyond dispute.... Movies cannot be dismissed as mere entertainment and diversion. Rather, they are life stories that both interpret us and are being interpreted by us.*
> —ROBERT K. JOHNSTON, *Reel Spirituality: Theology and Film in Dialogue*

But in a sense the argument regarding messages in movies is a moot point. Regardless of the questionable cries of the dream factory artisans for entertainment without message, the very nature of moviemaking (storytelling) and moviegoing itself incarnates the transmission of myth much in the way that it did for the ancients. As author Geoffrey Hill reveals in his dissertation on the mythic power of film entitled *Illuminating Shadows*,

As ironic modern worshippers we congregate at the cinematic temple. We pay our votive offerings at the box office. We buy our ritual corn. We hush in reverent anticipation as the lights go down and the celluloid magic begins. Throughout the filmic narrative we identify with the hero. We vilify the antihero. We vicariously exult in the victories of the drama. And we are spiritually inspired by the moral of the story, all while believing we are modern techno-secular people, devoid of religion. Yet the depth and intensity of our participation reveal a religious fervor that is not much different from that of religious zealots. (3)

WATCHING WITH DISCERNMENT

Two of the most frustrating replies to hear when asking people what they thought of a movie are, "I liked it," or "I didn't like it," *accompanied by an inability to explain why.* But with an elementary understanding of the nature and structure of storytelling, an informed moviegoer can intelligently watch a film, enjoy the story, and also engage his or her critical faculties to understand just what the movie is trying to say about the way in which we ought or ought not to live. Instead of being manipulated by the suspension of disbelief and suppression of the intellect, moviegoers can exercise their responsibility in discerning what they are putting into their minds and hearts. This is particularly important for the Christian, who is commanded by God not to be conformed to this world but transformed by the renewing of the mind (Romans 12:2).

We have already established that stories do not exist in an "entertainment vacuum." Prevailing myths and cultural values are being communicated through movies. And this cultural effect is far deeper than the shallow dangers of excessive sex and violence. It extends to the philosophy behind the film. The very way we view the world and right and wrong is actually embodied in the redemptive structure of storytelling itself.

A variety of Hollywood screenwriting gurus flood the market with their theories and models of good storytelling. Whether it's Syd Field's three acts, two plot points, John Truby's twenty-two steps, Chris Vogler's mythic structure, or Aristotle's beginning, middle, and end with reversals and revelations, screenwriters follow an organizational framework in their writing that requires certain things and directs them toward a certain goal. While no one theory fits all stories, there are nonetheless common elements to many of these theories. And it is these elements that incarnate the storyteller's message of redemption.

For purposes of illustration, I will apply the essential elements of a movie to two classic movies—the 1993 winner of seven Academy Awards, *Schindler's List,* and the 1946 Frank Capra classic and all-time favorite, *It's a Wonderful Life.*

Theme

The first element to consider when analyzing a movie is the *theme*. Every good movie has one or more themes. Some call it "the moral of the story," while others call it "the message." But the theme is what the story is ultimately all about. A theme can be expressed as a proposition that leads to a conclusion. It can usually be stated in terms of "x leads to y," or some other prescriptional equivalent. It is the *purpose* or *moral* of the story and can be told in one statement. If we claim that a sequence of events is inevitable from a character's beginning behavior, then we are making a moral claim about the world, namely, that x leads to y. If we behave in such a way, such an end will result. Our story fleshes out our theme.

To tell a story…is to create a world, adopt an attitude, suggest a behavior.

—JOHN SHEA, *Stories of God*

Schindler's List is about Oskar Schindler, a womanizing German war profiteer during World War II who tried to capitalize on the free labor available through the incarcerated Jews. By the end of the movie, Oskar realizes the true evil of his exploits and sacrifices all his wealth in order to save eleven hundred workers who helped him make his fortune. One of the themes of *Schindler's List* is that treating people as objects or means to an end leads to evil, while treating people as sacred or as ends in themselves leads to redemption.

It's a Wonderful Life is the story of George Bailey, who has dreams of breaking out of his small-minded small town, Bedford Falls, to build great achievements but who sacrifices them all in order to save those in trouble around him. He begins to resent the suffering his sacrifices bring upon himself, but eventually he returns to his traditional values. The theme embodied in the story of *Wonderful Life* is that the meaning of life is not found in selfish pursuits but in sacrificing for others. Selfishness versus selflessness is the core of the movie.

Both movies have similar *themes*, yet widely divergent *stories*. Other examples of themes are the following: *Jurassic Park:* science without moral restraint leads to self-destruction; *E.T.:* fear of differences in others ("aliens") leads to hostility, while acceptance leads to reconciliation; *Babe:* biology can be transcended by personal choice (a pig proves that he *can* be a sheepdog); *Fatal*

Attraction: infidelity turns against itself; *Dead Poets Society:* conformity kills the spirit, but individuality frees it; *Terminators 1* and *2:* technology turns against humanity.

The theme of a movie is its intellectual and moral core. The task of the screenwriter is to elaborate the central theme in as many aspects of the story and characters as possible. For example, the theme of *Schindler's List* that respecting people leads to moral redemption is worked out by means of an ever-present conflict between dehumanization and humanization. We are given variations on the theme of dehumanization with scenes of people standing in line and being called out randomly or deliberately, people wanting to be selected or avoid being selected, and Jews being carted in trains like cattle, yet maintaining dignity through it all.

The story embodies the theme, which is the moral equivalent of the way we ought or ought not to live our lives. As "x leads to y," so events in a story lead to a conclusion and incarnate the theme.

Basic Structure: The Protagonist / Hero

In its simplest form, a movie is about redemption because it takes a protagonist (hero) with a problem who tries to solve it but is opposed by an antagonist (villain) until he almost fails, finally finding a solution. This process of problem/plan/failure/solution is the exact process of paradigm change or conversion in an individual. We as individuals have a problem (a lack or want). We seek to solve it but are often unaware of the real need. It is not until we are brought to the end of our want in almost total failure that we finally realize our true need and are able to submit to it. We change our minds or behavior (conversion, redemption).

So the protagonist wants something but has a fault/problem/need that hinders him from achieving his goal. At the beginning of the story the protagonist sees life in the wrong way, and by the end of the story he learns the right way to behave or think. This progression or change is the *character arc*—the process by which a character changes his paradigm, seeking a want but discovering a need and responding to that need appropriately or inappropriately. If the character learns to respond appropriately, the result is comedy or drama; if he does not respond appropriately, the result is tragedy. Both paradigms are the stuff from which redemption is made.

In the beginning of *Schindler,* Oskar is a profiteering opportunist who sees people only as a means to his end of making profit. In a discussion with his wife, he says he wants to be remembered for doing something extraordinary, namely making big bucks. And the only thing missing in his life to make it possible till then was war. His weakness is his view of people as means to ends and his belief that the meaning of life is found in worldly riches. In the beginning of the movie, Oskar rationalizes the cruelty of the Nazis under the rubric of necessary evils of war. His protection of his workers is mere profit motive.

Stories that emphasize character portray issues of human need or potential. They deal with the question of human nature by offering paradigms of possibility…. There are also movie stories that are plot-driven…. Movies that portray…how our lives reveal patterns that can take on meaningful shape have plot as their center…. Third, movies can find their center of power and meaning in the story's atmosphere, the unalterable given(s) against which the story is told and the characters developed.

—ROBERT K. JOHNSTON, *Reel Spirituality: Theology and Film in Dialogue*

George Bailey, while romancing Mary after a dance, tells her, "I'm shaking the dust off my feet of this crummy little town. I'm gonna see the world, go to college and then I'm gonna build things. Bridges and skyscrapers so big, they reach the sky." He tells his father that he wants to do something "big and important." He is seduced by personal ambition and achievement and is blind to true value being found in the people's lives whom he has helped.

The Self-Revelation
Protagonists usually have a moment in the film where they explain what they have learned, where they were wrong, or how they have changed their mind. This is the view that the writer/storyteller is trying to convey to the audience regarding the way they should or should not live. This moment is the character revelation of the hero, and it represents the premise or moral. As we sympathize with the protagonist, so we will sympathize with his revelation.

At the end of *Schindler,* Oskar breaks down in front of his workers and expresses that he did not do enough. He decries the potential redemption of people that each of his remaining material objects might have brought. He has completely converted his original belief in money as the supreme value in life to having no value at all compared to the value of people. Human life is so sacred that no material sacrifice is enough to compensate for it. As Stern quotes from the Talmud, "Whoever saves one life saves the world entire."

Similarly, George, with the help of Clarence his guardian angel, sees the devastation on people's lives that he has stopped. Clarence shows that if George had not been born, his brother would have drowned as a child, that he would not have become a war hero, and that his whole battalion would have been killed. Mary became a spinster and Violet a whore, all because George wasn't there to redeem them. Bedford Falls became the riotous empire of Pottersville because George wasn't there to stop Potter from pillaging and plundering. And so on. When George's friends bail him out of his $8,000 debt, he realizes that he is "the richest man in town" because, as Clarence writes to him on a Christmas card, "No man is a failure who has friends." George learns that the values he resented for keeping him from his dreams are really what life is all about after all.

The Antagonist / Villain

The second element of story structure is the antagonist, the villain who opposes the protagonist in his goal. In essence, the antagonist represents the opposing belief system to the protagonist's, resulting in a story that is ultimately a clash of worldviews or ways of thinking about the world. An antagonist may be an individual like Scar in *The Lion King*, or a force like chance in *Forrest Gump*, or nature in *Alive*. An antagonist can be totally evil like a Darth Vader or a complex character with virtues like Sally Field's character in *Mrs. Doubtfire*. But the main characteristic of the antagonist is that he or she impedes the protagonist from achieving the goal.

The antagonist in *Schindler* is the Nazi system as embodied in Amon Goeth the Commandant. Oskar must seduce Amon in order to get what he wants. The antagonist in *Wonderful Life* is the stingy old banker Mr. Potter, whose greedy quest for power over others contrasts with George's selfless sacrifice for others.

The antagonist usually has a speech in the film where he explains his rationale for why he opposes the protagonist. Better movies will make this rationale as realistic as possible so as not to create cardboard villains. The antagonist's rationale represents the worldview that the writer or storyteller does not want us to accept as the way to see the world.

The antagonist's rationale is often expressed in an "obligatory scene" where the protagonist and antagonist meet face to face and their worldviews come into conflict. It is here that the hero faces what he (and vicariously, we) should most detest. Often the hero's revelation is that he is very much like his enemy and must change his behavior or viewpoint to have victory or redemption. So we the audience ought to realize in ourselves what we are capable of becoming and reject such ways of living.

In the American cinema especially, the story reigns supreme. All the other language systems are subordinated to the plot, the structural spine of virtually all American fiction films, and most foreign movies as well.
—LOUIS GIANNETTI, *Understanding Movies*

Schindler catches Goeth drunk one night and the two talk. Goeth has observed that Oskar's goal is a "subcamp" of his own, another form of the same kind of control. Goeth says that "control is power," and "the Jews fear us because we can kill arbitrarily." Schindler then disagrees and pontificates the meaning of power as the justified ability to destroy withdrawn by the decision to pardon. Goeth is temporarily attracted by this thought of emperor-like godhood. But his forgiveness of his servants and slaves soon bores him, and he returns to his evil nature of wanton and indiscriminate destruction. Power through fear can only lead to pain.

George faces off with Potter twice, first when Potter tries to take over the Building and Loan after the death of George's father. Potter criticizes the values of George's father of helping others as encouraging laziness, rabble, and irresponsibility. George responds that these so-called "rabble" are the backbone of the community. People are human beings, as George's father saw them, not cattle, as Potter, the "warped, frustrated old man," sees them. And so two ways of looking at the world clash when worldviews collide.

Inciting Incident / Allies

With the protagonist and antagonist set, the story will usually unfold from the starting point of an *inciting incident*. The inciting incident is an event that acts as a catalyst for the inevitable unfolding of events that becomes the movie. It happens fairly early in the movie, and it changes the direction of the protagonist's own story. In *Schindler*, the invasion of Poland and subsequent persecution of Jews is the inciting incident that gives Schindler's idea of slave labor impetus, which in turn makes the story. In *Wonderful Life*, George's father dies, thereby throwing the first of many wrenches in George's plans and leading him to sacrifice his European trip and his plans for college.

The inciting incident sets the stage for the conflict between the hero and villain by solidifying the hero's goal and catapulting him toward it. Once the inciting incident has established the hero's problem, he sets off with a plan of how to achieve his goal. Along the way, he often gathers allies and is countered by the opposition of the villain. Itzhak Stern, played by Ben Kingsley, is Schindler's ally, and Mary and Clarence are George's allies.

Apparent Defeat / Gauntlet

The key to the middle of the story is that everything the protagonist does is blocked by the antagonist and/or the protagonist's own weakness. There is wide latitude here for plot complications and reversals, betrayals, etc., but at some point the hero ultimately has what is called an "apparent defeat" or "supreme ordeal" wherein his attempts to achieve his goal are frustrated to the point of total futility. Nothing he has done works, and he is left with nothing. In *Schindler*, Oskar meets his apparent defeat when he is thrown in jail for kissing a Jewess and loses all his workers to Auschwitz. In *Wonderful Life*, Billy loses the bankroll of the Building and Loan to Potter, and George, after struggling years to keep afloat, faces final bankruptcy and total annihilation at the hands of Potter.

After suffering apparent defeat, the protagonist has a "visit to death" or enters "the gauntlet." "Running the gauntlet" is an old phrase used to describe a form of punishment in which men armed with sticks or other weapons arrange themselves in two facing lines and beat the person forced to run between them. The gauntlet can be literal, as it is in *Star Wars*, where Luke has to ride through a narrow canal of the Death Star while being fired upon from both sides by canons and Tie fighters. Or it can be metaphorical, as in *Wonderful Life*, where George faces suicide by jumping off a bridge. Schindler faces his gauntlet vicariously through the women he was trying to save. Their train is rerouted to Auschwitz, and they face near extermination in the showers. Oskar bribes the commandant and marches right through the "gauntlet" of guards to get them out.

Final Battle

The gauntlet usually ends in a "final battle" between the hero and villain. The hero either has had a self-revelation that helps him win the battle, or through the battle has a self-revelation that makes him victorious. In either case, the self-revelation of the hero is what forces him to make a moral decision, thereby reinforcing the premise of the story. The decision he makes will determine his ultimate victory or defeat. Will he change his paradigm and approach the world as he ought, or will he remain in his original state and refuse to redeem himself from his need? Oskar Schindler faces Goeth to save his workers from Auschwitz and realizes that the only way to save them is to buy them back with the money he made. He also makes a promise to his wife to stop his adulteries. Then he uses all his money to fake manufacturing artillery shells in order to foil the war and save his workers.

George Bailey's revelation is the angelic vision of all he has done for others. He decides not to commit suicide and faces his fate from Potter with courage. The townspeople then pull through by providing the needed money to redeem George. What goes around, comes around. We reap what we sow. Courage is doing the right thing, even when it hurts.

CAVEAT EMPTOR: RIVAL VERSIONS OF REDEMPTION

Most films today operate within a humanistic framework of the world. The kind of redemption portrayed usually reduces to self-actualization or redemption through self-righteousness, with man as the measure of his own potential. In *Dead Poets Society*, the redemption is asserted by the schoolteacher Keating that since man is food for the worms and there is no afterlife, he must "seize the day" by casting off social and moral restraint to find one's self or potential.

Another popular form of this humanistic redemption is called Existentialism. This is the postmodern view that man exists in an ultimately irrational universe that leads to despair (angst). The way of redemption is through the seizure of responsibility for creating ourselves through personal choice or commitment. *Forrest Gump* is the popular form of this redemption. Others include most of Woody Allen's movies, *City Slickers, Groundhog Day, Legends of the Fall, Babe,* and others.

Another increasingly popular type of redemption in film is Eastern mysticism, especially in the forms of monism and dualism. Dualism is the *Star Wars* paradigm of redemption, with the dark and light sides of the Force. *Ghost* is a good example of dualism: The bad people get sucked into spiritual punishment, and the good people who embrace their light side by "letting go" of their control over others enter Nirvana. Here we see salvation by good works. *Phenomenon* and *Powder* are examples of the monistic view of redemption. In *Powder,* the main character, a boy turned freak genius by an electrical storm accident, tells his beloved that humanity's problem is that we see distinction or separation between ourselves. If we only saw everything as "one" (monism), we could live in peace. John Travolta's character in *Phenomenon* has a very similar scene with the same belief: Enlightenment comes through shedding ignorant thinking by experiencing oneness with all things.

The power of film can change lives and communicate truth; it can reveal and redeem.

—ROBERT K. JOHNSTON, *Reel Spirituality: Theology and Film in Dialogue*

A fourth kind of redemption is the Judeo-Christian notion of substitutionary atonement and people's need for forgiveness from God. This is extremely rare in movies, which is no surprise, in light of the well-attested Hollywood antagonism to Christianity. Every once in a while movies like *Chariots of Fire, Tender Mercies, Shadowlands, Les Miserables,* or *The Addiction* come along that portray Judeo-Christian redemption in their characters. It seems that the true rebel in Hollywood is the writer who dares to defy convention and tell a story that redeems the hero or heroine through repentance and faith.

As a caveat, not all stories of redemption are complete and deeply woven philosophies. Often they are simple values like self-worth being based on self-acceptance, not peer approval *(Toy Story; Stand by Me),* or the dangers of trusting technology *(Jurassic Park; Terminator).* But even these values are ultimately about how we ought or ought not to live in this life—in other words, about redemption.

And so the story goes. Movies are finally, centrally, crucially, primarily only about story. And stories are finally, centrally, crucially, primarily, mostly about redemption. With the proper tools in hand, one can accurately discern the messages, worldviews, and philosophies of life promoted through the agency of movies. The suspension of disbelief need not require the negation of one's critical faculties. And the enjoyment of entertainment need not result in thoughtless abdication of the mind for manipulation of the emotions. Movies are, after all, not merely movies.

How Should We Then Write?

While the foregoing discussion has focused on the art of watching movies, the principles have obvious implications for the Christian writer of screenplays. In our postmodern literary theories, there is a tendency to negate all rules as limiting and oppressive, structure as arbitrary and relative. While there is validity to the need for flexibility and rule-breaking, the Christian should always be cautious when assimilating or creating new structural approaches in his writing. The Christian's task is to utilize story structure to express truth, not fashion.

In so doing, Christian screenwriters must be more careful than their contemporaries in the choices they make. For instance, nonlinear narrative is sometimes used in current postmodern movies as a stylish mode of consciousness with great effect (*Pulp Fiction, Go,* and others). But if this tool is not encompassed within a larger context of linearity, the storyteller is implicitly asserting that reality is ultimately nonlinear, which means there is no ultimate purpose guiding life. Linearity is a teleological concept, expressing intelligence behind events. And the linear notion of history is intrinsic to Christianity, with its beginning (creation), middle (fall) and end (redemption). From Genesis to Revelation, the Scriptures communicate that God is leading history to a linear conclusion, a final climax. This was not a cherished notion when Moses first introduced God's script of history to the world. Surrounding pagan cosmologies and literature expressed eternal time, cyclical histories, and a disregard for factuality in events.

Another postmodern storytelling technique with which a Christian writer needs to be careful is perspectivalism. This Nietzschean viewpoint denies people's ability to know absolute truth because of their epistemological entrapment in their own subjective perception. This epistemic relativism leads to an inability to distinguish between reality and illusion. It was used richly by famous foreign filmmakers, such as Fellini *(Juliet of the Spirits)*, Buñuel *(Belle de Jour)* and Bergman *(Silence; Hour of the Wolf)*, and it is becoming fashionable in mainstream movies like *The Game, The Usual Suspects, The Matrix,* and others. As long as there is a real world with which to compare the lies, deceptions, or multiple perspectives, then perspectivalism can be a helpful literary tool for truth. But if there is no ultimate standard of reality even hinted at in a story, then the story is communicating that there is no ultimate standard but only relative perceptions. In such a scenario, we are awash in a sea of personal subjective experiences, without a way or truth to life.

Film has become the medium in which stories are told that tend to be central to the concerns, problems, preoccupations of a society. It is one way in which society reflects upon, communicates with, and negotiates the meaning of everyday experience.

—MIRIAM HANSEN, as quoted by Robert Jewett,
Saint Paul Returns to the Movies

Though Christian writers must recognize and understand the effect that certain styles and structure have on the final meaning of a story's redemption, they can ultimately rest assured in the intrinsic Christian philosophy behind the act of screenwriting itself. The act of writing stories comports with the Christian doctrine of God's sovereignty in the scripts of our lives. When we watch a well-crafted movie, we see characters that are alive and real to us. We see them freely making choices that result in consequences, along with other events that seem to happen by chance. But in reality, behind the curtain is a writer who has crafted absolutely everything that a character says and does, every word spoken, everything that happens to that character. And it is all done with the author's original goal in mind: how the writer wants the story to end.

A character in a movie acts, but behind that act are two intentions—the actor's and the author's. This is not the wooden "fate" or unmoved mover of pagan worldviews, nor the absurd random chance of atheist ideology. This storytelling reflects the Christian God, who as ultimate Author of all, directs all events toward His purpose (Ephesians 1:9-12; Romans 8:28), while not negating man's free responsibility for his actions (Genesis 50:20; Acts 4:28; Isaiah 10:5-15). So the art of storytelling reflects the perfect balance of divine sovereignty and human responsibility.

Works Cited

Goldman, William. *William Goldman: Four Screenplays.* New York: Applause Books, 1995.

Hill, Geoffrey. *Illuminating Shadows: The Mythic Power of Film.* Boston: Shambhala Publications, 1992.

Medved, Michael. *Hollywood Versus America.* New York: HarperCollins, 1992.

Vogler, Christopher. *The Writer's Journey.* Studio City, CA: Michael Wiese Productions, 1992.

Viewpoint: C. S. Lewis

On Stories

If to love story is to love excitement then I ought to be the greatest lover of excitement alive. But the fact is that what is said to be the most "exciting" novel in the world, *The Three Musketeers,* makes no appeal to me at all. The total lack of atmosphere repels me. There is no country in the book—save as a storehouse of inns and ambushes. There is no weather. When they cross to London there is no feeling that London differs from Paris. There is not a moment's rest from the "adventures": one's nose is kept ruthlessly to the grindstone....

Good stories often introduce the marvellous or supernatural, and nothing about Story has been so often misunderstood as this.... Nor are the marvels in good Story ever mere arbitrary fictions stuck on to make the narrative more sensational. I happened to remark to a man who was sitting beside me at dinner the other night that I was reading Grimm in German of an evening but never bothered to look up a word I didn't know, "so that it is often great fun" (I added) "guessing what it was that the old woman gave to the prince which he afterwards lost in the wood." "And specially difficult in a fairy-tale," said he, "where everything is arbitrary and therefore the object might be anything at all." His error was profound. The logic of a fairy-tale is as strict as that of a realistic novel, though different.

Does anyone believe that Kenneth Grahame made an arbitrary choice when he gave his principal character the form of a toad, or that a stag, a pigeon, a lion would have done as well? The choice is based on the fact that the real toad's face has a grotesque resemblance to a certain kind of human face....

But why should the characters be disguised as animals at all? The disguise is very thin, so thin that Grahame makes Mr. Toad on one occasion "comb the dry leaves out of his *hair.*" Yet it is indispensable. If you try to rewrite the book with all the characters humanized you are faced at the outset with a dilemma. Are they to be adults or children? You will find that they are neither. They are like children in so far as they have no responsibilities, no struggle for existence, no domestic cares.

Meals turn up; one does not even ask who cooked them. In Mr. Badger's kitchen "plates on the dresser grinned at pots on the shelf." Who kept them clean? Where were they bought? How were they delivered in the Wild Wood?... But in other ways it is the life of adults. They go where they like and do what they please, they arrange their own lives.

To that extent the book is a specimen of the most scandalous escapism: it paints a happiness under incompatible conditions—the sort of freedom we can have only in childhood and the sort we can have only in maturity—and conceals the contradiction by the further pretense that the characters are not human beings at all. The one absurdity helps to hide the other. It might be expected that such a book would unfit us for the harshness of reality and send us back to our daily lives unsettled and discontented. I do not find that it does so. The happiness which it presents to us is in fact full of the simplest and most attainable things—food, sleep, exercise, friendship, the face of nature, even (in a sense) religion.... And in the same way the whole story, paradoxically enough, strengthens our relish for life. This excursion into the preposterous sends us back with renewed pleasure to the actual....

If I am right in thinking that there is another enjoyment in Story besides the excitement, then popular romance even on the lowest level becomes rather more important than we had supposed. When you see an immature or uneducated person devouring what seem to you merely sensational stories, can you be sure what kind of pleasure he is enjoying?... He may be seeking only the recurring tension of imagined anxiety. But he may also be receiving certain profound experiences which are, for him, not acceptable in any other form.... The nearest we can come to a test is by asking whether he often *re-reads* the same story.

It is, of course, a good test for every reader of every kind of book. An unliterary man may be defined as one who reads books once only. There is hope for a man who has never read Malory or Boswell or *Tristram Shandy* or Shakespeare's *Sonnets:* But what can you do with a man who says he "has read" them, meaning he has read them once, and thinks that this settles the matter? Yet I think the test has a special application to the matter in hand. For excitement, in the sense defined above, is just what must disappear from a second reading. You cannot, except at the first reading, be really curious about what happened....

The re-reader is looking not for actual surprises (which can come only once) but for a certain ideal surprisingness.... We do not enjoy a story fully at the first reading. Not till the curiosity, the sheer narrative lust, has been given its sop and laid asleep, are we at leisure to savour the real beauties. Till then, it is like wasting great wine on a ravenous natural thirst which merely wants cold wetness. The children understand this well when they ask for the same story over and over again, and in the same words. They want to have again the "surprise" of discovering that what seemed Little-Red-Riding-Hood's grandmother is really the wolf. It is better when you know it is coming: free from the shock of actual surprise you can attend better to the intrinsic surprisingness of the *peripeteia*....

To be stories at all they must be series of events: but it must be understood that this series—the *plot*, as we call it—is only really a net whereby to catch something else. The real theme may be, and perhaps usually is, something that has no sequence in it, something other than a process and much more like a state or quality....

Shall I be thought whimsical if, in conclusion, I suggest that this internal tension in the heart of every story between the theme and the plot constitutes, after all, its chief resemblance to life? If story fails in that way does not life commit the same blunder? In real life, as in a story, something must happen. That is just the trouble. We grasp at a state and find only a succession of events in which the state is never quite embodied. The grand idea of finding Atlantis which stirs us in the first chapter of the adventure story is apt to be frittered away in mere excitement when the journey has once been begun. But so, in real life, the idea of adventure fades when the day-to-day details begin to happen. Nor is this merely because actual hardship and danger shoulder it aside. Other grand ideas—home-coming, reunion with a beloved—similarly elude our grasp. Suppose there is no disappointment; even so—well, you are here. But now, something must happen, and after that something else. All that happens may be delightful: but can any such series quite embody the sheer state of being which was what we wanted? If the author's plot is only a net, and usually an imperfect one, a net of time and event for catching what is not really a process at all, is life much more?...Art, indeed, may be expected to do what life cannot do: but so it has done. The bird has escaped us. But it was at least entangled in the net for several chapters. We saw it close and enjoyed the plumage. How many "real lives" have nets that can do as much?

In life and art both, as it seems to me, we are always trying to catch in our net of successive moments something that is not successive.... But I think it is sometimes done—or very nearly done—in stories. I believe the effort to be well worth making.

—"On Stories" in *Essays Presented to Charles Williams*
Oxford: Oxford University Press, 1947

Viewpoint: Amos N. Wilder

How Stories Interest Us

How is that we account for the appeal of a story whether to children or grown-ups? There is first of all a natural interest in, a curiosity about, *what happened*, especially if it was something unusual, something marvelous or creepy or ridiculous. With this goes an interest in what happened *next*, and *next*, in how the recital unfolds. One is on a road and one wonders what is around the corner and about how the road forks.

But besides the interest in what is strange there is also an interest in what may be familiar, in *recognition*. Yes, we say, that is the way things are; that is the way things happen. That feature is lifelike.

There is also the interest in where the story *begins*. As the stage is set, and as the hearers are in expectation, out of all the innumerable possibilities of what could be recounted, what shall we hear about? The very first words of a tale come as a surprise. There is, moreover, the interest in the *end*. Beyond the interest in what happened next and next there is the interest in how it came out.

There is the interest, more or less conscious, in what the story *means*, in what the storyteller is "getting at." Finally there is the interest in the *art of telling*, in the performance. Audiences appreciate virtuosity, mastery, dramatic skill.

It will be noticed that all these aspects of story are referred back to *interest*. This is cardinal. The first axiom of good storytelling is that it should capture and hold our attention. Whatever else they do, the teller-of-tales, the novelist, even the gossip, must "hold" their audience or reader.

Apart from the appeal of the narration itself—the scenario, the plot, the characters—there are other factors and strategies which nourish the power of the recital. Important among these are what we may call the rituals of storytelling. The teller-of-tales from of old has always had something of the character of a charmer, and the initiates willingly enter into what they recognize as an artifice. They are happy to be transported.

All stories have their presuppositions. But with the more significant kinds it becomes clearer. These all posit a scheme or order in the nowhere of the world. We are glad to lend ourselves to [a story's] persuasion because though it may be fictive it answers to our gropings and lights up our obscurities and confusions. The storyteller does more than organize his tale and plot. His fable responds to and organizes an inchoate fund of longings, anguishes, obscurities, dreams. His narrations orchestrate our most urgent impasses and gropings. The story holds us because it lights up our own adventure. Fictions do not take us out of time and the world. Even tales of the marvelous do not take us out of time and the world. Their sequences and vicissitudes are woven of the same contingencies, surprises and reversals which attend on our own....

—"Story and Story-World"
Interpretation 37 (October 1983): 353-364

ONCE UPON A TIME:
REFLECTIONS ON STORYTELLING

The narrative mode is uniquely important in Christianity.... A Christian can confess his faith wherever he is...by telling a story or a series of stories.
　　　　　　　　　　　　　—Amos N. Wilder, *Early Christian Rhetoric*

⌒

Qua story, it can only have one merit: that of making the audience want to know what happens next. And conversely it can only have one fault: that of making the audience not want to know what happens next. These are the only two criticisms that can be made on the story that is a story.
　　　　　　　　　　　　　—E. M. Forster, *Aspects of the Novel*

⌒

It is from the kind of world the writer creates, from the kind of character and detail he invests it with, that a reader can find the intellectual meaning of a book.... The novelist makes his statements by selection, and if he is any good, he selects every word for a reason, every detail for a reason, every incident for a reason, and arranges them in a certain time-sequence for a reason.
　　　　　　　　　　　　　—Flannery O'Connor, *Mystery and Manners*

⌒

The art of storytelling lies within the storyteller, to be searched for, drawn out, made to grow. It is compounded of certain invariables and these can be stated. Experience—that faring forth to try one's mettle.... The building of background—that conscious reaching out and participation in all things that may contribute to and illuminate one's art. Creative imagination; the power to evoke emotion; a sense of spiritual conviction. Finally a gift for selection.... But the secret of the gift lies in the sixth sense of the true storyteller. Here is an indefinable something that acts as does the nose for the winetaster, as fingertips for the textile expert, as absolute pitch for the musician. I think one may be born with this; but it is far more likely to become ingrained after years of experience.

—Ruth Sawyer, *The Way of the Storyteller*

"The king died and then the queen died," is a story. "The king died, and then the queen died of grief," is a plot.... If it is in a story we say "and then?" If it is in a plot we ask "why?"

—E. M. Forster, *Aspects of the Novel*

From the writer's seat the plot…is what you are thinking about…. My characters are not drawn from life; they are drawn from my plots. I know, for example, that a child will be pushed from a cliff in the later part of my story. I ask myself what kind of person will do that.

—Jill Paton Walsh, "The Lords of Time," in
The Openhearted Audience, ed. Virginia Haviland

Fielding…made use of the fact that accomplishing the artistic end of…a work depended heavily on how successful its creator was in controlling our sympathy and antipathy toward, our approval and disapproval of, characters, thoughts, and actions at every stage of his work. Such attempts to control are implicit in devices of disclosure.

—Sheldon Sacks, *Fiction and the Shape of Belief*

Some good stories—and we can think here also of the novel or the epic—turn upon the fortunes of men, the ups and downs of life, success and failure, surprise and disappointment. The appeal of such stories and of such wisdom as they have is identified especially with the plot and its surprises. Other good stories turn on the perennially interesting topic of character in men, their varying traits and types, and the consequences of these. Or a good story may have its chief appeal in the sheer surface delineation, the absorbing detail and concreteness of the portrayal.

—Amos N. Wilder, *Early Christian Rhetoric*

TELL ME A STORY: REFLECTIONS ON CHILDREN'S LITERATURE

Fairy-tale motifs...are experienced as wondrous because the child feels under-stood and appreciated deep down in his feelings, hopes, and anxieties, without these all having to be dragged up and investigated in the harsh light of a ration-ality that is still beyond him. Fairy tales enrich the child's life and give it an enchanted quality just because he does not quite know how the stories have worked their wonder on him.

—Bruno Bettelheim, *The Uses of Enchantment*

Books written entirely for children are poor even as children's books.

—J. R. R. Tolkien, "On Fairy-Stories"

I never met *The Wind in the Willows* or the Bastable books till I was in my late twenties, and I do not think I have enjoyed them any less on that account. I am almost inclined to set it up as a canon that a children's story which is enjoyed only by children is a bad children's story. The good ones last.... I now enjoy Tolstoy and Jane Austen and Trollope as well as fairy tales and I call that growth: if I had had to lose the fairy tales in order to acquire the novelists, I would not say that I had grown but only that I had changed.... I think my growth is just as apparent when I now read the fairy tales as when I read the novelists, for I now enjoy the fairy tales better than I did in childhood: being now able to put more in, of course I get more out.

—C. S. Lewis, "On Three Ways of Writing for Children"

On the whole, my books are concerned with children tackling the problem of an adult world in which things have gone wrong.

—Joan Aiken, "Between Family and Fantasy,"
in *The Openhearted Audience,* ed. Virginia Haviland

⌒

What I wish for the writer for children...is the ultimate compliment—the return of the child in maturity to read the same book with new insight, new discovery, new joy.

—Ivan Southall, "Sources and Responses,"
in *The Openhearted Audience,* ed. Virginia Haviland

⌒

I don't think you have to actually know children to write for them. Some of the best children's writers don't even *like* children. But they do know very well the child within themselves. And they're willing to listen to that child.

—Katherine Paterson, interview

⌒

Most of us have in common a tragedy to forget what childhood is about.... We ignore the truth (until violently reminded) that anything that can happen to a grown person can happen to a person not grown. We forget the vividness and brilliance and breathtaking wonderment of the world a kid finds each morning when he slams the door and rushes out. We forget its terror, its violence, its bewilderment.

—Ivan Southall, "Sources and Responses,"
in *The Openhearted Audience,* ed. Virginia Haviland

⌒

One cannot know what is fine in children's books without having an appreciation of literature as a whole.

—Ruth Sawyer, *The Way of the Storyteller*

Acknowledgments

Grateful acknowledgment is made for permission to reprint the following material:

To A. P. Watt, Ltd., for permission to reprint an excerpt from "Man and Myth-ologies," from *The Everlasting Man,* by G. K. Chesterton, published 1925 by Dodd, Mead and Company. Permission granted by A. P. Watt, Ltd., on behalf of The Royal Literary Fund.

To Baker Book House for permission to reprint "Christian Poetics, Past and Pre-sent," by Donald T. Williams, from *The Discerning Reader: Christian Perspec-tives on Literature and Theory,* © 1995 by Baker Books.

To Cambridge University Press for permission to reprint excerpts from *An Experi-ment in Criticism,* by C. S. Lewis, © 1961 by Cambridge University Press. Reprinted with the permission of Cambridge University Press.

To *Christian Herald* for permission to reprint excerpts from "Christian Imagina-tion," by Clyde S. Kilby, © 1969 by *Christian Herald.*

To *Christianity Today* for permission to reprint excerpts from "Flight to Fantasy," by Miriam Hendrix, printed 1974. Used by permission, *Christianity Today,* 1974.

To the Estate of Chad Walsh for permission to reprint excerpts from "A Hope for Literature," originally published in *The Climate of Faith in Modern Literature,* ed. Nathan A. Scott Jr., © 1964 by Seabury Press. Permission granted by the Estate of Chad Walsh, Damaris Walsh McGuire, Literary Executor.

To Farrar, Straus and Giroux, for permission to reprint an excerpt from "The Re-sponsibility of the Poet" from *What Are People For?* by Wendell Berry. Copy-right © 1990 by Wendell Berry. Reprinted by permission of North Point Press, a division of Farrar, Straus and Giroux, LLC. Also for permission to reprint "Novelist and Believer" from *Mystery and Manners* by Flannery O'Connor. Copyright © 1969 by the Estate of Mary Flannery O'Connor. Reprinted by permission of Farrar, Straus and Giroux, LLC. Also for permission to reprint "One Art" from *The Complete Poems 1927–1979* by Elizabeth Bishop. Copy-right © 1979, 1983, by Alice Helen Methfessel. Reprinted by permission of Farrar, Straus and Giroux, LLC. Also for permission to reprint "Filling Station" from *The Complete Poems 1927–1979* by Elizabeth Bishop. Copyright © 1979,

1983 by Alice Helen Methfessel. Reprinted by permission of Farrar, Straus and Giroux, LLC.

To Harcourt, Inc., for permission to reprint an excerpt from *Of Other Worlds: Essays and Stories,* by C. S. Lewis, copyright © 1966 by the Executors of the Estate of C. S. Lewis and renewed 1994 by C. S. Lewis Pte. Ltd., reprinted by permission of Harcourt, Inc. Also for permission to reprint "Religion and Literature" from *Selected Essays* by T. S. Eliot, copyright © 1950 by Harcourt, Inc. and renewed 1978 by Esme Valerie Eliot, reprinted by permission of the publisher.

To HarperCollins Publishers, Inc., for permission to reprint an excerpt from *Acts: The Word Set Free,* by Larry Woiwode, copyright © 1993 by Larry Woiwode. Reprinted by permission of HarperCollins Publishers, Inc. Also for permission to reprint excerpts from *Telling the Truth* by Frederick Buechner, copyright © 1977 by Frederick Buechner. Reprinted by permission of HarperCollins Publishers, Inc.

To HarperCollins Publishers, Inc., for permission to reprint an excerpt from *Living by Fiction* by Annie Dillard, copyright © 1982 by Annie Dillard. Reprinted by permission of Harper Collins Publishers, Inc.

To Harvard University Press for permission to reprint poem 712 "Because I Could Not Stop for Death" from *The Poems of Emily Dickinson.* Reprinted by permission of the publishers and the Trustees of Amherst College from *The Poems of Emily Dickinson,* Thomas H. Johnson, ed., Cambridge, Mass.: The Belknap Press of Harvard University Press, Copyright © 1951, 1955, 1979 by the President and Fellows of Harvard College.

To Hope Publishing Company for permission to reprint an excerpt from *Lift Every Heart* by Timothy Dudley-Smith, © 1984 Hope Publishing Company, Carol Stream, IL 60188. All rights reserved. Used by permission.

To Houghton Mifflin Company for permission to reprint excerpts from "On Fairy-Stories," *The Tolkien Reader* by J. R. R. Tolkien. Copyright © 1966 by J. R. R. Tolkien. Reprinted by permission of Houghton Mifflin Company. All rights reserved.

To *Interpretation* for permission to reprint excerpts from "Story and Story-World," by Amos N. Wilder, *Interpretation* 37 (October 1983) 353-364. Permission granted by *Interpretation.*

To InterVarsity Press for permission to reprint excerpts from *Art and the Bible,* by Francis A. Schaeffer, © 1973 by L'Abri Fellowship. Used with permission from InterVarsity Press, P.O. Box 1400, Downers Grove, IL 60515.

To Lescher and Lescher, Ltd., for permission to reprint "Is It Good Enough for Children?" by Madeleine L'Engle. Originally appeared in *The Writer.* Copyright © 1990 by Madeleine L'Engle. This usage granted by permission of the author.

To New Directions Publishing Corporation for permission to reprint an excerpt by Denise Levertov, from *New and Selected Essays,* copyright © 1992 by Denise Levertov. Reprinted by permission of New Directions Publishing Corp.

To Oxford University Press for permission to reprint an excerpt by C. S. Lewis from "On Stories," originally published in *Essays Presented to Charles Williams,* © 1947 by Oxford University Press. By permission of Oxford University Press.

To Sven Birkerts for permission to reprint excerpts from "The Woman in the Garden," originally published in *Agni* 35 (1992): 66-75; permission granted by Sven Birkerts.

To University of Notre Dame Press for permission to reprint an excerpt by Jacques Maritain from *Art and Scholasticisim,* © 1974 by the University of Notre Dame Press.

Reasonable care has been taken to trace original ownership and, when necessary, obtain permission to reprint material in this book. For material not in the public domain, selections were made according to generally accepted fair-use standards and practices. Should any attribution be found to be incorrect, the publisher welcomes written documentation supporting correction for subsequent printings.

This book would not have been possible without a generous grant from the Wheaton College Alumni Association to cover permissions fees.

About the Author

Leland Ryken is professor of English at Wheaton College, where he has taught since 1968. He has published nearly two dozen books on such subjects as literature in Christian perspective, the Bible as literature, Milton, the Puritans, and work and leisure.